Reinventing Democracy

Reinventing Democracy succeeds in covering all the major issues of Portuguese democracy and the society in which it is based. Analysis covers the creative, social and political experimentation by citizen and popular movements during the revolution of 1974/75, to more recent episodes of alternative economic organisation. We are also treated to a thorough account of issues as diverse as popular mobilization over the claim of local populations to self-government, local environmental conflicts, the transformations in trade-unionism, and citizen participation on territorial planning. *Reinventing Democracy* explicitly explores the relationships and tensions between difference and equality, citizenship and difference, state/society relationships and local identities, and European integration, as part of broader processes of globalisation and of the emergence of the new experiences of active citizenship.

This volume was previously published as a special issue of the journal *South European Society and Politics*.

Boaventura de Sousa Santos is Professor of Sociology at the School of Economics and Director of the Centre for Social Studies at the University of Coimbra, Portugal.

João Arriscado Nunes is coordinator of the Graduate Studies Programme and Associate Professor at the School of Economics as well as researcher at the Centre for Social Studies of the University of Coimbra.

Reinventing Democracy

Grassroots Movements in Portugal

Edited by
Boaventura de Sousa Santos and
João Arriscado Nunes

LONDON AND NEW YORK

First published 2006 by Routledge
2 Park Square, Milton Park, Abingdon, Oxon, OX14 4RN

Simultaneously published in the USA and Canada
by Routledge
270 Madison Ave, New York, NY 10016

Routledge is an imprint of the Taylor & Francis Group

© 2006 Taylor & Francis Ltd.

Typeset in Sabon 10/12 pt by the Alden Group Oxford
Printed and bound in Great Britain by
Antony Rowe Ltd, Chippenham, Wiltshire

All rights reserved. No part of this book may be reprinted or
reproduced or utilised in any form or by any electronic,
mechanical, or other means, now known or hereafter invented,
including photocopying and recording, or in any information
storage or retrieval system, without permission in writing from
the publishers.

British Library Cataloguing in Publication Data
A catalogue record for this book is available from the British
Library

Library of Congress Cataloging in Publication Data
A catalog record for this book has been requested

ISBN 0-415-34808-0

CONTENTS

Notes on Contributors   vii

1. Introduction: Democracy, Participation and Grassroots Movements in Contemporary Portugal   1
   BOAVENTURA DE SOUSA SANTOS and JOÃO ARRISCADO NUNES

2. Local Citizen Action as a form of Resistance Against the New Wave of Worldwide Colonization: The Case of the In Loco Association in Southern Portugal   16
   ALBERTO MELO

3. 'Decent Housing for the People': Urban Movements and Emancipation in Portugal   46
   JOÃO ARRISCADO NUNES and NUNO SERRA

4. The Territory as Space for Collective Action: Paradoxes and Potentialities of the 'Strategic Game of Actors' in Territorial Planning in Portugal   77
   ISABEL GUERRA

5. A Beira Town in Protest: Memory, Populism and Democracy   98
   JOSÉ MANUEL DE OLIVEIRA MENDES

6. 'Don't Treat us Like Dirt!': The Fight Against the Co-incineration of Dangerous Industrial Waste in the Outskirts of Coimbra   132
   MARISA MATIAS

7. Sexual Orientation in Portugal: Towards Emancipation   159
   ANA CRISTINA SANTOS

8   Who Saved East Timor? New References for
    International Solidarity   191
    JOSÉ MANUEL PUREZA

9   Portuguese Trade Unionism vis-à-vis the European
    Works Councils   218
    HERMES AUGUSTO COSTA

10 The Reinvention of Trade Unionism and the
    New Challenges of Emancipation   253
    ELÍSIO ESTANQUE

    Index   285

NOTES ON CONTRIBUTORS

Boaventura de Sousa Santos is Professor of Sociology at the School of Economics and Director of the Centre for Social Studies of the University of Coimbra, Portugal. He has published extensively in the sociology of law, political sociology, globalisation and epistemology, based on his research in Portugal, Mozambique, Colombia, Brazil and Macao.

João Arriscado Nunes is coordinator of the Graduate Studies Programme and Associate Professor at the School of Economics as well as researcher at the Centre for Social Studies of the University of Coimbra. He has published extensively in the fields of the social studies of science, political sociology, sociology of culture, globalization and social theory.

Alberto Melo was born in Lisbon in 1941. After taking a post-graduate Diploma in Adult Education, in the UK, he has opted for a professional career alternating periods of academic work (Manchester, Milton Keynes, Southampton, Paris, Faro) with top administrative positions (Director-General for Lifelong Education, Educational Counsellor in the Portuguese Permanent Mission at UNESCO), consultancy assignments (OECD, BIT, Council of Europe, EC, UNESCO, UNCTAD, etc.) and the direction of citizens' organisations (In Loco, 'animar', etc.).

Nuno Serra is a geographer. His research interests include housing and urban policies in Portugal in recent decades, which was the subject of his MA thesis. He is currently working as an evaluator of projects in the field of education.

Isabel Maria Pimentel de Carvalho Guerra is Professor at the Instituto Superior de Ciências do Trabalho e Empresas (ISCTE) and Lecturer in the disciplines of Urban Sociology, Territorial Sociology, Methods and Techniques for Evaluation and Planning. Her main areas of research are urban sociology, housing, education and social exclusion.

José Manuel de Oliveira Mendes is Professor of Sociology at the School of Economics of the University of Coimbra, and a researcher at the Centre for Social Studies. His main interests are in the fields of social inequalities, social movements and identity processes. He is the author of *Do Ressentimento ao Reconhecimento: Vozes, Identidades e Processos Políticos nos Açores* (2003) and (with Elísio Estanque) of *Classes e Desigualdades Sociais em Portugal: Um Estudo Comparativo* (1998).

Marisa Matias is a sociologist and researcher at the Centre for Social Studies (CES). Her research interests include the sociology of the environment and public health, social studies of science, and public policy and participation. She has published on environmental conflicts and scientific controversies in Portugal, especially in relation to waste management policies.

Ana Cristina Santos is a sociologist and researcher at the Centre for Social Studies of the University of Coimbra and teacher at the High School of Education of the Piaget Institute of Viseu. She has published on sexual rights, sexual identities, AIDS and social movements. Her research interests also include patriarchy, gender mainstreaming, power struggles and human rights.

José Manuel Pureza is Professor of the School of Economics, University of Coimbra (Portugal) and Senior Researcher at the Centre for Social Studies. He is also coordinator of the Peace Studies Group and author of 'The Common Heritage of Humankind. Towards an International Law of Solidarity?' (Porto: 1998).

Hermes Augusto Costa is a lecturer at the Faculty of Economics, University of Coimbra, and a permanent researcher at the Centre for Social Studies of the same University. His research interests cover industrial relations and trade unionism, particularly the globalization and regionalization of trade unionism.

Elísio Estanque is a professor of sociology at the Faculty of Economics and a permanent researcher of the Centre for Social Studies, University of Coimbra. He has published works on themes such as class and inequalities, labour relations, trade unions and social movements, youth cultures and civic participation.

NOTES ON TRANSLATORS

This volume includes translations from David Jackson, Isabel Pedro, Karen Bennett, Sheena Caldwell and Sofia Ferreira. All the translations were revised by John Mock and Teresa Tavares. We would like to express our gratitude to each of them.

Introduction: Democracy, Participation and Grassroots Movements in Contemporary Portugal

BOAVENTURA DE SOUSA SANTOS and
JOÃO ARRISCADO NUNES

The last three decades have witnessed a succession of processes of political and social transition in various regions of the world which brought with them a spread of the institutions of liberal, representative democracy beyond the European-North American setting where they originated. From southern European countries like Portugal, Spain and Greece in the mid-1970s to several Latin American, Asian and African countries, Eastern Europe and the former Soviet Union and South Africa in the 1980s, democratization followed different paths associated with a diversity of historical experiences and dynamics of political and social conflict. At the turn of the twenty-first century, in what some have seen as the culmination of these 'waves of democratization', the Washington consensus version of a new, post-Cold War world championed a convergence towards a common, minimal model of representative democracy and a global capitalist economy as the condition for peace and prosperity at the global scale. International organizations like the World Bank included the establishment of democratic institutions and free elections among the set of conditions required for loans and development projects. Over the last few years, however, the promises that the virtuous combination of parliamentary democracy and global capitalism would bring in its wake more development, more equality and less injustice were added to the already long list of the unfulfilled promises of modernity. It will hardly come as a surprise, then, that as different forms of resistance and opposition to the dynamics of neoliberalism emerged, the debates on the theory and practice of democracy and on its links to social, environmental, cognitive and cultural justice gained in visibility and intensity.

The studies included in this volume have their origin in an international research project, 'Reinventing Social Emancipation', whose aim was to identify and study in detail experiences taking shape through resistance to hegemonic, neoliberal globalization and to its consequences in different areas of social life. The path taken by the project was to look at popular movements and citizen initiatives in a range of semiperipheral countries, that is, countries occupying an intermediate position within the world system in terms of levels of development as measured by conventional standards such as those used by the UN, and located in different regions of the world. The five selected countries were Brazil, Colombia, South Africa, India and Portugal. A peripheral country, Mozambique, was added as a 'control' case. The research team gathered more than 60 researchers in the six countries.[1] Rather than following the conventional path of defining a common theoretical and methodological framework, the project was organized around a thematic core which captured a range of issues defining crucial areas of contestation and resistance to hegemonic globalization and of experimentation with alternative, solidaristic and democratic forms of action. The five thematic areas were the following:

Democracy and Participation

Democracy and participation includes experiences of participatory democracy in both urban and rural contexts which, against the trivialization of citizenship, promote high intensity forms of democratic life, articulating participation and representation and recognizing the legitimacy of a range of forms of expression and public action and a diversity of public spheres associated with the latter.

Non-capitalist Production and Economic Organization

Included here are experiences in solidaristic and cooperative economic activity, associative projects of local development, collective management of land and other resources, alternative forms of access to credit, the creation of translocal and transnational networks of solidaristic economic activity.

Redistribution, Recognition, Justice and Multicultural Citizenship

This head encompasses struggles for the recognition of difference by indigenous peoples, sexual minorities, womens' movements and movements struggling for multicultural conceptions of human rights, for cosmopolitan citizenship, and for broader, multicultural concepts of justice that articulate recognition and redistribution.

INTRODUCTION 3

Biodiversity, Rival Forms of Knowledge and Cognitive Justice

Included here are the range of responses to the attempts at commodifying biodiversity and different forms of local knowledge and establishing new regimes of intellectual property, as well as the modes of asserting and protecting forms of knowledge on the environment, health and the management of land and space currently under threat by the expansion of hegemonic forms of knowledge and of neoliberalism.

New Forms of Labour Internationalism

The characteristics of the new forms of conflict between capital and labour and the emerging responses by the labour movement and its experiments with innovative forms of action and alliances with other movements and initiatives are here considered in their links to local forms of struggle and resistance to exploitation.

The conception of knowledge and of social scientific research that informed the project deviates from conventional social scientific work in several respects. The production of knowledge is, here, inseparable from a critical engagement with the subjects and the settings of the research. By 'critical', we mean that the task of the researcher is not just to describe and deal with what can be identified and analyzed using dominant social scientific theories and research procedures. Reality should not be reduced to what exists at a given historical juncture according to these theories and procedures. Uncovering the absences of official discourse and the silenced voices of past and present struggles and identifying the emergent forces that give shape to alternatives are crucial means for the production of a knowledge which does not see the current dynamics of neoliberal, hegemonic globalization and the low intensity forms of democracy and social apartheid it generates as ineluctable, as a fatality to which people should adapt in order to survive. Other futures and another, solidaristic globalization are possible, and grassroots movements and struggles are crucial contributions to the project of a multicultural and cosmopolitan world, a world built on social and environmental justice, solidarity, active citizenship and high intensity democracy. Cognitive justice and epistemic democracy are an indispensable part of such a project.

This form of critical engagement with the world does not mean that rigour and objectivity are sacrificed. The five thematic areas were explored through specific extended case studies selected by each national team, mobilizing a range of techniques available to social scientists. The 'strong' version of objectivity adopted ensured that the assessment of research would take into account the whole range of social, political, cultural and cognitive conditions framing each of the case studies.

A broader comparative approach including southern hemisphere countries allowed for a different range of questions to be asked and for the specificities of the semiperipheral condition within particular regions of the world system to be highlighted without the imposition of theoretical and analytical frames based on the analysis of core or 'developed' countries. This approach aims at the 'de-provincializing' of the discussion of current issues of democracy and citizenship in Europe both through its relocation to a broader space of comparison and through the detailed analyses of a country which is both a part of one of the core regions of the world system – the European Union – and a subaltern space within this region, thus concentrating in an exemplary way many of the contradictions that characterize the world system in its current historical stage. The following sections explore some of the contributions of this fresh approach to critical and comparative research to the discussion of the current predicament of democracy in Europe as it faces the challenge of neoliberalism and of the emerging responses to it.

NEOLIBERALISM AND ITS CHALLENGES TO DEMOCRACY

Even in the countries regarded as the cradle of democracy, the decreasing participation of citizens in elections, the lack of accountability of elected officials, the growing exclusion or marginalization of significant sectors of their populations from participation in social and political life or from gainful employment, the limitations of political and social rights, the dismantling of public welfare provision and the privatization of the public services that were at the core of the welfare state are regarded by many observers as symptoms of severe pathologies that affect the democratic order and its legitimacy.

The current situation is characterized by a predominance of forms of 'thin' or low-intensity democracy (Santos 2002b: 293), with democratic life reduced to steadily less mobilizing periodical elections to choose those who will exercise power on behalf of citizens. Both economic and financial globalization and the securitarian turn in the wake of the events of 11 September 2001 are accelerating the erosion of both the space of genuine political choice and the rights of citizens. Global economic constraints are invoked as a fatality to which all countries have to adapt in order to be able to survive in an increasingly competitive environment which escapes regulation by national governments. Threats by terrorist organizations or by so-called 'rogue states' allegedly justify the enactment of a wide range of liberticide measures, some of them aimed selectively at some groups defined by their ethnic background, nationality or religion – and, more generally, at the movements and organizations labelled as

INTRODUCTION 5

'anti-globalization' – but striking more generally at the heart of the very 'negative liberties', the rule of law and the respect for basic human rights once celebrated by even the most conservative liberals – all this in the name of collective security. Exclusion, xenophobia, increasing inequality, these are the visible consequences of a 'de-intensification' of democracy which is rapidly extending towards attempts at limiting the very rights of expression and association.

In the core countries of the world system, the experience of the welfare state as a response to the tension between capitalism and democracy through a 'virtuous' circle of economic growth and redistributive policies has given room to the mysterious disappearance of that very tension, with the spread of the market to every domain of social life, the narrowing down of democracy to a minimalist version and the push towards deregulation and the dismantling of redistributive policies. In semiperipheral and peripheral countries, even the limited attempts at public policies aiming at the reduction of inequalities and at the provision of basic services in health, education and welfare were swept by the tide of neoliberal economic and financial policies. The collapse of the experiences of state socialism in the former Soviet Union and in Eastern European countries added to the widespread belief that capitalism in its neoliberal version would become the unchallenged form of economic organization dictated by historical necessity. This state of affairs has not gone unchallenged, however. Some see in the capacity for self-criticism and renewal of the constitutional order and the institutions of liberal democracy the key to effective responses to the pathologies of actually existing representative democracy and to neoliberal globalization. Others, instead, point to innovative forms of citizen participation and social movements arising from subaltern groups and collectives throughout the world and to their struggles for broader, participatory conceptions of democracy and of citizenship (Santos 2001).

Valuable insights into the current crisis of democracy have been provided by the critiques of 'aggregative' democracy advanced by 'deliberative' theorists. Whereas the former assumes that citizens have preformed and fixed interests and preferences that will not be changed through their engagement in political struggle and public debate – and thus the voting process, as the main means of expression of the will of citizens, amounts to an aggregation of individual preferences and interests – the latter have underlined the way in which debate and persuasion through rational argument may lead participants in deliberative processes to change their views on the subjects under discussion and thus either to reach common or convergent positions on these or, at least, to have a better and clearer understanding of one another's positions when they disagree. The value often put on consensus through deliberation as the 'normal' (or, at least, the most desirable) outcome of the democratic process, however, tends to neglect a crucial feature of democracy: its recognition as an agonistic play of conflictual and diverse perspectives, aimed at dealing with the tensions between liberty, equality and difference, between the struggle for recognition and the struggle for redistribution, in order to construct common worlds where differences and contradictions can be dealt with through non-violent means.[2]

It is not enough to search for more participatory and deliberative modes of exercising democracy as long as the problems of inclusion and exclusion, of both ensuring access to the material means for a decent living and of broadening the means and forms of democratic expression are not taken up as crucial for the survival and quality of democratic life. Citizens often express their concerns in this respect through repertoires that are not reducible to debate based on rational argument. Forms of story-telling, performance, music, dance and other modes of expression or public protest are all legitimate, democratic means of non-violent participation in public life. This broad conception of democracy is all the more needed when governments and administrations increasingly tend to ignore public expressions of discontent that do not follow the 'orderly' path of voting, petitioning or responding to opinion polls and display a rejection of the political choices offered by the traditional actors of representative democracy.

DEMOCRATIZING DEMOCRACY: THE ROAD TO ACTIVE CITIZENSHIP AND PARTICIPATION

In the European context, discussions of the pathologies of democracy and of their implications for governance, citizenship, social justice and the struggle against different forms of inequality and of oppression were strongly influenced by Michel Foucault's later work on power, resistance and governmentality and by a range of neomarxist, feminist and poststructuralist orientations. More recent work has focused on the need to redefine the political in heterogeneous societies where claims for the recognition of differences based on gender, sexual orientation, ethnicity or religion are prominent (Featherstone and Lash 2001), as well as on the implications of the emergence of supranational arenas of governance and political struggle. How can citizenship and democracy be redefined so as to take into account the emerging versions of a *demos* which is no longer based on clear-cut definitions of national citizenship? A further issue is that of the scope of the domains of social life which should be subject to democratic control. The economic and the domestic domains figure prominently among the latter (Santos 2002b). The need to extend democratic debate and democratic control of these different domains of social life beyond the national context raises other pressing questions on the capacity of extant democratic institutions and practices to deal with the effects of economic, political and cultural globalization. How to reconcile the need for more participation and the increasingly mediated forms – through information and communication technologies – of public debate and deliberation required for the creation of new kinds of public spheres at the transnational level?

Another area of debate relates to the need to rethink the governance of societies deeply transformed by a range of new technologies and of their impacts, variously described as information societies, risk societies, knowledge societies or knowledge-based societies.[3] Neither traditional representative democracy nor expert intervention have provided adequate answers to the problems arising from these developments, as can be seen form the responses to the BSE crisis, to AIDS, to environmental hazards or to the new expectations and uncertainties associated with genetics and biotechnology and with the new information technologies. A range of interesting initiatives and experiments in citizen participation in areas like technology assessment, environmental impact assessment and urban and regional planning, among others, suggest that the response to these issues may well provide one of the most promising laboratories for the reinvention of participatory democracy and of its articulation with representative democracy.[4]

These areas of controversy have recently converged with the debate within political philosophy on forms of democracy – aggregative, deliberative and radical – and on the relationship between representation and participation. The issue of participation has been linked to the notion of democracy as 'agonistic pluralism', as a mode of institutionalizing and channeling conflict within heterogeneous societies or within transnational spaces. As stated above, this requires the recognition, on the one hand, of the plurality of forms of citizenship within a national or transnational space, and, on the other hand, of the plurality of languages and repertoires of action that citizens bring to democratic debates and initiatives. This debate brings to the fore issues such as the need to reconstruct appropriate notions of justice, recognition, redistribution and participation in order to promote new forms of multicultural citizenship. Included here are concerns with cognitive and epistemic justice, as experiences in participatory technology assessment and in environmental struggles have shown. The recognition of a diversity of forms of knowledge and experience provides relevant resources for dealing with problems which cannot be appropriately dealt with as 'technical' or 'scientific'. Identifying the repertoires of rival knowledges and how to articulate them into new configurations of knowledge appropriate to respond to specific problems in particular situations is a crucial part of radical democratic initiatives.

This debate is, of course, interesting and relevant in terms of its implications for political theory. But it often fails to connect with the experiences and practices of democracy as they are enacted by collective actors in different cultural and historical contexts, on the one hand, and with the research orientations and programmes that explore these experiences and practices. This has been the territory of studies of 'contentious politics', of social movements and citizen initiatives, of identity politics and of the struggles for recognition, of labour movements and new global solidarities, of struggles for livelihood and redistribution, in short, of the new forms of resistance and construction of solidaristic alternatives to hegemonic, neoliberal globalization. These have gained increased visibility over the last years, through the successive massive demonstrations against the World Economic Forum starting in Seattle in 1999 and, in particular, through the three editions of the World Social Forum held in Porto Alegre, Brazil, since 2001, as well as the many regional and national social forums that have been organized in the wake of the Porto Alegre initiatives.[5] A further display of the power of organized citizens at the global level were the huge anti-war demonstrations held throughout the world against the announced strike on Iraq by the USA in February 2003.

Studies on Europe are far from having given to experiences of radical democracy in southern hemisphere countries the attention they deserve, nor have they explored in a more sustained and comparative way experiments in the articulation of aggregative and representative and deliberative, radical, participatory forms of democracy.[6] Some research streams have explored the ways in which social movements and the broader range of forms of collective action subsumed under the label 'contentious politics' contribute to the debates on democracy and, in particular, on its agonistic and radical dimensions.[7] As Barry (2001: 175–96) has argued in his detailed examination of instances of protest and collective action within the space of the European Union – which political theorists like Mouffe or Dryzek would label as forms of radical democracy or of discursive democracy, respectively – current experiences in this field are not just coalitions or mobilizations of previously existing collectives or groups: they correspond to the emergence of new collective actors who come to existence and define their goals and their identities through the very struggles they engage in. There seems to be a parallel

INTRODUCTION

here with the dynamics described by the critical versions of deliberative democracy mentioned above.[8]

This is particularly relevant for countries where the access of citizens to decision makers and the accountability of elected officials and public administrators is limited, or where spaces for public debate and deliberation which are not subject to the control or manipulation of the state or of powerful economic and financial interests are rare or non-existent. The case of Portugal is particularly interesting in this respect, in so far as, over the period following the 1974–75 revolution, it has revealed persistent weaknesses in both the redistributive action of the state – which thus fails to provide both the means and the opportunities for citizen participation in public life – and in organized civil society, in the form of social movements and citizen associations and initiatives. Given this context, both the experience of the revolutionary period and the more recent popular movements and citizen initiatives that are dealt with in the contributions to this volume raise intriguing questions on the conditions and the difficulties of the emergence of participatory action in times of hegemonic, neoliberal globalization.

There are obvious points of contact between some of the approaches mentioned in this section and the project that generated the studies gathered in this volume. We believe that a convergence is needed between debates on democratic theory within political philosophy, research on contentious politics and comparative approaches to emancipatory initiatives in the South and in the North informed by postcolonial studies and carried out by local research teams connected through transnational networks based on a non-hierarchical approach to knowledge production. This convergence will bring fresh perspectives to the debate on the limits of actually existing democracy and the alternatives to the latter.

PARTICIPATION AND GRASSROOTS MOVEMENTS IN CONTEMPORARY PORTUGAL

Portuguese society is characterized by an intermediate level of development and, historically, has fulfilled a role of intermediation between Europe and other regions of the world system, first as a 'subaltern empire', a colonial power dominated, in turn, by core European powers like Britain, and, after decolonization and following integration into the European Communities in 1985, as an intermediary between the core countries of Europe and the peripheral and semiperipheral countries of Africa and Latin America formerly subject to Portuguese colonial domination.

For almost half a century, from 1926 to 1974, Portuguese society was subject first to an authoritarian military government and then, from 1933 onwards, to a dictatorship strongly inspired by Italian fascism – the 'Estado Novo' – which suppressed political rights, proscribed any form of free political or labour organization, exercised severe censorship over the press and held on to a colonial empire ranging from Africa to India and East Timor. After World War II, political and social tension grew within the country, with successive waves of vigorous oppositional activism, associated with some opening during the manipulated elections the regime was forced to stage. The colonial empire started to crumble with the fall of the enclaves of Goa, Damão and Diu to the Indian forces in 1960 and the beginning of armed struggle led by the liberation movements of Angola, Mozambique and Guinea-Bissau, in 1961. The modernization projects advocated by a technocratic faction within the regime from the 1960s on, including industrialization and an expansion of education, contributed to limited but real structural changes, among them a change in the composition of the active population, with a considerable increase in the numbers and concentration of the industrial working class around the urban areas of Lisbon and Porto. The promise of a 'political spring' in the wake of Salazar's replacement by Marcello Caetano in 1969 soon turned into an intensification of repression of all opposition to the regime. Internal foci of tension and conflict, translated into labour activism, student protest and political mobilization during election periods converged with a deteriorating military situation in the colonies, growing discontent among a considerable faction of the military, particularly among those drafted as officers for the colonial wars, increasing international pressure on the Portuguese government and the oil crisis, bringing about the collapse of the regime.

On 25 April 1974, a military coup by the Movement of the Armed Forces (MFA) opened up a new era in the history of modern Portugal. The coup was followed by a revolutionary period characterized by intense popular mobilization and creative political activism, but by fierce political struggle as well, overseen by the different factions of the MFA. The first free elections for the assembly in charge of drafting the new Constitution were held in April 1975. That same year, in November, an alliance of moderate and conservative sectors of the armed forces took control, and Portuguese society entered a period of 'normalization', whose landmarks were the voting, in 1976, of the new constitution and the first free presidential, legislative and local elections after the fall of the dictatorship. In 1985, after a long period of negotiation, Portugal was admitted into the European Community, joining it formally

INTRODUCTION   11

in 1986 and thus starting the process of 'Europeanization' of the democratic regime.

The revolutionary period (1974–75) witnessed a range of fascinating experiences of active citizenship and of attempting to bring together the two traditions of representative and participatory democracy. As the process unfolded based on the tension between an emerging revolutionary legality and democratic legality, under the tutelage of the armed forces, a plethora of social movements and citizen initiatives gave rise to the invention of new forms of participatory democracy. The 'normalization' that followed the revolutionary period led to the establishment of a parliamentary democratic regime and to the drafting of a constitution which tried to inscribe both the institutional framework of parliamentary and representative democracy and the innovative forms of participatory democracy. Successive revisions of the constitution over the next two decades tended to erase the memory of the revolution and to 'normalize' the constitutional architecture by getting rid of those formulations that were seen as direct expressions of the vigorous popular movements of the revolutionary period and their achievements. Participatory democracy was inscribed in the constitutional text, to be sure, but more as a principle and a right than as a set of specific institutionalized forms of citizen involvement in public affairs. The almost three decades following the revolution witnessed a decline, first, of the vigorous experiences of active citizenship of the revolutionary period, and the fading away of many of its organizational achievements. But the memory of the revolution has not failed to feed onto the experience of those who underwent the consequences of the insertion of Portuguese society into a world steered by neoliberal, hegemonic globalization. Despite their often localized expression and their dismissal from dominant discourse on Portuguese society, recent initiatives point towards a revitalization of active citizenship in pace with trends identified worldwide, especially in the wake of the Seattle demonstrations of 1999.

Studies of the recent historical experience of Portugal have brought to the fore features such as: the absence of a strong, organized civil society, of social movements and citizen organizations and associations; a weak and incomplete welfare state and a strong welfare society based on family, kinship and neighborhood ties compensating for the weaknesses and shortcomings of the former; a discrepancy between the formal definition of citizens' rights and the actual access to these rights; and a discrepancy between advanced legislation and conservative social practices. European integration brought with it new versions of the gap between legal and institutional frameworks and social practices, namely the role of the state as providing the 'imagination of the core' that presents Portugal as a backward but rapidly catching up version of the core countries of the European Union (Santos 1993). If it is true that membership in the European Union did not lead to the overcoming of the discrepancy between legal frameworks and the enactment of citizens' rights, its relevance in opening up new spaces for citizen action and struggle and in providing a source of legitimacy for the latter was significant.

The authoritarian mode of relationship between the state and citizens has persisted despite the change in political regime and the advanced framework of rights which is still one of the most important legacies of the revolution. The absence of spaces for public debate and deliberation outside the formal settings of parliament, local government and legislatures and courts of law is conspicuous. Non-state public spheres are still foreign to Portuguese society, despite the vibrant but short-lived experiences in popular mobilization and organization during the revolutionary period. This makes all the more interesting the emergence, in recent years, of locally-based citizen movements against what are seen as situations or actions involving some degree of injustice or violation of the rights or of the well-being of the population. The cases studied by the contributors to this volume explore movements and forms of collective action that have given rise to a number of experiences of articulating different kinds of struggles, of movements and of associations, of alliances with local government, state institutions, members of Parliament, political parties or actors within the legal and judiciary system. They often mobilize resources made available by European integration, such as directives on the environment, consumer rights or human rights. But they also draw, if not always explicitly, on the memory of the revolution and on different traditions of local struggle and popular action.

Rather than considering Portuguese society as a 'latecomer' or 'laggard' to a converging space of states following a common blueprint for economic and social organization, citizenship and democracy, the approach taken here focuses on the 'bottom-up' dynamics of the relationships between difference and equality, citizenship and diversity, forms of democracy, state and society, state and economic organization, capital and labour, citizen initiatives and social movements, 'Europeanization' and national social and political processes, the global and the local.

THE CASE STUDIES

The contributions to this volume provide an alternative approach to issues which, from the perspective taken here, often look parochial in the narrow Eurocentric frame within which they are usually analyzed.

INTRODUCTION 13

Each of the case studies is located at the intersection of several of the five themes enumerated above. They are exemplary in the way they bring to the fore the complex dynamics of struggles against different forms of oppression and the specific modes in which a variety of collective actors converge or cooperate, revealing their ambiguities and hesitations. They focus on the way processes at different scales – local, national, European, global – are articulated. Although they deal for the most part with grassroots initiatives and movements, they are attentive to the multiple ways in which their protagonists resort both to forms of contentious politics and radical democracy and to the means and channels provided by the institutions of representative democracy. Whereas citizen initiatives are highlighted, attention is given as well to the different ways in which their success is contingent on the responses of national and transnational political actors and institutions. The new collectives emerging from these processes are thus more than just an aggregation of previously existing actors and of their interests. They define new configurations of interests and identifications which may be more or less durable, depending on how the specific struggles they are engaged in develop, how heterogeneous interests and aims are translated into common purpose and action and on the responses of the state and of other actors to their claims and to their initiatives.

NOTES

1. The project was funded by the Macarthur Foundation and, for the work on Portugal, by the Calouste Gulbenkian Foundation, and directed by Boaventura de Sousa Santos. For a detailed description of the project and of its results, see www.ces.fe.uc.pt/emancipa. The results are currently being published in Portuguese (in Brazil and Portugal), English, Spanish and Italian. See Santos 2002c, d, e. For an extended discussion of the themes dealt with in the project see Santos, 2001.
2. On this debate, see Habermas 1996; Benhabib1996; Laclau and Mouffe 2000 (originally published in 1985); Mouffe 1992; Dryzek 2000; Santos and Avritzer 2002; Santos 2002b. Geoff Eley's recent history of the European left defines as its backbone the themes of democracy, active citizenship and collective, grassroots mobilization (Eley 2002). As the author himself acknowledges, his extensive and detailed historical reconstruction is heavily indebted both to scholarly work in social history to recent historical experiences in grassroots activism, feminism, environmentalism and the peace and anti-racist movements and the theoretical and political debates over these experiences.
3. This is the focus of social science research within the European Commission's Sixth Framework Programme.
4. Among recent contributions to a growing body of literature dealing with these issues, see Callon *et al.* 2001; Barry 2001; Fischer 2003; Jamison 1998.
5. For a detailed discussion and analysis of the World Social Forum and its contribution to innovative democratic and solidaristic practices, see Santos 2003b.
6. Experiences like participatory budgeting, adopted by more than two hundred municipalities in Brazil and in other countries of Latin America and endorsed as good

practices in urban government by the United Nations and even by an organization like the World Bank, have scarcely made their way into debates on democracy and citizenship in Europe, despite their obvious relevance to many of the concerns of those who participate in those debates. See, for instance, Santos 1998, 2002a; Avritzer and Navarro 2002; and several of the contributions to Santos 2002c.
7. See, for contributions to this literature, Fox and Starn 1997; Giugni *et al.* 1998, 1999; McAdam *et al.* 2001; Tarrow 1999. The timely issue of political violence and its relationships to democracy is dealt with in a recent book within the same research tradition (Tilly 2003).
8. Barry's approach is strongly influenced by science and technology studies and by the latter's studies of the material practices of science and of how they make use of the power of *demonstration* to confer visibility and 'matter of factness' to the objects or phenomena they deal with. For an argument along the same line, see Callon *et al.* 2001.

REFERENCES

Avritzer, L. and Z. Navarro (eds.) (2002): *A Inovação Democrática no Brasil*, Rio de Janeiro: Cortez.
Barry, B. (2001): *Political Machines: Governing a Technological Society*, London: The Athlone Press.
Benhabib, S. (1996): *Democracy and Difference: Contesting the Boundaries of the Political*, Princeton: Princeton University Press.
Callon, M., P. Lascoumes and Y. Barthe (2001): *Agir Dans un Monde Incertain: Essai de Démocratie Technique*, Paris: Seuil.
Dryzek, J.S. (2000): *Deliberative Democracy and Beyond: Liberals, Critics, Contestations*, New York: Oxford University Press.
Eley, G. (2002): *Forging Democracy: The History of the Left in Europe, 1850–2000*, 1850–2000, Oxford: Oxford University Press.
Featherstone, M. and Lash, S. (eds.) (2001): 'Recognition and Difference: Politics, Identity, Multiculture', in *Theory, Culture and Society*, 18/2–3, special issue of, pp.1–281.
Fischer, F. (2003): *Reframing Public Policy: Discursive Politics and Deliberative Practices*, New York: Oxford University Press.
Giugni, M., D. McAdam and C. Tilly (eds.) (1998): *From Contention to Democracy*, Lanham, MD: Rowman and Littlefield Publishing.
Giugni, M., D. McAdam and C. Tilly (eds.) (1999): *How Social Movements Matter*, Minneapolis: University of Minnesota Press.
Habermas, J. (1996): *Between Facts and Norms: Contributions to a Discourse Theory of Law and Democracy*, Cambridge, MA: MIT Press.
Jamison, A. (ed.) (1998): *Technology Policy Meets the Public*, Aalborg: Aalborg University Press.
Laclau, E. and C. Mouffe (2000): *Hegemony and Socialist Strategy: Towards a Radical Democratic Politics*, second revised edition, London: Verso.
McAdam, D., S. Tarrow and C. Tilly (2001): *Dynamics of Contention*, Cambridge: Cambridge University Press.
Mouffe, C. (ed.) (1992): *Dimensions of Radical Democracy*, London: Verso.
Santos, B. de S. (ed.) (1993): *Portugal: Um Retrato Singular*, Porto: Afrontamento.
Santos, B. de S. (1998): 'Participatory Budgeting in Porto Alegre: Toward a Redistributive Democracy', *Politics and Society* 26/4, pp.461–510.
Santos, B. de S. (2001): 'Nuestra America: Reinventing a Subaltern Paradigm of Recognition and Redistribution', in Featherstone and Lash (eds.), pp.185–218.
Santos, B. de S. (2002a): *Democracia e Participação: O Caso do Orçamento Participativo de Porto Alegre*, Porto: Afrontamento.
Santos, B. de S. (2002b): *Toward a New Legal Common Sense*, London: Butterworths.

Santos, B. de S. (ed.) (2002c): *Democratizar a Democracia: Os Caminhos da Democracia Participativa*, Rio de Janeiro: Civilização Brasileira.

Santos, B. de S. (ed.) (2002d): *Produzir para Viver: Os Caminhos da Produção Não Capitalista*, Rio de Janeiro: Civilização Brasileira.

Santos, B. de S. (ed.) (2003a): *Reconhecer para Libertar: Os Caminhos do Cosmopolitismo Multicultural*, Janeiro: Civilização Brasileira.

Santos, B. de S. (2003b): *The World Social Forum: Toward a Counter-Hegemonic Globalization*, available at www.ces.uc.pt/bss/documentos/wsf.pdf

Santos, B. de S. and L.Avritzer (2002): 'Introdução: para Ampliar o Cânone Democrático', Santos/2002c, pp.39–82.

Santos B. de S. and Arriscado Nunes João (2002), 'Introdução: Para Ampliar o Cânone do Reconhecimento, da Diferença e da Igualdade', Santos (2003a), pp. 25–68

Tarrow, S. (1999): *Power in Movement: Social Movements, Collective Action and Politics*, Cambridge: Cambridge University Press.

Tilly, C. (2003): *The Politics of Collective Violence*, Cambridge: Cambridge University Press.

Local Citizen Action as a form of Resistance Against the New Wave of Worldwide Colonization: The Case of the In Loco Association in Southern Portugal

ALBERTO MELO

PREFACE

An Inner Search

This essay represents a subjective and no doubt biased account and analysis that gradually evolved out of an intense personal experience. Life is made out of a mix of hazard and choice, as options always result from ideas and emotions somehow entangled. Therefore, this essay does not intend to be a piece of academic research, but rather an 'inner search' (obviously conditioned by a self-made mix of theories, ideologies, social contacts and material conditions) focusing on factors that, between 1985 and 1998, reflected my personal involvement in the launching and the day-to-day running of a local development project in the rural interior of southern Portugal.

The Political Dimension

I became aware of myself as a social being in the extremely conservative and authoritarian Portuguese society of the 1950s. Not surprisingly, very early in life the political dimension came to dominate most of my concerns. And also fairly soon, some fundamental options were made that shaped my adolescent 'political consciousness'. After an initial strong and emotional commitment against both the right-wing dictatorship and the widespread poverty within Portuguese society, a firm and lifelong conviction emerged: all despotisms are right-wing, notwithstanding their seeming divergences or antagonisms, because all regimes based on physical intimidation and brain-washing propaganda can only aim at protecting the vested interests of the powerful and at thwarting the free flow of social change meant for the benefit of the vast oppressed majority. Rather than trying to find my place amidst the traditional 'left–right' dichotomy, I looked for a formal political commitment along the continuum 'personal autonomy versus external constraint'. Later on, this evolved into yet another type of continuum, 'social self-determination versus state diktat', and later still into 'local collective enterprise versus extinction/exclusion resulting from hegemonic economic globalization', in other words, 'citizens' awareness and collective will versus profit- and power-based totalitarianism' or simply 'life energies versus death impulse'.

Critical Education

Until the end of the 1970s, at a time of fierce ideological dispute, I found myself in a very uneasy position. I was not among those who primarily claimed the need to 'take power' in order to define and carry out an entirely different state policy, in which all measures would pursue a 'pure Left' design. Rather than taking power, my personal and permanent concern was 'to split the existing power' into millions of 'particles' that would be taken and increasingly used by each and every citizen. That made me realize that, firstly, I had no place in any political party and that no existing political party would make any use of my ideas and leanings. Secondly, that if I still wanted to be involved in politics, I had to find a much wider meaning for politics than the conventional 'power politics'. Now, the type of 'political' work that encourages people to continuously become more autonomous, better informed, increasingly powerful in all sectors of personal and social life, is what is called (critical) education. And that is why, after many years of a rather unhappy and often rebellious experience as a student, I felt obliged to re-enter the educational domain. Nonetheless, when analysing Education from a political angle, I realised how urgent it was to build up – through a 'learning by doing and doing by learning' approach – a new kind of education that would be much more than just another expression of the hegemony of a few over the many; and not yet an extra pillar for the sustained support of conventional powers and their dominant culture and ideology.

Now, such a critical, constructive and transformative education would necessarily mean taking it away from the teachers' hands and their classrooms, and building close links with social movements. A process whereby 'teachers' and 'learners' alike would be actively involved in a common search for solutions to the local problems that daily affect people at large and, particularly, the more socially and culturally deprived. Adopting this concept, education can no longer aim at giving pre-determined answers (for questions that have not generally been raised by others than the educationalists themselves), but rather the opposite: it means listening to the problems most people face and need to overcome, and then searching for, and producing, the necessary knowledge, attitudes and skills that may contribute to the design and implementation of appropriate and efficient responses.

The 'Laboratory' of Social Action

Meanwhile, I heard and read a great deal of information and opinions, and also uttered a few (but very little was written, as I was never a natural, fluent writer). Two more fundamental realizations thus dawned in my mind that were decisive for the later course of events. First, the fact that defining, arguing, demonstrating – while remaining at the mere level of discourse – was not after all a real 'scientific' method, because the 'proof of the pudding is in eating it'; an understanding of society demands that one enters the 'laboratory' of social action. Secondly, that after the mid-1970s, the 'world of politics' was rapidly receding and increasingly taking an ancillary role under the aegis of economic, chiefly financial, powers. A consequence of this realization was my decision, taken in the early 1980s – as a self-appointed 'social scientist' – to become an 'alert practitioner', directly involved in a process that would, somehow, somewhere and no doubt at a nearly imperceptible scale, touch some of the crucial issues facing contemporary society.

A Meaningful Crossroads

For the purpose of achieving a better insight into existing social realities, while simultaneously engaging in practical politics, the chosen ground for personal and collective involvement, in the mid-1980s, was the then quite novel area of local development. Obviously, this choice does not mean that local development is the only or the best sector to materialize one's political commitment. It is merely one among many. There is no such thing as a 'best option' here. Whoever wants to pursue their vision of a better society will have to find the right way (and this means the 'field' and the 'manner' that make them feel at the same time more useful and better fulfilled), at the right moment and in the right place. Such an option can and does widely vary according to each individual, and also during a person's lifetime. For someone like myself who had just returned to Portugal, on the eve of its integration within the European Community, and more specifically, who was then settling in the Algarve – where the disorderly growth of the tourism-tailored seaside sharply contrasted with a vast rural interior under threat of extinction – local development appeared in the early 1980s as the proper choice, a meaningful crossroads of crucial and strategic contradictions in Portuguese society.

A Personal Journey

The pages that follow are an attempt to disclose the factual and ideological environment in which a personal and collective experiment of local development took place. Naturally, the whole process was a collective endeavour – commonly understood, desired, decided upon, enjoyed and endured by all those women (as a majority) and men, who have taken (and most of them are still taking) a significant part in this challenging, sometimes distressing, but more often rewarding, adventure. However, I do not intend to represent here the views of anyone but myself. In this text I am looking for a deeper understanding of the pros and cons, the ups and downs, of my own commitment to local development since 1983. And this attempt is not merely done for the sake of an individual introspection, as I believe this exercise may also be useful for others who want to better discern their own personal journey through and towards social commitment.

Can there be any personal authorship when writing texts that have resulted from merging one's own ideas and opinions with those of others that became naturally ingrained within one's own 'mental capital'? I certainly do not claim to have written this essay alone and therefore hold no copyright on it. I have thought it through and typed it, certainly, and at a great expense of effort. But so many people, dead and alive, have also strongly contributed to it, that I cannot claim to be the author. Finally, let me warn the reader that I do not usually make very faithful quotations (for which I do apologize to my academic friends), as I have generally lost track of a clear border between what others wrote and said and what I agreed with, digested and absorbed. Nevertheless, whenever I can recall the author or the book that most influenced me on a certain issue, a specific reference will be duly made at the end of the text.

THE BEGINNINGS OF THE IN LOCO ASSOCIATION

A Lifelong Project

In 1983, when I started preparing a definitive return to Portugal, after living and working abroad for nearly 18 uninterrupted years, I drafted a project for 'participatory community development' in a given territory. Coming home would only make sense if it allowed me to carry out an entirely new activity, a meaningful endeavour that could really become a lifelong project. The proposal – then called the 'Green-Blue Project' (as it was intended for a rural area neighbouring the Atlantic Ocean) – was sent to two municipalities in central western Portugal, a region that I had known very well during childhood and adolescence. To my surprise, I had no reaction whatsoever from the local authorities. As I was later to understand, in the 20 years or so following the Portuguese democratic revolution of 1974, there had been a shift from a regime of 'planned backwardness' to one in which the newly created borough councils were exclusively concerned with physical infrastructure and had neither time nor disposition for the so-called 'immaterial' initiatives. That project was, nonetheless, inside my luggage when, a year later, I accepted an invitation to move to the Algarve, the southernmost province of Portugal, and join in the process of establishing the Polytechnic Institute of Faro (the Algarve's capital city).

The 'Hidden Interior'

Not knowing this region, which lies some 300 kilometres south of Lisbon, the first months after arrival were spent in reconnaissance missions across the 'hidden interior' in addition to some menial administrative work. And it was such a big surprise to discover, right behind the glossy cosmopolitan shores of the Algarve – one of the best-known resorts in the world for 'sea, sand and sun' holidays – an entirely different scene, a rural society which still kept most of its essential features. The Serra do Caldeirão is a semi-mountainous area that, despite its skin-deep soil and abrupt slopes, has provided the necessary living and feeding grounds for the people who have settled here since time immemorial. Human subsistence in the area has traditionally relied on a diversified utilization of the land (Mediterranean forest and fruit trees, small irrigated vegetable plots, animal husbandry, and so on) and on a deeply ingrained culture of self-reliance.

A Negative Identity

This Serra is one of the innumerable rural territories of Europe that have been 'set aside', earmarked for gradual extinction by the 'macro-architects' of the modern economy. Here was, then, a natural arena for the contention between the new economic ideologies and the determination to 'put people first' and to demonstrate in practice that human thought, emotion, willpower and action may succeed against the destructive designs of the hegemonic world economy. The first barrier to be hurdled was the widespread defeatism that prevailed among the local population. They had internalized a negative identity: being born and bred in the Serra had been for a long time, in the eyes of town people, synonymous with being backward and slow-witted. This is why when travelling around and asking

LOCAL CITIZEN ACTION IN SOUTHERN PORTUGAL   21

'is this part of the Serra?' the answer inevitably heard was 'no, no, the Serra is further up'. And further up we went, until we were already descending on the other side, without having found the 'Serra'...

Particularly after the 1960s, successive years of emigration had taken away the more active and energetic members of the local communities, a fact that strongly aggravated that rather gloomy attitude. 'This is only the land of those who have been or of those who are still to be', was the way some of the residents defined their area, as a territory where only the very old and the very young could find a place to live. Parents were the first ones to persuade their offspring to leave early and look for employment and better living conditions elsewhere.

A Provisional Action Plan
With the help of a few colleagues from the Faro Polytechnic Institute, a provisional 'action plan for integrated development' was prepared during 1984, and later submitted to the Dutch Bernard van Leer Foundation in view of an eventual grant. It so happens that this Foundation specializes in the support of community projects that cater for early childhood. Therefore, our initial proposal had to be revised in order to give first priority to this specific aspect. (And here was one of the first lessons to be learnt: although human life is manifold and, consequently, any process that is geared towards solutions to existing local problems has to cope with every facet of society, the 'application form' to be submitted to available sponsors has to clearly underline that particular field which is most likely to 'tickle' their selective attention).

After a visit to the area and some months of negotiation, their decision was favourable and our project – which initially was located in just one village – was approved for funding and, by suggestion of the Foundation itself, expanded to three more localities, and not only for a year (as we unassumingly had requested), but for a first phase of three years. This was certainly a unique occasion in my fund-raising experience, when the sum I had originally requested was, by a decision of the sponsors, multiplied by ten!

The RADIAL Project
It was now possible to start building a full-time team. However, colleagues at the Faro Polytechnic Institute were now much too busy in pursuing their academic assignments and careers, in which 'community action' is not validated or recognized. Therefore, in order to carry out the RADIAL Project (an acronym for 'Support Network for the Integrated Development of the Algarve'/'*Rede de Apoio para o Desenvolvimento Integrado do Algarve*'), which was about to start in

October 1985, new members had to be recruited from the outside. And not only outside the Polytechnic, but outside the Algarve. The three-person team who initiated this process included no one who was born in this province, probably because those who were more familiar with the territory and its crucial issues did not believe that anything could be done to alter the course of events. (This situation has now been entirely reversed, and more than two-thirds of the active members in the In Loco association come from the region, and many of them were actually born or still live in the rural interior).

A Preliminary Consultation

Even before the RADIAL Project started, a preliminary consultation meeting was held (in May 1985). Three representatives were invited from each of the eight rural parishes (or *'freguesia'*, the lower unit of the two-tier local administration system in Portugal) included in the territory selected for the initial phase of activities: the elected mayor, an entrepreneur or 'natural leader', and an unemployed young person. The main public services operating in the Algarve were also present (all the regional branches of government departments, the University and the Polytechnic, the concerned municipalities) as well as members of the OECD and the European Commission – although Portugal was only to join the European Community the following year. Local representatives were the first to be 'given the floor' and asked to make a brief presentation of their locality, focussing on its potential for employment creation (for example, under-utilized resources) rather than on its shortcomings. After each of these 'local resource audits', the officials present were questioned about programmes and measures their departments could offer that were appropriate to supporting the suggested local initiatives. The general conclusions were, first, that everywhere local resources existed and needed to be tapped and, secondly, that significant public funds were available but not accessible to local people, who lacked both the information and the technical skills to successfully prepare the required applications. Between the local level and the sphere of public services there was a 'no man's land' that needed to be covered by means of a structure and a process of animation, liaison, information and training. Such was the rationale behind the launching, five months later, of the RADIAL Project.

Immediate Action

Four villages, and their rural surroundings, were initially selected for immediate action and three main issues were chosen as springboards for local integrated development: early childhood care, training for self-employment and support to local associations. Next, local meetings were convened and the whole population invited to come and debate 'the future of our children'. This 'children issue', although statutorily imposed by the Van Leer Foundation, proved indeed to be a very useful and consensual topic for the start-up of a course of community action leading to a gradually all-embracing local development process. The question of 'local consensus' is in fact of the utmost importance for territorial fieldwork, particularly in its early stages, as small communities are invariably divided by bitter cross-generation feuds.

These meetings were very well attended (60–80 participants in each) and produced a collectively assumed decision to create village centres that would provide pre-school and out-of-school care and activities for local children. Parents' committees were then formed to search for suitable premises, gather equipment and raise funds. It could have been possible for the RADIAL project to invest some funds in buildings and materials and then open and deliver these centres to the local families. Our main objective, however, was to foster the empowerment of the local people and not to turn them into mere receivers of 'gifts' coming from the outside. And, for that to happen, it seemed essential to involve the largest possible number of residents from the very beginning of the process. The local 'children activity centres' had to be their own centres, not ours. In less than a year, the four village committees were formally constituted as parish-level associations, each taking in charge the management of a newly created centre.

The Children Activity Centres

After the initial phase of local mobilization and organization, the RADIAL team could then concentrate on the question of selecting and training 'animateurs' to operate the children centres. Given the lack of employment prospects for local youth, it was decided to recruit from among them the 'para-professionals' who would carry out the daily running of these centres. Obviously, they had no specific training to be qualified 'child-minders' and their schooling was generally below average. However, as we were continuously to learn through this entire process, any actual drawback can usually become the source of a very promising innovation. Training was then organized by the RADIAL team and, because opening the centres could not be deferred for a couple of years while waiting for all the necessary training to be provided, in-service 'sandwich' courses emerged as the natural answer. This operational dilemma – organizing training for people already working in the field they have to be trained for – actually became a 'trademark' of the RADIAL project and, after 1988, of the In Loco association too, as this methodology was further elaborated and adopted for, among others, the training of local development agents.

Training for Self-Employment

During 1986, while the local children's centres were beginning their activities, the first training courses for self-employment were also launched in the same villages, all within the scope of the RADIAL Project. Since the process carried out by local families and the RADIAL team had led to the opening of the first children's centres in the villages, several mothers – who now enjoyed some extra free time – asked the Project to provide support for new income-generating activities, as no local employment was available nor predictable for them in the short or medium term. The general approach adopted by RADIAL, in all its current fieldwork, was never to start from what the local people were lacking, from limitations or shortcomings, but rather from their resources, experience and knowledge. And this principle was also adopted in regard to training. Local artisans monitored the initial courses catering for traditional crafts (hand-weaving, dress-making, doll-making). The aim of the training, however, was to advance much further once the local lore was duly recognized and registered. A second generation of training courses followed, two years later, on wooden games and toys, knitting, aromatic herbs and cake baking. As a result, in 1989, seven new village-based production units had been formed, providing an independent paid occupation for the 50 women involved. The contents of each course and the ensuing self-managed workshops were the result of several confluent factors: namely, local tradition, potential commercial outlets, use of untapped resources and multiplying impact on the local economy.

The Question of the Trainees' Grant

Turning housewives who live in remote rural villages into skilled producers and managers, able and willing to cooperate in a commonly owned workshop, was not an easy task. Fortunately, at that time there were some European-funded training programmes that offered two to three-year long courses on a full-time basis, also providing a trainee's grant that was the equivalent of a minimum wage. This question of individual grants raised a crucial problem that was eventually transformed into yet another opportunity for a very appropriate innovation. A minimum wage was a relatively high income in those villages, especially for women who generally had had no previous paid employment. And we knew that after the end of the training course, when the women would start their business activity, the expected income was bound to be, at least during the initial months, no more than 25 to 30 per cent of the amount they had previously received as trainees ... An infallible formula for a premature death of the new enterprises!

The following scheme was therefore conceived and proposed to all applicants to the courses run by RADIAL (and later by In Loco): trainees were requested to save a share of their grant every month; this amount was then credited into a bank account commonly owned by all the women enrolled in each course. The money thus saved would be used when the trainees collectively decided to invest in equipment, raw materials or participation in fairs, and later on, when the grants had stopped, in order to supplement the meagre initial incomes of their enterprises.

To Produce and To Sell

With regard to productive activities, in remote rural areas like Serra do Caldeirão, crucial problems emerge at both ends of the line: to produce and to sell. In fact, it is not easy to mobilize local people for the revival of products and processes that they tend to associate with past times of backwardness and dire poverty. And if and when a few local people become interested, then it is not viable to merely recreate the old production process. New markets, new consumer trends and new requirements in terms of the producers' time and income are factors that all point towards a radical change in the organization of work. New technology is generally needed, but its introduction has to be combined with a vivid awareness that the products and most of the processes are still deeply rooted in the cultural history of the producers. Each single product is not just an item to be sold, but is also the expression of a culture, of a local society, of the producers' and their families' determination to live and work in the territory of their choice. And this no doubt raises new problems but also new opportunities.

Small-scale Dimension

One of the problems to face and solve relates to the scale of the local production: too small will not ensure an economically viable activity; too large will certainly degrade its hand-made and home-grown nature. Another crucial question is selling the local products. Given their small-scale dimension and the existence of numerous and scattered producers, conventional marketing strategies do not apply here.

Genuine local products do not aim at conquering the world markets. They have to combine quality with rarity. Ideally, they should be sold at the doorstep, to visitors attracted by a surviving local culture and keen to take with them some living evidence under the form of 'cultural products'. And a territory that becomes highly attractive, given its natural and cultural assets, can also engage in different forms of rural tourism, owned and managed by the residents. To manufacture distinctive and highly appreciated products in order to attract visitors and, at the same time, to promote family-farm based tourism in order to increase the direct sale of locally produced articles: this is indeed the most promising formula for integrated local development in rural areas like Serra do Caldeirão. However, short of reaching such an ideal situation, several other outlets will have to be tested, such as town shops and certain fairs with a strong 'rural or local development' image.

A Multiplying Effect

In 1992, the In Loco association invented just such a new fair for the Algarve region, the 'Feira da Serra', exclusively designed for the local producers to display and sell their goods, amidst a festive environment where the expressions of the local culture as well as the different local structures and projects are constantly featured during the three or four days of this event. This fair draws every spring and summer over 20,000 visitors, most of them in search of the 'genuine Algarve', and more than a hundred local producers. Some of the latter have stated that at least half of their annual income derives from sales here. What is more, in all the 20 times this fair has so far been held, a strong feeling has developed among the producers who trade there that they are not there just to sell their products, but also as 'ambassadors' of the 'Serra', and spokespersons for its 'difference', its local culture, and this makes them feel quite proud too.

In some instances, local producers have started to act as development agents themselves, stimulating others to initiate local enterprises, organizing local events – festivals, crafts and food fairs, gastronomy contests, local museums... This multiplying effect is indeed a hallmark of the strategy designed and carried out by the In Loco association from its early days. In the four villages where the work started, the original initiatives were closely interrelated: the wooden toys workshop also produced playthings for the children's centres; the hand-weaving women received local children and helped them with their school assignments on local culture and crafts, and also entered the administration board of local associations or created traditional music and dance groups; the trainees at the herbs course collected information and recipes from the elderly at the local aged people centre. And this principle has been implemented and reinforced ever since.

The Creation of In Loco

Now, it is time to properly introduce this association. In August 1988, as an offshoot of the original RADIAL Project, 12 founding members formally constituted the In Loco Association. After the initial stage of

LOCAL CITIZEN ACTION IN SOUTHERN PORTUGAL 27

about three years, when the Faro Polytechnic Institute (a public institution) was responsible for all official dealings, the existence of an autonomous, private and flexible structure was seen as a strong and urgent necessity. One of the objectives of the whole enterprise was, indeed, to demonstrate that citizen action was not only possible but also necessary, as it could be more relevant and efficient, particularly with regard to environmentally and socially sustainable local development, than the routine and anonymous procedures of public administration. Furthermore, as in the meantime Portugal had joined the European Community, new opportunities had been opened for diversifying and multiplying the potential sources of financing for initiatives undertaken for the benefit of the Serra do Caldeirão.

An association of citizens: In Loco was thus created as a non-profit association of individuals, of citizens concerned with the ongoing 'misdevelopment' of the world as a whole and, in this specific case, of the rural interior of the Algarve. Their commitment was to dedicating their time and professional expertise to the design and implementation of activities aiming at 'the improvement of the cultural and material conditions of the local communities of the rural interior', as formulated in the In Loco charter. Most of its founding members were already actively engaged in the RADIAL Project and the others had, at different times, joined the informal network that had naturally been woven among professionals, employed by different public or private bodies, who shared the same concerns. In contrast with other local development associations in Portugal (which were later to mushroom, especially after 1991, and generally under the auspices of local authorities), In Loco was an initiative taken by individual citizens, and until today none of its members is or represents a collective organization. To affirm the capacity and the power of concerned citizens and to guarantee total independence from 'party politics' in the conception and running of local development initiatives were, in fact, two very strong factors behind the constitution of In Loco which are still put into practice today.

Promoting sustainable development: During the initial years, and in addition to its central mission of promoting active citizenship and sustainable development through local entrepreneurship, In Loco carried out many projects whenever national or European programmes made grants available for specific ventures which In Loco deemed beneficial for the people and the region of the Serra do Caldeirão. At the time of the creation of In Loco, the RADIAL Project was still thriving thanks to the steady support of the Van Leer Foundation. It then became one of the several sectors of activity within the new association and was put to the service of the overall strategy for local development. Thus, after the local children activity centres were consolidated, it was decided in 1989 to extend their work from each parish seat to other smaller neighbouring localities. And this was done through a new project of 'mobile education': at first, regular tours by car were organized, with a qualified child-minder visiting the dispersed settlements and, later, 'play-buses' were launched. This principle of taking the necessary services to where people actually live, instead of expecting them to always come to the 'centre', was later adopted by some local municipalities when they planned and implemented local health care provision on the same basis.

Original fields of activity: From its outset until 1992, In Loco activities were mainly undertaken within the fields of training (in local and regional planning), transnational exchanges on environmental issues (for example, four one-month long 'summer campuses' for university students on natural and cultural heritage), applied studies and the organization of seminars and conferences (for instance, one in December 1991, on behalf of the European Commission, DG V, on the evaluation of social projects). These activities have increasingly given In Loco a wide visibility at both European and national levels, particularly at a time when very little had yet been done, in Portugal, under the name of 'Local Development'. It can certainly be said that In Loco was initially recognized at the European level, a factor that later led to official acknowledgment by the Portuguese government. General acceptance by local and regional politicians took a bit longer to emerge: not until In Loco achieved the status of a 'para-public' institution, as later happened under the EU LEADER Programme.

MATURATION OR TRANSMUTATION?

The EU LEADER Programme

In fact, a new phase began in early 1992, when In Loco was invited by the Portuguese Department of Agriculture to draw up a 'local action plan' as part of the preparatory stage of the EU LEADER Initiative. The 'catchment area' of In Loco was suddenly increased from the original four rural parishes to 29 (and later to 32), and its range of activities expanded in order to embrace all sectors likely to contribute to 'integrated rural development'. Moreover, the relationship of In Loco with public administration and local authorities underwent a radical change.

An organization that previously used to contact them 'cap in hand' to plead for their material support, had now become an equal partner and could sit at the same table for negotiations and decision-making over matters related to the running of the LEADER 'local action plan'.

According to EU regulations, each accredited private (non-profit) agency in charge of a LEADER territorial programme is allocated a specific fund which is expected to cover both its own running expenses (up to a limit of, originally, 10 per cent and later 15 per cent) and the adjudication and distribution of grants to initiatives taken by local entrepreneurs and institutions. The prerogative to actually manage 'public funds' (ca. €11 million over 15 years) which was bestowed on In Loco in 1992, when it became one of the 20 Portuguese LEADER 'local action groups' (after 1995, one of the 48 licensed Portuguese LAGs, under LEADER II; and between 2000 and 2007, under LEADER +, one in 52), was most certainly the cause of a deep mutation in its posture and image, which has yet to be thoroughly analysed.

A Network of Local Animateurs

With the start of the LEADER Programme, in May 1992, there is no doubt that In Loco made a decisive leap forward, in both quantitative and qualitative terms. A first important decision was to establish a network of local development animateurs. If the previous work in a small number of parishes had required a core team of seven to eight members, keeping now a similar methodology based on intensive local contacts would undoubtedly require a core team of at least 40 (and this only for the purposes of this EU Rural Development Programme), which was not viable nor desirable. Consequently, a two-tier organization was designed: local animateurs and core team. The whole area, some 3,500 square kilometres, was thus divided into seven zones, each under the coordination of a 'veteran', who would work there in close cooperation with selected residents, initially 30, remunerated on a full-time basis while attending a parallel training course organized by the In Loco core team.

This methodology has proven very fruitful and demonstrated how enthusiastically and effectively young adults (mostly women, in this case) can work on behalf of their own communities, when they become aware of the local needs and issues at stake and of their own ability to positively influence the existing situation. The animateurs support every potential or actual, social or economic, local entrepreneur in turning their ideas into viable projects. They have also started to collect information, opinions and local agendas, and to produce a very popular monthly 'neighbourhood newsletter' which is delivered to every resident's home.

Below are the words of a local animateur, who has been working since 1992:

> Many people were afraid to say that they lived in the rural interior. Now it is different, people are actually proud to have it known that they live in the Serra. That is because we have a different and better quality of life. I am personally committed, because deep inside I enjoy this kind of work. Perhaps I am too involved, which is sometimes unbearable, but I am strongly attached to the people here and to their initiatives. Our employment is precarious and we have no real prospects for the future, as this work may well finish all of a sudden. But that doesn't worry me. Each day is a new day. Something will crop up. What is important is that this work is my primary motivation. I do believe in the Algarvian interior and also believe that it is possible to do something, even small things, which once put together and interrelated, can offer better conditions to the local people and make them give its due value to the land where they live. This structure of animateurs set up by In Loco has allowed a whole series of projects to emerge and to develop, which would have been impossible without our action. Initially, it was rather frustrating, because I kept looking around and could not see the results of my work. I cried a lot in those early days. Today, I can see new tourism facilities, new or improved production units and restaurants, much more active local associations and a lot of new activities and initiatives of all sorts. A few years ago, people used to say: 'the Algarve is just sea and sand!' Today, even the mass media have discovered the 'other Algarve'.

Among many other effects, the In Loco animateurs have been very influential in the creation or the reinforcement of local associations and some of them have already stood for local elections at the parish level.

A Coherent Strategy

With the innovative EU LEADER Programme, In Loco finally guaranteed the necessary means – both human and material – for seeking to develop a coherent strategy of integrated local development. Naturally, this assertion has to be taken within some significant limits. The funds available were, on the one hand, just enough to support a few 'pilot projects' but not any overarching strategy (it was actually estimated by a Regional Director of Agriculture in 1995 that the LEADER Programme in the 'In Loco area' had received less than one hundredth of the European funds available to finance 'mainstream (petrochemical) agriculture' in the Algarve). On the other hand, the LEADER grant never covers any project on a 100 per cent basis, but usually 50 per cent to 75 per cent of the total outlay. Private projects with expected profits in the short term can easily find the necessary matching funds. The same, however, cannot be said regarding the poorer residents or the innovative initiatives of general interest that In Loco had to launch in order to guarantee or reinforce the success of the whole operation. Without its own financial resources, in such cases, the Association had to look for partners who eventually agreed to partly cover the total investment. And this was not always an easy operation, also due to the fact that In Loco was now supposed to be a 'very rich' association, overseeing 'millions' and even awarding grants to local people and institutions...

New and Critical Problems

The quasi-official new role of In Loco, under the LEADER Programme, raised really crucial problems: externally, concerning its image with regard to the local people – from whom it now had to demand all sorts of documents (social security, income and VAT taxes, birth certificates, building permits, etc.) whenever they wanted to apply for an eventual grant; and internally, as several members, previously occupied in essential fieldwork, now had to be drawn back to the 'headquarters' in order to cope with the colossal amount of 'red tape'. A very high price to pay, indeed, in order to guarantee that some novel and exemplary projects could finally be carried out in the rural inland and start paving the way to a sustainable process of local development. And it soon became quite noticeable that most of those who were very competent at dealing with personal, educational and organizational matters at the local level were hopelessly inept when facing the huge and complex stacks of paperwork on their desks. As a result, a small number of the In Loco staff had to volunteer and gradually specialize in 'bureaucratic martyrdom', not without a certain degree of resentment towards those colleagues who 'just wanted to eat the lean without taking the bones'. Uneven workloads, unequal shares of personal involvement and stress, an increasing gap between those who undertake this sort of work out of their belief in, and commitment to, personal and social values and those who want little more than a paid job, are indeed aspects that generally affect the life of any civic and solidarity-geared organization, and In Loco has been no exception. Regular conflicts emerge between effectiveness, which is indeed very high, and efficiency, which is generally low, thus causing undue stress and an avoidable waste of time and other valuable resources. It seems that most activists, even when they are full-time professionals, somehow resent managerial organization. Working interactions between veterans and newcomers can also bring about some misunderstandings and disputes, the former sometimes insisting on vested prerogatives, the latter tending to adopt an 'employee attitude'.

So far no serious upheaval has occurred within In Loco. Perhaps its continuing success, the very positive image it has managed to build among the Serra residents and the different public and private bodies, the deep and selfless commitment of its leaders and collaborators, have been factors that have helped to overcome the inevitable and inherent conflicts that are part and parcel of any human group. Also, the internal democracy of the In Loco structures and its daily running procedures, based as they are on decentralized and relatively autonomous projects or task forces, the easy access to the leadership figures, as well as the periodic (if and when funds are available) resident plenary debate on all aspects of In Loco internal and external activities, can explain its relatively untroubled existence.

External Impact

It is fair to say that the impact of In Loco was not felt at the local level alone. Often, its activities, opinions and publications (brochures, books, magazine, monthly newspaper) have made some meaningful inroads into existing regulations, institutional thinking and administrative procedures. It was also very important for the emergence of other similar organizations in different parts of Portugal, for the creation of a nationwide network of local development agencies and specialized professionals (ANIMAR), and for the design and organization of a biennial 'parliament', festival and fair of civic and solidarity organizations, local products, alternative and traditional cultures which has been held in Portugal since 1994 ('Manifesta').

As an example of a short-term impact on public policy, it can be mentioned that the very fact that In Loco (as also the other fellow-associations all over the country) earned – thanks to the EU LEADER Programme – a decisive say on the type of projects to be selected for European funds, eventually resulted in the introduction of more 'democratic' forms of rural tourism in Portugal. Before LEADER, the Directorate-General of Tourism, in Lisbon, had adopted a very restrictive and elitist policy with regard to rural areas. Only outstanding historical buildings and large aristocratic farms were usually licensed and subsidized to offer tourist accommodation, while applications for converting small cottages into self-catering lodgings, or for opening bed-and-breakfast facilities in the countryside, were inexorably refused. When all the LEADER Portuguese associations realized the strategic weight of the supplementary income resulting from 'small-scale tourism' for a rural family budget and started co-funding hundreds of similar projects all over the country, the national policy had to be changed, despite a fierce opposition by that Directorate-General.

Local Products

Small-scale local products represented yet another momentous battlefield. Existing laws and regulations had practically banned small-scale, home made products. In fact, due to the huge investments required to ensure all the necessary conditions for 'legal production', such sectors as cheese making, liqueur distillation, sausage and ham preparation, or food processing as a whole, were being handed over to mass-producing industries. And yet there were many consumers who still favoured the higher-quality and special products with a 'traditional and personal touch'. Once again macro-decisions were being taken against the interests and wishes of the majority of producers and consumers, a fact that has become only too evident in regard to the EU Common Agricultural Policy, and obviously to many other spheres.

As was already mentioned, during the first year of the LEADER Programme, in November 1992, the first 'Fair of the Mountain' was organized by In Loco. For the first time, all local producers from the 'Serra' (either legally registered or not) were invited to exhibit, describe to the public and sell their own food-products or crafts in an 'open fair' (*'feira franca'*), organized in a town located halfway between the depleted northern hills and the congested seaside. The success of this In Loco initiative was, no doubt, enormous. Enthusiasm ran very high among organizers, visitors and producers. Besides the wide range and high quality of activities and of products on display, the large volume of sales and of paid entrances, the fair also revealed its potential as the best possible 'training course' for local producers on how to present and market their goods and on the actual preferences of city dwellers and foreign tourists. This fair had indeed been designed, not only as a commercial event, but mainly as a vivid and picturesque 'shop-window' of the Serra do Caldeirão, where social, cultural and environmental activities – here closely intertwined – could be adequately represented. After organizing the first editions, relying on partial funding from the LEADER Programme, In Loco has now transferred the responsibility for the '*Feiras da Serra*' to the municipality of the town in which it is organized. At present, the aim is to hold one of these fairs in every season, with four different municipalities rotationally taking charge of its organization.

Recently, after strong lobbying on this issue of small-scale production by Rural development agencies, most of them strengthened by their involvement in the LEADER Programme, some rules of exception have finally been adopted by the Portuguese government concerning some local products, perhaps not the ideal ones but at least revealing for the first time some degree of empathy with the principles and aims of local development.

Partnerships

Naturally, numerous and very diverse partnerships were set up between In Loco and other private and public institutions, including local authorities, in order to design and implement specific projects under LEADER and many other national or European programmes of smaller dimensions. One of the several partnerships has involved, for instance, the already mentioned training and supervision of rural development animateurs. Some 30 residents were selected in 1992 to attend a two-year in-service training course on local development and to simultaneously stimulate their communities and assist their neighbours in designing and carrying out viable local projects, mainly of an economic nature. Every project was later thoroughly and jointly analyzed and debated by the promoter, the animateur and the In Loco core team, and further advice was often requested from the local authorities, local leaders, external consultants or representatives from public services. The local authorities agreed to pay the necessary matching funds (as the EU never covers 100 per cent of costs) with regard to the trainees' fees and, later, the salaries of these local animateurs (whose number has been gradually reduced given financial constraints), and also provided the suitable premises and indispensable equipment.

Towards Local Democracy?

However, despite the many instances when residents of the Serra do Caldeirão villages have freely and openly participated in this process of local development, displaying their own opinions, attitudes or decisions, there has never been a formal structure especially designed to guarantee a regular public consultation on all issues of local collective concern. And, in my view, this is obviously indispensable if one wants to improve representative democracy at both the parish and the borough levels by introducing some rudiments of participatory local democracy. Municipalities should, therefore, initiate everywhere an increasingly participatory process leading to the elaboration and periodic monitoring, assessment and revision of local development plans.

Until now, the task of setting up a participatory structure at municipal level could hardly have been undertaken by In Loco. Its role within a far-reaching vision of participatory democracy has generally been played through the diverse tasks – mainly of an educational nature (in its widest sense) – performed by its members, committed as they generally are to both causes of furthering active citizenship and of promoting integrated local development. So far, in fact, In Loco has not overtly adopted a political or ideological stance through its many and varied activities. Nonetheless, it could, of course, and certainly should become an important partner in such a process, if and when a local authority takes such an initiative. And it could even start advocating some new and more participatory decision-making approaches at the level of municipal governance.

This would be a novel and promising switch from the In Loco current strategy. Time may soon be ripe for In Loco to take a further step towards more participatory and empowering local structures and decision-making procedures. The main problem is that an association like In Loco has no independent funds and, consequently, always relies on projects it previously drafted, submitted and that are eventually approved in order to cover all its personnel and running expenses. Under such circumstances, how could In Loco make people and time available for additional, even though very decisive, tasks other than the ones supported by strictly earmarked grants? Has In Loco, therefore, inevitably to accept the role of an extra arm of public policies, with only a slight hope of gaining now and then some fleeting opportunities to 'throw a spanner in the works'?

According to Isabel Guerra (this volume) these local projects and structures can be considered as 'new forms of social regulation', which may be regarded as either extensions of the state apparatus, embryos of participatory democracy or managers of existing social conflicts. In the case of In Loco, it would seem that a civic and solidarity-based organization, when involved in a sustainable local development process, takes on different roles according to contextual and strategic parameters. In Loco has certainly been all of that at certain moments in its short history, and nobody can predict with any degree of certainty what will be the dominant pattern in the years to come.

Up to now, its ultimate goal has been to support local people – as individuals, families or groups – and help them to become more aware of the factors that most influence their society and to be increasingly capable of controlling their own lives. As a confirmation of what Isabel Guerra wrote, it is a fact that the local people who actively cooperate with In Loco are indeed a minority and it cannot be generally stated that those who do it invariably represent wider common interests. In this type of social action, however, it is not so much the number that counts, but rather the relevance and the quality of the initiatives and of their local, and sometimes global, impact in the short and long run.

In Loco has also been fairly successful in overcoming some ingrained parochial attitudes and in pushing an all-embracing concept of 'Serra' to the forefront; which is now a common reference for the more than 30 parishes and nine boroughs involved in the In Loco territory-based venture. It was under this banner that the fairs were held, that a new monthly newspaper was published (*Jornal da Serra*), that shops were opened (*Casa da Serra*) and festivals organized (that is, *Réveillon da Serra*). As these initiatives are gradually taken over by local authorities and other organizations, which is indeed no more than the very materialization of its continuous strategy, In Loco could in the near future start to take on a less technical but more political role (on behalf of a more active and participatory citizenship) within the Algarvian region. It will all depend, most obviously, on the collective will of its present membership and on the social and institutional context, namely the degree of acceptance by elected political leaders.

Living Precariously

Today about 30 people constitute the core of the staff, management board and general assembly of In Loco. At a peak time, when over 50 different projects were simultaneously running, the monthly payroll included more than 70 people. Precariousness, though, has been, and still is, the rule. A financial inflow is only guaranteed for the duration of any approved project, and this means that while current assignments are still being carried out, new proposals always need to be designed and prepared for submission. And even during the implementation of approved and financed projects, the actual regulations, the unjustifiable delays in payments and the absence of an interest-free loan system force In Loco and all other associations in a similar situation to endure a very hard and anxious existence in order to deliver 'public goods' for the well-being of society.

In Loco has neither a regular institutional support nor any political or religious allegiances. In order to survive and be efficient, In Loco has to keep searching for partners, to negotiate and compromise in order to reach commonly accepted agreements. Naturally, it has attempted to foster more participatory approaches within the existing power structures and administrative procedures. In fact, the ongoing work in local development and the pressure made by citizens' organizations are still pushing towards the creation of a non-partisan Third Sector Forum designed for a permanent enlarged debate and eventually for promoting some common, more democratic endeavours among diverse local, regional and national partners. In Portugal, so far, this process has undeniably led to a few but yet undeveloped breakthroughs in the domain of local democracy and, hopefully, will in the future contribute to a more participatory democracy on a nationwide basis.

Relationships with Formal Powers

Obviously, the future of this development will always depend on the global, political and institutional contexts that shape the relationships between the formal political powers, at their different levels, and the civic and solidarity organizations (or CSOs – a better denomination, in my view, than the definition 'by negation' which is implied in NGOs).

Taking into account the fact that local development associations do produce 'public goods', it would be fully justified that they regularly received a grant from the state budget, irrespective of their ongoing projects, and simply based on evidence of past activities and established according to mutually agreed performance indicators. This grant should cover the basic level of functioning (a permanent core team and essential running expenses), thus guaranteeing a permanent 'springboard' from which the necessary projects and initiatives would be elaborated, funded by various sources and carried out by task forces composed of both permanent and temporary professionals.

However, at present, the general outlook does not seem to point in such a direction. In view of the increasing and often absurd administrative and financial constraints which are built into both European and national programmes, as well as the 'power stance' that many public institutions and their individual decision makers and other officials still display in debates, negotiations and 'enforced' agreements, I dare say that the future does not look very bright for CSOs or public-private partnerships, at least in Portugal. At best, the power structures will still 'tolerate' them as long as CSOs strictly carry out the tasks they are delegated, insofar as they operate within a highly inhibiting legal framework that prevents any free room for innovation or a more autonomous and adequate local work. Rather than acting as sources of social creativeness, are CSOs bound to become mere 'extensions' of established, change-resistant policies?

A disturbing financial straightjacket is currently pushing CSOs into a Damoclean deadlock. If they wish to carry out activities of a highly professional nature, they cannot rely on voluntary work alone and they also require fully operational premises and equipment. All of this demands a regular inflow of funds as well as a strict managerial attitude. When, on top of this, there is a strong commitment to work for the benefit of populations and territories which are unable to pay for the 'development services' they receive, it is only too easy to conclude that CSOs will always have to be at the receiving end of public funds (hopefully with 'no political strings attached'). And there is no reason to feel demeaned by that. CSOs receive such a minute share of public money, when compared with big business. And whatever they get is unquestionably justified by the fact that – within some areas and regarding some targets – they fulfil 'state functions' in a more relevant and efficient way than the '9 a.m. to 5 p.m. public services' could ever do. Moreover, the specific activities that are undertaken by CSOs under different public schemes should not rely on subsidies but, as a rule, be covered by previously negotiated 'programme-contracts' – not exhaustively pre-defined but flexible enough to allow for the necessary revisions and adjustments, as demanded by the specific territorial and social contexts of their implementation.

Networking

The institutional weakness of each individual CSO, and also their natural disposition to cooperate in different degrees, has led to several processes of networking at both national and international levels. In the case of those which, in Portugal, are active within the various realms of local development and citizens' social action, this 'federating movement' started in 1992. In Loco was then one of the ten partners of a process that culminated, in September 1993, in the creation of the Portuguese Association for Local Development, ANIMAR, which is now the nationwide reference for individuals and agencies who work in integrated and participatory development, either in urban or rural areas. Among other initiatives, ANIMAR has launched the biennial MANIFESTA: since 1994, this 'Local Development Parliament, Festival and Fair' – which aims at raising the visibility of the whole movement and at increasing the morale and the 'societal weight' of all those involved – has had five editions. The fourth, in April 2001, co-organized by In Loco, gathered more than 300 different Portuguese agencies and thousands of agents, supporters and visitors (including the President of Portugal) during its four-day run.

A great deal still needs to be done in regard to international networking. Most Portuguese CSOs (and In Loco is certainly not an exception) have established regular or occasional links with transnational counterparts. However, much more could and should be done in order to built up a stronger alternative movement, following the lines of an antihegemonic globalization. Local development associations and other Portuguese CSOs should, for instance, become as a whole much more closely involved with the World Social Forum held in Porto Alegre, Brasil.

A Work Never Done

As happens with any other venture undertaken in a similar vein, when one attempts to advance in a direction that runs opposite to the mainstream, there are no conclusive victories in the local development projects which are carried out through local citizen action. Any eventual success, which is invariably achieved through a disproportionate outlay of personal exertion, is nothing more than the 'starting block' for yet another exhausting course of hurdles. The general feeling for all those participating in this movement is similar to one's constantly trying to climb up an escalator that is always going down... However, once inside such a movement, it is impossible to stop or step out, for every minute of such a struggle becomes an invigorating moment of 'feeling alive', a worthwhile step in one's personal effort to improve society and the world at large and, in so doing, to continually improve ourselves.

ACTIVE CITIZENSHIP FOR SUSTAINABLE LOCAL DEVELOPMENT AS A CREATIVE FORM OF RESISTANCE

Lessons from Spinoza

When someone is faced with a course of events – at a local, regional, national or worldwide scale – which strongly challenges their philosophy and values, what is to be done? Where is the opportunity for adding one's own input in order to reinforce what we believe to be the forces of life, culture and civilization, against the current destructive trend, however largely predominant or hegemonic, that is inevitably leading humankind and all other forms of life to strife, unhappiness, degradation and death?

Some 320 years ago, Baruch de Spinoza, in Amsterdam, built an extremely 'modern' concept of the 'individual' and of the right and the duty of everyone to become an active member of society. For Spinoza, each person is not the indivisible isolated atom of Anglo-Saxon liberalism, but rather a coherent set of relationships, either physical or intellectual, with nature, with all things, with other people. And these relationships unremittingly affect each human being. Consequently, no individual can ever be a strictly isolated individuality.

The coherence that is inherent in these relationships can and should continuously be strengthened, deepened, improved, but it may also deteriorate and vanish. In order to relentlessly foster this internal coherence, each person must fully understand the kind of relationships which are positive and useful, thus reinforcing their autonomy, but also be aware that what is useful is not only that which is convenient on a purely individual basis. Useful is above all what makes every person feel and act in solidarity with the natural and social world in which we all live.

Now, in order to attain this threshold of wisdom and to be able to undergo a relentless personal process of self-improvement and actualization, it is necessary, according to Spinoza, to undergo a daily practical experience: acting upon the world, searching and trying out innumerable and diverse relationships with the physical and the social world. Or, to summarize his own words, constantly being active through 'work' and 'politics'.

Conversely, there is an inalienable obligation on the part of political society, of any state, to constantly create and promote the most favourable context to the full personal development of all citizens through those two fields of human activity.

More recently, we find in the words of Paulo Freire a very similar message, when he writes that 'to be cultural and to be aware is the radical form of being human' and that 'human beings, when re-making the world they have not made, are making their own world, and in this making and remaking they remake themselves' (Freire 1975).

A Worldwide Movement of Active Citizenship

Certainly inspired by a similar humanistic philosophy – which sustains that whatever is related to the social sphere can never be submitted to immutable, inexorable laws – numerous organizations of active citizens have been created in recent years, searching for local answers to the daily problems brought about or exacerbated by the dominant macro-economic trends of today's globalized world. This is an extremely diversified and scattered movement, in which every local project and group is looking for those solutions – in terms of organization, of methods and of contents – which are the most appropriate to their specific context and to the capacities, needs and expectations of the people involved.

In most cases, these initiatives emerge to fight back the 'productivist steam-roller', although they do not usually try to withdraw from the outside world or from the economic domain. Instead, they attempt to find and validate some alternative, viable and sustainable ways in which to combine economic and social concerns. They are generally rooted in either a given territory or to a specific group of people threatened by marginalization or exclusion, if not eradication, as they are considered to be 'dispensable' by the hegemonic powers that be. According to the currently dominant ideology, whatever diverges from the parameters of the 'one and only economy' (that is, the globalized economy kept under the thumb of financial capital) has no place in today's society.

The Three Layers of the Economy

Within this wider trend, the worldwide anti-hegemonic movement, known as Sustainable Local Development, starts by denying the existence of a unique economy. In doing this, it assumes the pluralistic structure proposed by the French economic historian Fernand Braudel, who, in 1980, defined three relatively independent economic spheres, each with its specific rules and features: the world economy, the economy of the local market, and the family (or subsistence) economy.

In a more recent work (Verschave 1994), it is held that this tripartite Braudelian structure allows, even in the near-totalitarian world of today, some margin of human freedom and social creativity. There is communication and also interdependence among the three layers of the economy, but no over-determination: the deadlocks or contradictions that occur in each one of the three strata can also influence the others.

The top layer – the world economy – has been mainly conquered by the 'new conquistadors', the giant corporations and the huge financial trusts that can overnight build or destroy most national or regional economies. Within such a novel and singular context, the functions of the state have been reduced to mere financial, legal and bureaucratic engineering, with the main aim of ensuring the most favourable conditions for the maximal monetary accumulation by national and transnational corporations. In this way, the essence of the state, as a political expression of the common public interest, seems to be dying out. The state has also been privatized. The alliance between the state and economic interests is now well established, to the detriment of democracy and the citizen. The state, which should be the political arm of human society, has thus become the delegate, if not the hostage, of the world economy. Individual states are now under close and relentless scrutiny: public funds have to be invested according to the whims of the world economy and not with regard to the will and the needs of the citizens. Consequently, those governments which, at a given time, may feel more concerned with the ordeal of marginalized localities or of excluded social groups, and which intend to launch important public programmes for their benefit, are immediately rebuked by their 'supervisors' and punished for contravening the norms of 'financial convergence'. If they persist, they will be put on the 'black list' of investors and international banks, and their national economies will soon suffer the negative effects of inflation, stagnation and unemployment.

Building Alternatives from the Bottom-Up

Given the existing constraints upon governmental institutions and policies, I daresay that the possibility for a genuine – equitable and sustainable – worldwide development starts at the local level, because all macro-economic measures forcibly focus on growth, and accordingly adopt quantitative, 'monetary-obsessed' and 'productivity related' criteria and indicators which are incompatible with human-centred development. And while taking growth as a goal is always conducive to increasing concentration and totalitarianism, Sustainable Local Development is strongly biased towards liberation, as it tends to further the autonomy, the awareness and the cooperative participation of the majority.

Today, the question is not only that of trying to find an economically viable response at the local level, but engaging in a process that – in the long term and through the networking of a plethora of local structures and experiences – will produce a worldwide alternative (or rather alternatives, as local development inherently means diversity) to the dominant destructive economy and to our crumbling societies. It is not, however, a new system replacing the old system, but rather, I believe, the slow but steady establishment of a creative and fruitful co-existence of different sub-systems, as diversified forms of working, producing, consuming and living together. And this is no doubt a decisive step forward in the advancement of democracy: achieving a plural economy as part and parcel of a truly open and free society.

We are not really nearing the 'end of History': our societies are now, and will always be, undergoing a permanent process of creation, of construction (or destruction?) of the future. And the possible future is being built – today, every day – within the cultural, social, economic, and environmental 'fissures' of the dominant system, through multiple and varied experiences, including those that occur within the vast range of local development activities in urban and rural territories. Now, the adoption of the Sustainable Local Development approach in contemporary societies means a process of constantly challenging the illegitimate claim of a unique, hegemonic, political and economic system, and favouring instead the eruption of the most diverse initiatives and choices, thus ensuring pluralism and diversity, which are vital dimensions not only to organic but also to social life.

Within this new trend, there is a strong need to resist domination as imposed by world financial capital. Local projects, therefore, have to achieve certain degrees of autonomy, at different levels (from local to inter-local and international), and it will become necessary, in addition to other measures, to reduce dependence in regard to the world trade and, consequently, to escape from the disruptive manipulations of the currency stock exchange. Surely, in today's world there is no longer room for an excessive autarky and protectionism. But nothing should prevent a locality, a region or a country from implementing strategies based on a certain degree of economic self-reliance, namely within the strategic food sector. For that to happen, current policies have to undergo an about-turn and to start redesigning and reorganizing social and economic life from the 'bottom up'. We need to test the 'principle of subsidiarity' also within the economic domain: detecting basic needs, listing actual and potential resources, locality by locality; then, only in relation to those goods and services not locally available would regional markets and, following the same logic, national, continental and world markets, be called for. After the food sector, all the other fields of economic and social life could follow this same approach.

On the basis of audit and diagnosis surveys, carried out at the local level, it is possible to elaborate an integrated plan concerning sustainable development and quality of life. This would lead to an 'asymmetric developmental framework', that is, decentralized and differentiated strategies for different territories and sectors: in some instances, there would still be room for economic growth, in others the priority should be given to a steady-state economy of zero-growth and, in the excessively congested localities, the goal could well be that of a negative growth rate, at least for a period of time; in all cases, the global aim should be to constantly enhance life and its quality for present and future generations (of all living forms).

The Urge for a More Favourable Political Context

At the same time, a favourable institutional framework has to be built in order to promote micro-initiatives everywhere. For instance, encouraging intermediate agencies – such as local committees for development and associations for local development – to emerge and to be active by means of 'programme-contracts' supported by a decentralized fund designed to promote Sustainable Local Development. Obviously, new legislation and rules need to be adopted, not penalizing but encouraging the creation of micro-firms and self-employment at a small scale, namely with regard to the legal requirements of production (nowadays exclusively grounded on the needs of the mass, industrial scale), to fiscal matters and to social security deductions. It will be necessary to stimulate universities and research centres to focus an increasing part of their activities upon local communities and economies, as well as small-scale production. It will also be necessary to have new decentralized credit agencies and risk capital and insurance companies, in order to channel local savings towards initiatives within the neighbourhood. Another necessary innovation, already under way in many instances, is the creation of 'local money', which can remove from the world market an important part of the exchanges that are locally carried out. Certain subsidies, for instance, could be paid in this currency, by means of 'cheques' only valid for the purchase of locally available goods and services that need to be protected and stimulated, despite the fact that they are not competitive within the wider markets. In this way, it would be guaranteed that at least part of the allowances and grants locally paid would actually strengthen local economies instead of further reinforcing the dominant forces of the worldwide economy. These 'local cheques' could also be issued to institutions, such as schools, hospitals, homes for the elderly, etc., as these could represent an invaluable outlet for local products and services – for example, agricultural crops and food products considered as non-marketable by the yardsticks of the macro-economy. Moreover, all public tenders should include social and ecological clauses, thus giving preference to bidders who guarantee, for instance, the creation or upgrading of local employment as well as a real respect for environmental issues.

Given this short list of examples (many more could obviously be mentioned), it is easy to understand the scope and depth of the changes that could be induced in our societies by giving priority to the implementation of Sustainable Local Development by means of territory-based plans and initiatives. Hence the vital importance of all those social experiments that are now taking place all over the planet and that can be included under this banner. Within this context, 'local' means much more than just the 'fourth level' of enforcement of macro-economic measures. It is indeed the only echelon at which it is possible to attain, in a given and manageable territory, the actual integration of sector-based programmes and, at the same time, to ensure the full, daily and empowering participation of an increasing proportion of all citizens. And it is also at the local level that citizens' associations can carry out their political, social and economic projects, for it is only at this scale that the creativity of civil society can clearly be expressed and materialized.

Still a Very Complex Matter

Sustainable Local Development has so far proved to be a very positive answer for groups and territories that have been left behind by the world economy. However, local development is in itself a very complex affair. To create, out of indigenous resources, alternative ways that also need to be viable, at least partly, within the wider economic context, is no easy task. To request the indispensable support from society at large, by means of start-up grants and other aid schemes, without falling prey to a situation of permanent dependence, also poses rather intricate problems. And to combine local and external know-how in order to design projects that will help revive the social and economic fabric of local communities is certainly not a straightforward process, as it is prone to constant conflict. To turn conflict into creativity is a rare skill that has to be acquired and deployed by everyone active in these processes and structures.

Furthermore, how can we foster 'the culture of development' or 'the urge for autonomy' in the more deprived and unstructured areas so deeply affected by isolation, acculturation, dependence, emigration, low esteem? It is a fact that, in declining rural territories suffering from pre-desertification, in both demographic and ecological terms, as well as in marginal, disadvantaged urban areas, a social movement for change – for a better quality of life, if not just for life – will generally have to be introduced from the outside. There are obviously some local – human and natural – assets on which to build a viable action strategy. However, given the social and cultural disruption caused by strong external constraints and also by a deeply ingrained disbelief in available resources and capacities, the following paradox has to be well understood and accepted within local development: any process leading to endogenous development requires, by and large, an external energy input, certainly in the initial phase, but very frequently also as a collateral driving force for many years, until the local organizational capacity reaches a mature and self-sustaining stage.

Does In Loco Have a Viable Future?

The In Loco Association, as already described and analysed, has carried out such a role since the mid-1980s. The definite proof of its success would be its eventual disbandment as new local – village and borough – associations come into being. This process is actually under way, though still in a timid and uneven manner, and In Loco has always fully supported local organizational capacity building. Such a development, however, does not seem to make In Loco redundant, for new requests are continuously being made by local as well as regional bodies. Its nature, nevertheless, can radically change as a result of a better structured territory, and In Loco will possibly become technically more specialized and politically more vocal, concentrating its expertise and practical experience on such strategic matters as technical assistance to local authorities and associations on matters of Sustainable Local Development, and also having a mediating role leading to territorial and inter-local partnerships, experimentation and demonstration. Thus, it can act as a 'power station' for technological and organizational innovation, as a training centre for activists-cum-professionals, as a practical school for active citizenship.

REFERENCES

Freire, P. (1975): *Pedagogia do Oprimido*, Oporto: Afrontamento.
Verschave, F.-X. (1994): in Syros (ed.), *Libres Leçons de Braudel. Passerelles pour une société non excluante*, Paris: Fondation pour le progrès de l'homme.

'Decent Housing for the People': Urban Movements and Emancipation in Portugal

JOÃO ARRISCADO NUNES and NUNO SERRA

Over the last two decades, western-style parliamentary and representative democracy, offered to societies around the world as the 'natural' way of organizing political life and citizens' participation, has usually been defined in a minimalist way, as a 'low intensity' model of democracy (Santos 1999a), stressing individual rights and voting in elections held periodically as the essence of democratic life and of citizens' participation. The same period, however (and the 1990s in particular), also witnessed an apparently opposite increase in criticisms of 'actually existing' democracies and of their deficits and pathologies. The modes of participation of citizens in the definition of political agendas and in deliberative processes grew in importance as central topics of a debate which, although under different guises, has emerged in societies of both the northern and the southern hemispheres.

It is interesting to note a peculiar feature of the debate as it has taken place in several countries of Western Europe, in the United States, Canada and Japan. The problem of the legitimation of the state and of democratic orders in these countries has tended to be brought up in connection with issues involving science and technology and the intervention of experts – in fields like energy policies, transportation, telecommunications, the environment, biotechnology, human genetics, health and food safety, among others. Political decisions and administrative practices based on secrecy and on the exclusion of citizens from debate and deliberation were seen to be particularly frequent when a strong component of expertise and technical and scientific knowledge was present. As some authors like Ulrich Beck or Anthony Giddens[1] have noticed, science, technology and expertise tend to generate new forms of uncertainty and hazards whose consequences fall disproportionately on 'ordinary' citizens, who are actually excluded from any debate and deliberation on these 'manufactured risks'. We shall not go here into the details of this discussion. But the recognition of this problem – in the wake of several crises involving contaminated blood for transfusion, the AIDS epidemics, the BSE affair or serious environmental disasters – as well as the difficulty in dealing with it in a credible and effective way has led governments, parliaments, regulatory agencies, NGOs, scientists and other actors to search for new modes of public participation in debate and decision making, in the context of a 'precautionary' approach to politics.

As a member country of a core region of the world system, the European Union, Portugal has not been absent from this debate. However, the debate has some specific features which arise, to a great extent, from the semiperipheral condition of Portugal, as a space which can be defined as an interface between North and South, or as an instance of the 'South of the North'. This means that many of the issues and questions raised in societies of the South are likely to be relevant, at least in part and in specific versions, for Portugal. What will interest us here and now is the fact that the new approaches to participation, which have been enacted in the form of consensus conferences, citizens' juries or forums in several countries since the mid-1980s, raise three issues which, as we shall see, were at the centre of the short but intense experience of participatory democracy during the Portuguese revolution of 1974–75. These include the conditions and dynamics of participation and its organizational forms; the key role of the articulation of different forms of knowledge and of experience; and, finally, the role of the state as a promoter or, alternatively, an obstacle to citizens' movements and participation.

The experience of the Portuguese revolution concentrates in an intriguing and, at the same time, exemplary way features which will allow us to look in more detail into these three topics. We shall examine them, focusing on the process known as 'Operation SAAL', an intervention in the field of urban and housing policy.

Before moving on to an account of this case, however, some clarification is required of a number of aspects bearing on the relationship between citizens and the 'carriers' of specialized forms of knowledge commonly described as 'experts'. The role of the latter, as we shall see, was crucial to the experiments in participatory democracy in the field of housing and in urban planning policies which will be dealt with in detail later. The links between knowledge and political action were traditionally associated with the figure of the intellectual. The mobilization of specialized forms of technical knowledge in the context of movements aiming at radical political change, however, suggest that a redefinition of the intellectual is needed, as well as a specification of his/her links to the figure of the 'expert', of the specialist in a bounded domain who is in a position to draw on scientific and technical skills. This link, as we shall see, is far from being linear, and how it is articulated may well make the difference between the promotion of emancipatory dynamics and the emergence of new forms of regulation legitimated by forms of expert knowledge.

INTELLECTUALS, KNOWLEDGE(S) AND POLITICAL PARTICIPATION

Michel Foucault's concept of the 'specific intellectual' – who stands in contrast to the 'universal intellectual' and the 'organic intellectual' – appears to be an adequate starting point for the definition of the 'experts' or 'technicians' involved in processes of political and social change. The specific intellectual's business is not the production of a universal discourse, or of posing as the spokesperson for a universal subject (or, in the Gramscian version of the organic intellectual, as the spokesperson arising from a class, group or institution), but a kind of intervention which is based on specific modes of technical–scientific knowledge – 'expert' or specialized knowledge – and on their relations to particular 'truth regimes'.[2]

In their role as specific intellectuals, these actors may get into a collision course with the system, with institutions or with power relations, and as a consequence align themselves with other actors as participants in emancipatory struggles. This alignment does not rest upon the privileged means of producing public texts, but upon their interventions as specialists or carriers of a given type of skill or of knowledge. According to Foucault, the emergence of the specific intellectual is a phenomenon of the post-World War II era. Its exemplary figure would be a nuclear physicist like J. Robert Oppenheimer, first known as the 'father' of the atomic bomb, and later becoming an active opponent to the use of nuclear weapons. But the intervention of specific intellectuals was also highly visible in struggles around psychiatry, prison systems or, more recently, social welfare, the environment, public health, planning or cultural policies. Authors like Paul Rabinow (1989), though, point out that the presence of specific intellectuals can be traced back to earlier periods, linked to the figures Rabinow describes as 'middling modernists', agents of urban and social planning who, from the first third of the nineteenth century onwards, were in charge of 'engineering' the modernization of both imperial metropoles and colonial territories. They acted on behalf of what was regarded, at the time, as the universalist mission of promoting progress and welfare.

Foucault's and Rabinow's proposals raise two interesting problems with the concept, which are particularly noticeable in the case of revolutionary Portugal. The first is related to the tension between hegemonic and counterhegemonic tendencies among specific intellectuals. Their professional ideologies may lead them to embrace interventions regardless of who the actors involved are (the state, corporations, social movements, citizens), as long as these interventions are seen as 'progressive' from the point of view of professional or technoscientific cultures. The counterhegemonic dynamics of these interventions is strongly associated with their articulation with citizen and social participation. In the case dealt with here, the specialists in housing and urban planning (architects, engineers) were very central in articulating the technical, the social and the political around housing and urban issues. This process emerged with a particular shape in the circumstances of revolutionary Portugal, which in turn leads us to the second problem with the concept, namely that of the tendential blurring of the categories of 'specific' and 'organic' intellectual under conditions in which it is impossible to sustain in a credible way the boundary between the 'technical' and the 'political'. 'Taking sides' in situations of technical controversies which are not separable from the political debate on the implications and consequences of these controversies was – and still is – seen by architects, engineers and other professionals committed to neighbourhood activism as an ethical imperative.

In spite of these qualifications, however, the concept of specific intellectual is still useful in defining the predicament of those intellectuals who engage in social and political activism by mobilizing a particular kind of expertise or of scientific–technical competence, rather than by claiming more generally to speak 'for' the justice of a cause. For many of these specific intellectuals, taking sides with urban populations in their struggle for decent housing and social justice during the Portuguese revolution was seen as an extension, in a new historical situation, of their previous involvement in oppositional political action during the dictatorship or, in some cases, of the experience of intellectual and political radicalization during exile in countries like France in the 1960s, particularly during the May 1968 events.

Seeking ideological and theoretical inspiration from the 'new' marxist currents – particularly from authors like Henri Lefèbvre and Manuel Castells, whose work was translated into Portuguese and had been circulating for some time, even before its publication, mostly in the form of mimeographed texts or limited editions (Lefèbvre 1972; Castells 1976) – the specific intellectuals associated with movements and initiatives in the field of housing and urban policies tried to put architecture, urban planning and other forms of technical and scientifically and academically legitimated knowledge at the service of populations, of their struggle for changes in social relations and for individual and collective welfare. This generated a tension between the claim by 'experts' to be able to define blueprints for emancipatory social change and the acknowledgement of the need to articulate the search for the most adequate and effective technical solutions for housing and urban planning with the different forms of local knowledge, aesthetic preferences and identity-building associated with the places where populations were struggling for decent housing and a more democratic appropriation of urban space. We shall see, further on, how these tensions came to the surface and how they were managed throughout the development of 'Operation SAAL'.

THE PORTUGUESE REVOLUTION OF 1974–75 AND THE CONTEXT OF 'OPERATION SAAL'

The 25 April 1974 military coup opened the way to a historically unique period of experiences of social and citizens' movements and popular participation. The military organized in the Armed Forces Movement (MFA) overthrew the longest lasting dictatorship in Europe (1926–74), which had deprived the Portuguese people of basic democratic rights and had been engaged, since the early 1960s, in a war against the liberation movements of the African colonies of Angola, Mozambique and Guinea-Bissau. Opposition to the dictatorship and to the colonial wars had taken a variety of forms, both in the shape of underground resistance and of overt challenge to the regime, through street demonstrations, workers' and students' strikes and, during the last decades of the regime, participation in elections staged by the regime. (see Introduction, this volume).

The long-lasting and unpopular colonial wars and the increasingly obvious impossibility of a military defeat of the liberation movements fed internal tensions within the military, particularly among junior officers. The MFA was the organized expression of common concerns which brought together officers with very different political leanings, some of them even without clearly defined political objectives. A minimalist programme of reinstating basic democratic rights seemed to hold the movement together during the first phase of the revolution. It soon became apparent, however, that under the growing pressure of social movements and of political struggle under the new conditions of freedom of speech and of freedom of association, the MFA was splitting into a range of factions, more or less aligned with different constellations of political currents and organizations, with the more radical wings claiming for themselves the role of a revolutionary avant-garde. Radical concepts of democracy, with socialism as their horizon, based on popular participation, on grassroots organizations and freely elected councils took shape and were central to the political debate throughout the revolutionary period.

A peculiar feature of this situation was the coexistence of these radical experiments and concepts with more 'traditional' blueprints for a western-style parliamentary regime or a more state-centered, Soviet-inspired model of society. As for the colonies, the early lack of definition as to the form of 'autonomy' to be granted to them soon became obsolete in the face of the unavoidable recognition of the independence of the new African States of Guinea-Bissau/Cape Verde, Mozambique, Angola and S. Tomé e Príncipe.[3]

Throughout this period, the state went through a period of paralysis. A series of provisional governments (a total of six) were formed on the basis of coalitions of political parties and organizations and of different left-oriented factions of the MFA. They were under the protective intervention of the military and highly sensitive to the pressure of social and citizen movements. Rather than a duality of power, the situation seemed to be one of a 'duality of impotence' (Santos 1990), with revolutionary legitimacy and democratic legality playing each other out in a game which would come to an end in November 1975. This situation was made even more complex by the pressures and counter-pressures arising from the geostrategic dynamics of the Cold War, which were translated internally into the programmes and strategies of the different political forces. Over a period of a year and a half, industrial, agricultural and service workers, neighbourhood movements, students, intellectuals and the military carried out an extremely rich and unprecedented range of experiments of mass mobilization, grassroots organization and participatory democracy. Meanwhile, a constitutional assembly was elected in 1975 – the first free elections in half a century – and a Constitution drafted which inscribed the tensions and contradictions of this period. This period of broad political and social change came to an end in November 1975, when a coalition of conservative and 'moderate' wings of the military and of the political 'centre' resumed control of the political process.

Despite its short duration, the revolutionary period left its imprint in the Portuguese constitutional order and in the historical and collective memory, both as a source of new energies and experiences for the renewal of social and citizen participation, and as an 'abnormal' hiatus in the 'normal' path to representative, parliamentary democracy. The 1976 Constitution defined the construction of socialism as its programmatic aim, and the range of forms of participatory democracy and of very advanced social and economic rights which had arisen during the revolution were explicitly acknowledged in the constitutional text. In the same year, the first legislative elections were followed by a presidential election, which provided a last upsurge of popular movements supporting the platform of the left-wing candidate, Otelo Saraiva de Carvalho, one of the military leaders of the revolution. This candidate (who got 16 per cent of the vote) was committed to the full implementation of the 1976 Constitution, namely the various forms of participatory democracy and the whole range of social and economic rights. Lastly, the year 1976 was also the year of the first election of local governments.

During the revolutionary period, experiences of participation mushroomed, and some of them concentrated in exemplary form some of the successes as well as the dilemmas and tensions of the period. One of these experiences was the process known as SAAL (Serviço Ambulatório de Apoio Local/Mobile Service for Local Support). Launched by a sector of the state in several urban areas of the country, it involved architects, engineers, lawyers and other specific intellectuals, students and, above all, urban dwellers from impoverished or run-down neighbourhoods, who organized themselves in local neighbourhood committees in an effort to define and enact new rights and new conditions of urban life centred on housing and on what some of the core actors of the process called the 'right to place'.

As part of a revolutionary dynamics, the operation, which was developed in the urban areas of Lisbon, Setúbal and Oporto, probably took its more theorized and consistent shape in Oporto. Its success in fostering a dynamic of popular organization and an alliance between sectors of the state, specific intellectuals and popular movements rested upon a definition of precise sectoral aims – decent housing and the right to place – within the more general objective of building a socially just, socialist society. SAAL/Norte thus showed a possible route towards this alliance of the specific and local with broader projects of global social change.

In the following section, a narrative presentation and chronology of the process is offered, including a characterization of the actors involved and an identification of their alliances and articulations, as well as of their strategies and modes of intervention. The memory of SAAL/Norte, invoked today by actors involved in struggles for housing and the right to place, is then explored as a resource for the reinvention of new forms of participation. This memory is set against the identification and discussion of the main issues raised by the analysis of neighbourhood movements in the context of this project. These include: the dynamics of popular mobilization and organization; the role of sectors of the state and of the military 'enrolled' in emancipatory and solidaristic projects; the central role of holders of different forms of knowledge and expertise in the definition of how to fulfil the objectives of the movement, as well as their alliance with neighbourhood movements; and, finally, the importance of the revolutionary situation to the 'feasibility' of the process.

The materials we drew on for this case study include, on the one hand, published reports, analyses and documents of the period, and, in particular, those produced by, or otherwise related to, SAAL/Norte.[4] A second type of source consisted of interviews with key informants, all of them participants in the process. Finally, we also drew on our participation in recent debates on housing and urban policies, involving former and current activists of neighbourhood movements, specific intellectuals linked to housing and urbanism and members of political organizations active in this area.

THE EXPERIENCE OF SAAL/NORTE: THE STRUGGLE FOR HOUSING IN A TIME OF REVOLUTION

A Break with the Past

The SAAL process was undoubtedly – and from several points of view – a singular moment in the history of housing policies in Portugal. The specificities of the historical moment following the 25 April military coup opened up the space for a convergence of new forms of state intervention and popular struggles for housing, giving rise to an unprecedented experience of popular participation.

The model of public intervention in housing policies which had been followed until then, and particularly during the almost five-decade-long *Estado Novo* dictatorship, was based, in its first phase, on the building of single-family dwellings. This option was justified by the belief of policymakers and 'experts' that collective housing provided a fertile ground for 'subversive' and revolutionary movements. In its second phase, this was replaced by the building of social housing, with flats for individual families, built in peripheral urban areas, which required families to move away from more central urban areas where they had been living before, closer to their workplaces and with more accessible public transportation. The outcome of this second phase of housing policies of the *Estado Novo* amounted to the emergence of socially segregated neighbourhoods, located in urban peripheries.

In both instances, interventions started from certain conceptions of housing held by the state and by the bodies of technical experts who were involved with urban problems, such as engineers, architects and social workers. Under the cover of a pseudo-public welfarism, the housing policies of the *Estado Novo* focused on minimalist responses to the more extreme cases of deprivation of housing conditions. There was a concern about avoiding the emergence of possible foci of opposition to the government and to the regime, and no concern at all with the recognition and promotion of the right of citizens to urban space and to access to decent living conditions for all. Never as during this period were housing policies used as a tool of social control and as a means of promoting the authoritarian and repressive values upheld by the regime. This approach to housing policies thus excluded any attempt at taking into account the expectations and representations of populations in matters of housing, spatial organization of neighbourhoods or the appropriation of urban space.[5]

This was the world the 1974 revolution sought to disrupt, creating conditions for the emergence and development of multi-shaped and relatively spontaneous social movements. In this new context, these movements found a fertile ground for the opening up of public space to the active expression of claims in different areas of social life, including housing, and for experimenting with new forms of participation and political and social intervention. At the same time, the revolution created the conditions for a radical change in the working and organization of public institutions and of the state, feeding a trend towards a democratization both of the procedures for policy making and of the relationships between 'experts' and administrators, on the one hand, and citizens, on the other.[6]

A Convergence of Actors and Dynamics

This was the context in which the SAAL process was launched. Its creation derived from the convergence of a variety of conditions and dynamics, rather than from the intention of any one of the actors involved. In other words, the formal creation and further development of SAAL as a process arose from the virtuous effects of the articulation – complex and ambivalent, to be sure – of a set of collective actors:

(a) the residents of urban neighbourhoods facing housing problems, their movements and organizations;
(b) the scientific and 'expert' bodies involved in housing and urban policies;
(c) the state, through its sectoral and locally based agencies and departments; and
(d) political parties and organizations.

To these, one should add the 'tutelary' presence of the Armed Forces Movement, which was crucial for the enactment of a variety of forms of popular action based upon revolutionary legitimacy.

It would be hard to deny, however, that one of the main engines of the process was the struggle of residents in run-down neighbourhoods and of families living in precarious conditions. These struggles took shape through different forms of action. In the case of Oporto, where the struggle for housing already had a long history, going back to the nineteenth century, the main actors of urban neighbourhood movements were social housing residents.[7] On the day following the 25 April coup, there were several demonstrations demanding that the regulations for social housing be revoked. These regulations were denounced as means of interfering, in a repressive and violent way, in people's private lives, violating basic principles of dignity and freedom.[8] Throughout June and July, these demands were followed by a second wave of protests, involving the residents of '*ilhas*',[9] who called for immediate action aimed at the improvement of their housing and living conditions. A third popular movement was launched several months later by the dwellers of subleased buildings, against the '*subalugas*', the tenants who made large amounts of money by subdividing houses 'into such minimal spaces, that even a corridor or the space under a staircase is leased out, and even receiving phone calls or having access to some hours of electrical lighting during the night . . . have to be paid for' (Coelho 1986: 622). The over-exploitation by '*subalugas*' remains one of the strongest memories of those who are still active in neighbourhood organizations. Finally, a more radicalized expression of the struggle for housing was the occupation of vacant houses, often organized by neighbourhood committees and in many cases legalized, at a later point in time, through a leasing contract. The success of this form of popular action depended, to a significant extent, on the armed forces, as a warrant of the legitimacy of occupations based on the principle that 'there shall be no houses without people as long as there are people without houses'. From the point of view of formal legality, however, these occupations were defined as violations of the right to private property.

A highly visible feature of these movements was the leading role and the very active participation of women. According to the dominant sexual division of labour, women were assigned a place within the private domain of the household, and 'governing' it was seen as a female task. It will come as no surprise, then, to find women appearing as activists and leaders of movements when housing problems flowed from the 'private' domain of governing the household to the emerging public sphere as political struggles for the right to decent housing. Many of the participants in the movement still recall the day a demonstration led by women living in social housing neighbourhoods invaded the City Hall of Oporto and forced the mayor to come out of his office and speak to the crowd assembled in the foyer.

From very early on, these popular movements caught the attention and the imagination of architects, engineers, students, intellectuals and professionals with a variety of academic and scientific backgrounds who had been involved, in one way or another, in the search for 'alternative forms which would give a new impetus to the production of social housing, replacing state-controlled or statist forms' (Portas 1986: 636). Interest for the city as a privileged stage for social change and the search for new paths in architecture and urban planning created a broad space for the convergence of these specific intellectuals with popular movements and neighbourhood organizations. This convergence, however, was loaded with tensions and misunderstandings, involving a difficult process of learning and dialogue.

In the case of SAAL/Norte, and according to participants in the process, the attempt at articulating the functional and urbanistic dimensions with the residents' aesthetic conceptions and preferences usually amounted to the definition of a field of technical solutions, whose limits were set by budgetary and locational boundaries. Within this field, households and neighbourhood committees could make their choices, so as to configure and personalize their habitat according to their life experiences and preferences. The process involved participation and mutual apprenticeship, despite the emergence of divergences and the confrontation, sometimes charged with conflict, of different perspectives, as would be expected of such a process. The assumption that architecture should be put at the service of people, of neighbourhood communities, led to a recognition of the crucial role of the latter in the definition and enactment of interventions. This assumption, as well as the acknowledgement of the difficulty in separating technical and political responses to problems would leave a strong imprint, sometimes a permanent one, on a whole generation of architects, urban planners and other professionals.

Many of these specific intellectuals thus shared a vision of the city as a space which was politically earmarked and appropriated by the capitalist system. Evidence of this vision was the harsh competition for space and the production of inequalities and exclusions associated with territorial and spatial policies. This, in turn, seemed to confirm their belief that the then existing revolutionary situation constituted a unique historical moment in which the transformation of the urban space and the defeat of the capitalist system would go hand in hand. Under the prevailing atmosphere of vigorous popular mobilization and the apparent 'doability' of a socialist transformation of society, an alliance started to take shape between popular movements and specific intellectuals, opening the way to new articulations of 'lay' and expert – though critical – forms of knowledge.

The joint participation of these two broad categories of collective actors in what was to be the SAAL process, despite the many tensions that crossed it, allowed two very precise aims – already mentioned – to be defined for the movements and for urban and housing policies: the right to decent housing and the 'right to place'. These were seen to be realistic and tangible aims, precise enough to allow a broad mobilization of a range of different actors, above all local populations, and progressive enough to 'fit' into the broader project of socialist transformation of Portuguese society.

Whereas the first aim – decent housing – spoke directly to the most basic needs of large sectors of urban populations, the second aim – 'the right to place' – found its roots in a long history of resistance of populations living in urban neighbourhoods of Oporto to being displaced by force or by administrative decisions – even with the best intentions – to other neighbourhoods, usually located in the urban peripheries. The 'right to place' may thus be defined as the right to have housing conditions improved – including the dimension and quality of dwelling spaces, as well as access to water, electricity or sewage systems – but also the right to urban and social equipment installed *in loco*, so that residents in a given neighbourhood might be able to 'create roots' and develop forms of sociability anchored in the appropriation of local space. Adequate public transportation, infrastructures, play grounds for children, schools, day-care centres for the elderly, green areas, spaces for the practice of sport or entertainment – these were, and still are, specific claims through which the 'right to place' took shape. Forceful removal of populations – total or partial – in exchange for better housing was not an option, from this point of view. After 1976, however, this kind of housing policy, entailing a denial of the 'right to place', was often used as a way of redistributing populations according to the dynamics of speculation on land for construction, giving rise to severe situations of social exclusion. Populations of several neighbourhoods of Oporto are still resisting this policy.

Going back to the 'lay'/'expert' articulations, it should be added that many of the specific intellectuals involved in the process, such as architects, engineers and lawyers, held positions within different state agencies, thus bringing the state into the emerging social and political dynamics. As Boaventura de Sousa Santos (1990) has argued, the period following the 25 April coup witnessed a 'duality of impotences', which balanced the forces of permanence against those of change, rather than the classical duality of powers scenario. This situation cut across the state itself. According to Santos (1990: 33),

> [t]he most characteristic, if not the most original feature of the crisis of the Portuguese state during this period is precisely the capacity of the state to keep itself intact throughout a generalized administrative paralysis for quite a long time and amidst very acute social struggles.

This, however, did not prevent a transformation within the state itself, both in the composition of its agencies and in the heterogeneous modes of its action, under the specific conditions of strong popular mobilization. The Coordinating Committee of SAAL/Norte, for instance, would sometimes come forward as an 'alien body' within the state apparatus, according to one of the specific intellectuals who belonged to it. Due to its strong and permanent entanglement with popular movements, this structure worked, to a large extent, as the representation, within the state, of urban residents' interests. This gave rise to frequent tensions and conflicts with those sectors which were more reluctant or impotent in the face of the changes in bureaucratic forms of functioning and of the direction of political and social change itself, at the levels of both the central and the local state. As a heterogeneous entity itself, the state may engage in heterogeneous relationships with society. This is more likely to be the case in periods of revolutionary crisis. How the state will relate to citizens and to social movements may well vary as a consequence of two forms of heterogeneity. The first, which we may call 'horizontal' heterogeneity, is related to the different dynamics of the diverse state agencies and departments. Some of these may be closer to citizens and social movements, others to the forces upholding 'law and order' who try, for instance, to protect the inviolability of private property; some may side with revolutionary legality, others with democratic legality, and still others attempt a fusion of different legalities and legitimacies.

The second form of heterogeneity, which may be described as orthogonal to the first, is 'vertical' heterogeneity. At different levels or scales (central administration, local administration, services depending on local government or local agencies of ministries, for instance), agents or services which are part of the same state agencies or departments may act differently and generate diverse kinds of articulations with different actors and movements. This may happen, at times, through a greater proximity or outright fusion of lower level services or departments with citizen and social movements or, conversely, with those opposing these movements (interests linked to real estate or construction, for instance). But it may also happen that at the national or central level certain agencies or departments adopt a clearly counterhegemonic orientation which may be actually followed by the whole agency at all levels, translated into more or less radical forms of intervention at lower levels or simply opposed, passively or actively, at the bottom or at intermediary levels. This kind of heterogeneity is particularly relevant to understanding how the 'duality of impotences' cuts across the state itself. Two other dimensions should be added to this double heterogeneity: spatial diversity and temporal evolutions. As we shall see, both the actions of the state department dealing with housing and members of government responsible for the sector and of SAAL are to be understood according to this play of heterogeneities, differences and evolutions over time.

Many specific intellectuals seized the chance to mobilize state agencies to support, facilitate and, in some cases, direct popular initiatives. New ways of defining and implementing housing policies were promoted, and the right to decent housing for all citizens was inscribed in the 1976 constitution, like several other advanced social and economic rights which had been banners of popular movements during the revolutionary crisis.[10] On the other hand, as Nuno Portas would later note, the active participation of populations in dealing with their housing problems through cooperation with the state and with the technical teams brought together by SAAL provided a significant push towards a more rapid response to housing problems, and gave a relevant contribution to the credibility and legitimacy of the emerging social and political order (Portas 1986). This is perhaps the most significant feature of the singularity of this period and of the SAAL process in the history of housing policies in Portugal: for the first time, an attempt was made to build a bridge connecting the energies of an emerging welfare state and the energies of a welfare society rooted in forms of sociability which were mobilized for the achievement of specific aims within a broader horizon of social change.[11]

Political parties and organizations influenced the development of this process, of course. Having been deprived of any participation in organized political activity before April 1974, many citizens became involved with left-wing organizations and parties which, until then, had been illegal or did not even exist before the revolution. Many of these organizations joined the popular movements and social struggles, supporting their causes and goals – even if opposing or criticizing the actual forms of action of the movements, as was often the case with the Communist Party throughout most of the period – but they also tried to influence them and to recruit their leaders in order to widen their political base. This often led to internal conflicts and disagreements within the movements. In fact, and SAAL/Norte is a good example of this, the ability of these organizations to influence, control and monitor popular movements was generally contained, and sometimes even unsuccessful, when faced with the spontaneity and social heterogeneity of the movements themselves. The conflicts between the left-wing parties and organizations active within the neighbourhood movements often focused on issues of strategy or on ideological divergences which appeared to many of the activists and participants in the movements to be of limited relevance to their struggle for what were seen as more urgent and tangible objectives. It often happened that these contradictions caused internal strife and disruption within the movements. But quite often political organizations also provided many of the resources – mostly organizational knowledge and, at times, material support – which allowed the movements' actions to be effective.

A reference should also be made to the military. Their intervention during this period was often in active support of popular movements, and they were called on to act as arbiters in many situations of conflict – particularly during the occupation of vacant houses – which, otherwise, would have ended in physical violence. The headquarters of the army in Oporto actually created a 'Division for Civil Affairs' which took up this role of mediator.

The roles of both political organizations and the military were thus crucial to the survival of neighbourhood movements, but their effects on them were ambiguous. As far as political organizations are concerned, they offered models of organization, activists with organizational and leadership skills, and sometimes logistic and material support. But they were also responsible for the rise of internal hierarchies within neighbourhood movements, first by channeling support and resources to certain activists who would later be recruited to the organization and act, in Leninist style, as 'chains of transmission' between the organization and the elected committees of the movements; second, by 'importing' into the movements and their committees interorganizational conflicts related to the definition of aims for the movements, of links of the neighbourhood movements to broader political objectives or even to the daily workings of the movements themselves and of the committees; and thirdly, through the promotion, within the movements, of a split between the 'enlightened' political 'avant-garde' and the 'masses', deprived of any autonomous capacity for defining their aims and modes of political intervention. These three features tended to encourage the reproduction of top-down modes of dealing with issues which the movements were supposed to engage with in active and creative ways through participatory mechanisms. Thus, they helped to perpetuate previous and deeply rooted experiences of paternalistic modes of relating to the state in Portugal.

As for the role of the military, it should be remembered that the alignment of their more radical wings with popular movements ensured that their actions, grounded on what was then labelled 'revolutionary legitimacy' – such as squatting in empty houses – would be given some protection, and that the military would neutralize attempts by other forces, like the police, to reinforce conventional property rights. When this protection was withheld after November 1975, neighbourhood movements and other popular movements had to seek to consolidate their newly gained rights through the legislation enacted as part of the 'normalization' of society and of the political order. These two orders of factors undoubtedly account for many of the weaknesses which underlie the defeat of popular movements and experiences of participatory democracy once the revolutionary crisis came to a close.

The Aims and Operational Logics of SAAL

On 6 August 1974, the Ministry for Internal Affairs (MAI) and the Secretary of State for Housing and Urban Affairs (SEHU) issued a joint legal document whereby, as part of a first set of initiatives in the area of housing policies, the decision was made to create an entity called 'Serviço Ambulatório de Apoio Local' (Mobile Service for Local Support), or SAAL. According to Nuno Portas, an architect who was Secretary of State at the time:

> SAAL was born after several representations of neighbourhoods from Lisbon and two from Oporto came here to declare that they would start constructing on their own initiative, as long as they were provided with financial resources and technical support (Ferreira 1987: 84).

A crucial moment preceding the formalization of the process corresponded to several meetings with neighbourhood residents, such as the ones held at Teatro S. Luís, in Lisbon, 'organized by members of the technical staff of public agencies involved in housing problems'. The aim of these meetings was to 'put pressure on the closed, bureaucratic and technicist structures of state institutions', in order to 'facilitate the actual participation of the population and of local organisms and entities in decision and implementation' (Conselho Nacional do SAAL/SAAL National Council, 1976: 9–10).

According to Nuno Portas, the purposes underlying this legal document rested upon four main pillars. First, the connection 'of the state to some more dynamic sectors of civil society, through some mechanism of decentralization. Not a decentralization in terms of devolution to local government ..., but an actual decentralization – even if its legal coverage was to be enacted much later – for those involved, as long as they were organized, sometimes shortcircuiting attributions of state agencies' (Portas 1986: 638).

Secondly, the SAAL programme aimed at 'linking technical functions performed within or without state agencies to the agents they were supposed to serve', thus reversing the trend towards 'deciding initiatives within the state machinery, in a more or less centralized way, and regardless of the will and the non-monetary resources of the residents they are aimed at' (Portas 1986: 639).

Thirdly, through SAAL, an attempt was made to counteract the urban impacts of the housing policies implemented until then, acknowledging that residents in specific neighbourhoods had 'a right to stay in the place their communities were located in', that is, 'acknowledging some continuity to communities which lived in conditions of deprivation, but in areas they probably were satisfied with', as long as there was some consensus on existing conditions of habitableness in those places (Portas 1986: 639). Finally, a further innovative aim was the need to 'define a way of acting which would maximize the application to housing of all sorts of resources provided by residents' (Portas 1986: 641), be they material or human, in order to optimize the effectiveness, adequacy and swiftness of public investment.

SAAL operations, as they were then called, started with the identification of the areas of intervention and of the types of actions to be carried out. This first step was followed by the joint programming of each intervention, involving the technical teams and the residents and their committees. Institutional responses to demands for the means needed to carry out different tasks were the responsibility of the working group of the Fund for the Promotion of Housing (*Fundo de Fomento da Habitação* – FFH), the state agency in charge of the management and organization of SAAL, channeled through local governments. This was seen as a way of defining policy interventions which would impose some coherence on each intervention and on the programme as a whole. The energies summoned through this process had a threefold origin:

(a) the state, both the central state and local government, which was in charge of accomplishing work related to communication and sanitary infrastructures, and acquiring or providing land and materials for construction;
(b) technical and scientific resources made available through multi-disciplinary teams, which were active both in the identification of areas and in the work of construction itself;

(c) the populations themselves, who were actively involved in the operations, contributing either with labour or financial resources, or with both.

One of the first positive results of operation SAAL/Norte was the conversion of land which had been earmarked for parking lots to land for housing. Since this land belonged to the municipality, it was possible to give a quicker response to the political urgency of accomplishing the interventions, as well as to the need to erect 'mobile houses', in which families would be installed while construction was carried out in the places where they would continue to reside after the operations came to an end. The intertwining of wills and energies of the neighbours and their committees, of specific intellectuals and of parts of the state machinery involved in the process allowed the field of intervention to be gradually broadened, until almost the whole of territorial planning and management in Oporto was included. It is worth stressing that this strategy had not been outlined or explicitly announced in advance.

Another area where SAAL appeared as an innovative experience is that of legislative production. In fact, from its very beginning, the programme proposed an inversion of what had been, until then, current and undisputed practice. Programmes used to be implemented after the regulation of their operational procedures was defined. SAAL, in contrast, opted for an explicit view of legislation as process. Initiatives were 'vaguely defined from the start, as an accepted risk and not as a shortcoming' (Portas 1986: 637). Legal aspects were gradually defined and established according to information and knowledge obtained through the experience of the interventions themselves.[12] This option allowed problems to be dealt with 'considering their local specificity', which meant that there was an attempt to attend to the socio-spatial peculiarities of each operation and to the modes of participation of the populations involved. This, in turn, was linked to the promotion of a kind of organizational plasticity, experimenting with flexible ways of organizing neighbourhood committees or associations, in order to adapt their forms of institutionalization to local specificities. This plasticity and gradualism in defining the normative and regulatory framework of SAAL was responsible, however, on different occasions, for the deficit of legal legitimation of the process, not so much because of the strategy that was followed as because of the frailty and ambiguity of the prevailing political situation. The need to legislate and to legitimate procedures like making land available, occupying run-down empty houses, funding operations, changing plans or creating neighbourhood associations, among others, and the lack of swift or clear responses by the state prevented or slowed down, as was true of some cases within the purview of SAAL/Norte, the actual work of carrying out the operations, thus compromising a more rapid and determined pursuit of the operations themselves.

SAAL as a Process of Social Emancipation and Participatory Democracy

One of the most fascinating issues raised by the historical reconstruction of the SAAL process is directly linked to its features as an experience in social emancipation and participatory democracy. A particularly challenging aspect is the internal diversity of motivations, expectations and practices of the various actors that had a leading role in the process.

On what grounds did neighbourhood movements mobilize, and what were their thresholds of expectation for social and political change? Were they motivated by claims of improvement in housing and housing conditions and of an effective response to people's needs, or by the more broadly articulated demand for housing to be acknowledged as a right inscribed in the constitutive documents of the new political regime emerging from the revolution? According to sociologist Vítor Matias Ferreira, writing in 'real time', urban social movements could be categorized on the basis of the scope of their motivations. He identifies the following categories:

(a) *movements based on claims*, struggling for more immediate demands, such as those related to the material survival of populations;
(b) *protest movements*, directed towards a political–institutional opponent, adding a political motivation to the more immediate material claims; and
(c) *social movements*, properly defined, articulating a project of social change, with impacts reaching beyond the response to specific problems and reformulating the more strictly functional logics of political action (Matias Ferreira 1975: 14–17).

We suggest that the mobilizations of urban residents around SAAL display an ambiguous dynamic which is expressed, on the one hand, through a progressive transformation towards a more emancipatory dynamics – which would probably have gone a lot further if the process had not been as short-lived as it was – and, on the other hand, a recurrent propensity of urban movements to depend on a heterogeneous state and on the military and, sometimes, on political organizations, to achieve their aims of decent housing and the right to place. As for the first point, the sequence of aims articulated by popular movements during the three phases of the SAAL/Norte process described earlier, from the revocation of council regulations, can be read as a symbolic expression of the demand for putting an end to the housing policies defined during the *Estado Novo*, to claims related to the qualification of residential areas and legal solutions to degrading situations, like those associated with subleasing. Throughout the whole process, and due to its growing politicization – to which political parties and organizations made a substantial, though debatable, contribution – the wider claim of the right to housing was to be consistently and coherently expressed. Neighbourhood movements thus acquired the ability to learn from experience, in which interactions with other actors, such as the state and the technical teams, played a very significant role. This, however, often translated into a propensity to rely on the state and on other actors as providers of resources on a top-down and often paternalistic basis. This contradictory dynamics is well illustrated by the relationship between neighbourhood movements and committees, on the one hand, and SAAL, on the other.

Within the state itself, in turn, transformatory dynamics could also be identified, as well as attempts at incorporating innovative procedures, more open to social participation. It would be fair to say that – even within limits – SAAL fostered a simultaneous process of change within the state itself and in its relations to society. Crucial mediators in this process were the scientific and 'expert' bodies which, from the beginning, had a fundamental role in 'pushing' for these dynamics, framing technical interventions within a project of political change. As it struggled to create a 'new dynamics in administration', promoting its 'interconnection with the surrounding social tissue' (Coelho 1986: 623), the SAAL process thus stimulated the state's configuration as an active facilitator of social emancipation and participatory democracy.

The analytical wealth and complexity of the process is further displayed in the way interesting ideological questions were raised, regarding the role and intervention of political parties and organizations, for instance, but also of state agencies and departments. One of the most heated debates, at the time, focused on the very methodology of SAAL, which included the active participation of local populations, as providers of both human and material (monetary) resources. This methodology was justified by the advantages which could be gained from valuing and mobilizing energies and resources that populations were willing to draw upon,[13] thus allowing a smoother execution of the planned interventions. But, within the political party field, this option was often criticized, sometimes in rather heated terms, the argument being that if housing is a right, it did not make any sense that the population should be called on to carry the burden of its actual fulfilment.[14] Thus, SAAL actually encouraged interesting contributions to the opening up of new areas of ideological debate within the left, particularly around topics related to the nature of the revolutionary situation and of state power, or of the emancipatory sense of state interventions.

The process was also perceived as a challenge by the 'experts' or specific intellectuals who were part of the multidisciplinary teams intervening in the field. The challenge arose from the acceptance of the principle of democratizing technical rationality and making information widely available to 'ordinary' citizens, who would be able to compare them with their own expectations concerning the right to housing and to an adequate space for living. Of course, and as might be expected, the dialogue was not always easy or peaceful, but it involved an exchange of forms of knowledge and of experiences which ended up being beneficial to all the actors involved. One of the architects we interviewed stated that his participation in the process, despite its short duration, left a deep imprint on his subsequent professional activity and identity, forcing him to struggle with the tension between the more aesthetic and technical aspects of his activity and the need to engage with the social functions and impacts of architecture – a tension which is currently not felt by many architects, who tend to have a more 'internalist' view of their profession and social role.

The Demise of SAAL

On 27 October 1976, about two years after its official beginnings, a joint decision from the Minister of Internal Affairs and the Minister of Housing, Urban Planning and Construction suggested the extinction of both the method and the organic structure of SAAL. According to the two ministers, 'after two years of experience, we have come to the conclusion that some of the teams within SAAL have deviated in a visible way from the spirit of the legal decision which had established their organization, acting independently of FFH [the Fund for the Promotion of Housing] and of local government itself', thus concluding that populations who had no access to adequate housing had not been 'attended to as they should have been' (*Conselho Nacional do SAAL*, 1976: 452).

The factors leading to the extinction of SAAL were, however, far more complex and differentiated.

Soon after the decision to extinguish SAAL, public investment in housing slowed down, in a clear inversion of what had been the trend of previous years. The end of SAAL was the result of 'the government's non-definition', which could be 'traced back to the beginnings of the process, and which never ceased to grow until it reached the breaking point. The response of political power emerged only where, when and in so far as there was pressure from the populations and often after action had been taken by the latter' (Brochado Coelho 1986: 657).

Within the legislative arena, there was a significant delay in the drafting and publication of legal decisions which would have consolidated the funding procedures for the operations conducted within SAAL as well as the acquisition of land, the legal work performed during the process often being ignored (Brochado Coelho 1986: 657). The administrative and technical machinery of the state, in turn, proved increasingly incapable of responding, from the administrative point of view, to the dynamics of requests to join the programme and to the growing number of requests for interventions, either due to financial constraints, or to obstructions often arising at the municipal level, sometimes linked to issues of urban and local planning. In addition, there were increasing demands from residents, parallel to the progressive institutionalization of SAAL. In the words of Nuno Portas, 'the claims for inputs by the state increased to 100 per cent, and people withdrew all other resources'. At the same time, residents became increasingly demanding as far as the architecture and the materials used for completing the houses were concerned, with many situations arising in which experts ended up imposing their solutions on members of residents' associations. The latter, however, on the margins of the interventions, often invested in their dwellings at their own expense (Portas 1986: 643).

There are good reasons to believe, however, that the extinction of SAAL was due, above all, to political, social and historical factors linked to that particular moment, rather than to any factor linked to the 'intrinsically' ephemeral features of the programme.

SAAL had been conceived as an initiative for the provision of housing based on a decentralized and decentralizing dynamics which was oriented, form the very start, towards the empowerment of local actors (municipalities and neighbourhood associations), namely in areas such as management and decision making. The central state, however, due to a convergence of factors, including the very rapid and intense rhythm of the process, proved unable to regulate the institutional framework of SAAL as an initiative in housing policy through agencies such as the General Directories in charge of this area of public policy and, in particular, the FFH (Portas 1979).

The government took advantage of the lack of a solid legal framework to move to local government the process of decision making concerning the support or, alternatively, the suspension of interventions without the parallel transfer, however, of financial means and even of some indispensible legal tools, such as the power to decide on the final approval of projects. This amounted to a *de facto* dismantling of SAAL.

The lack of capacity of the state at the start of a period of transition from dictatorship to democracy to keep up with the pace of the process, during a period of 'duality of impotences'; the absence of past experiences and of a memory of social and political participation and civic intervention and of confrontation and dialogue of different forms of knowledge and experiences; and, finally, the dynamics of 'normalization' underlying the post-revolutionary period, with its attempts at eliminating or condemning as irrelevant any experiences which might appear as alternatives to 'normal', parliamentary and representative democracy: these seem to be the main explanatory causes of the demise of SAAL and of the failure of the maturation, consolidation and continuity of one of the most important experiences of popular participation during the revolutionary period.

We believe that SAAL was, in fact, a movement/process with a strong emancipatory potential and a singular experience of participatory democracy in Portuguese society, if we consider it in terms of the configuration of actors involved and of their relationships. Each of the intervening collective actors tried, in its own way, to articulate energies which were expected to produce a set of wide-ranging political, urbanistic and 'methodological' changes. Understanding the social movements associated with SAAL requires a close look at this particular configuration and at the dynamics of the interaction of the actors involved. This, in turn, suggests a concept of a dynamics of social emancipation involving not only social movements or initiatives arising from civil society, but also specific alliances between social movements and citizens' initiatives, sectors of the state and 'experts'.

THE MEMORY OF THE REVOLUTION AND OF SAAL/NORTE: A RESOURCE FOR THE REINVENTION OF PARTICIPATION?

Over the years, the 'official' memory of the Portuguese revolution has sought to erase all the episodes which, in some way, pointed towards the possibility of an alternative way of organizing society or of involving citizens in the political process, or of extending the very notion of politics into those areas usually excluded from the institutionally bounded field of 'legitimate' political activity. Despite the growth of inequalities and of exclusion, and despite the unfulfilled promises of a more equal and just society, critical interventions have been made increasingly difficult by the widespread notion that the supreme value of democracy is consensus. Any critical position towards 'centrist' notions of the 'public good' or 'political realism' is invariably denounced as 'fracturing' and, as such, a threat to the stability and unity of the national polity. The memory of

URBAN MOVEMENTS AND EMANCIPATION IN PORTUGAL   69

the revolution (with all its successes and mistakes, its hesitations, its excesses and its compromises) is itself actively purged of any notion that the revolution was a process of social and political change, crossed by contradictions, played out by a heterogeneous set of collective actors, of social movements and of popular initiatives, giving rise to a wealth of experiences in collective action and participatory democracy, but also attempts at articulating the state and grassroots organizations, the armed forces and social movements, political parties and organizations and popular initiatives. The revolution is often seen, in fact, as an abnormal 'hiatus' in a process which should have run its 'normal' course from the overthrow of the dictatorship to the creation of the institutions of western-style, parliamentary democracy. The successive revisions of the Constitution of 1976 – which still inscribed the contradictions and the alternative political projects of the revolutionary period – were particularly significant moments in the deletion of the memory of participatory democracy and of the role of social movements in the new democratic order. This tends to induce conformity to the prevailing social order and accommodation to prevailing inequalities and injustices. As Boaventura de Sousa Santos reminds us, conformity to the present seems to feed on conformity to the past, a past whose celebration is reduced to a public holiday and to an asseptic 'celebration of freedom and democracy' which, in the name of consensus, is blind and deaf to everything that justifies non-conformity and criticism: 'we cannot rethink social change and emancipation without reinventing the past' (Santos 1996: 7).

Defining possible articulations between that reinvention of the past and the reinvention of participation, through an active and creative retrieval of the memory of social movements and of the will to emancipation during the revolutionary period, is far from being an easy task. On the left, the frequent reference to the unfulfilled promises of the revolution is often at risk of turning into nostalgia – and as such deprived of the indispensable energy for mobilization – for an irrecoverable past without any 'power of irruption' in the present. Another obstacle has to do with how to take into account the differences between the contexts of 1974–75 and of the present, in order to identify the emerging constraints and opportunities in the path that leads to a future different from the one that has been naturalized as necessity by the neoliberal present.

Let us start with an account – necessarily brief, incomplete and provisional – of the various ways in which the memory of popular movements and participatory democracy has been neutralized or deleted from the 'official' narratives of the revolution. These experiences are usually minimized or condemned as a set of unnecessary and perverse excesses which have amounted to no positive contribution to Portuguese democracy. The 'normalizing' chronology of the building and institutionalization of democracy in Portugal includes the military coup which overthrew the dictatorship on 25 April 1974, the elections for the Constitutional Assembly in 1975, the conservative military intervention of the 25 November 1975, the voting of the new constitution in April 1976 and the legislative, presidential and local elections of 1976. Even the military movement responsible for overthrowing the dictatorship is 'normalized' through a distinction between those who, appearing as the precursors of the 'proper' role of the armed forces, subject to legitimate political power, limited their role to that of overthrowing an illegitimate regime and then turned political power to civilians, and those who, exceeding that mandate (retrospectively entrusted), had an active intervention in the process of social and political change.[15]

It is also significant that most of the narratives of how democracy was restored in Portugal tend to focus, on the one hand, on the military coup itself and on its preparation, and, on the other, on the period following the voting of the 1976 constitution. At most – though with some important exceptions[16] – the whole two-year period between the military coup and the voting of the constitution is reduced to a confrontation between two opposed political dynamics strictly aligned with the two sides of the contending forces in the Cold War, the stakes being whether Portugal would become a western-type democracy or a Soviet-type regime. The net result of these versions of the recent history of Portugal is the deletion of one of the most vigorous and creative periods of Portuguese history, and with it, of the memory of social movements and participatory democracy.

The vitality and diversity of experiences arising during that period included new forms of organization and participation of citizens in the 'government' of the workplace, in factories, offices and fields, neighbourhood movements and committees, new experiences in the field of education, solidarity campaigns with colonial populations and anti-colonial movements and with the victims of dictatorships and repressive regimes, women's and minority movements, the emergence and spread of new experiences of alternative modes of organizing daily life and the first public expressions of ecological concerns and mobilization around environmental issues. This particular historical moment thus concentrated with an unusual density the passage from a five-decade period of repression and persecution of citizens' initiatives, social movements and demands of political participation to an apparently boundless experience of participation which did not fit into the limited definitions of parliamentary and representative democracy.

The apparently unique and unrepeatable experience of the Portuguese revolution of 1974–75 raises understandable and well-founded questions about the possible relevance of that experience to the shift from a low-intensity to a high-intensity democracy in the current context of globalization. One of the most conspicuous differences between the two contexts is the absence of a clear strategic goal for social movements and participatory initiatives, and the well-known difficulties of articulating specific issues with a wider prospect for social change. In 1974–75, socialism was the name of that wider prospect. Struggles around specific issues, like housing, were seen as part of a more wide-ranging process of change based on equality and social justice. The blueprint for change – in spite of the heterogeneity of the conceptions of socialism, of democracy and of participation then circulating within Portuguese society – was largely identified with the 1976 Constitution, which stated explicitly as its aim socialism and a classless society, and established forms of participatory democracy as part of the constitutional order. The successive revisions of the Constitution in the 1980s brought it in line with the liberal conceptions of state and society, eliminating the reference to socialism. The central role of the state as a crucial actor in the process of change was thus gradually deleted. In the absence of a comparable blueprint for comprehensive social change, what other forms of solidarity can be imagined that allow, at the same time, local mobilization and translocal linkages of emancipatory dynamics, as well as the dual obligation – vertical, between citizens and the state, and horizontal, among citizens and citizens' organizations – upon which the radical reinvention of democracy will have to rest (Santos 1999a,b)?

The loss of the mobilizing power of terms like 'revolution' or 'socialism' and their association with historical processes which, in many cases, led to outcomes contrary to the expectations of emancipation and radical democracy suggest that beyond the words we should look for emerging signs of alternative, non-teleological ways of conceiving and promoting social change.

We live in a period of turbulence, when small causes may generate wide-ranging effects, extended fluctuations in political and social processes and economic dynamics, fostering an increasing instability and uncertainty within the capitalist world system. Choices made through social mobilization and active intervention by citizens may well make a difference in the kind of future we will be living in (Wallerstein 1995). The opportunity for an emancipatory future, a future which will have to be constructed through partial, unequal and contradictory processes, inscribing irreversible paths of historical development, may dwell in grassroots initiatives and in the search for new ways of bringing the state – or sectors of the state – into emancipatory and solidary alliances with citizens' initiatives and social movements (Santos 1999).

Several lessons from the SAAL/Norte process are relevant for the purpose of this case study. They have been drawn by some of the more reflexive actors who have been involved in the process themselves, and they converge with the preceding outline.

One of the strengths of the SAAL/Norte process was its capacity for mobilizing a heterogeneous set of actors around specific and achievable aims. 'Having a decent house' and the 'right to place', as we have seen, seem to summarize these aims in an appropriate way. They allowed the opening up of spaces of democracy and respect for differences rooted in class, gender, ethnicity and religious and party affiliations. The very diversity and heterogeneity of movements rooted in the struggle for the right of living in places recognized by residents as their own, and to supplement housing with a range of urban equipments that enabled an active appropriation of those places not just as places for dwelling but as spaces for living and building locally-based solidarities, was the condition of their success. The connection to place is a crucial dimension of the process. The compulsory relocation of dwellers from one specific neighbourhood to other places, sometimes in a piecemeal fashion, and without the conditions for forging solidarities and a sense of community which can only arise from long-term face-to-face interaction proved to be fatal to most of these movements. It is interesting to note that the struggle against forced relocation is one of the long-lasting features of urban popular struggles, especially in Oporto, and can be traced back to several attempts at urban reform and relocation of urban populations in the early twentieth century. This makes it easier to understand why a range of committed actors are still struggling for what an architect described as the most durable achievement of the SAAL/Norte process, the 'right to place'. An interesting feature worth recalling is the role of women in bringing what is traditionally defined as a private issue into public space. It will come as no surprise to see that the most active leaders of neighbourhood movements in Oporto, today, are women, and that women are also the bulk of the specific intellectuals working in the field in neighbourhoods described as 'difficult'.

But there are other relevant dimensions for the revitalization of neighbourhood movements and struggles. A crucial issue is the need for alliances between 'experts' or specific intellectuals committed to social change and to social emancipation and neighbourhood movements. During the SAAL/Norte operation, many architects, engineers, lawyers, social workers and volunteers were compelled to enter into negotiation and dialogue with neighbourhood movements and committees, and to negotiate the meanings and specific ways of bringing about 'decent housing' in practical terms. Although there were asymmetrical attempts at imposing aesthetic and functional views by some architects, many of those involved in the process struggled to incorporate 'lay' views and preferences in the design of housing and to maximize those features seen by dwellers as crucial for sustaining patterns of sociability largely organized around specific spatial arrangements. The 'rival knowledges' of 'experts' and 'lay people' thus became, in some instances, resources for designing new concepts of housing, articulating a new range of aesthetic and functional preferences and possibilities. Some of these concerns have been taken up, again, in the design of social housing for specific groups of dwellers, such as gypsy families. The current situation, however, is one where 'experts' are mostly seen by neighbours as siding with power, particularly with local government, and imposing their views, legitimated by their technical credentials and diplomas, on neighbours, who are disqualified and deemed incompetent to decide on issues defined as 'technical'. The need for new alliances with experts willing to side with the neighbours on a symmetrical basis is seen as a crucial condition for contesting the authority of 'official' experts, bringing into full light the existing controversies among experts and the social and political dimensions of urban and housing policies. The pattern, here, follows closely the one that is arising in other fields where 'expert' knowledge is seen as crucial, and which were evoked in the introduction to this essay.

Another feature of the experience of SAAL, particularly that of SAAL/Norte, suggests a set of very interesting and promising means to think about the current possibilities of facilitating and fostering forms of participatory democracy: the dimension of active learning of citizenship and of participation in public space. It has to be built gradually and progressively, starting from the experiences and expectations more directly linked to the daily life of individuals. The plurality of actors and the participatory features of the process, besides the demand for its progressive broadening, actually allowed a widening of the field of citizens' concerns, centered at first on their homes and their communities. Over time, those concerns extended to a broader public space, less directly linked to the more local experiences of the subjects involved. The nature and direction of the process, consistently and gradually built up from micro-social contexts, may well inspire a viable strategy for debate and citizen participation around the many issues which, in more or less direct ways, affect the daily life of individuals and collectivities.

Another central issue is the relationship with the state. This was a fundamental feature of the SAAL/Norte process. Its success and legitimation depended on a strong backing from state agencies and actors linked to the state or with a mandate from the state. The final demise of the process was a direct consequence of the state pulling back from and delegitimating the process as a challenge to 'real' democracy and to the normalization of the institutional framework of the young Portuguese democracy. To what extent can this alliance with the state or with sectors of the state be rebuilt, on a participatory and solidaristic basis (Santos 1999a,b)? It would seem that the doability of such an alliance rests upon the recognition of what we have described as the 'double heterogeneity' of the state, that is, of the capacity of different levels of the organization of the state and of state agencies and departments to open up spaces for alternative experiences in dealing with grassroots movements or initiatives. This has hardly happened up to now, but opportunities are emerging which are strongly linked with the issue of the 'enrolment' of 'experts' for the promotion of alternative policies.

NOTES

1. The two most influential versions of this line of argument are developed in Beck 1992 and Giddens 1991. The critical debate triggered by the work of these two sociologists gave rise to a considerable – and growing – number of publications, of which the following should be singled out: Beck *et al.* 1994; Lash *et al.* 1996; Adam *et al.* 2000; Irwin 1995. On the political implications of these arguments, see the contributions to Franklin 1998. The broadening of the discussions on the relationships between experts and citizens to include southern hemisphere societies can be found, among others, in Silliman and King 1999, and Fischer 2000.
2. 'Each society has its truth regime, its general politics of truth, that is, the kinds of discourses society accepts and enacts as true; the mechanisms and instances which allow the distinction between true and false statements to be made and the way statements of either kind are sanctioned; the techniques and procedures which are valued as means of producing truth; the status of those to whom the task is committed of stating what will work as true' (Foucault 1994b: 158).
3. Guinea-Bissau had unilaterally declared independence in 1973.
4. For a detailed historical account of the struggles and movements of urban populations in Oporto during the Revolution, see Rodrigues 1999.
5. For a more detailed analysis of the housing policies of the *Estado Novo*, see Gros 1982.
6. It was not possible, within the limits of this case-study, to explore some of the experiences of intervention in popular housing under the dictatorship, namely those carried out by some progressive Catholic organizations.
7. Social housing (*bairros camarários*) consists of apartment buildings owned by city councils, for accomodating families with scarce economic resources.
8. The neighbourhoods where social housing was located were in a permanent state of surveillance by council inspectors who, in their reports, did not fail to record the situations which, according to their judgment, fell under the category of violations of the regulations. They proposed penalties for alleged violators which might go as far as expulsion from the neighbourhood, a penalty which entailed the loss of entitlement to social housing, as if the latter were an undeserved privilege. Some of the statements found in inspectors' reports reveal much about the harsh regime of surveillance and

control social housing residents were subject to: 'Has an illegal chicken (...). Laundry on the balcony (...). Plastic vases on the front of the building (...). Has animals; the cat died (...). She entertains a man (...). She has a lover, while being a spinster (...). He bought a motorcycle' (Costa et al. 1979: 29).
9. The 'ilhas' consisted of 'rows of small, single-floor houses (...) built in the backyards of old bourgeois houses' (Teixeira 1992: 67), which were often deprived of water supply. They emerged as a response, even if a precarious one, to the search for inexpensive housing by the working class of Oporto. Estimates of the proportion of the population of the city living in 'ilhas' at the end of the nineteenth century are as high as 50 per cent. The 'ilhas' were identified with patterns of spatial organization and of sociability which could not be reproduced under different forms of social housing, particularly those organized in the form of single-family flats. On the housing conditions of the popular classes in Oporto in the late nineteenth/early twentieth centuries, see Pereira 1995.
10. The actual implementation of these rights is a different story, which has been discussed in detail by Santos (1990).
11. See Santos 1993, and the thematic issue of *Revista Crítica de Ciências Sociais* (42, 1995, 'A Sociedade-Providência').
12. ' [...] the projects would start as soon as the neighbourhood committees were created; the land for construction was in the process of being selected while the legal decrees which would consolidate the process were drafted' (Portas 1986: 637).
13. '[...] the idea that all the residents who are in need of help from the state are incapable of contributing in any way because they are already exploited was, of course, a simplistic view which did not fit the actual problems the country was facing (...). For the question was: either the state would build only a few houses and people would pay 'political' rents, covering the cost of housing through payments in money, be it in the form of rent or of mortgage, or one would have to resort to other means, probably interesting to the residents, of reducing the amount of investment by the state' (Portas 1986: 641–42).
14. As they were forced to deal with this debate, some political organizations on the left ended up defining SAAL as an obvious instance of a bourgeois strategy based on 'buying time' for the recomposition of state power as it had existed during the dictatorship.
15. Different versions of this 'normalized' narrative circulate in Portuguese society, taking a more explicit and coherent form in the moments of commemoration of the 25 April and 25 November.
16. See, namely, Santos 1990, and the contributions to the special issues of *Revista Crítica de Ciências Sociais* (15/16/17, 1985, and 18/19/20, 1986), on '1974–1984: Ten Years of Social Change'. The creation of archives and documentation centres of the history of the Revolution is decisive for the reconstruction of its memory. The 'Centro de Documentação 25 de Abril' of the University of Coimbra harbours the most important collection of documents related to the period. It has provided the information for detailed and commented chronological reconstitutions of the revolutionary period, as well as for a set of educational materials for primary and secondary schools. See, for instance, Santos *et al.* 1997.

REFERENCES

Adam, B., U. Beck and J. Van Loon (eds.) (2000): *The Risk Society and Beyond: Critical Issues for Social Theory*, London: Sage.
Beck, U. (1992): *Risk Society: Towards a New Modernity*, London: Sage.
Beck, U., A. Giddens and S. Lash (1994): *Reflexive Modernization: Politics, Tradition and Aesthetics in the Modern Social Order*, Cambridge: Polity Press.
Brochado Coelho, M. (1986): 'Um processo organizativo de moradores (SAAL/NORTE – 1974–1976)', *Revista Crítica de Ciências Sociais*, 18/19/20, pp.645–72.
Castells, M. (1976): *Lutas Urbanas e Poder Político*, Porto: Ed. Afrontamento.

Coelho, M. (1986): 'Uma experiência de transformação no sector habitacional do Estado. SAAL – 1974–1976', *Revista Crítica de Ciências Sociais*, 18/19/20, pp.619–34.
Conselho Nacional do SAAL (1976): *Livro Branco do SAAL, 1974–1976*, Volume I: Edição do Conselho Nacional do SAAL.
Costa, A.A., Á. Siza, C. Guimarães, S. Moura and M.C. Fernandes (1979): 'SAAL/NORTE. Balanço de uma experiência', *Cidade/Campo*, 2, Lisbon: Edições Ulmeiro, pp.16–60.
Ferreira, A.F. (1987): *Por uma Nova Política de Habitação*, Porto: Ed. Afrontamento.
Fischer, F. (2000): *Citizens, Experts, and the Environment: The Politics of Local Knowledge*, Durham, North Carolina: Duke University Press.
Foucault, M. (1994a): 'La fonction politique de l'intellectuel', in *Dits et Écrits*, Paris: Gallimard, Vol. 3, pp.109–14.
Foucault, M. (1994b): 'Entretien avec Michel Foucault', in *Dits et Écrits*, Paris: Gallimard, Vol. 3, pp.140–60.
Franklin, J. (org.) (1998): *The Politics of Risk Society*, Cambridge: Polity Press.
Giddens, A. (1994): *Modernidade e Identidade Pessoal*, Oeiras: Celta.
Irwin, A. (1995): *Citizen Science: A Study of People, Expertise and Sustainable Development*, London: Routledge.
Lash, S., B. Szerszynski and B. Wynne (orgs.) (1996): *Risk, Environment and Modernity: Towards a New Ecology*, London: Sage.
Lefèbvre, H. (1972): *O Pensamento Marxista e a Cidade.*, Lisbon: Editora Ulisseia.
Matias Ferreira, V. (1975): *Movimentos Sociais Urbanos e Intervenção Política*, Porto: Ed. Afrontamento.
Pereira, G.M. (1995): *Famílias Portuenses na Viragem do Século*, Oporto: Ed. Afrontamento.
Portas, N. (1979): 'Depoimentos: Nuno Portas', *Cidade/Campo*, 2, Lisbon: Edições Ulmeiro, pp.111–24.
Portas, N. (1986): 'O processo SAAL: Entre o Estado e o Poder Local', *Revista Crítica de Ciências Sociais*, 18/19/20, pp.635–44.
Rabinow, P. (1989): *French Modern: Norm and Forms of the Social Environment*, Cambridge: Massachusetts: MIT Press.
Rodrigues, M. (1999): *Pelo Direito à Cidade: O Movimento de Moradores no Porto (1974/76)*, Oporto: Campo das Letras.
Santos, B. de S. (1990): *O Estado e a Sociedade em Portugal (1974–1988)*, Oporto: Ed. Afrontamento.
Santos, B. de S. (1993): 'O Estado, as relações salariais e o bem-estar social na semiperiferia: o caso português', *Boaventura de Sousa Santos* (ed.), Oporto: Ed. Afrontamento, Portugal: Um Retrato Singular, pp.16–56.
Santos, B. de S. (1996): 'A queda do Angelus Novus: para além da equação moderna entre raízes e opções', *Revista Crítica de Ciências Sociais* 45, pp.5–34.
Santos, B. de S. (1998): *A Reinvenção da Democracia*, Lisbon: Gradiva.
Santos, B. de S. (1999): 'A Reinvenção Solidária e Participativa do Estado', *Oficina do CES*, p.134.
Santos, B. de S., M.M. Cruzeiro and M.N. Coimbra (1997): *O Pulsar da Revolução: Cronologia da Revolução de 25 de Abril*, Coimbra/Oporto: Centro de Documentação 25 de Abril/Ed. Afrontamento.
Silliman, J. and Y. King (orgs.) (1999): *Dangerous Intersections: Feminism, Population and the Environment*, London: Zed Books.
Teixeira, M. (1992): 'As estratégias de habitação em Portugal, 1880–1940', *Análise Social* XXVII/115, pp.65–89.
Wallerstein, I. (1995): 'Mudança Social? A mudança é eterna. Nada muda, nunca', *Revista Crítica de Ciências Sociais* 44, pp.1–24.

The Territory as Space for Collective Action: Paradoxes and Potentialities of the 'Strategic Game of Actors' in Territorial Planning in Portugal

ISABEL GUERRA

THE NEED TO UNDERSTAND THE NEW FORMS OF BUILDING COLLECTIVE ACTION IN TERRITORIAL MANAGEMENT

Today, we need to recognize the deep crisis in territorial policies and in the foundations and objectives of public action in the organization of space: they are scarcely operative and are subject to constant criticism from various actors who are increasingly demanding and less likely to reach consensus. Similarly, the authority, values and reference frames of urban planning experts are increasingly put into question. This situation leads us to search for the causes of such criticism and to experiment with new forms of urban governance.

The question involves not only a process of territorializing public policies; it involves above all the redefinition of ways of doing. If 'territorial' implies a policy's capacity to frame the demands for belonging, it also implies managing resources – horizontally and transversally – and mobilizing horizontal relations between different groups of actors. In order to act within these new contexts, new tools of analysis have been created, and new concepts have emerged, such as urban governance, regimes, political networks, concrete action systems, and so on. How can these notions renew our thinking about public policies and go beyond the analysis of the relations of dependency and autonomy between the state and territorial collectivities? To what extent do they clarify new ways of living together and negotiating social change in a specific system of action?

As a participant in different processes of territorial strategic planning, I would like to focus on a central issue: the new forms of collective action and the rules of the 'strategic game of actors' in a local context. This 'local strategic game of actors' derives from a complex dynamics of actions and territorial organizations, in which power relations and conflicts of interest guide the behaviours of a great diversity of actors that emerge as a function of the various situations.

The value system on which public action was based, and which allowed it to be organized in a relatively simple way, has been put into question, or at least is the subject of debates and uncertainties. The values of the republican state or of the welfare state, their legitimacy and efficacy, are being questioned, and public institutions rarely manage to garner significant support. Since dominant actors are not enough to structure action, this depends increasingly on a myriad of other actors, while the administration works hard to reinvent consensual values that can serve as foundations for action.

However, this strategic game often establishes a view of urban planning as a commodity, subject to permanent negotiation, thus minimizing or retracting political responsibility. The 'transactions' do not always have clear rules, nor are the competencies of public and private agents defined. According to some views, urban planning is nothing more than a strategic act of fluid negotiation, disintegrated and sporadic, the product of compromises between different influences. Still according to the same views, public authorities do not have the distinctive characteristics of other agents. However, as Wachter asserts (1998), if urban planning cannot be defined as a technique, it is certainly more than a procedure of conciliation that regulates the agreements and conflicts of the protagonists of territorial organization.

As François Eymard-Duvernay (1999) mentions, although rationality is not enough to understand the complexity of interactions between actors, the starting point of the analysis of the strategic game of actors is the recognition of their differences, the heterogeneity of their projects and the existence of contradictory interests.

In the context of these dynamics, the object of an interactionist sociology is that of clarifying the forms of constructing collective action, the roles of the different actors, and particularly the role of the public agent. In other words, this sociological approach seeks to understand the way in which conflicts and agreements are processed, in terms of the power relations that are present in any society or specific situation. According to the pragmatic field where all these questions arise, this interactionist sociology starts from the premise that the 'social significance' of living together is only recognizable through the analysis of specific processes, and this demands a strong involvement from researchers.

These questions are central for planning technicians because they need to clarify their action environment and their own role. Thus, the paradoxes of a participatory and contractual urban governance raise questions which remain largely unanswered: what is the degree of openness of the negotiation to the different economic, political and social actors, and therefore to the diversity of powers and status. What is the specificity of the public actor? What is the legitimacy of actors who are not elected but are called to participate? Is not the same traditional bureaucratic logic, clientelism, and the return to a certain kind of state (now expanded due to the new alliances) behind this apparently participative game? How are the interests of those who are excluded represented?

Looking for answers, I will connect three kinds of empirical materials. First, the evolution of electoral participation and associational involvement of the Portuguese; second, the different forms of intervention of stakeholder organizations in strategic planning processes; and, finally, I present a typology that seeks to interrogate the different logics of social action of the different kinds of actors.

In Portugal, the traditional 'let it be' concerning the ways of constructing the city has been translated into 'the law of the strongest' (obviously real estate interests dominate, but they are not the only ones). This has resulted in a huge disqualification of the urban structure, a deep neglect of public spaces and an increasingly marked socio-urban segregation. The new challenges that we are facing today do not allow such a disastrous situation to continue on pain of the city becoming impossible to live in.

We have been hearing, since the 1980s, that there is a growing crisis in urban management, which derives by and large from the multiplicity and fragmentation of interests and from the growing prominence of real estate groups in the management of built space. This crisis has taken different shapes, but the decline of the legitimacy of elected municipal officials, the increasing complexity of expectations and, above all, the growing demands by increasingly heterogeneous social groups, have generated increasing political and financial tensions between rising expenses and decreasing resources, due to the progressive retreat of the central state from local intervention (Gabriel and Hoffman-Martinot 1999).

For many, the growing anomie of local populations, often expressed in the low level of electoral participation, especially at the municipal level, is a worrying sign of a separation between political power and the citizens' daily concerns. Demands are seen as 'savage manifestations', manipulated by some for the purpose of furthering different kinds of interests, and amplified by the media.

Anomie or Growing Level of Demand?

In Portugal, there is a great diversity of forms of participation in 'city government', which have different levels of impact and visibility, as well as different fields of action. The 'partnership trend' is present across almost all sectors of intervention. At the social level, there are local committees for the monitoring of the guaranteed minimum income, committees for the protection of children, local education councils, social networks, and so on. At the economic level, there are different entrepreneurial associations, unemployed associations, trade associations, farmers' and fishermen's associations, etc.

Despite the proliferation of forms of associations of interests, central questions remain both in relation to the reinforcement of corporative interests (as well as the related decrease in collective solidarity) and the growing lack of interest from large groups of the population. Some available information on the evolution of electoral voting and forms of association has shown that the ways in which citizens participate have been changing in recent decades, but the interest in what is public is far from being on the decrease. New, less institutionalized, forms of political behaviour, such as those activities happening within citizens' initiatives, participation in demonstrations or petition signing, have been added to the more traditional forms of political influence. All of this has given rise to different interpretations. In any case, surveys have been showing the compatibility between old and new forms of political manifestation (Wilde 1999).

Taking the larger cities of Portugal into account, the participation in elections – both local and national – has been decreasing since the first elections after 1974. But this decline in participation has been relatively stabilized and there is no difference between urban and rural areas. The observed decrease seems to be better explained by the different political conjunctures than by the decline in the forms of electoral participation.

Taking into account other forms of political participation, the survey conducted by Cabral et al. (2000) concluded that electoral abstention was directly related to the refusal and/or inability of people to define themselves in ideological terms. It was also stated that the number of absentee voters (about 27 per cent) was not enough to conclude that there was any alienation from politics.

Other forms of political participation have been reinforcing the idea that the Portuguese population is far from being anomic, and the participation in local associations is of particular relevance in this respect, although only 20 per cent of those surveyed said they belonged to an association. Despite the public recognition of high levels of membership, the associative participation of the Portuguese population is lower than the European average, and we need to find the deep cause of this fact, which, for many, is counterbalanced by the existence of networks of informal relations.

The results from the last survey to the social attitudes of the Portuguese (1999) tend to show a decrease in association membership in the rural areas and simultaneously an increase in the participation of

TABLE 1
PERCENTAGE OF SURVEYED PEOPLE WHO BELONG TO ASSOCIATIONS BY TYPE OF ASSOCIATION AND AREA 1999

	Urban	Suburban	Rural
Local collectivities	16.1	17.0	13.8
Sports clubs	19.2	15.5	13.2
Unions	13.5	9.7	6.6
Occupational/economic associations	7.9	7.4	3.1
Political parties	3.4	3.7	5.7
Leadership bodies	14.5	18.9	26.6

Source: Survey on the Social Attitudes of the Portuguese, 1999.
[The author thanks the team led by Professor Manuel Villaverde Cabral for allowing the use of this unpublished information.]

inhabitants from these areas in leadership bodies (Table 1). Thus, it seems that there is no specific model of participation in urban politics, and that the 'old' forms of citizen participation still have some meaning to the majority of the Portuguese people. However, this doesn't mean that there are no problems. It seems obvious that only a minority is actively involved, and there is no way of knowing whether mobilized groups are representative of wider interests.

The multiplication of associations[1] is accompanied by a multiplication of interests and forms of demand, which by and large characterize the forms of social organization of 'semiperipheral' countries (Santos 1985). Frequently, authors underline the difficulties that political leaders have in governing due to the fragmentation of the political–administrative system and the growing complexity of actors' networks. It is this fragmentation that leads to the search for new concepts: 'The concept of urban governance allows us to recognize fragmentation and incoherence, and suggests that we should develop the forms of horizontal and vertical coordination of public action' (Novarina 1997: 215).

Strategic Planning: Methods, Results and Questions

It is in this context that the new forms of participation in the city potentially emerge as ways of expanding participatory democracy. Today, new forms of structuring diverse interests have been set in motion through concrete processes of participatory planning, at municipal and regional level. This has been expressed in the notion of 'strategic planning'. Its major challenge lies not only in the fact that it is procedural and participatory, but also in that it aims to maintain partnership forms of management and monitoring which can guarantee its rigorous execution, as well as its adjustment throughout relatively long periods of time.[2]

This essay discusses the forms of decision making which are related to quotidian urban planning and management, focusing on the practical experience of accompanying different levels of planning processes during the 1990s. The references used are based on different structures of participation: neighbourhood committees, local development associations, cultural and recreational collectivities, environmental associations, social and business associations, and so on. Among the large amount of work relating to municipal and regional planning forms, my research references are: *Forms of Management and Organization of Council Neighbourhoods*, Observatório de Habitação, CET (Centre for Territorial Studies)/Câmara Municipal de Lisboa, 1994; *Ways of life and expectations of the population of Pinhal Novo*, CET/Câmara Municipal de Palmela, 1997; *Prospective Analysis of the Pombal Downtown*), CET/Câmara Municipal de Lisboa, 1997; *Strategic Plan for the Peninsula of Setúbal*, CET/Associação de Municípios da Península de Setúbal, 1999/2000; *Recommendations for the Strategic Plan for the Peninsula of Setúbal*, 2000/2001.

However, my discussion is mainly based on the following studies about the region of Lisbon, the West and the Tagus Valley: *Social and Urban Dynamics of the Region of Lisbon, the West and the Tagus Valley* (preparatory work for the regional Plan for Economic and Social Development), CET/*Comissão de Coordenação da Região de Lisboa e Vale do Tejo*, 1997/1999; and *Strategic Plan for the Region of Lisbon, the West and the Tagus Valley*, CET/*Comissão de Coordenação da Região de Lisboa e Vale do Tejo*, 1998/1999, in which I participated, especially in what concerned its elaboration and the preparation of its implementation in the Western region.

In the above mentioned case,[3] and for the two sub-regions, the studies that were made used different methodologies: one, the preparatory study for the regional strategic plan, used Michel Godet's methodology, but introduced some innovations developed by CET's research team; about two years later, the elaboration of the strategic plan made use of more traditional methodologies, such as SWOT and the creation of work groups for each of the dimensions considered important to the strategic plan.

M. Godet's actors' strategy: This research work stemmed from a request made by the Coordinating Committee of the Region of Lisbon and the Tagus Valley (CCRLVT) to the Centre for Territorial Studies (CET) for the preparation of the launching of the Strategic Plan. The use of the methodology proposed by M. Godet, supported by the software MACTOR, could lead to the identification of the key actors, their alliances and conflicts, as well as the degree of mobilization and conflict of the strategic objectives for change in the region.[4] The objectives of MACTOR can be summarized as follows: to identify and characterize the key actors, to identify the principal conflicts and alliances, to help understand the social dynamics and improve actors' participation, to understand and evaluate power relations, to define strategies for the planning process by taking into account the social dynamics. In both regions (the metropolitan area of Lisbon and the West), individual interviews were conducted with a large group of actors: the Coordinating Committee of the Region of Lisbon and the Tagus Valley, the Metropolitan Board, several municipalities, departments from several ministries (Territorial Planning and Urban Development, Environment, Transportation, Regional Development, National Housing Institute, Education), real estate agents, entrepreneurial associations, trade unions, ecological, social and local cultural associations, and so on. Based upon these interviews, the study identified the objectives of each actor regarding the region and their position of adherence or conflict in relation to each of the strategic objectives established for the region. At the same time, the 'solidarities' and 'conflicts' of several actors vis-à-vis the proposed objectives were identified. These results allowed the regional organ to define a strategy for launching the discussion and execution of the strategic plan.[5]

The planning process of the strategic plan for the region of Lisbon, the West and the Tagus Valley[6]: The context of this study (made after the one previously mentioned) was the elaboration of the strategic plan for the Region of Lisbon, the West and the Tagus Valley[7] for the period 2000–06. The board of directors of CCRLVT created a work team with experts from different fields, who followed the elaboration of the plan. The objective was to design several sub-regional plans with the participation and contractualization of actors. These plans should guide the structuring of the Third Community Support Framework and establish monitoring structures for that framework, within the defined period.[8] The structure behind the elaboration of the strategic plan (which lasted about one year) can be presented as shown in Figure 1:

CCRLVT and the local municipal associations (in this case, three municipal associations, that is, AML, AMO, AMVT[9]) coordinated on equal terms the organic structure at sub-regional level. A forum with representatives of 'local actors' (trade unions, entrepreneurial, cultural, environmental and religious associations, and so on) was created. After assessing the problems, work groups were created in order to elaborate programme and project proposals and to identify and programme those projects considered 'structural'.[10] In March 2001, the local structures responsible

FIGURE 1
STRUCTURE BEHIND THE ELABORATION OF THE STRATEGIC PLAN FOR THE REGION OF LISBON

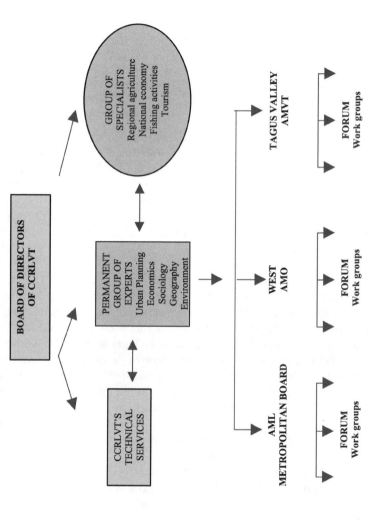

Source: Author

for monitoring the projects were organized. The team of experts who prepared the project is now elaborating the matrix for external evaluation.

We are facing two different methodologies with different scopes as well. In the first case, the aim was only to identify the key actors and their positions in relation to the interests that were to be mobilized by the plan, so as to devise a strategy that would allow the plan to be executed without any drawbacks from the viewpoint of the synergies of the actors and interests involved. In the second case, the aim was to elaborate, in a participatory way, a plan with its programmes and to ensure the necessary momentum for its future management.

Both methods have advantages and drawbacks. What MACTOR gains in terms of rigour, it loses in terms of actors' mobilization and involvement. M. Godet's actors' strategy leads to a greater systematization in terms of thinking and collection of information and outputs – conflict/agreement and mobilizing/non-mobilizing variables emerge more clearly. The major advantage of the methodology of participation in planning through discussion groups is that it socializes information and consequently involves the actors directly. However, there is the risk of attributing too much value to the expectations and interests of some groups to the detriment of others, due to the fact that there is no control over those actors who are involved[11] (and especially over those who are not[12]) (Table 2).

We can, however, raise questions not only about actors' representativeness and the meaning of their participation, but also their practical efficacy and the interests that are represented.

Unfortunately, there are very few research studies that answer these questions, or that analyze how agreements are achieved and conflicts are managed.[13] We should also recognize that not all actors are represented, and that, even when they are, not all have the same power or are legitimated by the authorities in the same way, or even have the same degree of legitimacy. The various forms of participation and criticism are recognized and valorized differently, and 'politically correct' behaviours are required as a *sine qua non* for 'participation'.

Considering the experiences of participation, we could construct an empirical typology of the forms of collective action present in several forms of grassroots organizations. These would be as follows:

(a) 'claiming action';
(b) 'critical action';
(c) 'local and/or global participatory management action and concerted negotiation action';
(d) 'pedagogic and/or innovative action'.

TABLE 2
COMPARISON BETWEEN TWO METHODOLOGIES OF PLANNING

M. Godet's actors' strategy	CCRLVT's process of participation in planning
Content:	Content:
More precise in terms of clarifying issues of conflict and agreement but more limited in terms of the number of actors involved	Questions are discussed in a more dynamic and conflictual manner but it is difficult to distinguish between essential and non-essential questions
Alliances are clearer and conflicts are more easily expressed	The number and types of actors are limited due to institutional and operational constraints
There is time to listen to individuals, which allows us to gather information which cannot arise in a collective discussion	Conflicts (personal, political or of interests) sometimes override content questions and disturb meetings and decision making
Method:	Method:
Less involvement	Actors are more involved, relationships can develop over a longer period, and thus personal relationships based on trust can be established. Potential management structures are clarified in the course of time.
Actors are more central and their choice is controlled	Involvement depends largely on the potential benefit each actor expects from the process.
The supervising institution controls the information	Actors with lesser impact or who are less organized (which are often the carriers of social interests and social cohesion) present discourses which are 'too local' or have difficulty in verbalizing their interests
	Socialization of information

This typology can help us to explore in depth the forms of construction of collective action, to clarify the roles of the different actors (especially of the public agent), and to identify conflicts and agreements in terms of the power relations that exist in a society or a particular situation.

Claiming Action

This type of action emphasizes the satisfaction of immediate needs considered to be fundamental or opposes actions that are considered to be clearly prejudicial to local interests. They are usually started by local associations, which have very specific objectives, although these objectives can be maintained for a long period of time or can emerge from specific situations. The relationship of these associations with established power is generally problematic because their demands and the way the demands are made threaten the power structure, or at least strongly put it into question. Claiming actions are sometimes aggressive; although they are not just typical of lower-class groups, they are very present in certain neighbourhood associations of lower-class areas. They can emerge in middle-class neighbourhoods through groups that feel harmed by the administration.

This may be the case, for instance, of a neighbourhood association which decides to abandon the procedures of strategic planning when it realizes that there is no budget for housing in the planning process. Considering that this is its central objective and that the need for housing is fundamental, the absence of this objective leads it to undervalue the whole process of municipal strategic planning. The argument that housing financing is not a municipal responsibility has no bearing in the case, since the logic of needs is clearly more important than the understanding of the means through which bureaucratic administration works.

Critical Action

This type of action seeks not only to provide a solution for immediate problems, but also, and above all, to raise the population's awareness about their rights and local identities and to create opportunities for experimenting with new ways of managing and organizing the territory. They are usually made up of associations that last longer than more immediate demands, and that are usually, but not always, organized at a more global level. Some local groups can indeed be long-lasting.

These associations seek to mobilize people by using original forms of struggle and consciousness raising; their search for answers is based on a global questioning of a certain model of development, and propose alternative models. This is a form of demand that is feared by existing power structures, due to their extra-local, and often international, roots. Most of these local associations see themselves as a counter-power that corrects the supposed or real imperfections of representative democracy, stimulating a participatory democracy. It is difficult to deny that these organizations have an irreplaceable role in that they serve as intermediaries in the production of relations of solidarity in spaces where processes of social de-structuring are developed, or where sustained development is threatened.

In these types of association, relationships are often characterized by either instability or permanent negotiation in relation to the problems that need to be solved. However, the management of competencies and knowledge, which are very important in these networks, is not supported by stable professional organizations and administrative hierarchies, and is constantly changing. The role of these associations is rendered fragile due to the instability of their presence in the public sphere.

Most ecological associations are a paradigmatic example of this type of action. Their spectacular (and sometimes original) manifestations are by no means a sign that they do not have an effective and pragmatic action in many situations, since they often have a detailed understanding of the issues at stake.

Local and/or Global Participatory Management Action and Concerted Negotiation Action

This is a type of action undertaken by actors who seek to 'participate' actively in everyday city management, defending their own interests, which are often corporative. Actions are frequently carried out by important public figures, and they aim to aggregate the maximum possible number of represented people, since numbers are here a measure of the degree of political legitimacy and strength. The means of struggle are formal and 'politically correct': meetings, collaboration in certain actions, negotiation, and so on. The relationship with established power is formal, institutional and cordial, although these forms of participation are often sporadic (they happen, for instance, when a plan is implemented, when particular actions are initiated, etc.). This type of action is even encouraged by public powers and frequently gives rise to more formal structures of management, such as local development associations, social and economic forums, and so on.

Their field of action may be more local – as happens with some private social solidarity institutions, housing cooperatives, neighbourhood associations – or more global – such as entrepreneurial associations, certain industrial associations, etc. The most paradigmatic example in the situations of strategic planning that I have been following is the entrepreneurial associations, especially in industry (in the Setúbal peninsula and in the West).[14] These associations have several advantages: most of the financing is directed toward them; they have a deep knowledge of the entrepreneurial structure and its needs (which are diverse and wide ranging); they often have a medium-term perspective; they have technical support staff and their presidents are usually people with local charisma. These characteristics make them strong partners, with a wide range of proposals in the fields of education/training, urban quality, and the different dimensions of economic activity. In this sense, their participation can confer a strong legitimacy to planning processes, and they end up winning because they manage to direct considerable financial resources and support to many of their proposals.

Pedagogic and/or Innovative Action

The actors who use this type of action aim to innovate through the creation and diversification of economic and social activities, as well as through the involvement of all the members of the associations which propose them. They offer a model of local development that is alternative to the Fordist models of development. Their pedagogic action is not only directed to the outside world, but mainly to their own members. These forms of association have had a central role in the development of a very interesting discussion not so much about the modernization of the state system, but about 'repairing the social fabric' and, mainly, about the role of 'associativism' in institutional networks, and the articulation of associative logics (solidarity, altruism, etc.), state logics (general interest) and business logics (efficacy, profitability).

Their action is strongly marked by the interests of those that are excluded and which they aim to represent, seeing themselves as spokespeople for populations deprived of citizenship rights and participation. Their actions are achieved by those elements that aim to satisfy their individual needs, and although they want to have a less localized reach, they frequently have difficulty in overcoming their local dimensions. Their relationship with the administration is paradoxical. They are supported, ignored or opposed depending on whether the actions at stake are convenient or not for the established power.

Some local development associations, cultural or patrimonial groups can be identified with this form of action. They come up with items for reflection that raise problems and question assumptions that were considered as givens. In the west, the Association of Young Farmers often presented aspects about the rural way of life and the needs of young people in this social context, drawing attention, in a significant and pedagogic manner, to what is changing but is still not clear to many. However, the intimate and cultural character of many of their original proposals does not have an impact on the established technocratic rationality.

In a generalizing, and therefore imprecise way, Table 3 can allow us to reflect on the diversity of forms of mobilization and the political impact of the different types of 'associativism' at urban level in Portugal. It is possible to see that mobilization is not always a sign of a greater degree of impact on the proposals of urban planning and management.

TABLE 3
POLITICAL STRENGTH AND MOBILIZATION OF THE DIFFERENT TYPES OF
ASSOCIATIONS IN RELATION TO FORMS OF MANAGEMENT

Political strength Mobilization	Strong	Weak
Strong	Municipalities and municipal associations Entrepreneurial associations related to industry and advanced services Real estate associations Ecological and other environment-related groups	Cultural, sports and associations
Weak	Commercial associations Universities and public higher education schools Regional and municipal offices of political parties Churches and religious associations	Regional organs of administration Neighbourhood committees and associations Trade unions

The methods of participation in the processes of urban planning and management in Portugal are still just beginning and are only used marginally. Therefore, they have not yet had the chance to prove their efficacy. Unlike other European countries, Portugal does not have formally established local or regional bodies that follow and assess municipal, regional or national planning. The role of social and economic actors is still modest, sometimes only formal; they are only present as consultants (rather than decision makers) during the stages of study and diagnosis. Most actors who are invited to participate belong to the economic sphere, whilst associations belonging to the cultural, social or sporting spheres are clearly marginalized.

Furthermore, the selection of valid interlocutors is still an open question as it relates to the fact that the goals of these forms of participation are not very clear. It is frequently difficult to find interlocutors who represent general interests instead of particular ones. The respect for the principle of 'globality' should lead to the involvement of some groups that, although less structured, are not less representative of the needs of territories.

Decision processes are not carried out in a participatory way, although they sometimes share specific tasks in certain fields during the stage of execution. However, functions and responsibilities are not clearly defined, and potential compromises are not formulated with clarity and precision;

there are no sanctions provided in cases of non-compliance, and contractualization is precarious. The legal forms that support the planning process are fragile, despite the fact that the law already allows support through local development associations, mixed societies, and so on.

THE PARADOXES AND POTENTIALITIES OF SOCIAL INTERVENTION

In the context of decentralization and the transformation of local conditions and needs, there is today an urgent need for a localized management of social risks, as well as for social prevention, which requires the renovation of the ideas and practices of urban public policies. This change in problems has contributed to the strong modification of work relationships between public and non-public actors and is producing changes in institutional functioning. If, for the time being, the specifically urbanistic effects of this type of collective action are not totally convincing, its impact on administrative practices and political and social relations is deep and certainly durable.

According to this logic, an increasing number of problems are raised in a paradoxical manner, due to the evolution of our ideas and due to modern pragmatism, which was introduced into our way of doing things and which questions the traditional paradigms of social science and the competencies of urban planning. Questioning the emancipatory potential of the new forms of urban government is thus totally relevant. These questions have to do with the forms of participation or integration, and with a managerial democracy or a collective project democracy based on the construction of forms of collective action.

The value system on which public action was based, and which allowed it to be organized in a relatively simple way, has been put into question, or at least is the subject of debates and uncertainties. The values of the republican state or of the welfare state, their legitimacy and efficacy, are being questioned, and public institutions rarely manage to garner significant support. Since dominant actors are not enough to structure action, this depends increasingly on a myriad of other actors, while the administration works hard to reinvent consensual values that can serve as foundations for action.

Emancipation Versus Integration

The 'new planning' calls for new forms of collective action. One of the paradoxes of this new collective action derives from questioning whether the new forms in which 'civil society' is involved in public action are forms of integration or of emancipation. The question is whether actors' involvement in the administration of the public means a widening of representative democracy or new alliances among the most powerful.

Most authors believe that the dimensions of emancipation and social control (although not directly connected to class domination) are both active in associative life. Even if we do not know the specific ways in which the game of negotiation (present throughout society) is played today,[15] it seems to be this tension between emancipation and social control that generates the current forms of regulation. It can be hypothesized that these two dimensions do not oppose each other but, on the contrary, are to a large extent complementary. Due to its mobilizing, as well as integrating (and therefore regulating) effects, participation can strongly contribute to the exercise of social control. It can even be thought that the expectations of political powers in relation to associations derive precisely from this attitude, which makes participation an important vector of socio–political integration (Palard 1998).

To understand this paradox implies a different conception of power. Traditionally, power is seen in many different ways: jurists define it through norms and institutions; some sociologists highlight the role of arbitration between economic and social interests; and, more recently, political scientists – Pierre Muller and Bruno Jobert – have stressed the mechanisms of production of hegemony. Most of these authors develop an approach to power in terms of social control. Nowadays, however, there is a group of authors who follow different currents of thought, such as the theory of justification (Luc Boltanski, Laurent Thévenot), the sociology of organizations (Erhard Friedberg), or the theory of urban regimes (Clarence N. Stone), proposing an interactionist approach to power.

These authors refuse the idea that social positions and roles are forever fixed. They believe that there are changing dynamics that imply various types of positions in time and space, because they derive from different statuses in the social and economic structure or from an unequal distribution of wealth and cultural capital. This postulate allows us to reintroduce the subject into the model of the analysis of society; although subject to constraints, the subject is able to make autonomous decisions. These constraints do not derive from internal determinations but from situations of interaction. Group restructuring derives from these situations of interaction and from the networks of relations that are constituted on such occasions, in order to obtain resources and gains.

It is obvious that this 'variable geometry' of interests and groups does not cancel out the indispensable dimensions of power relations which structure social organization. It just does not fix them as eternal dimensions, such as 'social class' or social status, but takes into account other social divisions, namely those that are relevant to the issues

I have been discussing, and that relate to the possession and use of scarce urban resources.

The paradox emancipation/integration brings to the fore a Hegelian conception of 'being together' by admitting that these groups can build consensus from shared experiences. So, power needs to be analyzed not only in terms of social control or domination but also in relational terms, based on the ability to interpret situations, construct objectives, obtain other actors' assent and get the resources needed to fulfil projects.

In the context of planning, power can be understood as a social construction that depends on the ability of certain actors to structure exchange relations to their own advantage. But the construction of a plan requires group unity. As the product of common objectives, internal cohesion makes the strength of the agreement depend on the degree of consensus. If power can be analyzed as a social construction with interactive dimensions in a concrete situation of decision making about planning, able to create networks in relation to objectives commonly accepted, emancipation can be (pragmatically) 'measured' by the dimensions of social justice that are expressed in the equity of the goals and programmes that derive from this process.

From a Managerial Democracy to a Project Democracy

The negotiation of the territorial project is not a simple process of equitable distribution (with different degrees of conflict) among diverging interests, and the state is not an actor like the others. Public entities cannot be mere managers of a power under construction, but should act according to pre-established and, as far as possible, consensual values and objectives. The management and organization of a territory are classified as public actions of a redistributive character – their objective is to allot the various resources according to the principles of equality and equity (Wachter 1998). Thus, in order to clarify the emancipatory dimension of the forms of participatory management of what is public, we need to know what is being negotiated and what are the results of the negotiation.

There are some who oppose a 'managerial democracy' to a 'political democracy', establishing a difference between the conception of the state as an intermediary for the interests of some and the state as guarantor of equality for all. According to Wachter (1998: 27), 'what separates a managerial democracy, based on negotiation and the search for compromises, from a political democracy is that the latter rests on values, principles and rules that are translated into political objectives and choices which are legitimated by the rules of the electoral game'.

Sometimes the 'culture of consensus' appears to be based on an inability to assume compromises or to erect a true culture of negotiation, different from one in which 'everything is negotiated all the time' and which establishes rules without a real content:

> By aligning the methodology of projects with a simple rationality of procedures, this 'strategic planning' invites us to prefer the consumer instead of the citizen, while efficacy invites us to prefer 'management' instead of democracy. Blinded by the false virtues of pluralism, it consecrates the virtue of compromise, a sort of average of wills that is obtained by dismantling conflicting interests. Thus, urban democracy is assimilated to a game of commodities (Wachter 1998: 180).

Unfortunately, experiments show that the current practices of participatory urban planning are far from being part of a direct urban democracy, despite the available potentialities. The following are all urgent tasks: to ensure the representation of the interests of the dominated (often rendered invisible because of the very logic of the forms of domination) and the goals of equity and social justice, bearing in mind that economic development and social development are not concomitant; to appeal for a larger participation of social and environmental interests, fighting the obvious over-valorization of economic interests at the level of the instruments of planning, and insisting on the idea that economic competition is not possible without social cohesion; to demand that public entities clearly express the assumptions that guide their actions in each specific context; to clarify the responsibilities of the different actors and find institutional forms of coordinating the planning structures throughout the process; to ensure that compromises are unambiguous and contractualized, and that forms of independent evaluation are established.

What seems to be specific in a project of local development is exactly the collective construction of the rules of the game, which all respect regardless of differences vis-à-vis immediate interests. Although these differences are important, it seems possible to find points of convergence in the identity processes connected to the sharing of a space/time of common work (Nicourd 1997). If a 'development project' can endure in the context of diverse interests, it is because it is connected to a concrete territory which has a history, an identity and forms of collective action (Denieuil 1997: 28). Thus, many values are not conflictive.

If participatory democracy, on one hand, overcomes some of the contradictions of formal democracy, on the other hand it gives rise to a considerable number of new questions, related fundamentally to the forms of management of contradictory interests and to the need for a critical reading of hegemonic interests.

The 'strategic game of actors' now takes centre stage, and the ability to analyze these dynamics gives the social scientist a new role. But it appears that it is in this 'strategic game' that both the germ of modern dictatorships and the emergence of new forms of social regulation can be found:

> To govern a territory means much more than to offer a service to its inhabitants. It means the possibility of creating and maintaining the social bonds without which living together stops being meaningful. This implies that the system of actors, within a concrete territory, can give meaning to collective action, i.e. can create and set in motion common projects and an overall view that all perceive as legitimate (Lefèvre 1997: 215).

NOTES

1. In Portugal, the levels of formal associative membership are considerably smaller than the European average. Participation is clearly more important in the northern European countries than in the southern countries. Participation is highest in Denmark (59 per cent) and lowest in Greece (13 per cent). In Portugal, 18 per cent of adults belong to a club or association. This difference has been interpreted as the result of the specificity of local forms of social organization; at the local level, the absence of institutionalized participation is accompanied by a greater degree of informality in the forms of participation. Thus, participation in groups and associations does not have the same sociological meaning in the different countries (Loison 2000)
2. We should remember that an important part of these plans is based on six-year programmes which are financed by the Community Support Frameworks.
3. The Lisbon region is made up of four sub-regions and these two studies concentrated only on the metropolitan area of Lisbon (the Lisbon and Setúbal districts) and the sub-region of the West.
4. See the many reports of this research project by CET and CCRLVT.
5. This study was not made public, at least at the level of political decision makers, due to the CCRLVT's change of direction between the time it was made and the launching of the plan.
6. I will only present here the general features of its organic structure, since the process of organization was complex, as were the results obtained.
7. A summary of this work can be found in CCRLVT (1999), *Strategic Plan for the Region of Lisbon, the West and the Tagus Valley – 2000–2001, The Horizon of Excellence*.
8. At that time, the management of the different funds was not clearly defined.
9. AML – Lisbon Municipal Association; AMO – Western Municipal Association; AMVT – Tagus Valley Municipal Association.
10. The Metropolitan Board decided that this organizational model would not be applied to the Lisbon city area. The operational logic of the work groups was not exactly the same in the sub-regions of the West or the Tagus Valley.
11. A number of institutions considered 'representative' of different local interests are invited to be involved.

12. Some groups are excluded from being involved, because the processes of exclusion imply political participation itself. Groups with fewer resources are often represented by social solidarity associations.
13. Most EU financing focuses on economic and employment issues and has little impact on 'social questions'. Thus, actors who represent interests in this area easily demobilize because they believe that their needs are not being addressed.
14. It is difficult to make generalizations since my experiences relate to the Lisbon area. However, commercial associations represent mostly small and medium merchants 'threatened' by the new big chains. This puts them in a more defensive position, which leads them to have a less significant role in the negotiation context. Conversely, those associations that represent real estate interests have a very active role, but are directed by their specific interests. They also resort to strong pressures outside the negotiation context of the planning process.
15. It is important to explore the following questions: who are the actors? How does social negotiation take place? How are compromises established? And how can their actual performance be controlled? The examples of the Council for Social Concertation and the agreements concerning territorial planning seem to point to the need for developing 'strategic interactions' between actors who do not represent individual interests but collective ones.

REFERENCES

Cabral, M.V. (1997): *Cidadania Política e Equidade Social em Portugal*, Lisbon: Celta.
Cabral, M.V., J. Vala and A. Freire (2000): *Trabalho e Cidadania*, ICS/ISSP.
Callon, M., P. Cohendet, N. Curien, J.M. Dalle, F. Eymard-Duvernay, D. Foray and E. Schenk (1999): *Réseau et coordination*, Paris: Economica.
Eymard-Duvernay, F. (1999): 'Les compétences des acteurs dans les réseaux', in C. Michel (ed.), *Réseau et coordination*, Paris: Economica, pp.153–78.
Friedman, J. (1996): *Empowerment: Uma Política de Desenvolvimento Alternativo*, Lisbon: Celta.
Gabriel, O.W. and V. Hoffmann-Martinot (1999): *Démocraties urbaines: L'état de la démocracie dans les grandes villes de 12 pays industrialisés*, Paris: Harmattan.
Gaudin, J.P. and G. Novarina (1997): *Politiques publiques et négociation: multipolarités, flexibilités, hiérarchies*, Paris: CNRS Editions.
Genestier, P. (ed.) (1996): *Vers un nouvel urbanisme, faire la ville, comment?, pour qui?*, Paris: La Documentation Française.
Godard, F. (ed.) (1997): *Le Gouvernement des villes – territoire et pouvoir*, Paris: Descarte & Cie.
Guerra, I. (1991): *Changements urbais et modes de vie dans la Péninsule de Setubal de 1974 a 1986*, Ph.D. dissertation, François Rabelais University, Tours, France.
Lefèvre, C. (1997): 'Démocratie locale et production institutionnelle: le cas des aglomérations francaises', in G. Loinger and J.C. Neméry (eds.), *Construire la dynamique des territories acteurs, institutions, citoyenneté active*, Paris: Harmattan, pp.215–22.
Loinger, G. and J.C. Neméry (1997): *Construire la dynamique des territories acteurs, institutions, citoyenneté active*, Paris: Harmattan.
Loison, L. (2000). 'Mecanismos compensatórios do desemprego em Portugal: família e redes sociais', Fourth Portuguese Conference of Sociology, Coimbra.
Neveu, É. (1996): *Sociologie des mouvements sociaux*, Paris: Editions La Découverte.
Nicourd, S. (1997): 'Processus identitaires et dynamique de projet et organisation', *Lien Social et Développement Économique*, Paris: Harmattan, Pierre-Noel Denieuil (org.), pp.99–110.
Novarina, G. (1997): 'Les réseaux de politique urbaine: concurrence et coopération entre acteurs', in F. Godard (ed.), *Le Gouvernement des villes – territoire et pouvoir*, Paris: Descarte & Cie, pp.213–54.

Palard, J. (1997): 'Dynamique associative, integration socio-spatiale et systéme politique', in G. Loinger and J.C. Neméry (eds.), *Construire la dynamique des territories acteurs, institutions, citoyenneté active*, Paris: Harmattan, pp.253–65.
Perestrelo, M. and J.M.C.Caldas (2000): 'Instrumentos de Análise para a Utilização no Método dos Cenário II – Estratégia de Actores', *Dinamia* 99/17, pp.1–40.
Ruivo, F. (2000): *O Estado labiríntico. O poder relacional entre poderes local e central em Portugal*, Oporto: Afrontamento.
Santos, B.de S. (1984): 'A crise e a reconstituição do Estado em Portugal – 1974/1984', *Revista Crítica das Ciências Sociais* 14, pp.7–29.
Santos, B.de S. (1985): 'Estado e Sociedade na semiperiferia do sistema mundial: o caso português', *Análise Social*, pp.869–901, 87/88/89.
Santos, B.de S. (1990): *O Estado e Sociedade em Portugal*, Oporto: Afrontamento.
Thuderoz, C. and A. Giraud-Héraud, (eds.) (2000): *La negociation sociale*, Paris: CNRS Editions.
Wachter, S. (1998): *Politiques Publiques et Territoires*, Paris: Harmattan.

A Beira Town in Protest: Memory, Populism and Democracy

JOSÉ MANUEL DE OLIVEIRA MENDES

'The universal is the place without walls' (Miguel Torga)

In this essay it is my intention to see how, in practice, a struggle is produced and maintained, what arguments, resources and relationships are mobilized, and what adversaries and allies are named. In a more descriptive logic, it is my goal to understand the dynamics, the contradictions, the paroxysms and the continuities of protest, that is, to understand the practice and the mundanity of protest actions.

Taking the common categories of indignation as object, I inquire about the conditions and constraints that lead to the distancing that is necessary for criticism (Boltanski and Chiapello 1999; Heinich 1999). For this I try to answer the following questions: When do indignation and criticism turn into collective action? How democratic and participatory is that process of mobilization? What allies and adversaries are produced? What material, relational, and discursive resources are used? What is the role of the leaders? Can these be bypassed?

For this case study, I chose the Movement for the Restoration of the Municipality of Canas de Senhorim (MRCCS).[1] From the outset it has been a working class movement with some support from the middle classes. Although the town's economic and cultural elites were not hostile to the movement, due to their social and political networks outside the locality, they never directly participated in the movement's activities. The Movement's main aim has been to restore Canas de Senhorim as a municipality, reinstating the lost status in the nineteenth century and reaffirming its autonomy from the mother municipality of Nelas. This expresses a strong and deep radical localism that is crucial in the construction of personal and social identities in the town.

Since 1998, this Movement has acquired great visibility in Portuguese national public opinion, due particularly to the spectacular nature of the actions undertaken. This greater visibility derives from a change in the Movement's leadership, and the consequent expansion of its network of contacts. The Movement now takes as interlocutors the political bodies at the national level. Thus, the demand for political recognition has entailed, in this case, the attempt to project and give visibility to the local space at the national level.

In a country with a long tradition of political and administrative centralization, it was after the Carnations Revolution of 1974 and after more than 40 years of a totalitarian regime, that local government and municipalities became symbols of the democratic process. As Ruivo (1999, 2000) has shown, it was only after this date that municipalities really obtained some administrative autonomy and could begin a process of local development. Local authorities, being elected, became the legitimate representatives of local populations and a new and important layer of political power in Portugal. Being a municipality made possible the access to financial resources and enabled the investment in infrastructures and in social services. It also allowed the municipalities to implement policies to attract investment. Furthermore, local government implied an administrative structure that meant opportunities to hire qualified personnel. The status as municipality became practically the only way for local development, especially in localities situated in the periphery of the country. However, the decentralization process was ambiguous and complex, and was established with the existing municipalities in 1974. There was much reluctance from central political power to create or redefine the administrative boundaries of the country, mainly for fear of igniting localism and old rivalries between local territories.[2]

This essay has two sections. In the first section there is a long and detailed description of the Movement, its beginning and marking events, its formal organization and the role of its leaders, its repertoire of actions, the important participation of women, the presence of violence and emotion, and the personal and collective identity processes of the Movement's participants. In the second section I reflect on the emancipatory potential of this concrete struggle.

THE CONTEXT AND THE REASONS FOR A STRUGGLE

Canas de Senhorim is located in the district of Viseu (interior centre region of Portugal), on a plateau between the River Mondego and the River Dão (Mouraz 1996). It is a town of around 4,000 inhabitants, mainly constituted by popular classes. Having received its charter in 1196 – confirmed by a second charter in 1514 (D. Manuel I) – it was governed as a municipality until 1852. At this time the former municipalities of Aguieira, Canas de Senhorim, Folhadal and Senhorim merged, thereby creating the municipality of Nelas (Various, 1975). The new administrative organization of 1867 allowed Canas to regain its status of municipality. With the January revolution of 1868, Canas de Senhorim once again became a parish of the municipality of Nelas.

It was only in 1975, a year after the Carnations Revolution, that the claims for the restoration of the municipality in Canas de Senhorim began.[3] The town's population wanted administrative autonomy and the recognition of its economical and demographic weight in the existing municipality and in the region. Mainly supported by the local factory workers and miners, its leaders were local trade union leaders and primary teachers that used the trade union and leftist political parties' organizational structures as ways to mobilize the population. The left-wing middle classes supported the struggle for administrative autonomy, mainly in the years following the Revolution.

The great strength of the movement was based on a memory and symbolic work that invoked more than 650 years history of the town as a municipality, along with the symbolic and power rivalry with the town of Nelas, now the municipality's capital. This rivalry was also a factor that united different classes and social groups in the parish under the idea of a local and autonomous administration. This strong localism was, and still is, the motive force behind the will for autonomy in the town.

In 1975, after some popular meetings, a list of demands and a petition were drawn up and sent to the Home Secretary. In this claims book one can read that, 'despite its ample participation in the national economy and exchequier, [Canas] has always been a victim of the most severe oppression and exploitation' (Various 1975). The action of the Nelas Municipal Council was accused of overtly withdrawing infrastructures from the parish of Canas de Senhorim, and the signers of the petition appealed for the legal establishment of a decentralized local administration. They set a term of 90 days for receiving answers to their demands, and at the end of this term the popular assembly of Canas would delegate powers to the parish council to collect and apply taxes locally. Furthermore, according to the manifesto, the head offices of the large companies operating in the region should be transferred to Canas, as 'Nelas and Lisbon cannot continue to colonize Canas'.

The claims book emphasized the legitimacy of the local population to self-government due to the ostracizing policies from the municipality of Nelas and demanded the localization of economic power in the town.

The entities mentioned in this document as legitimate interlocutors for the application of the proposed measures were freely elected representatives of the people of Canas, delegates of the government or

MEMORY, POPULISM AND DEMOCRACY

of the MFA (Armed Forces Movement), any negotiation with the municipal authorities being considered impossible. The action's leaders sought to project the issue of Canas's municipal autonomy to a level of national relevance, trying to mobilize the authorities recently constituted in the ambit of the ongoing revolutionary process in the country. They did this stressing the large working-class base of the population of Canas and the socio-economic power of this town in the context of the municipality, the district and the country.

Basically, the arguments are the same today. In a document included in the 'Process Relating to the Restoration of the Municipality of Canas de Senhorim', drawn up by the Movement for the Restoration of the Municipality of Canas de Senhorim (1999), they plead: 'Let Canas de Senhorim be free and dignified once and for all, definitively purging it of the old provocations in the form of the so-called *internal neo-colonialism* [emphasis in the original]'. In this document, the Movement also proposes, as a way of getting around the demographic criteria imposed by the Law on the Creation of Municipalities, two processes for creating municipalities: by law (quantitative, urban or administrative municipalities) and by the will of the people (qualitative, rural or historico-municipalist). It is the arguments submitted to justify this second method that I want to stress. They are justified by the idea of interiority and the need for balanced and sustained socio-economic development. Thus, in order for a municipality to be created, according to the Movement, the following aspects need to exist: conditions and structures equal or similar to those of the mother municipality; the will of the people, shown in several public acts (the argument of local representation); and municipalist traditions (a historical argument).

However, there is an important difference between the earlier demands and protests and the current ones. Before, constant references were made to the fact that Canas was one of the most populous and industrialized towns in the district of Viseu, contributing half of its gross domestic product. At present, after the closing of the Portuguese Electric Oven Company in 1987, and the consequent loss of economic influence in the municipality and the district, the Movement's documents now stress the spirit of progress and the high level of skills of the human resources in the town of Canas. It is felt that one of the main obstacles to the development of Canas is the need that the skilled workers feel to seek work outside the parish.

After the factory closing, and due to their professional skills, almost all workers found employment in factories in nearby localities.[4] Other became small entrepreneurs or administrative clerks. The consequent economic instability forced also women to look for jobs.

This was a great change in the family and social dynamics of the town. It really increased living standards for most families and, most importantly, brought women into the public sphere creating new sociabilities and consumption patterns. On the other hand, it left women with the burden of the double shift, as the traditional sexual labour division in the households remained almost unchanged.

With the normalization of the national political life and the end of the revolutionary period in 1976 in Portugal, the population of Canas participated in the first free national, municipal and local elections. The Movement's activities were restricted to sparse local meetings and some reunions with leftist political parties. The elected Mayor of Nelas for the first two mandates (1976–79; 1979–82) was José Correia from the PPD (Popular Democratic Party).[5] He established a policy of non-investment in Canas and this orientation, reinforced with his being from a party from the right, created a negative impact on the working class population of Canas.

The presentation in March 1982, by the Social Democratic Centre (CDS) of a bill in Parliament for the creation of the municipality of Canas de Senhorim, reactivated the local demands for autonomy. This legal initiative, politically institutionalizing for the first time the fight for the municipality, united the different social classes and groups of Canas. It was a proposal by a political party that participated in the national government, in coalition with the Popular Democratic Party (PPD).[6] Although the Movement leaders were from the left wing parties, namely Popular Democratic Union, a maoist party, the Socialist Party (PS) and the Portuguese Communist Party (PCP), they saw here the opportunity to give a national dimension to the struggle and a way of responding to the grievances by the Mayor of Nelas.

In May 1982, the newly named Committee for the Creation of the Municipality gave a press conference where it submitted the following demands: a specific postal code should be created, express trains should stop in Canas, there should be a health centre, and the bill submitted by the CDS should be discussed in Parliament (*Jornal de Notícias*,[7] 1 May 1982). These demands were strategic to mobilize the feeling of localism in the population and were presented as signifiers of the ecomomic and symbolic power of the town. At the time, the newspaper JN took up a position favourable to the demands of the Canas Committee, publishing several pieces condemning the deplorable state of the infrastructure in the town and putting the struggle for the municipality into a historical context (JN, 20 May and 1 July 1982).

On 30 July 1982 the CDS's bill was not voted on in Parliament for lack of a quorum. On 2 August 1982, the population of Canas gathered outside the Post Office to prevent the mail from leaving and to demand a postal code. This action was a response to the Parliament's refusal to discuss the bill about Canas de Senhorim. It was also a demand for a visible and concrete measure that could signify the real importance of the town and its autonomy from Nelas. This was done also in a national context of social and political instability, the national government having faced many labour strikes and a general strike on February 1982. For many of the Movement's leaders, the national government was weakened and this was the time to push forward by a spectacular action that presented the local struggle to the national public opinion.

On 2 August 1982, when the people realized that the mail had been removed earlier, the building was taken over. Spontaneously, they then decided to block the railway line. As the JN writer stresses, this measure had a great impact, as it was an international line and was used by many emigrants at this time of the year. More than 100 metres of rails were taken up. As word was passed that the Republican National Guard (GNR) was outside town ready to take action against the population, the fire siren and the church bells began calling for the population. Hundreds of factory workers and miners with their relatives and wives gathered on the railway, turning this event into an instance of the local resistance against centralism and its representatives, mainly the security forces. Many years of ostracism by the local and national authorities converged on this event, and beyond political or social differences, the population had an opportunity to unite and bond around a feeling of community, in an almost mythic fusion of minds and bodies, as many of the interviewees told me.

Meanwhile, the GNR had taken advantage of the absence of the people who had gathered at the railway line to occupy the Post Office building. The fire siren sounded again and the people returned to the Post Office. The GNR used force. The population retook the building, and mounted a picket line. When the people returned to the railway line they found the GNR's riot troops there. An agreement was reached with the GNR commandant. The police did not intervene, and the people remained on the railway line.

The next day, after a meeting with the authorities at the Viseu Civil Government, the movement, in a popular assembly, decided to raise the blockade. It was also decided that from then on 2 August would be observed as the symbol of the future municipality of Canas, as against the Nelas municipal holiday, which is celebrated on 24 June (JN, 4 August 1982).

On 26 September 1982 a plaque commemorating the 2 August would be unveiled. Since then, there has only been one year when that day was not commemorated. The commemoration is of a popular and solidary nature. Sardines, wine and corn bread are distributed freely to all who are present. As one of the interviewees said, after that date:

> the Movement's only action was the 2nd of August. ... It didn't happen only once, one year ... The 2nd of August became the people's holiday. The people's holiday. We had lots of people here, sometimes people who came and said, 'hey, mate', emigrants and foreigners who appeared, 'Hey, mate, this is different, in a country like this, to have a party where people eat, drink and don't pay. Where else can you see this?' ... We clubbed together, and people went round collecting money (Carlos Henrique,[8] 8 August 2000).

But more importantly, this date recorded the population's capacity for mobilization around the ideal of the restoration of the municipality in the collective memory, projecting the struggle to a national level (Ruas 1994). It was the first violent action in the municipality's political demands process, showing the local will to resist the impositions of the municipal, district and national authorities. The annual commemoration of this date is part of the practice and the memory of popular resistance and solidarity, and celebrates the communion of all the people in a decommodified event with no social distinctions or privileges. It is the only moment, together with the town's famous Carnival, that class differences and social hierarchies are bracketed and the community commemorates together. By gaining its own postal code in 1983, this was a small reward for those who believed in the possibility of gaining administrative autonomy, and a sign that sometimes violent action can bring some results. To date, this was the only visible national policy success in the long history of the Movement.

In the local elections of December 1982 the candidate of the PS, José Albuquerque Vaz, was elected as Mayor of Nelas. Being a native of Canas he began a strong policy of investment in infrastructure in the town. The Movement maintained its informal meetings, participated in only by the leaders. The only public presence of the Movement from 1982 onwards was the yearly political rally of 2 August.

Another politically important date, and a local policy success for the Movement was later when, in 1986, it stood for the parish council elections with its own list of candidates, the only opposition being the PS. The Movement won by a large margin. This date coincided with the beginning of the crisis at the Portuguese Electric Oven Company. The parish council took up many positions condemning the critical situation at the company, and the difficult labour situation came to overshadow the demands for the administrative autonomy of Canas. Also the Nelas Mayor elected in 1985, José M. Lopes de Almeida from the Social Democratic Party (PSD), maintained a policy of strong support for the town of Canas. With the closing of the factory and the dislocation of workplaces, the Movement entered a long period of stagnation.

In the remaining parts of this essay, I will concentrate on the most recent years of the struggle for the restoration of the municipality of Canas, which has been renewed and intensified since 1997.

Formal Organization and Leaders

At the end of 1997, some of the leaders of the Movement who had remained since 1987 contacted Luís Pinheiro, a local high school teacher, to reactivate the movement. He had been the president of the parish assembly, for which he was elected by the PSD from 1993 to 1997. He was also the defeated PSD candidate to Mayor of Nelas in the local elections of 1997.

This reactivation of the Movement can be explained by two factors. José Correia Lopes, the Mayor of Nelas from 1976 to 1982, had been re-elected in 1989, now by the PS.[9] He maintained his personal orientation of not investing in Canas, and the fact that he was now a candidate for the PS caused many socialists from Canas to withdraw their support from the local policies of their political party and to appeal to a more vigorous political presence by the Movement. On the other hand, the majority of the town's workers and their families now had more stable economic situations, and they felt that only administrative autonomy could stop the declining position of their town when compared with the mother municipality or other neighbouring towns.

Luís Pinheiro sought to institute a collegiate leadership structure for the Movement which would bring together representatives of all the political parties. This was a strategy to unite all social groups around the struggle for the status of municipality. In an extended meeting he was elected leader. The Movement's leadership would maintain the presence of the former leaders, who symbolized the continuity of the struggle and its popular roots; but it included also representatives of the PS, the PSD, the Social Democratic Centre/Popular Party (CDS/PP) and other parties of the left. At present, the PS has just one permanent representative, and the other parties of the left have none. Despite the effort to keep the Movement above the parties, party political logic turned out to be the factor that caused most friction within the movement and its supporters.

Indeed, party political identification is a crucial identity marker, especially because of the personal, family and relational divisions it creates. At this stage of the struggle, the Movement's great enemy is the PS, especially some important figures, such as the Mayor of Nelas (José Lopes Correia), the leader in the Viseu district, the Speaker of

Parliament, and the leader of the parliamentary benches. Those in Canas who are PS members and also feel close to the Movement are divided between local solidarities and pressures and the biographical, political and ideological allegiance to the party. The resolution or lessening of the ideological dilemmas in which they are entangled involve the personalization of their party's negative attitudes. In order to protect the party, which has always received strong electoral support in Canas, they attribute negative positions to personality traits, as well as to the personal interests of some municipal, district and national leaders.

The personal party orientation of some of the people I interviewed, in almost all cases decided after 25 April 1974, has a decisive and important influence on the identity levels activated and the broader levels of political and social involvement. These levels include the personal and unique, intermediate spatial and institutional identifications, as well as broader identifications, such as the country (Augé 1998). For reasons of identification with the party leader, ideological choice, influence of local dynamics, hatreds and passions, and especially the choice of party of personal and family adversaries, the chosen party indelibly marks opinions and political positions.[10]

Although the Movement's supporters in their majority put the local struggle above their political allegiances, it is predictable that when Canas obtains its status as a municipality all the force of party identifications will come to the fore and new alliances and confrontations will be established.

In the Movement today, we are faced with the crossing of different memories, with different temporal depths. For the new leader, the important references belong to the most recent years (1998–2000). For those who have been in the Movement since 1975, what is important, with its highs and lows, is the permanence of the struggle and the capacity for resistance. Some interviewees made a clear distinction between the current Movement and the former one in terms of goals and methods. The strategic capacity for mobilization therefore depends on an appeal directed towards different memories and common histories and narratives. As Jeffrey Rubin says, 'these ambiguities and contradictions suggest that it is the coexistence of multiple forms of difference that animates a radical social movement' (1998: 160).

The strategic appeal by the Movement's leader to the localism ideology and the rivalry with Nelas town, along with the mobilization of the strong local identities of those who were born in Canas de Senhorim or have lived there for many years, puts the Movement above the political parties. This is also facilitated by the fact that the Mayor of Nelas has been in power for more than ten consecutive years, not investing or attracting factories or other investments to the town of Canas. These facts allow a clear identification of the local adversary and create an ideological consensus around the main goal of becoming a municipality. This is an ideological binding force that overcomes particularisms and party identifications. The political fight, as the new Movement's leader says, is against the local and the national governments and demands allegiance to this cause and no other. This demands a constant identity work of defining the in-group against all the adversaries from the outside, be they in the municipality, the region or the national level. The Movement has a core group of five people around the leader, constituted mainly of small entrepreneurs, all former factory workers and some in the Movement since 1975. The Movement has weekly meetings with the population. The people who go to the meetings regularly[11] are, on the whole, thought of as political mediators and people of privileged opinion in the locality. They have wide networks of contacts and knowledge, and are given a respected position in the hierarchy of local credibility.

Of those who regularly attend the meetings, the majority are factory workers, some are teachers, administrative clerks and peasants. Of the women who attend, the majority are housewives, along with some factory workers and administrative clerks. The most striking feature is the complete absence in the meetings of the representative of the economic or cultural elites, this being a clear indication of explicit reinforcement of the popular composition and ideology of the Movement after 1997.

At the organizational and logistical level, the support of the Canas parish council is important to the Movement.[12] The Movement's weekly meetings with the population are held in its offices. These meetings, instituted in 1998, are an exercise in confrontation and an explanation of arguments. As one person remarked in conversation,

> The meetings are educational. At the beginning there was great confusion. Everything under the sun was talked about. People came with personal hatreds and grudges. There were intentions to give up the meetings. People learned how to behave at these meetings. They learned to submit pertinent topics, not to get excited and to explain their points of view.

This learning of a democratic debate materializes and ritualizes the closeness of the Movement's leadership to the people. Although the meetings are guided by topics submitted by Luís Pinheiro, given his privileged relationship with the national political bodies and the media, many people take an active role in the meetings. These meetings are seen by the leaders as an opportunity to control the more radical elements, allowing their discontent to be voiced and arguments to be rationalized.

But they also force the leaders to face resistance, to explain attitudes, affirmations and actions. Although the decisions to be taken regarding the Movement's concrete actions are made by a restricted group of leaders, the weekly justification of these decisions has become an imperative.

It should also be emphasized that the participants in the meetings constantly activate a policy of vigilance in relation to everything that is said or written in the local, regional and national media about Canas. The participants in the meetings conduct a practice of careful, deconstructive reading of the news stories and reports, imputing intentions, defining allies or adversaries, categorizing favourable and unfavourable positions, and consequently placing the reports analyzed into a continuum of closeness and localism (valorization) or distance (devalorization).

To maintain a close relationship with the general population, the new leader also initiated monthly rallies, where the Movement could expose its initiatives and lines of action, and maintain a constant arousal against its political adversaries. These rallies were normally attended by 400–550 people, the majority of them from the popular classes with some from the middle classes.

The greatest tension that runs through the Movement, visible at many of the meetings I participated in, comes from the precarious balance between the radicals and the moderates. The moderates, represented by the leader, have a more political, medium and long-term vision. They place the struggle in a logic of party political strategy, favouring negotiation and institutional viability, waiting, if necessary, for a national alignment of political forces which will be more favourable to the process of establishing the new municipality.[13] The radicals, less closely linked to party logic and closer to a fundamentalist working class ethic, base their arguments on a moral logic, of personal and collective offence and indignation. The central argument on which this moral position is founded was well summarized by Manuel Alves when he said that:

> It's like this. There are people who like to live under the control of others. There are others who don't. Canas de Senhorim doesn't. It's a place which thinks it should never be dominated by others. So they think it should be set free, like any other place. Just as Portugal thought, and as other nations thought, so as never to be dominated by others (24 August 2000).

What prevents the polarization of positions and allows some tolerance is the ideology of brotherhood and the crucial role of the family in the structuring of social relationships. The great closeness between the men comes from a common past as employees of the Companhia de Fornos

Eléctricos or of the Minas da Urgeiriça. Many participated together in protest actions, and the fact that they had worked together gave them a sense of community and a capital of trust that are very hard to break. This idea of brotherhood and the common memory of work prevent the radicalization of positions against those who are less favourable to or against the Movement. Although some voices are heard threatening more extreme actions against those who are against the Movement, these have never been carried out. In many cases, the example of the radicalism of Vizela is invoked[14] with the idea of regretting that similar actions were not applied locally. Basically, we have a counterpoint between a political pragmatism and a moral vision based on the principles of dignity, honour and familism.[15]

The weekly meetings, a populist and demanding democratic exercise, force the leaders to present and justify their opinions and decisions before the people they represent.[16] Leadership is never a given, and demands the constant exercise of rhetoric, argument and justification. It is always seen and read as provisional, as demanding a constant labour of affirmation and confirmation. Knowing how to listen to and accept criticisms in the meetings is an indication of the leadership's democratic nature. Knowing how to speak and explain points of view shows the leader's ability to represent the Movement to the outside (media, politicians), where a good command of language, a good physical appearance and a persuasive argumentation are needed.

The provisional nature of leadership, always dependent on concrete results and achievement of the goal of administrative autonomy, as well as on the balance of forces between the more radical elements and those who propose a political, negotiated strategy, was clearly evident in the interview Luís Pinheiro gave me.

> I tried, and I only managed to get people to be on my side and to rise above the logic of the parties and each one's party. Each one's party has always been respected. This has been the great exercise of my mandate, let's call it that, in the Movement. It was to open the game to the people. To open everything to the people. We have meetings open to everybody. No politician does that. And if I wanted to I wouldn't. I'd be respected just the same. People would follow me just the same. ... And it's difficult to face the people every week. Because they don't all think the same way. Everyone can give their opinion. Some think we should take action, others think we shouldn't do that. This is very difficult to manage, and few people want to be exposed to situations of this kind. ... I've learned a lot from people and people teach me a lot. ... Now I understand that at

a political level, in any chamber, this can't be opened up in this way, or chaos would set in. But it's good that people realize that the people are increasingly less stupid. The people increasingly know more and see more. And now nobody is smarter than anybody else. We see these politicians increasingly going under from one moment to the next because really they think they're still working for idiots. They can't understand that nowadays the people around them study. Nowadays people have a different level of culture, they have the Internet, they have television, read newspapers, listen to the radio and are informed. They are beginning to understand the system. There has to be a different kind of respect for people. ... And I think that this is an exercise that I'm going to undertake and continue to the end. And if I go under with this, I'll go under with pleasure and I'll go under with honour. Because I'll go to any length to tell people the truth (19 September 2000).

Here the interviewee again emphasized his intention to maintain the Movement as a means of uniter regardless of the party political options of each individual. Stressing that he considers himself a democrat, he mentions that the weekly meetings were his idea and he has always had the option not to hold them. Here, he emphasizes his role as leader, as capable of imposing a direction and a practice. But, having instituted the ritual of the meetings, doing away with them would be dangerous to his leadership. He himself recognizes that people are much better informed, and the meetings also serve to channel passions, emotions, and feelings, and to clarify criticisms and radical positions and make them public. Without the meetings, it would be almost impossible to control the more radical elements. Without a framework of some kind, their actions would become unpredictable and could put the Movement's entire strategy of institutional negotiation at risk. The voicing of radical ideas makes them visible and the arguments put forward can be contested, normalized and soothed.[17]

What separates the Movement's leadership from the other supporters has to do with the means for achieving the goal of raising Canas to a municipality. While the former adopt an overtly political pose, reflecting on and strategically weighing every action, seeking to mobilize the political bodies at local, regional and national level, the latter, with memories of long hard struggles, demand immediate results, proposing drastic actions, especially directed against the local government that dominates them. This gap between strategies and territorial levels of relevance of action creates ambiguities, contradictions and compromizes which have to be constantly negotiated, assessed and controlled.

Following Santos's suggestion (1995: 482), the relationship of the Movement's leadership with its supporters appears as a negotiated form of the transformation of power into shared authority. The dilemmas of choice between institutionalized/non-institutionalized action, between legal/non-legal actions and between violent/non-violent actions, which all social movements face (McAdam and Tarrow 2000), are felt more by the leadership of movements than by their supporters, and the latter often end up going too far or forcing the leaders into unplanned, unprogrammed, more radical actions.

Besides his organizational and rhetorical skills, the current leader's great trump card is that he mobilized and interested a party with a great national profile like PSD in the cause of raising Canas to the status of municipality.[18] The bill submitted in 1982 had been an initiative of CDS, and in the years that followed (1983, 1986 and 1988) the initiative came from the PCP,[19] two parties with unimportant representation in Parliament. The support of the PSD after 1998 reignited the hope of those who fought for the municipality and broadened the Movement's support base, reinforcing the new leader's legitimacy and his calls to unity above party identifications.

The Repertoire of Actions

From 1998 the Movement adopted a set of action strategies which projected it to the national level, and appeared as a break with past actions. Modernization of the repertoire of actions included extreme attention to the effect of the struggle on the media and the adoption of spectacular forms of action. The Movement's leader acknowledges that getting media attention was the most difficult part of the struggle, because there is always the risk that statements or actions will be interpreted negatively, harming the Movement's goals. The targets of the actions, with occasional exceptions, had now become political bodies and institutions at national level, especially Parliament. There was an explicit will to be innovative and radical at the actions chosen, with the sole aim of getting the attention of national media and public opinion. This was done with a clear symbolization and aestheticization of all actions, carefully selecting the rituals, the props and the chants to be used.

The most important moment in the intensification of the struggle occurred on 19 November 1998, when discussion on raising more than 20 places to the status of municipality was scheduled in the Parliament. The conference of leaders in the Parliament ended up agreeing to discussion and voting on only two new municipalities, Trofa and Odivelas (JN, 19 November 1998). For the people I interviewed, this was the most negative moment of the whole process of the struggle since 1975. Party alignment at this time was favourable to Canas. The news of the non-tabling of Canas was received by those who were in the Parliament with great emotion. As Carlos Henrique told me:

> When we were in Parliament, some time ago, when it arose, when it was supposed to come up for discussion, and when only Vizela [it was Trofa, not Vizela] and Odivelas came up and we did not come up, I was there in Parliament. And when they came to us saying 'Hey, Canas didn't come up!' Hey, some were crying, there were four of us, some were crying and I shouted. ... We were crying, some on one side, some on the other. We were shouting, we were crying. We stormed the Parliament, we shouted, everyone was fleeing, watching, everything. It was... it was the most dramatic moment, for me it was (8 August 2000).

From then on the attitude of those most directly linked to Canas's struggle was characterized by indignation against political power and its strategic games. It was an indignation against the asymmetry of power and the failure to respect political promises. As Carlos Henrique mentioned, 'This is shocking. They make fun of us, and later when we see that they're playing with us, there's nothing we can do. Have you seen? They think they are the bosses, above everyone, they are the greatest. They are the MPs, they're the greatest, and you put up with it and that's that'.

In January 1999 a petition was sent to the Speaker[20] asking for the discussion of, and voting on, the bills about Canas. On 2 February there was a demonstration outside Parliament with 234 citizens, one for each MP. On 2 March, 12 Canas men began a hunger strike on the steps of the Parliament building. This was suspended the following day, after appeals from some PSD MPs, and this party's promise to schedule discussion of the Canas project. On 9 March people from Canas demonstrated outside Parliament with nooses around their necks. The scheduling of the discussion about the parties' bills concerning Canas was due on that date. The press attributed the fact that this did not happen to the direct intervention, for the first time since he had held the office, of the Speaker, Almeida Santos from the PS (*Diário de Notícias*, 24 March 1999).

These last actions had notable repercussions in the national media. The cartoons published in the *Diário de Notícias* and *Público* were significant.[21] On 18 March, after the Movement held a rally in Canas, people blockaded the Beira Alta railway line. On 28 March, at the Almeida Garrett (a national writer from the nineteenth century) commemorations in Porto, attended by the President of the Republic, the people of Canas demonstrated for their municipality. According to the report by journalist Domingos de Andrade of the JN, Jorge Sampaio did not like this action, and appealed for national unity against administrative divisions (JN, 28 March 1999). More important was the symbolic act of refusing political citizenship by many demonstrators, who on this day burned their voting cards in an improvised ballot box. In this way they showed their distance from the national institutions and the political system, abdicating their right to vote.

These actions show an explicit strategy of continual pressure on the organs of sovereignty, seeking to raise the profile of the Movement and embarrass the national authorities. However, they also show great ability to mobilize the town population, which has managed to be present in significant numbers in different scenarios and situations.

On 19 April 1999, ten members of the Movement's leadership began a hunger strike on the steps of Parliament which lasted until 25 April. This extreme action taken by nine men, the leader and the core leadership, and an old woman, was strategically intended to project nationally, through the suffering bodies of this small group, the struggle of the town. The date chosen, to coincide with the commemorations of the Carnations Revolution (25 April 1974), intended to show that there was a town that claimed freedom in the spirit and the tradition of the 1974 political revolution. The chosen action was an indicator of how radical and strong-willed they were fighting for their town's autonomy. It was an unexpected action that had great media impact.

The memory of this action is painful for those who participated in it. The Movement's leader was accompanied on the strike by his mother, a lady of advanced age, which made him more vulnerable and sensitive to the suffering of the other strikers. When I interviewed one of the participants in the hunger strike, his wife remembered those days of expectation and absence in silence, and her eyes were full of tears which she tried to hide.

But what most impressed the participants and the people of Canas was the indifference of the MPs and politicians to the strikers. Nobody came to talk to them or ask them about their complaints. This extended strike culminated on 25 April, with the beginning of the commemorations of the April Revolution. The ceremony took place in Parliament, in the presence of the Speaker of Guiné-Bissau and the President of Mozambique. The demonstrators from Canas called the Speaker and the President of the Republic fascists when they arrived for the ceremony (JN, April 1999).

An element of the stories told by the people of Canas, which was not reported by the newspapers, is the surprise they had at how little security there was at the Parliament, which allowed them to get very close to the Prime Minister and see the fear and surprise stamped on his face. It was a desacralization of power, and a momentary inversion of the hierarchy of power.

But the actions most aimed at the media were reserved for the official commemorations in the Parque das Nações. The demonstrators who came from Canas with banners decorated with black carnations as a sign of mourning were following what was happening at the Parliament by radio and communication with acquaintances and family members. According to later reports, spirits were exacerbated and when they got to the Parque das Nações they were prepared for the worst. The principal figures of the state, especially the President and the Speaker, were met by the people of Canas with cries of 'fascist, fascist'. When the national anthem was played, the protests, shouts and chants continued. Some of the participants claim they did not even notice the anthem. Most of the people I interviewed consider this to be the most significant moment in Canas's struggle to become a municipality. Press coverage was enormous, and, some argue, they managed to show the foreign leaders and the diplomatic corps the situation of injustice and oppression that exists in some regions in Portugal.

These events were assessed very negatively by commentators in the national media.[22] As an example, in his article in *Visão* magazine (29 April to 5 May 1999), with the title 'The 25th of April Deserved Better', Cáceres Monteiro, after writing that the commemorations of 25 April had been disappointing and routine, goes on to tackle the action of the people of Canas. To quote:

> Also seen was the regrettable demonstration by the inhabitants of Canas de Senhorim, on the steps of São Bento (including insults to the President and the Speaker) and at the military parade – with hoots and whistles at the national anthem. After this act of extremely poor civic education, unless the population of Canas discredits the delegation of political hooligans, the place had better give up on its aims. Wretched parish![23]

This commentary forms part of a journalistic logic, inherent in the very format of the opinion article, which Shanto Iyengar (quoted in Jasper, 1997: 79) calls episodic framing (stories told as single events) as against thematic framing (events set in a broader social context). No information is given by the writer about the reasons for the demonstration. In addition, the application of the label 'hooligans', normally associated with disorderly young football supporters, denigrates the demonstrators of Canas, lumping together women, people who had just finished a long hunger strike, children, young people, labourers with a long tradition of struggle and resistance, civil servants, employers, and so on.

In Canas's long tradition of populist struggle, the demonstrators, against an intellectual and journalistic vision of 25 April, and in a logic of appropriation, normalization and institutionalization, sought to deconstruct in practice the reified categories of freedom, democracy and people. By intoning the slogans of the revolution, they sought to create a spectacle within a spectacle, undoing and denouncing the exhibitionist logic of the commemoration. They were recuperating, through invocation, the revolutionary and popular celebration of freedom. This can be read in the arguments put forward by Manuel Alves:

> The press has not been correct in their not getting adequate information about the reasons behind these demonstrations, these struggles. It's not enough to show up and criticize. As they did, for example, on the 25th of April [1999], when they criticized what I feel should not have been criticized. Because, see, they failed even there, because the 25th of April is a time of struggle and freedom. That wasn't done by chance. Precisely to free the people. And we thought the 25th of April was the ideal time for us to plead for our freedom. And so we did. Now, to say there were excesses, which there were, but what struggle doesn't have excesses?[24] (24 August 2000)

The Movement's leader, Luís Pinheiro, also considers this date to be the most important since he took over the leadership, although his vision is more strategic:

> I think the most important moment we had, which may have been negative from the media's point of view, was the 25th of April. The 25th of April registered decisively in the politicians' heads that this was a problem that they had to treat differently. It may have been a complicated way, but it was decisive.... It was a process we had to go through to get that media coverage, to gain a position in the head and spirit of the politicians. And we did it. In the end we succeeded perfectly.... Today I enter Parliament and everybody knows me (19 September 2000).

The Movement's actions would continue throughout the year, with great media visibility. They would be present in Tondela when the Prime Minister opened a landfill site. They would jeer at the Speaker when he was honoured by Dão gastronomic fraternity (*Público*, 24 May 1999). And, on 10 June, the day commemorating Portugal, Camões and the Portuguese communities, they would appear, gagged, in Aveiro (*Público*, 10 June 1999). They would also boycott the European elections (in June) and the parliamentary elections (in October), and the elections for a new parish council.

To finish this point, it seems pertinent to mention that an article from *Visão* magazine (25 November to 1 December 1999) indicated that the President had reviewed his position on Canas de Senhorim. To quote, 'His advisers have mapped out the historical and sociological causes behind the desire for separation from the municipality of Nelas, and Jorge Sampaio promises to follow the case closely, helping to tackle the fundamental problems of that community'. The President became a potential ally, and today still has an adviser in regular contact with the Movement's leaders.

In the prosecution of the goal of raising Canas to municipal status, the Movement's actions, very intense and frequent in 1999, can be seen as attempts to redefine the state's positions and actions, setting a localism of resistance against a centralist and centralizing vision, a democratic law against a despotic law (Santos 1995: 482), based on the memory of a struggle and on populist and egalitarian ideals. In the structural space of citizenship the appeal is for a radical democracy, both in its vertical component (relationship between citizens and the state) and in its horizontal component (relationship between citizens and their associations) (Santos 1995: 486).

Women's Participation

The women of Canas have had a powerful and constant presence in the public actions carried out by the Movement. They sing the chants at demonstrations and rallies. They were present at the electoral boycotts I witnessed, keeping a permanent watch throughout the night. They also take part in the weekly meetings. Thus, the women have their own, visible standing in the public space. However, they have never had important positions in the Movement's leadership structure. The role and the presence of women is a given for the people, and they do not question the sexual division in the political work of representation.

Some interviewees have attributed their visibility in the public space of protest to a personality trait in the Beira's women, who have always been very determined and active in issues that affect them directly. Others look for socio-economic reasons, because since the closure of the large companies which were based there, it was the women who most felt the first years of recession and economic difficulties as they were forced to look for work, often shift work, outside Canas.

The Movement's leader himself recognizes that this is a topic he has had difficulty in tackling and explaining, though he has stressed that the women are often the most radical and most difficult to control in the public actions conducted by the Movement. In the Movement's weekly meetings, the women intervene with comments and suggestions, but rarely assume leading roles. Delegating to men the work of representation and mediation with the outside is taken as natural, and I never witnessed an occasion when this situation was questioned or even discussed.

The arguments put forward by Clara Simões in the interview she gave me seem interesting:

> JM: I've noticed that there are many women who go to the meetings and go to the demonstrations, but there are none in the leadership.
>
> CS: Yes, really they haven't put any women in the leadership. I don't think there is a single one, right? Though there are plenty who work with them.
>
> JM: But there have never been any in the leadership?
>
> CS: No, I don't think so.
>
> JM: Why do you think that is? Do you think it would be important to have...?
>
> CS: Well, at that time, in my personal opinion, I think it was still in that phase when men were men, men knew how to talk to politicians, because they had a little, okay, machismo. Today, obviously, things are still the same and have continued, and they haven't yet remembered to put in a female warrior, I don't know! And us, as we know it's in good hands, we let it go, right? (uh uh) Really, they've been extraordinary, they've been, poor things, they've slept badly at night on the way to Lisbon and coming back. Poor things, really they've been marvellous. As for there being no women yet, let's hope that in the next, the next elections they elect one, right? I don't know (27 July 2000).

The interviewee, who until that concrete question had spoken of the Movement as a structure that united the local residents, especially in surmounting individual party logic and identifications, always using the pronoun *we* in a clear process of collective identification, on this topic used the pronoun *they* to refer to the Movement. In arguing that the movement previously applied a sexist policy (machismo) in the choice of leaders, because men were considered to be better prepared for talking with politicians, she tried to distance herself from this sexist logic and practice. At the current stage, where greater equality in the relationships between men and women may be supposed, Clara Simões described the women who support the Movement as 'female warriors', and attributed the continuation of these sexist practices to forgetfulness, showing the extent to which this topic is forbidden in the rhetoric surrounding the Movement's actions.

Hoping that this situation will change in the near future, Clara Simões immediately tried to modify her statements, emphasizing the effort, the dedication, the sacrifice, and the self-denial of the current leaders. In the quick description she gave of the leaders' duties, such as, for example, the journeys to Lisbon, the long nights of work and meetings, she applies the traditional logic of men having more time available, the result of a sexual division between domestic work and the work of public presentation and representation. The resolution of the ideological dilemma my question raised led Clara Simões to reiterate the qualities of the leadership, so that for her there was no need for women to intervene.

Violence and Emotions

In the concrete case of Canas, this community is characterized by a strong distrust of everything that is external to it. A constant watch is kept on outsiders, seeking to assess their intentions and their orientations regarding the cause they find themselves involved in.

Having taken part in some violent situations since 1982, people see violence as a last resort to raise the visibility of their demands. As Carlos Henrique told me, commenting on the situation of development in Canas compared with 20 years ago, 'It only makes you want to throw stones at these guys. And kill one of them. This (Canas' struggle) will only have a solution when we kill people and people die. This only will end when people die. It could be me'. Carlos Joaquim also put forward similar arguments:

> We have to take the struggle forward, whatever the cost, we have to take a beating, this has to be resolved. We know the history of Portuguese politics. It's only when blood flows that problems are solved. Look at the IP5 (highway linking the city of Aveiro to the Spanish frontier). A hundred-odd people died before they built the third lane.... There has to be blood for them to sit round the table and sort things out. When things have to be sorted out beforehand.... We have active men here. If this causes problems, they [the politicians] are responsible (15 August 2000).

To describe the role of violence and emotions in the production and reinforcement of personal and collective identities and in the definition of possible words, I will relate two episodes I witnessed. The first had to do with setting a date for by-elections for the Canas parish council.

By agreement of all the local representatives of the most important political parties, no list was submitted, and the intention to boycott the elections remained in force. But to everyone's surprise, a list from the National Solidarity Party (PSN) appeared.[25] People's reactions in the weekly meetings were very negative. Their candidacy was considered an offence and a complete degradation of the integrity of political values, as an intrusion from the outside into local life and order, exacerbating the ideology of localism in the Movement's supporters.

The presentation of the PSN ticket was set for 6 p.m. on 8 May at the parish council building. Thirty minutes before this time there were hundreds of people in front of the building. The women, near the door, sang the chants about Canas' struggle. There was great impatience, and a near certainty that the party's candidates would not show up. Later, a tractor arrived, displaying a large Canas banner and a placard saying 'This [a stick with a hangman's noose] is for those who want to betray Canas'. This vehicle was received with loud applause from the people. In the garden of the building next to the parish council, where the Republican National Guard (GNR) station operated, an increase in the number of officers and the presence of one senior officer was noted.

At 6.15 p.m., to a murmur of surprise from the people, three vehicles approached, driving up the avenue. Minutes later one of these vehicles was surrounded by people who started to hit and smash it, managing to break the windscreen. The driver, in panic, accelerated through the crowd and left the area. The people were excited. They said to me, 'Did you see that? That's an offence. It's humiliation, their having the cheek to come here'.

One of the occupants of another vehicle, who later turned out to be a police officer in charge of the candidates' safety, went to talk to the GNR commandant, but ended up leaving, threatened by the furious population. Throughout all these events, the GNR never left the station's garden, nor intervened in any way.

This episode reveals several important facts. A population in momentary fusion against an external force, resisting the intrusion of the outside. The PSN candidates, apart from their status as candidates for the parish council, brought with them the asymmetric and oppressive logic of the national political power and crystallized in those brief moments years and years of struggle against the indifference, the superiority and the domination of the outside. The women posted at the door of the council building admitted that their first intention was to strip the female candidate, in an act of humiliation and despoiling, a clear intention to shame. The violence of this intention and the violence of the actual events were justified by the construction of the candidates as representatives of distancing categories, as politicians, as mercenaries, de-personalizing their traits or characteristics. Nothing could weaken this negative categorization, no belonging, no identity.

On the other hand, the inaction of the GNR clearly showed the absolute autarchy of the place, as well as the impotence of the state to claim the monopoly on violence and impose sanctions on the transgressors. I should mention that this episode received practically no media coverage, but was, and still is, a topic of people's conversation. Phrases, actions, gestures and intentions are recalled, and what was or was not possible rediscovered. Even those who admit to being direct actors in the events legitimize their actions with the uncontrollable strength of their emotions, the momentary blindness of reason, attributing the causes of the events to the abstract notion of 'the people'. For example, with phrases like 'The people in fury are uncontrollable', 'Who controls an offended mob?', 'With the mob this is unpredictable', 'With them on the loose, you can't do anything'. The appeal to an abstract entity such as the people or the mob is a culturally acceptable way of contextualizing and legitimizing violence, of activating extremisms without the actors feeling responsible and accountable (Despret 1999). Rather than heroes, what is produced is an entire community united against the outside. Nobody has the right, in this context, to demand protagonism with impunity.

The other episode I will analyze, on the other hand, had huge media coverage, and was the leading story on all the national television stations' afternoon news programmes and made the newspaper headlines. It was to do with the inauguration of the Polis programme, a national urban requalification programme, covering some medium-sized Portuguese cities, by the Prime Minister, António Guterres, in Viseu. A Movement demonstration was planned for that day in the district capital. Although an adviser had managed to arrange a meeting between the Movement's leaders and the Prime Minister, the demonstration was not called off.

In Viseu, after a march through the city's main streets, during which the Movement's chants were sung, the demonstrators gathered in the city centre. They were more than 600. The leaders had already gone to the Civil Government for the meeting with the Prime Minister. Some minutes later, some of the more radical elements began to pass around the information that the Prime Minister was sitting on the terrace with the MP and district chairman of PS, José Junqueiro. Tempers flared, and comments and jeers were directed at the two. The police cordon managed to hold off the demonstrators' advance.

The official retinue then began the walk which was planned in the programme. Although the majority of the Canas demonstrators were held back by the police, about 20 followed the retinue with shouts and jeers. After a frustrated attempt by the Prime Minister to talk with the demonstrators, the walk had to be cut short and the leaders and other important people were collected by buses.

The demonstrators returned to the city centre, where the Movement's leaders told them they had only been met by the Prime Minister's adviser. Tempers once again flared, since these events were seen as another example of the politicians' failure to keep their word, and people were indignant about the indifference of the national authorities. Now a solid group went towards the theatre where the ceremony for the presentation of the programme was taking place. At the end of the narrow street the police had set up a safety cordon. After some confrontations, in which the women and the elderly were much in evidence, the commander of the force allowed the demonstrators to gather in the square in front of the theatre. Chants were sung, and the Movement's leader appealed continually to the Prime Minister to be received, complaining of the failure to keep his promise of a meeting with the Movement. When the authorities left the ceremony, the demonstrators symbolically chanted the slogan 'We are Portuguese, we are Portuguese'.

This episode is one of a long series of actions whose goal is public demonstrations in the presence of national authorities in order to raise the Movement's profile. The goal, in addition to media coverage for the movement, is to publicly embarrass the national political authorities. In this case, the goal was achieved in full, placing - according to the Movement's leaders - the Prime Minister in a difficult situation, where he failed to keep his word in front of the national media.

I should stress the unpredictability of the events and their developments. The action of some of the more radical elements, away from the control and presence of the leaders, brought about a highly effective protest action with a high media profile, allied with the security forces' lack of coordination and inability to act. The later police blockade, confronting women and elderly people, showed the disproportion of the police action at that time. The state did indeed appear repressive.

However, the ludic and festive component of the demonstration must not be forgotten. The pleasure of marching and singing together, and more importantly, the sensation of desacralizing power, seeing fear, reproval and perplexity on the faces of the politicians and government members. These actions and, sometimes, the violence associated with them, are seen as legitimate because they place citizens, who are fighting for a cause they consider just, in confrontation with a distant, arrogant state, which has the power to mobilize large-scale forces of repression.

But, while the Movement is taken very seriously by its supporters and their personal and emotional involvement is deep, it is also important to mention the ironic tone with which the Movement's actions are analyzed. For example, on the day of the meeting after these events, all the comments concentrated on personal stories of experiencing those events. There was satisfaction and euphoria because of the media coverage of the actions carried out, and regret that these actions had not been more radical. When the man who had fallen during the confrontations with the police and been shown on television arrived, he became the centre of attention for a few brief moments. Many fired playful comments at him, and he, laughing, recounted everything that had happened. This irony relativized the events and allowed the episode to be reintegrated into the community's narrative, and more importantly, produced this very community, the shared closeness between the fallen man and those present. As Allen Feldman (1991: 14) states, 'The event is not what happens. The event is that which can be narrated'.

Personal and Collective Identity Processes

The collective identity of Canas is based on a past of economic vitality and working-class experience. As the leader of the Movement said in a meeting, 'We are not farmers or peasants. We worked in the factories with more than a thousand workers. We have an industrial, urban mentality. It is not rural, like the surrounding area' (14 March 2000). This working-class factory experience – materialized in the workers' collective struggles – spread a populist, radical culture, fiercely opposed to the local elites, who were often accused of having supported the integration of Canas into the municipality of Nelas at the time of the liberal struggles in the nineteenth century. As Manuel Alves said:

> Canas is a bit feudal. I'm against the attitude of those who are called rich. There are neither rich nor poor. Wealth is more in their inheritance or in the status they inherit. In life they are no more than us. The rich man is the one who works and knows how to work. They are not at all rich. The son of a factory employee gets a university degree and is still Manuel or João. The children of these individuals get a degree and insist on the title 'Doctor'. It still happens. I've never bowed down. I speak as equal to equal. I don't bow down. (24 August 2000)

What the interviewee valorizes is the work ethic against traditional hierarchies. He takes an attitude of resistance and of radical equality and mistrust in relation to the local elites.

The collective identity also forms part of a long course of struggle and resistance, on a journey of suffering and abandonment, in a framework of injustice (Gamson 1992). This communion of feelings feeds the struggle, and is the support for the most recent arguments for socialization of the younger generations in the reasons that underlie the Movement and its supporters. It is this long story of resistance, suffering and abandonment that unites and mobilizes the inhabitants around the idea of administrative autonomy, seen as the only way to consolidate and develop economically and socially their locality. Disinvestment by the local and national governments is the real indicator that reinforces the narrative of abandonment and what explains the actual strength of the Movement.

Personal identities and personal recognition are intertwined with this collective identity of struggle, resistance and suffering. Each person places herself, assesses herself and is assessed by others in the local hierarchy of credibility and moral conduct. Although birthplace is an important factor in the position in this hierarchy of credibility, some of those who are close to the Movement were not born there, but went to live in the locality when they were children. Two components allow them to legitimize and strengthen their moral position in the town:

(a) the status and behaviour of the family to which they were born; and
(b) personal and family integrity and coherence in their attitudes in favour of the Movement (tradition and biography) and in actions that benefited the town.

In the former, a factor of valorization is status as a worker (as against, for example, the engineers and technicians who came to the companies operating in the town) and the family's integration into the local social networks. In the latter, assessment is made of the individual's abilities to support and be close to the local values and ideals for the restoration of the municipality.

All the people I interviewed claimed as their first personal identification at the spatial level that they were from Canas. Those who were born elsewhere placed their birthplace on equal footing with Canas, or immediately below it in the intensity of identification.[26] Many also considered themselves to be from the Beira Province, and all said they were Portuguese. The long history of struggle against the local and central governments and the strong and radical localism did not affect the Canas residents' degree of identification with their country. Their discontent was turned against the national and local authorities and politicians, and not against the imagined Portuguese community.

The struggle for the restoration of the municipality allows an almost daily personal affirmation of values such as integrity, honour, suffering and a capacity for resistance, producing a deeply rooted spirit of community and solidarity.[27]

THE EMANCIPATORY POTENTIAL OF A STRUGGLE

In an attempt to reflect on the emancipatory potential of the concrete case I am analyzing, I use Santos's proposals when he seeks to establish the principles that can guide the construction of knowledge-emancipation and an emancipatory common sense (1995: Ch.8). Referring especially to the structural spaces of the community and citizenship (1995: 416–41), and paying attention to their specific forms of power (unequal differentiation and domination, respectively), I seek to define the different forms of resistance activated by the participants in the Movement for the Restoration of the Municipality of Canas de Senhorim and the alternative sociabilities they created.

In the communityplace, there is a need to gather the participants in the Movement under a strategy of unity and of concerted actions. This strategic unanimity, associated with severe mistrust of strangers and the outside world, could lead to the production of a fortress community, with strict internal hierarchizations (Santos 1995: 485). However, the practice of weekly meetings, a democratic exercise in power sharing, as well as the rallies for the general public, permit confrontation, debate, assumption of distinct ideas, identities and identifications, and coming together in a common but non-normalizing goal.

The collegial leadership and the weekly meeting with the Movement's participants are organizational innovations that favour the creation of a dialogic public space where people participate. While the existence of the leaders is seen as unavoidable in representing the Movement to the outside world, it is always a provisional leadership, forced by the democratic participation of the people into constant proximity to them and their opinions, problems and perplexities. The egalitarian and fraternal ideology, arising from the working-class history of the town and the vocabulary and repertoire of actions in the revolutionary post-25th of April period, obliges each voice and each opinion to be heard equally.

Simultaneously, the practice of debate and constant analysis of the events most relevant to the Movement and the locality induce a high degree of politicization of all the participants. The great tension derives – and here may reside one of the principal obstacles to the creation of an emancipatory common sense - from the need to subordinate the Movement's participants' party-political logics and identifications to the interests of the struggle for elevation to the status of municipality. As party identifications are an indelible part of the personal identities of the participants, this situation leads to profound dilemmas of ideology and identity, which can cause lines of fracture, silencing or even censure in the community. Furthermore, the popular base of the Movement excludes the majority of the representatives of the locality's economic and cultural elites. This assumed populism, associated with a negative and critical view of the logic of traditional domination, also establishes dynamic tensions within the locality and its connection to external powers and spaces.

The participation of women in the community's public space and in the wider political space takes on special importance in the analysis of this Movement. This visibility derives from women's decisive role in the events that left their mark on the locality in 1982, leading to the foundation of the Movement. Since then, their presence has been unquestionable and is completely legitimized. The major obstacle to a full emancipatory practice lies in the almost total absence of women from the Movement's leadership, reproducing the patriarchal logic dominant in the household place. And, as Boaventura de Sousa Santos says (1995: 441), struggles for emancipation have to pay attention to all the structural places, and not confine themselves to those where counterhegemonic practices are most visible. The interviews I conducted and my conversations with women of the movement show a clear awareness of this situation, and although they justify delegating the powers of representation to the men, it is hoped that in the future there will be greater pressure for the women to play a larger and more important part in the Movement's leadership structures.

It is in the structural place of citizenship that the Movement marks its position most clearly. Indeed, the strategy in recent years has been to confront the state and its national representatives, projecting the struggle into the national ambit. Claiming a participatory and radical democracy, the Movement's leaders and participants opted for rebel actions, trying, as Boaventura de Sousa Santos says, 'to redistribute the anxiety and insecurity socially, creating conditions for the anxiety of the excluded to be transformed into a cause of anxiety for the included' (1998: 32). In addition to creating space-times which promote democratic deliberations, as we saw earlier, they brought about a desacralization of the national and local representatives of the state. This real and symbolic distancing of the Movement's participants from the representatives of the national political system did not induce a distancing of the identity markers of an imagined Portuguese community. Criticism of the political system in force does not go further to a criticism of a democratic regime.

The favoured target of the criticisms of the Movement's participants is the inability of the state to draw up alternative institutional designs (Santos 1998: 47). The administrative division of Portugal has remained almost unaltered since 25 April 1974, and there are no institutional structures to allow effective inspection of discriminatory practices on the part of the municipal authorities. According to the arguments of the Movement's sympathizers, the alternative would include revision of the geo-demographic criteria for the creation of municipalities and greater attribution of autonomy and responsibilities to local governments at the parish level.

The most radical act of the Movement's participants and sympathizers was the destruction of their voting cards and the systematic boycott of all elections in the locality. These actions represented an extreme affirmation of their rights of political citizenship, forcing the national and municipal powers into continued attention to the locality's political process. It is a clear refusal and a denunciation of the total failure of representative democracy and of the current political system. This refusal of the formal rights of political citizenship placed the locality at the centre of the national political and media debate.

In this essay I have given special emphasis to the subjective and collective identification processes of the Movement's participants. To assess the production of emancipatory, individual and collective subjectivities, I turn to the topoi defined by Santos: the frontier, the baroque and the South (1995: 489–518). That is because, as the author states, these topoi 'preside over the reinvention of a subjectivity capable of and willing to explore the emancipatory potentialities of paradigmatic transition' (1995: 517).

The metaphors of the frontier and the south should be read, in the case of the Movement, as the affirmation of interiority, of a peripheral space in the country's interior, which allows a critical deconstruction of the hegemonic logic of a centralizing state. From the metaphor of the frontier, the important things seem to be retention of the selective and instrumental use of traditions, the invention of new forms of sociability and the production of weak hierarchies (Santos 1995: 491–3). An example of the first is the invocation of the fact that Canas had been a municipality for more than 700 years, giving historical legitimacy and solidity to the current demands. Furthermore, the locality's tradition of labour feeds the rhetoric of brotherhood and solidarity and the unifying dynamics of an ideological familism.[28] Traditions feed the town's political utopia.

As for the new forms of sociability and weak hegemonies, the weekly meetings, the rallies and the annual commemoration of the events of 1982 produce and reproduce a public space of proximity, of solidarity and, above all, a non-commercial communion between equal citizens.

From the metaphor that permits the development of a baroque subjectivity (Santos 1995: 499–506), I stress the predominantly local space linked to the movement. This radical localism mobilizes the Movement's participants politically and socially, and keeps the citizens informed about political and party life at the national level. As I described earlier, the Movement's activities, from the most banal to the most expressive, are marked by constant moments of ludic distance, of irony and laughter, and even by a logic of subversion. The refusal of the locality's minor position and the extreme egalitarianism are shown in constant expressions of non-conformism, of revolt and of counter-hegemonic logics and actions.

From the subjectivity of the South, the most relevant aspect in this context is the personal and collective memories which, in everyday conversations and some of the Movement's actions (hunger strikes), emphasize the idea of suffering, of a loss of decent and dignified living conditions in the community. This phenomenology of suffering (Santos 1995: 516) creates ties of solidarity and allows the construction of analogies with situations of exploitation and oppression which go from the national space to the world space. Several times I heard the case of Canas compared to the situation in East Timor or the Basque Country by the Movement's participants. If these comparisons may seem exaggerated to many commentators and journalists, they forget the thread which wove and connected them, the suffering, the refusal to accept lack of recognition and the ongoing search for greater dignity of the Movement's participants as people and citizens.

CONCLUSION

The stories and narratives recounted, the collective memory of struggle, crystallized into some important moments, besides being concrete indicators of the capacity for struggle and protest, represent a possibility for emancipatory practices that challenge the hegemony of the state.

The narrathemes of the Canas residents who support its Movement and its concrete actions of protest, seek to re-specify and deconstruct, on a basis of populism and radical egalitarianism, the concepts of freedom, democracy and power. In the intertwining of personal and collective memories, the dream is the affirmation of their autonomy and the practice is one of resistance and affirmation towards the outside, in the search for personal and collective recognition. These practices have produced alternative sociabilities in regard to women's participation in the public space and have given equal access to the possibility of all participants having their voices heard.

The greatest obstacles to the constitution of an emancipatory common sense are the reproduction of the patriarchal domination in the representation work of the Movement, that is, the non-access of women to leadership posts, and the populism which leads to the exclusion of the elites, creating internal tensions in the community and in its relationship with outside powers.

NOTES

1. This work is based on field observation, from Feb. to Dec. 2000, of the weekly meetings of this Movement with the population, on participation in the Movement's rallies and demonstrations, and on interviews with its leaders and supporters. For documental analysis I use documents produced by the movement, a systematic analysis of the JN from 1974 to 2000 and news from other daily and weekly newspapers, in addition to the minutes of the meetings of the Canas de Senhorim parish council, from 1977 to 1998.
2. The exceptions being the creation of the municipality of Amadora one year after the revolution of 1974 and the municipalities of Odivelas, Trofa and Vizela in 1998. The Law on the Creation of Municipalities (Law no 142/85, of 18 November 1985) was approved by the Parliament in order to restrain the creation of new municipalities. This law established that only localities with a territory of 10 square kilometres and more than 10,000 registered voters could apply to the status of municipality. These criteria excluded, in a small country like Portugal, almost every locality from the rural and the interior from the possibility of becoming a municipality.
3. It is important to note that until recently Canas de Senhorim was a highly industrialized parish. In 1924 the Calcium Carbide Factory began to operate, later becoming the Portuguese Electric Oven Company. This company would close in 1987. It came to have nearly a thousand workers. The mines of Urgeiriça are also located in this parish, operated today by the National Uranium Company, and are currently being deactivated. They came to employ a large number of workers, but now have only 50. It is forecast that in the near future there will be only two or three jobs left.
4. Men's unemployment rate is very low in the town, and although women's unemployment rate is higher it is below the district and national averages.
5. On the second mandate (1979–82) he was elected for AD (Democratic Alliance), a coalition government by PPD and CDS.
6. Later this party would change its name to PSD. The coalition was in power since 1980.
7. From here on I shall use the abbreviation JN for *Jornal de Notícias*.
8. All names are pseudonyms, with the exception of the Movement's leader, who because of his visibility, and by his own choice, agreed I should use his real name. Although some interviewees agreed to the use of their real name, I opted to use pseudonyms.
9. He has been reelected as Mayor of Nelas, for the PS, in the 1993, 1997 and 2001 local elections.
10. When CDS submitted the bill for the creation of the municipality of Canas in 1982, PS, PCP, and MDP (Portuguese Democratic Movement) – all opposition parties – showed themselves in favour. From 1995 to 2002, with PS in power, PSD, CDS/PP, PCP and BE (Left Bloc) showed themselves in favour of raising Canas to the status of municipality. And from 2002 on, with a coalition government by PSD and CDS/PP, only PS is against the raising of Canas to municipality.

11. A typical meeting will have around 30 people, the number varying according to the season and whether or not there are burning issues or imminent broader actions.
12. From the beginning of 1999 to 2002, owing to the parish council's resignation, the running of the Canas de Senhorim parish has been in the hands of an administrative committee (chairman and secretaries who were in office; the chairman is from PS, one secretary is from PSD and the other is from CDS/PP). Since then, elections to constitute a new council have been systematically boycotted by the population, and the Movement became the only accepted political force in town. The national political parties representatives in the town agreed not to interfere with the Movement's political actions. In 2002, now with a new national government, there were local elections in Canas and the only candidates were from the Movement. Since then the parish council and assembly have been run by the Movement.
13. According to McAdam and Tarrow (1991), all social movements are faced with the need to choose between three strategic options: institutionalized or non-institutionalized action; legal or non-legal actions; violent or non-violent actions. This favourable national alignment of political forces has, unexpectedly, become true in the general elections of 2002, after the resignation of former Prime-Minister António Guterres of the PS.
14. It was reported that, in Vizela, a town that also fought to become a municipality and managed to get this status in 1998, people who were against its elevation to the status of municipality were thrown out, although they had been born there.
15. Familism is a factor of union between people and of political mobilization. It is different from the so-called amoral familism proposed by Edward Banfield. For an application of the latter concept to the political processes and dynamics in Portugal, see Cabral (1999).
16. This democratic exercise can be defined as populist, not in the negative and pejorative sense given by many political and social scientists, but in the sense given by William Gamson (1992: 89–90) in his study about injustice frames used by interviewees of the working classes. For Gamson, populism includes a set of class images that oppose common citizens, simple people, to the powerful and rich, to the capitalist classes. Enrique Dussel also proposes the use of the concept of 'the people' that subsumes the concept of social class and allows us to transcend the dogmatism of class analysis (Gomez 2001: 36).
17. In a conversation I had with one of the more radical elements, he compared the situation of Canas with that of the Basque country, saying explicitly that what was needed was a practice similar to that of ETA. But, according to him, this would have to be done away from the structures of the Movement and of the older people, who maintain a logic of institutional political struggle, still connected with the ideas of negotiation.
18. Bill 478/VII, submitted on 28 February 1998. In this legislature (1995–99), PCP also submitted a bill for raising Canas to municipal status. In the following legislature (1999–2002), PSD again submitted a bill to the same end. CDS/PP and the BE have also submitted projects for raising Canas to the status of municipality. In the 2002–06 legislature PSD has submitted a bill, and the BE and PCP have taken similar initiatives.
19. The submission of bills by PCP distanced many sympathizers who were politically more to the right from the Movement's leadership, according to one interviewee.
20. Petition signed by more than four thousand citizens of Canas de Senhorim. The letter addressed to the Speaker that accompanied the petition mentioned the approval of new municipalities (Vizela, Trofa and Odivelas), as well as the fact that Canas had been forgotten. The letter questioned whether there were first-class and second-class Portuguese citizens.
21. In the *Diário de Notícias*, the cartoonist Bandeira published the following dialogue between a tourist and a character on 11 March: 'Character: Parliament? Let me see…, go down this street and turn left, then turn right. When you see "Canas de Senhorim in Struggle", it's next door'. In *Público*, on 10 March, Luís Afonso's cartoon had the following dialogue: 'Bar customer: Inhabitants of Canas de Senhorim say the situation

in the municipality of Nelas is like that of the Timorese in Indonesia. Barman: Damn. Another headache for the UN'.

22. A long article by journalist Pereira in the *Expresso* (1 May 1999) was entitled 'Canas de Senhorim without a shadow of sin'. Here several members of the Movement were interviewed, including the leader, and it was stated that they faced the condemnation of public opinion. At the institutional and legal level, the Attorney General filed a suit against the people of Canas de Senhorim for insulting the President. This lawsuit was eventually withdrawn at the request of the President himself (JN, 22 May 1999).

23. The opinion article by Valada in the JN (2 May 1999) concluded differently: 'The noisy demonstration by the people of Canas de Senhorim, beyond the scandal it may represent in terms of protocol, represents in itself only an act of civil liberty. Would it have been possible without the 25th of April? Would it have been possible without the calm of President Jorge Sampaio? Those who censure do not understand'. An interesting reading of the situation in Canas was put forward almost a year later, by Miguel Portas, leader of the BE, a party which also submitted a bill for raising Canas to municipality status. Reporting the rally he had held in Canas with Luís Fazenda, another BE leader, he said in his weekly column that 'The air we were breathing was that of a 25th of April announced, but not yet concretized ... For example, I do not believe it is possible to force people to be governed against their will and in conflict with their neighbour. When the majority of the population wants a separation, the Republic should help. Or the conflict of the people will come to be with the Republic itself' (*Diário de Notícias*, 11 May 2000).

24. One of the interviewees told me that the date was chosen strategically, because, due to the symbolism of the date and the great press coverage, they knew it would be almost impossible for there to be any police repression.

25. This is a small right wing party with no parliamentary representation.

26. The identities claimed depend on the context and the purpose of the narratives and stories they tell. As Harvey Sacks (Jayyusi 1991: 237) pointed out, in his writings on categorization membership mechanisms, one must distinguish, as regards identities, between the correct descriptions (man, husband, father, worker, trade-unionist, resident of Canas, resident of the Beira, Portuguese, and so on) and those that are appropriate for the concrete context of action (worker, resident of Canas, and so on).

27. Recently, on 12 June 2003, the Portuguese Parliament has approved an amendment to Law no. 142/85, of 18 November 1985. The approved amendment allows now the granting of the status of municipality to parishes that have strong historical traditions or exceptional features. Following this amendment, the Portuguese Parliament has approved a bill, on 1 July 2003, that allows Canas de Senhorim to regain its status of municipality. The status of municipality was also granted to the parish of Fátima, because of its international role as a Catholic sanctuary. Both the amendment proposal and the bill are waiting for the final decision of the President of the Republic. The amendment and the bill were made possible because, after the general elections of 2002, there is now in Portugal a coalition government of the PSD and the CDS/PP.

28. In the case of some regions of Colombia, a rather different context, Sanin and Jaramillo (2003) argue that the emancipatory potential is in the idea of the person and in the individualism which endows the subjects with differences and potentials. These concepts of the human person and of individualism may go against the micro-territorialized collective dynamics which, in the regions studied by the authors, give rise to levelling and uniformising territorial identities which inhibit the political and civic participation of the members of the different groups and movements. The action of the state is also marked by great ambiguity.

REFERENCES

Alvarez, S., et al. (1998): 'Introduction: The Cultural and the Political in Latin American Social Movements', in S. Alvarez (ed.), *Cultures of Politics Politics of Cultures. Re-Visioning Latin American Social Movements*, Boulder: Westview Press, pp.1-29.
Augé, M. (1998): *Les formes de l'oubli*, Paris: Editions Payot et Rivages.
Boltanski, L. and È. Chiapello (1999): *Le nouvel esprit du capitalisme*, Paris: Gallimard.
Cabral, M.V. (1999): 'Autoritarismo de estado, "distância ao poder" e "familismo amoral" – uma pesquisa em progresso', Brasil–Portugal Congress Year 2000, Sociology and Anthropology Section. Recife: Sept.–Oct.
Despret, V. (1999): *Ces émotions que nous fabriquent. Ethnopsychologie de l'autenticité*, Le Plessis-Robinson: Institut Synthélabo.
Feldman, A. (1991): *Formations of Violence. The Narrative of Body and Political Terror in Northern Ireland*, Chicago: University of Chicago Press.
Gamson, W. (1992): *Talking Politics*, Cambridge: Cambridge University Press.
Gomez, F. (2001): 'Ethics Is the Original Philosophy; or, The Barbarian Words Coming from the Third World: An Interview with Enrique Dussel', *Boundary 2*, 28/1, pp.19–73.
Heinich, N. (1999): *L'épreuve de la grandeur. Prix littéraires et reconaissance*, Paris: La Découverte.
Jayyusi, L. (1991): 'Values and Moral Judgement: Communicative Praxis as a Moral Order', in G. Button (ed.), *Ethnomethodology and the Human Sciences*, New York: Cambridge University Press, pp.227–51.
Jasper, J. (1997): *The Art of Moral Protest. Culture, Biography, and Creativity in Social Movements*, Chicago: The University of Chicago Press.
McAdam, D. and S.Tarrow (2000): 'Nonviolence as Contentious Interaction', *PS* June, pp.149–54.
Movimento de Restauração do Concelho de Canas de Senhorim (1999): *Processo Relativo à Restauração do Concelho de Canas de Senhorim*. Canas de Senhorim.
Mouraz, A. (ed.) (1996): *Canas de Senhorim. História e Património*, Canas de Senhorim: Junta de Freguesia.
Ruas, H.B. (1994): 'O poder local', António Reis (org.), *Portugal 20 anos de democracia*, Lisboa: Circulo de Leitores, pp.90–103.
Rubin, J. (1998): 'Contradiction and Ambiguity in a Radical Popular Movement', in S. Alvarez et al. (eds.), *Cultures of Politics Politics of Cultures. Re-Visioning Latin American Social Movements*, Boulder: Westview Press, pp.141–64.
Ruivo, F. (2000): *O Estado labiríntico: o poder relacional entre poderes local e central em Portugal*, Oporto: Edições Afrontamento.
Ruivo, F. and D. Francisco (1999): 'O Poder Local entre centro e periferias', *Revista Crítica de Ciências Sociais*, February, pp.281–306.
Sanín, F.G. and A.M. Jaramillo (2003): 'Pactos paradoxais', in B. de S. Santos (ed.), *Reconhecer para libertar. Os caminhos do cosmopolitismo multicultural*, Rio de Janeiro: Civilização Brasileira, pp.249–87.
Santos, B. de S. (ed.) (2003): *Reconhecer para libertar. Os caminhos do cosmopolitismo multicultural*, Rio de Janeiro: Civilização Brasileira.
Santos, B. de S. (1995): *Toward a New Common Sense. Law, Science and Politics in the Paradigmatic Transition*, New York: Routledge.
Various (1975): *Canas de Senhorim. O que somos o que queremos*, Canas de Senhorim: Comissão de Moradores.

'Don't Treat us Like Dirt': The Fight Against the Co-incineration of Dangerous Industrial Waste in the Outskirts of Coimbra

MARISA MATIAS

Although the history of the treatment of industrial waste in Portugal is now almost 20 years old, the choice of Souselas[1] (Coimbra) as a site for the co-incineration of dangerous industrial waste only dates back to December 1998. Since then, and until very recently, there has been a long process of opposition and redefinition of the initial political strategies, and it is this process which constitutes the particular 'scenario' of my analysis. The struggle at Souselas drew together a vast and complex set of issues which, as it grew, enabled a local protest movement, in its most 'heated' moments, to define the national agenda.

An analysis of the whole process would seem to indicate that Portuguese society is undergoing profound structural changes, which actually had already been made evident in other recent situations of public controversy. If, in the period immediately after the fall of the dictatorship (1974-75) Portuguese society was involved in countless popular campaigns and collective actions, in more recent years it has been experiencing some strange moments of apathy. However, particularly around the second half of the 1990s, it would seem that new forms of focus for public participation have been emerging, which, like the struggle in Souselas, have directly questioned the relationship between political decision-making processes, scientific knowledge and citizens'

This text is based on the research conducted throughout the preparation of a Master's thesis in the Faculty of Economics, University of Coimbra, with the support of Fundação para a Ciência e a Tecnologia (SFRH/BM/361/2000). Without wishing to exclude any of the other people who have helped me during my period of research on this subject, I would like to thank especially Prof. Boaventura de Sousa Santos and Prof. João Arriscado Nunes, whose comments and suggestions were invaluable in the writing of this text.

participation.² As this is relatively recent, it would be premature to characterize the changes that these movements will bring to Portuguese society, which, until now, has preserved two distinctive features: a weak organization of civil society and a lack of political participation (Santos 1993 and 1994). Will these movements actually bring about a more general change, or do they merely reflect a reinforcement of the already existing complexity of social practices that have resulted from the semiperipheral condition of our society?

Moreover, in controversial public situations the Portuguese administration has revealed itself as 'traditionally centralized and not very open, either to scientific opinion or public debate' (Gonçalves 1996: 136). Although in core countries science has functioned as an important ally of political decision making, in Portugal it has always been viewed as an autonomous sphere. However, what is nowadays evident in those countries is a decreasing credibility of science, since the risks associated with some of its applications have become clearer (Ezrahi 1996; Gonçalves 2000). In this context, it is also relevant that in some of the most recent demonstrations in Portuguese society, political decision makers have sporadically resorted to expert opinion in order to make informed decisions or even, as in the case of Souselas, to legitimize their position. In addition, there has also been a growing tendency to question the credibility of the results of scientific practice by both citizens and other actors involved in the processes. These 'new' developments have opened up a set of particularly important questions: what are the consequences of possible alliances between scientists and political decision makers? What 'doors' have been opened as a result of the association between scientists and citizens, or, namely, between scientific knowledge and lay knowledge, in the context of the protest movement?

These and other, more specific, issues will be analyzed later. First, I will contextualize the movement which is the subject of my analysis. In the second part of the text, I will identify the hypotheses which underpin this study and briefly describe the protest movement against the installation of a co-incinerator in Souselas. In the third section, I discuss the movement and examine its possibilities, that is to say, I will attempt to evaluate the extent to which this protest movement could contribute toward expanding the forms of emancipatory public participation.

In addition to the analysis of documentary and bibliographical material, this research draws on information gathered from interviews with representatives of the associations and entities which constituted the Committee for the Fight against Co-incineration (Comissão de Luta Contra a Co-Incineração), and also from the close contacts maintained with the protest movement.

GENERAL CONTEXT

There is, nowadays, a growing interest in matters relating to science and technology, as well as a growing denunciation of the risks and uncertainties which their various applications can create (Nunes 1999). In terms of the rising importance of environmental issues, science is nowadays considered as much a problem as a cure; if, on one the one hand, it provides a deeper understanding of common problems, it seems equally able to produce, in practice, results which mask some of the worst excesses of modernity. In fact, one of the characteristics that have been highlighted about the new environmental conceptions is the close connection between environmentalism and science and scientific knowledge, which are considered both a cause of environmental problems and a key element for their solution (Yearley 1993, 1996, Szerszynski et al., 1996).

Besides, there is another dimension we have to add to this problem, which is related with the attitude of those scientists who understand science as a 'special' form of knowledge which should be separated from local forms of thought, thus enabling it to shift from place to place and assume a universal character (Clark and Murdoch 1997). Moreover, following James Scott, 'the relation between scientific and practical knowledge is (...) part of a political struggle for institutional hegemony by experts and their institutions' (Scott 1998: 311).

Concerning environmental problems, certain developments have become evident which demand a rethinking of the articulation between the different forms of knowledge and environmental issues. If science and scientific knowledge are undoubtedly related to environmental issues, it is also true that the new environmental problems require more than a scientific intervention in order to be solved (Jamison and Wynne 1998). This context has favoured the involvement of citizens in controversial situations, similar to the one under analysis, which involve scientific and technical knowledge and a perception of the risks involved on the part of the affected populations.[3] Various models have been put into practice – consensus conferences, citizens' panels, focus groups and referendums, amongst others – corresponding to various forms and levels of citizen involvement (Fixdal 1997; Font 1998; Rowe and Frewer 2000). Nevertheless, whether in a consultative or a deliberative role, citizens have directly participated in the definition of policies at this level, even though, in terms of the choice of a model, there is no consensus on the most adequate methods of participation, since this depends very much on the specific nature of each situation.

Although it belongs to a core regional block (the European Union), there are no intermediate mechanisms for decision making on scientific and technological issues in Portugal, in contrast to what happens in some other European countries. One of the fundamental characteristics of the Portuguese state has been the abyss which separates the representatives from those they represent (Santos 1990, 1994). This tension has taken on changing contours to the extent that the country, as a result of its integration into the European Union, has adopted different legal frameworks and political practices which are even more distant from the existing social practices, because they have been conceived for other contexts (including strong scientific involvement, high levels of associationism and strong civil societies).

The question of the treatment of dangerous industrial waste exemplifies this, since the performance of the state in this area has been characterized by sudden bursts of activity interspersed with periods of stagnation. The net result is that it was only in 1985 that the first foundations of a national policy for waste management were laid (Decree-Law no. 488/85 of 25 November). It should be remembered that at that time Portugal was in the midst of negotiations for entry into the European Community, thus making it imperative that it made an effort to accommodate its legal frameworks to those of the EC. The state then assumed a high level of autonomy in the conduct of national affairs (Santos 1993). This posture may also explain the legislative void which followed in this field until 1990, when an attempt was made to define the destination of the waste produced in Portugal. Even so, the Integrated System for the Management of Industrial Waste (SIGRI) was only re-launched in February 1994. It was during the course of defining a policy on waste that the option of Souselas as a site for co-incineration was announced.

In broader terms, it may be affirmed that the protest movement against co-incineration in Souselas is one of the indicators of the repositioning of Portugal within the world context – whilst still remaining a semiperipheral country, it finds itself located within a core regional bloc (the European Union). If, in terms of economic development, its position has not altered, since the Portuguese economy remains semiperipheral, the fact is that, given the political nature of the European Union, Portugal has to act as if it were a core country, not only in terms of legislation but also in the field of political discourse. These factors eventually condition its own political struggles.

From another perspective, the European Union has also become a resource for social movements, a situation which can be analyzed from a dual perspective: firstly, as European legislation is more advanced than national legislation in some areas relating to the environment, social movements have frequently been helped by European directives which support their claims, whilst, in addition, they can take into account protest movements which have emerged in other European countries and can analyze the situations and solutions which have previously been presented. Bearing this in mind, it may be suggested that Portuguese social movements have attempted to compensate for their belatedness by taking a selective look at Europe in order to defend the most advanced positions and reject solutions which have proved fallible in other contexts. As we will see, the 'European dimension' is central for the case of Souselas.

On the other hand, the Portuguese state has little experience in risk management issues and these, therefore, have been subjected to conventional political strategies, revealing a complete lack of trust and belief in any form of citizen participation, to the point of transforming public consultations into mere formalities. In addition, the state has acted in an authoritarian manner in relation to issues of risk management. Yet, despite its enduring capacity to condition constellations of social practices (Santos 2000), some space has been left for social experimentation in matters relating to co-incineration. It only remains to be seen whether, due to the specific characteristics of Portuguese society, these transformations have the potential to lead to a growing politicization of different space-times, or whether they still need to be propelled and recreated by the state as a very new social movement (Santos 1998). Rousseau's principle of the community – which includes the idea of horizontal political obligation among citizens, as well as the idea of participation and solidarity in the formulation of the general will – is the principle which holds the most emancipatory potential. The possibility of a new political culture and a new quality of personal life derives from this principle, through decentralization and participatory democracy, cooperative principles and socially useful production (Santos 1994). Transformations associated with emancipatory struggles (the transformation of power into shared authority, the transformation of despotic might into democratic rights and the transformation of regulatory knowledge into emancipatory knowledge) occur in different forms according to different space-times at their own specific rhythms (Santos 1995; 2000). It is not a question of a single, unified transformation, but of actual transformations. In relation to this question, this analysis shows, in particular, the transformations that took place in the space-time of citizenship due to the unfolding of the protest movement, as well as an experience of citizen participation in direct confrontation with representative democracy.

Parallel to these issues, the analysis of the protest movement against co-incineration allows us to reconsider the role of science and technology in Portugal, both as an element associated with forms of power and regulation and as a resource for forms of public participation of an emancipatory nature, and, at the same time, to explore one in the articulation between modes of scientific and non-scientific knowledge. It should also be noted that, within the protest movement, two types of traditionally opposed knowledge became associated with the protest movement: 'local' knowledge and 'global' knowledge. The difference between these two types of knowledge, seen as 'rivals', is based on the premise that there are forms of knowledge which, due to the manner in which they are constructed, are independent of the contingencies and limitations associated with local forms of knowledge and are therefore considered to be universal in character, imposed globally on all other forms of knowledge. This separation – strongly linked to a modern conception of knowledge which is based on the split between science and common sense – devalues local forms of knowledge, misrepresenting them as sporadic and ungrounded manifestations, so that in contexts of confrontation between types of knowledge, local knowledge tends to be viewed as non-legitimate.

THE SOUSELAS PROTEST MOVEMENT AND THE CLASH OF KNOWLEDGES

Turning now to a concrete analysis of the protest movement against co-incineration, the three working hypotheses which I consider central are as follows:

(a) a science which is not solidly established is vulnerable to appropriation by political power and by protest movements;
(b) the politicization of science is the other face of the 'scientification' of political decision making;
(c) the movement against co-incineration demonstrates the strengths and weaknesses of social movements today in Portugal and how these are linked to the use of 'lay' knowledge and experiences.

Taking the first working hypothesis, in contrast to other countries, namely core countries, science in Portugal has succeeded over the years in retaining a high level of autonomy in relation to other social spheres. It is only very recently that some controversies, associated with protest movements, have been made public, leading to the questioning of some of the foundations of science. However, the high degree of autonomy enjoyed by scientific knowledge has not implied a reinforcement of its political authority. In fact, some studies have shown that the position of science and of scientists remains fragile, a factor which can favour the manipulation of this type of knowledge (Gonçalves 1996). In this respect, the movement presented here is undoubtedly the one which led to the amplification of these issues. Arguments based on scientific knowledge were incorporated in a dual sense: on the one hand as a means of legitimizing the protest movement and on the other hand as a tool for political decision making. In the latter case it can be seen that, although Portugal had never before produced any studies similar to those undertaken by the officially appointed commissions of scientists, the results obtained were declared the most valid, even though studies and debates in other countries might have indicated different solutions. Science became politicized and so part of the conflict. The conception of science as a unique and authoritative description of the world (Irwin 1996) gradually dissolved, as contradictions between the scientists themselves were revealed.

As far as the second working hypothesis is concerned, Portuguese society, as previously described, does not resemble core countries in this aspect either. Whereas in these countries the relationship between science and democracy was closely linked to modern development and progress, in Portuguese society this was one of the unfulfilled legacies of modernity. On the contrary, it was only when this relationship began to be questioned in other countries that Portugal began to make the first associations at this level. The situation involved in the process under analysis here represents much more than a simple association and, in fact, turned into something that had never been experienced before.

Finally, the protest movement grew and created alliances. During its first phase, associations and local institutions, local representatives of the political parties, local personalities and local scientists came together. The group was then enlarged to include the national scientific community as well as all the representatives of the opposition parties in Parliament. In the second phase, the local associations and entities themselves began to act in conjunction with other associations and entities from other areas. In over two years of protest and with a chorus of 'voices' and 'texts' associated with it, the movement always featured a plurality of positions and a heterogeneous membership. Nevertheless, the people who shouted the slogans were always the local people. There was the odd, timely demonstration in support of the movement but it never extended to the national or even regional population. On the contrary, the protest movement was the target of countless criticisms, of which the most notable was the one which always followed in its wake: that it was a locally based movement that defended particular local interests for selfish reasons (the NIMBY[4] syndrome), and whose arguments were based on irrationality and ignorance. It was mostly the government, some scientists and some national opinion makers that were at the origin of these criticisms. However, the protest movement reacted to this and changed its tactics, learning from its mistakes and developing and deepening the articulation between local protest and the various initiatives which were being developed nationally. Within this context, it gathered information about and questioned the chosen solution in the light of the practices and legal frameworks of other countries, in particular the European Community. Locally based arguments, whilst not ceasing to exist, retreated to make space for another type of foundation for the protest, even creating initiatives that were unique in Portugal for a movement of this kind. However, as we shall see later, the protest movement allowed itself to rest during the less 'heated' moments of the process, conserving most of its energies for the moments of political decision and thus suffered the consequences of allowing itself to 'switch off'.

Furthermore, there is one issue which was central during all the process: the way the problem was 'framed' by the different actors in opposition.[5] In fact, decision makers have considered the co-incineration process as an isolated situation related with the adoption of a new technology in order to solve the problem of hazardous industrial waste. As for the local populations, the decision around the installation of a co-incinerator was seen as another episode in the 25-year old history of the presence of a cement plant which has affected the population and the environment. The lack of transparency in relation to the labouring conditions at the cement plant and the consequent distrust of the population were crucial for the production of shared definitions and positions about the co-incineration process.

Antecedents of the Protest Movement

One of the decisive steps in advancing the decision in favour of co-incineration was the formation of Scoreco – a consortium of cement companies formed by Secil and Cimpor[6] in association with a French company (Suez Lyonnaise des Eaux) in 1996. The inclusion of Souselas as one of the possible locations for the co-incineration of dangerous industrial waste was confirmed during the month of July 1998, at the same time as Scoreco presented its study on Environment Impact Assessment (EIA). To push its strategy forward, the government suggested the creation of a Strategic Plan for the Management of Industrial Waste (PESGRI), together with environmental improvements for the areas involved. These measures became the 'banners' of the government in its defence of co-incineration. Both served to support the basis of the government's argument throughout the whole process: the urgent need to treat dangerous industrial waste.

Neither of these measures was, however, sufficient to silence the protest movement, which was seeking another solution and displaying a lack of confidence and uncertainty toward the policies which the government was attempting to carry out.

Important amongst the arguments that served as a basis for the protest movement was the negative relationship that the population had maintained with the cement company since it had begun operating in 1974 (which included damage to houses caused by 'explosions' at the cement factory, frequent work 'accidents' at the factory, constant pollution, the destruction of subsistence farming, local health problems, and so on) and the dangers that co-incineration could bring to public health, and which led to the presentation of two documents in support of the protest, as an interview with a representative of the Souselas Association for the Defence of the Environment (ADAS) confirms:

> when there was the public discussion on the study of environment impact assessment in Souselas, the ADAS presented two documents: one technical, presented by João Pardal, and the other relating to the accidents, presented by me (Joaquim Gonçalves, Private interview, 24 July 2000).

The position assumed by the ADAS shows that, from the beginning, there had been an attempt to mobilize diverse knowledge in order to reinforce a dimension that had been forgotten until then, namely the work carried out by the Anti-Pollution Commission which had existed in Souselas since 1976 and which had come to function as a kind of observatory on the cement company's activities.

In spite of the 'warnings' sent to the government that there would be resistance, the decision on the choice of locations was made public on 28 December 1998: Souselas was to be one of two sites in which a co-incineration unit would operate.

The First Phase: 'Measuring' or Redefining Forces

The first months of 1999 added a new dimension to the process: the struggle in Souselas descended on its city (Coimbra). The variety and intensity of the initiatives turned it into the principal issue in both national and local political debate. One of the movement's first initiatives was the establishment of the Committee for the Fight against Co-incineration (*Comissão de Luta Contra a Co-Incineração* – CLCC),[7] which informally brought together the 'movers and shakers' of the city. This committee brought together the diverse voices of protest which had attempted to speak out against the government's decision. One of the interesting features of this committee was the association of very different types of organizations which were not restricted to the civic and environmental ones, and it is particularly significant that two trade unions were involved. In Portugal, it is very unusual to see trade unions associated with struggles which are not related to labour and workers' issues. In this case, these trade unions have subscribed to and participated in all the committee decisions and initiatives that were more environmental and health oriented. However, the relation with the cement plant workers was, of course, mediated by one of the trade unions being involved (the Coimbra Federation of Trade Unions).

From amongst the various initiatives, it is worth mentioning the petition organized by the local newspaper *Diário de Coimbra* calling for the government's decision to be revoked[8] which obtained more than 50,000 signatures, representing around 50 per cent of the population of the municipality of Coimbra. During this phase, all the opposition parties represented in Parliament also joined the protest movement.[9]

Other arguments were added to those of the Souselas population, based particularly on the location of the co-incineration unit. The arguments presented against the government's proposal included: the fact that the co-incinerator would be located near a large population centre (Coimbra), the consequent 'devaluing' of the central region since, having never represented a high political cost to the party in power, as in many other previous situations (including under former governments), it had suffered discrimination in terms of economic and social development and had been the victim of some of the most unpopular initiatives, of which co-incineration was yet one more example; and the fact that Coimbra had a weak industrial base, which made it an inadvisable choice for the treatment of waste produced principally in other areas. In addition to these arguments, which dealt primarily with the location, it should be stated that the 'slogans' were very diverse and that there was no consensus on proposed solutions.

On 25 February, with the approval of the bill proposed by PSD, which called for the suspension of co-incineration until a scientific commission could determine whether or not it was the most secure method for the treatment of dangerous industrial waste, the protest movement 'celebrated' its first success. In order to achieve this victory, the president of the Coimbra Civic Association Pro Urbe went to Parliament to negotiate approval of the PSD document in conjunction with the opposition parties. All members of the opposition managed to overcome their differences and present a united front to the socialist government. In one of the more evident examples of an alliance between democratic participation and democratic representation, citizens managed to mobilize parliamentary representatives to support a political decision that would favour their movement. On the same night, the population of Souselas gathered in front of the local church and held a symbolic wake for co-incineration.

The legal framework for the Independent Scientific Commission (CCI) was completed with the passing of Law no. 20/99[10] by Parliament on 15 April, which established the 'Independent Scientific Commission for the Treatment of Dangerous Industrial Waste', and by Decree-Law no. 120/99, passed by the government on 16 April, which established the 'Independent Scientific Commission for the Environmental Control and Supervision of Co-Incineration'. This dual regulation of the CCI was 'solved' by Decree-Law no. 121/99, also of 16 April, in which the government stated that the two commissions should be considered one and the same.

With the CCI duly defined, the first 'chapter' in the history of the protest movement drew to a close, leaving behind it a kaleidoscope of opinions[11] which had 'swamped' the media in the preceeding months.

This chapter was characterized by demands for the intervention of experts in the decision-making process. The local population, together with the associations/entities which had joined the protest, had fought to ensure that co-incineration was discussed scientifically, since the government had paid insufficient attention to popular demands. The arguments of several scientists who were opposed to the process of co-incineration contributed greatly toward the realization of the citizens' wishes, and they established a belief within the protest movement that science was on their side. In fact, there were various other initiatives in which scientific knowledge was combined with other forms of knowledge in order to oppose co-incineration.

The Second Phase: The Establishment of Scientific Controversy

The second phase of the protest movement began to take shape during the election campaign for Parliament as a result of the heated debates which arose in this context. Having won the elections, the socialist government then appointed a new Environment Minister who continued determinedly to defend the policy of co-incineration.

During the month of December, the month in which the CCI[12] took office, the environmental and civic associations in Souselas and the surrounding areas drew up a joint strategy to fight co-incineration, based on already-established alternatives for the treatment of most waste material which required incineration.[13] The fight would now turn against the 'end of pipe' solution, regardless of the sites chosen for implementation. The protest movement was beginning to expand and redefine its arguments.

As in the first phase, co-incineration soon became the main item on the national political agenda. The debate it generated was now wider, both in terms of participants and contents. After the CCI took office, the internal divisions within the scientific community became more widespread, and discussion on the different positions regarding the process became a permanent feature.

One of the most significant initiatives of this period was the 'International Forum on Co-Incineration', which gathered national and European specialists on co-incineration. This forum would come to be divided in two: one section dedicated to the alternatives to co-incineration and the other to issues relating to public participation. Somewhat behind schedule, the results of the CCI study were strategically announced the day before the opening session of the Forum (19 May 2000), indicating that the process should continue, whilst recommending changes to the sites previously selected, with the Souselas cement factory remaining but the Maceira plant being replaced by one in Outão (situated in a Natural Reserve). The Environment Minister, in a statement to the *Público* newspaper, tried to put an end to the matter:

> Four scientists are in complete agreement. It is now time for a political decision on the matter based on science and objective knowledge and not on prejudice, ignorance or demagogy (20 May 2000).

The isolation of scientific knowledge in relation to other forms of knowledge became, in this phase, one of the main points in the defence of co-incineration, with the arguments of other scientists who were opposed to the continuation of the process devalued and relegated to a secondary place.

The controversy was thus reopened and the Commission's report heavily criticized. Some of the media, however, took up the minister's position very positively, believing that, although there was dissent, it was imperative to find measures and solutions to the problems, regardless of whether they were correctly formulated or not. This attitude was fostered to a great extent by the political climate in Portugal at the time, in which the socialist government was subject to sharp attacks for its passivity in the face of the country's problems.

The results of the Commission were based on the argument that co-incineration was the most economically and environmentally suitable method for the treatment of toxic waste. In the opinion of the Commission scientists, the fact that reduction and re-utilization processes were not being correctly implemented in Portugal made them unviable options. Similarly, they concluded that the burning of toxic waste in cement factories would not produce any increase in the level of atmospheric emissions beyond those produced by the cement factories during the course of their normal operation (Formosinho et al., 2000).

The session of the Forum dedicated to alternative solutions was characterized by a redoubling of efforts, since the decision of the CCI was, by then, already known. During this session, a specialist from the European Commission Directorate for the Environment also emphasized that Portugal was not following the hierarchy of options defined in 1996 by all member states, which stated that the treatment of waste should be dealt with in the following order: prevention, re-utilization, recycling, recovery for energy purposes (co-incineration or incineration), and landfill.

The protest movement accused the CCI of failing to carry out its mandate, since they considered that its study of the alternatives to incineration and co-incineration was simply limited to listing them, without taking into due consideration the options of 'reduction', 're-utilization' and 'recycling'. Moreover, criticism of the report did not end there. Many national scientists pointed out faults in the results obtained[14] and expressed their disagreement. The controversy within the scientific community reached a peak at this point and led to a radicalization of the diverging positions. Together with the protest movement, they accused the government of 'trying to put the cart before the horse', since data relating to the production and destination of waste in Portugal had not yet been made known.[15] Another argument which gained weight during the proceedings and which became a key point was based on the fact that treatment by co-incineration only dealt with a small fraction of the waste produced in Portugal[16] – and only part of the dangerous industrial waste – thus reducing the scale of the problem. The demands of the populations most affected by the operations of the cement companies remained constant. These demands were based, above all, on the negative relationship which they had maintained with the companies and on a lack of trust in the institutions that would implement the process and ensure its safety. The basis for their arguments lay in the long years of exposure to excessively high levels of pollution caused by the malfunctioning of the cement factories, with no sign of any efforts on the part of the political decision makers or company managers to reduce them.[17] Greater awareness of this type of local argument made the relationship between environmental problems and public health a more significant issue. In effect, living in dangerous situations gives local populations access to a lot of information about themselves and their local environment, even before dangerous situations become evident to the world at large (Kleinman 2000; Brown 2000). This type of denunciation of problematic situations forms part of the so-called 'popular epidemiology' (*idem*), which is currently a major issue. In addition to the arguments based on personal experience, there was one question that was never answered: why, independently of the selected locations, did all the envisaged situations point toward the establishment of co-incineration in two cement factories, one owned by Secil and the other by Cimpor?

As may be imagined, although the CCI had submitted its opinion,[18] which could have meant the end of the process, the protest movement did not back down and its initiatives gained pace. Important amongst them was the second session of the Forum dedicated to public participation.

Even at the end of this second phase, calls within the protest movement for a solution to the problem based on good sense began to gain strength. It was proposed that the conflict should be negotiated in such a way that all sides would emerge as winners, rather than adopting the traditional win-lose approach. In the words of the president of the Coimbra Civic Association Pro Urbe, the issue was as follows:

> If, after having opted for these [alternatives to co-incineration proposed by the protest movement], there is still waste to be burned, which is very likely, this should be distributed amongst all the cement factories according to their capacities. There are many reasons to support this idea: if all the cement factories are improved, as they should be, they will all have the same facilities for burning waste; if there is no risk to health or to ecology there should be no logical objection to this geographical distribution; if there are health risks, as countries which have already adopted co-incineration have realized, it is always preferable, in terms of risk analysis, to disperse the source of the threat rather than to concentrate it; and, in addition, with these measures it is possible to get rid of the 'not in my backyard' syndrome and promote a genuine national solidarity. Moreover, as the option of burning waste is now considered to be not only transitory but also fourth in order of priority, territorial distribution would make it easier to evaluate its impact and decide on reductions. As well as meeting EU requirements, the solutions I am proposing can be carried out in the short term and would enable us to put an end to the conflicts which are undermining the credibility of all those involved (*Público*, 14 June 2000).

After a parliamentary initiative by the Green Party, the *Assembleia da República* (Parliament) once more called a halt to co-incineration.

In fact, the party's proposal was based on the suspension of the process, through an alteration to Law no. 20/99, until the risks of co-incineration for public health were evaluated, and a new committee of experts – the Medical Working Group (GTM) – was formed to assess these effects. All the cards were back on the table. A new period of reflection followed. The petition organized by the *Diário de Coimbra*, which by January 1999 had received more than 50,000 signatures, was only debated in the Assembleia da República on 29 June 2000, once the major debates were over and after having been ignored for 17 months.

The Third Phase: Public Health

In this phase the concerns of the protest movement were focused on the defence of public health in the affected areas. The formation of the Medical Working Group (GTM) answered one of its main demands.

The findings of the GTM were made public in December 2000 and guaranteed that co-incineration had no harmful effects on the health of local populations. The report also stated that the risks involved in operating a co-incinerator were 'socially acceptable' (Barros *et al.*, 2000). Amongst the various members of the GTM, only one person declared his opposition to the findings and voted against the report. It was this vote that enabled the arguments of the protest movement to gain ground once again. One more factor lent credibility to the struggle: the silent recognition of an error committed by the CCI. The publication of the GTM report was accompanied by a 'new version' of the CCI Report, with certain descriptions and references, which had been those most strongly criticized by the opposition movement, namely, the comparison made with emissions from domestic fires, having 'slipped' from its pages. By doing this, the CCI, which had never admitted to its error and had always insisted that it was right, ended up supporting some of the arguments advanced by the protest movement.

During the period of public debate on the GTM report, which extended until March 2001, some of the most important initiatives of the entire proceedings appeared, including the presentation of a report on the state of health of the population of Souselas, based on the statistics made available by the health centres of the municipality, submitted by the CLCC in partnership with the University of Coimbra Institute of Hygiene and Social Medicine. This study came into being as a reaction to the findings of the GTM, in particular the fact that it had presented its conclusions on the effects of co-incineration on public health without having ever analyzed any of the existing data or making one single visit to the affected areas. The study presented by the CLCC concluded that the population of Souselas already had considerable health problems, particularly evident in the 'types of pathologies in which environmental factors are especially relevant, such as respiratory pathologies and breast cancer' (CLCC 2001),[19] which does show an alternative form of epidemiology.

Having stated that the 11,650 opinions against co-incineration submitted throughout the period of public debate had brought 'nothing new' to the discussion, the Minister decided to press on with the procedures and set the co-incineration test phase for the following months. It was also decided that members of the CCI should carry out epidemiological studies, but their results were heavily compromised by the fact that the local population boycotted the tests and only 2 per cent of the target group turned up at the appointed places.

By this time, the Director of the Scientific Unit of Greenpeace declared that the co-incineration of hazardous industrial waste in the neighbourhood of populated areas or of a natural park (the other site that had been proposed by the CCI) was an 'irresponsible' decision on the part of the Portuguese authorities, and as such should be condemned.

It should also be noted, however, that this decision of the Environment Minister also included the fact that only waste that could not be treated in any other way (excluding used oils and organic solvents) would be subject to co-incineration, which substantially reduced the proposal. The location of the treatment plant for the waste that would be burnt and a precise definition of what this waste would actually be, still had to be decided. The protest movement continued in its efforts to find alternatives for the remaining waste.

Moreover, during the Stockholm Convention (2001), the Portuguese government declared its opposition to any process that involves the production of persistent organic pollutants (POP). This position seriously threatened the defence of a risk-free process such as co-incineration was initially described. In addition, the Convention confirmed the preference of Member States for non-thermal alternatives for the treatment of toxic waste, since incineration and co-incineration are central to the production of POP. This is only one indication of the duplicitous discourse adopted by the national government, which assumes an external posture substantially different from the one it adopts at home (that is, backing a different approach in accordance with whether it is acting as a member of the European Union or a regulator of national space). The protest movement used this duality of discourses in order to reinforce their opposition to co-incineration.

Another crucial element during all the process was the use of several European directives related with waste management and environmental strategies, for instance, the use of Directive 2000/76/CE about waste incineration, defining the limits for the emissions of cement plants labouring with hazardous waste. In fact, this directive was used as 'proof' that there was a difference between the levels of emissions resulting from cement plants burning hazardous waste and those from average labouring conditions, thus refuting the government's and the CCI's claims that no such difference existed.

In December 2001, the party in government suffered a heavy defeat in local elections. The prime minister resigned and national legislative elections were held. The victory of the Social Democratic Party brought the process to a halt with the decision to drop co-incineration as a method for treating hazardous industrial waste and resuming the task of both completing an inventory of hazardous waste in Portugal and defining a comprehensive strategy for its management.

THE IMPLICATIONS OF THE MOVEMENT FROM THE DUAL VIEWPOINT OF KNOWLEDGE AND POWER

Clearing up the possible consequences associated with the government's decision had enabled controversy to emerge within the scientific community, which became one of the decisive elements in the entire process. The fact that part of this community became associated with the citizens' movement meant that it had gained in strength and visibility, and at the same time lent credibility to the protest. This was clearly recognized by those taking part in the opposition process, as some of their statements show:

> There really is a wide range of opinion on this matter within the scientific community. Although I'm an ordinary citizen and I don't have any training in this area ... what I'm saying is that the scientists have had so many, many differences of opinion that you can see that it's really problematic, this question of dangerous industrial waste ... [the opposition] has been working well because the scientific community, to a certain extent, has been listening to the community. I don't believe ... what some of them say, who are on the side of the government and economic power, that the bad lot [of scientists] are the ones who are on the side of the local people and that they are the good ones (José Figueiredo, interview, 18 July 2000).

The association between scientific knowledge and lay knowledge eventually became evident on two levels: on the one hand, it democratized the struggle, since it put both sides of the dispute on the same discursive level and, on the other, by carrying out the debate in scientific terms it led to a permanent demand for a space given to 'lay' knowledge and experience, making way for the need to accommodate and relate knowledge to specific socio-spatial contexts, in this case environmental problems.

In a process like this, which involved issues of risk and uncertainty, it became obvious that restricting the debate only to the realm of science would eliminate many of its dimensions. In effect, the questions raised by the local population about perceived risks are examples of the need to articulate different types of knowledge. We have to consider that in spite of being aware that risks that surround us are shared unequally, risks are still a part of everyone's daily life (Ross 1996). In this sense, the different actors involved in the process can all legitimately claim authority to define and solve the problem. The fact that we are facing a hugely complex movement, the implications of which are unpredictable, only reiterates the need for the articulation of different knowledges and the benefits which this may provide. Any partial perspective, as opposed to a limited one, should be seen as a privileged means of producing knowledge in conditions which extend beyond the practice of experimentation and observation in the sciences (Nunes 1999). In the case of co-incineration, in the first phase of confrontation a scientifically-based solution was chosen, ignoring other types of knowledge which would have been relevant in informing the decision. By relegating experience to second place, the problem was analyzed without taking into account information which only local residents in the directly affected areas could have known about, such as the frequency of accidents in the factories, the stability of the emissions produced by the same factories and whether or not particular types of illnesses were prevalent amongst local people and/or animals. In effect, local residents have living memories of what has happened over the years, they are aware of the risks and how to face them and, in the light of their everyday experience, have a deep sense of the morality (or lack of morality) of the decision. After more than 20 years of protest through the Anti-Pollution Commission, they united and felt threatened just by the possibility of anything else happening to the 'normal' workings of the cement factory. Knowledge of local conditions was, therefore, one of the most widely used arguments and served as the motto for one of the first protest documents presented by the Souselas Association for the Defence of the Environment. One of the interviewees posed the question: 'Pollution isn't only what comes out of the chimneys, it's everything that the factory does around us ... it is not the politicians from Lisbon or Porto or other places who come to visit Souselas who know what we are suffering' (Joaquim Gonçalves, interview, 24 July 2000). Another interviewee stated that 'science, theory without experience, is bankrupt' (Adriano Lucas, interview, 18 August 2000).

However, throughout the proceedings a huge imbalance was evident between the importance given to the arguments presented in the various scientific reports and the social conditions which the policies would apply to, or the living knowledge expressed through the opinions and experiences of the citizens, who were summarily classified as ignorant.

The kind of knowledge that was considered valid in resolving the problem indicated a typically modern solution, since the conclusions that were used to make the decision, in addition to not extending beyond scientific knowledge, created an alliance between the scientists who produced the results and the political decision makers. One of the problems of the use of science as a legitimizing instrument lies in the fact that it masks broader political and economic concerns (Irwin 1996). This did not escape the notice of those involved in the process, who soon understood the economic muscle behind the cement companies and their need to safeguard their own interests, initially negotiated with the government. Moreover, the protest movement felt impotent in the face of the economic power that lay behind the decision, and some of their declarations are symptomatic of this: 'I think business is behind all of this' (Mário Nogueira, interview, 27 July 2000); 'The cement companies would save millions of *contos* on fuel ... and this has to be taken into account' (António Moreira, interview, 19 July 2000). It should therefore be reaffirmed that the government's decision, which was based on scientific reports, was taken in opposition to the citizens of the areas directly affected, the opposition parties, the environmental associations and part of the scientific community.

In this case, however, the state's regulatory attitude was not accompanied by a lack of citizen participation; on the contrary, they continued to clash swords with the government. The relations that were established between the state and its citizens allowed the inequality between the two parties to become much more evident. In effect, in the movement we are studying, despite effective citizen participation, there was an ongoing effort on the part of the government to ignore citizens' demands on matters that directly affected them, a situation which, naturally, was criticized by the participants:

> The government ... has acted badly because, on the one hand it hasn't considered people's opinions, which I think is fundamental in any situation of this kind, and on the other it hasn't acted impartially either. ... People don't trust them any more because no one has ever proved to them that there is no reason to feel like this (Mário Nogueira, interview, 27 July 2000).

The fact that the protest movement had 'rested' in the periods of time between the scientific reports became a justification for the forces in favour of advancing the process to attempt to delegitimize its action. However, although we cannot identify it as a national protest movement and only to a slight extent as a general feeling of opposition to the government's decision, we cannot ignore the many 'doors' that were opened as a result of its actions.

One of the most common criticisms, as has already been mentioned, was the fact that it was a local movement defending merely local interests. However, it should be remembered that, in terms of environmental issues, the identification of problems at a local level is one is of the determining factors in ensuring that these are made visible, and therefore that the debate is enlarged. By accusing them of NIMBYism, the possibility of individuals being able to contribute to the debate and seek solutions to the problem using their own knowledge and experience was completely denied. If this criticism has in its favour the fact that it draws attention to the bias involved in a larger issue, it also risks creating an opposition between the local and the global. Added to this is the fact that, in this case, it is obvious that various types of knowledge were always present: in the first phase locally based arguments were much more in evidence, whilst in the second and third phases the more 'global' arguments predominated. The result of this development was that the movement gained momentum and was able to withstand the criticisms levelled against it. With the process still continuing and with countless examples of articulations having been developed between the different local initiatives as well as several alliances forged at a national level, what is missing is the involvement of civil society and the state for these initiatives and actions to be based on the NIABY (Not in Anybody's Backyard) principle. In fact, members of the protest movement have claimed advances in this area:

> ... this co-incineration process has gone really well. From the point of view of participation and the contributions made, I think it's one of the best ever. And I also think that it's opening up a lot of new paths here in Portugal, because many of these things had never happened before.

> ... there's no doubt that this whole story of co-incineration, which I hope will continue to prove controversial ..., has done more to promote these questions in people's minds than ten years of petty struggle or ten, or even 20, years of environmental education for children (João Gabriel Silva, interview, 29 August 2000).

> ... there have been some victories: for the people who had opinions and suggestions – both individuals and organizations – because

the suggestions they offered generated many others. No individual can have the answer to a global problem like this, no one can wave a magic wand and solve the problem, but there has been a victory in terms of the retreat of both the government and the scientific commissions' positions (António André, interview, 20 July 2000).

Regarding the stance of the scientists who favoured co-incineration, the discourse employed throughout the whole process set aside the principle of organized scepticism (Santos 1996), since they always affirmed definitive notions in relation to the problems presented. The texts of the scientific reports never allowed any notion of doubt to emerge, and thus simplified a discourse which is characterized by complexity. It is this combination of factors which explains why there was no public recognition of the original errors in the report on which the decision was based.

As to the effects of these movements on Portuguese society, thus far only small changes can be glimpsed; the major transformations, as we already know, are hidden from immediate view. The solutions to the problems take on a local shape, but at present we just do not know, in this particular case, whether they are really solutions or not. Knowing that 'the more global the problem, the more local and locally diverse the solutions should be' (Santos 1994), the actual dimension of the problem and the actual dimension of its solutions still need to be determined.

CONCLUSION

The protest movement against co-incineration has been marked by periods of different types of opposition. We have been able to identify three of these periods which display the following characteristics: in the first phase, a lack of attention to popular demands by governmental decision makers led to a call for expert knowledge on which a decision could be based; in the second phase, the position taken by the CCI, which was unreservedly in favour of continuing with co-incineration, made the opposition focus mainly on the scientific controversy that in the meantime had emerged; in the third phase, the widening of scientific analysis to include issues relating to public health reinforced the developing alliance between a section of the scientific community and the protest movement, and brought it unequivocally closer to the main concerns of the local population.

Amongst the various implications of this process, it should be emphasized that the developments promoted throughout the protest movement were constructed and defined on a dual basis of contingencies and universalities. There was undoubtedly a politicization of science and a 'scientification' of political decision making.

In spite of the fact that the opposition was, from the outset, accused of being parochial, the unfolding of events led to a dialogue about issues that had never been raised before in the country. Furthermore, the protest movement assumed a vanguard position against the so-called 'toxic culture', one of the most topical issues today.

In addition, what was, from the beginning, the movement's most obvious weakness should also be seen as a strength: the fact that minor visible transformations led to a rethinking about a process of transition, opening up a whole set of future possibilities.

The debate which emerged proved that scientific arguments, or rather the arguments of the sciences, like any other form of knowledge, are partial and culturally and socially circumscribed. If we recall the facts of the matter, it may be verified that an entire political decision was replaced by a scientific opinion. This process condensed years of a deepening relationship between science and political power in terms of the implementation of new technologies, without leaving any space for any other actors to participate. The relationship between the government and scientists was based on the 'certainty' and 'truth' of the results that would be obtained and on the competence of the scientists involved, which, in itself, delegitimized the protest movement. The result of this association between the government and the scientists from the CCI was seen as the consecration of science, as a victory of 'scientific results' over 'ignorance', 'irrationality' and 'emotion'. Following James Scott, we can say that one of the major reasons for denigrating practical knowledge is that its 'findings' cannot be integrated 'into the general conventions of scientific discourse' (Scott 1998). However, when it comes to this protest movement we witnessed an attempt to desacralize scientific knowledge. In fact, the union of scientific knowledge and lay knowledge also gained some ground, thus heralding a change. The weak development in this field and the slight knowledge accumulated so far would lead us to expect greater tolerance for the diversity of positions within science and greater attention to experienced knowledge. The successive retreats of the government's decision reflect an acceptance of some of the directions indicated by the protest movement, gradually diminishing the 'ghost of Galileo' initially brandished by the government. Thus, the process opened up the possibility of identifying and exploring experiential forms of knowledge in order to add a more democratic and emancipatory dimension to the use of scientific knowledge. The emergence of scientific controversy, associated with the 'rival' knowledges in dispute, has shown the way forward to the legitimation of so-called 'lay' knowledge, as well as new constellations of knowledges, since it was proved that science is also political.

By 'unveiling' the opposition between traditional political struggle and environmental struggle, the Souselas movement has taken the first step toward another means of carrying out a political struggle, which is different from that which is channelled through parties and traditional institutions. In effect, the actions developed by this movement sought to organize and give voice and visibility to emerging collective identities, which, on the basis of problems initially experienced on a local scale, became progressively linked to broader movements and struggles, centred on the defence of the environment and the right of citizens to participate in decisions which affect their lives, their health and their environment. Having claimed their right to participate, citizens gradually defined their own position in relation to the process as a whole, a position which became increasingly informed and critical.

NOTES

1. A small parish in the municipality of Coimbra, located about 5 km from the city centre, which had 3,144 inhabitants in 2001 (INE, 2001).
2. Amongst the many protest movements which have emerged, the following merit special attention: the struggle to preserve the Foz Côa pre-historic riverside engravings (threatened with submersion by the construction of a hydroelectric dam), 1994–95; the fight against the construction of an incineration station and a physio-chemical treatment unit in Estarreja, 1995–97; the fight against the construction of a sanitary landfill in Taveiro (Coimbra), 1997; the fight against the installation of a co-incinerator in Maceira (Leiria), 1998–2000; the fight against the construction of a sanitary landfill in Bigorne (Viseu), 2000; the fight against the installation of a co-incinerator in Outão (Setúbal), 2000–01. To these may also be added the fights led by Vizela and Canas de Senhorim for their recognition as 'concelhos' (the second of a three-tier local administration system).
3. With reference to the struggle under discussion here, it is also worth mentioning that similar situations have been multiplying in recent years in other countries, although leading to substantially different developments. From amongst a variety of struggles, we can highlight the models adopted in waste management in England (Petts 2000), the fight against the installation of a radioactive waste incinerator in the USA (Gusterson 2000) and the recent fight against co-incineration at a cement factory in Matola, Mozambique.
4. This syndrome is normally associated with the rejection, by a local population, of the installation of certain infrastructures which are perceived to involve a serious threat to the area. In this sense, a typical NIMBY (Not In My Backyard) reaction is set in motion when the intended measures are considered to be obviously unfavourable to the affected population. As Maria da Graça Martinho and Helena Freitas state, 'the potential benefits resulting from the installation of these infrastructures do not outweigh the costs, which include potential risks to the environment and public health, the inconveniences of noise, traffic, the devaluing of property and the lowering of the community's self-image, all of which lead to public opposition to the chosen location for these infrastructures' (*Público*, 23 February 2000). The issues associated with this

type of problematic demonstrate the importance of location in environmental management.
5. These processes are related to the ways in which the actors frame 'their claims, their opponents and their identities' (McAdam, Tarrow and Tilly 2001: 16).
6. These cement companies coexist in Portugal as a duopoly, with Cimpor holding a slightly larger share of the market than Secil.
7. This committee originally consisted of the Coimbra Civic Association 'Pro Urbe', the Souselas Association for the Defence of the Environment (ADAS), the Souselas Parish Council, the Central Region Teachers' Union (SPRG), the Coimbra Union of Trade Unions (USC), the Coimbra branch of Quercus and the Coimbra Commercial and Industrial Association (ACIC). Later, the Coimbra branch of the National Coordinating Committee against Toxic Waste (CNCT), the Ecology Group of the Coimbra Student Union and the 'Ruptura' movement also joined. Throughout the whole process, the *Diário de Coimbra* attended the meetings of the committee as a silent 'listener', as its representative stated, in order to help the newspaper 'keep its readers better informed' (Interview given on 18 August 2000).
8. In addition to the *Diário de Coimbra*, which promoted the initiative, many commercial establishments in the city also lent their support by allowing the petition to be displayed on their premises. For about a week and a half, the newspaper publicized the places where people could go to express their opinion on the issue of revocation. A similar initiative was developed by the *Diário de Leiria* in relation to the situation in Maceira (the other chosen location for co-incineration).
9. Despite the consensus against co-incineration, the reasons were significantly diverse: the Social Democratic Party (PSD) defended the construction of an incinerator from scratch; the Portuguese Communist Party (PCP), in addition to the platform defended by the Green Party, accused the government of not having correctly justified its choice of sites for co-incineration, and, finally, the Popular Party (PP) accused the government of a lack of respect for public health.
10. In addition to regulating the Independent Scientific Commission, this law also required that an inventory of waste be made and that the priorities of 'reduction, re-use and recycling' be fulfilled in the process of treating it. In fact, the government was obliged by Parliament to carry out a strategic plan which included making an inventory and description of the waste produced or existing in Portugal, and to implement short-term measures for its adequate disposal or storage under controlled conditions.
11. Given the intensity of the debates generated over this issue, it is impossible to reproduce here all the positions that were taken. I chose to present specific initiatives in favour of the suspension of co-incineration. However, it is only appropriate to mention some of the associations/entities that publicly expressed their opinion throughout these two intense months. Thus, the Portuguese Industrial Association and obviously the representatives of the cement industry were in favour of co-incineration in cement factories; taking an intermediate position, the District Federation of the Socialist Party objected to the choice of Souselas, although it agreed with the need for co-incineration; among those against co-incineration, we should highlight the positions of the Central Region Council, which also accused the government of having underestimated the region, the Social Democrat Youth National Council, the Scientific Committee of the School of Medicine of the University of Coimbra, the Oceanus Ecology Association, the Taveiro 'Marginis' Association for the Defence of the Environment, the Coimbra Agricultural Cooperative, the Bishop of Coimbra, and the associations and entities that compose the Fight Against Co-incineration Commission (CLCC).
12. The Independent Scientific Commission was composed of the following members: one Professor at the School of Engineering, University of Porto, and Researcher at the Porto Biomedical Engineering Institute; one Professor at the Environment Department, University of Aveiro; one Professor of Epidemiology at the School of Medicine, University of Porto; and one Professor at the Chemistry Department, University of Coimbra.

13. In fact, the waste destined for co-incineration treatment and which was the focus of the CCI study consisted, in general, of used oils, organic solvents and organic sludge. At a large gathering, environmentalists and representatives of other associations agreed on the option of regenerating the oils and solvents, since alternatives which were technically and economically viable already existed for this, thus leaving only the organic sludge, which, due to its variety and composition, needed to be studied more deeply.
14. The most controversial issue in this respect became known as the 'domestic fireplaces case': calculations contained in the Independent Scientific Commission's report claimed that the dangers associated with the emissions from a co-incinerator were no different from those resulting from 170 domestic fireplaces. As this was one of the strongest arguments in support of the method, other scientists came forward to reveal that the calculations were wrong: instead of the 170 domestic fires mentioned by the Independent Scientific Commission, the correct figure was around 140,000. In addition to this numerical 'minor detail', they also pointed out other factors which had not been taken into consideration, such as the qualitative difference in the emissions, bearing in mind the higher level of toxicity of the waste that would be burned, as opposed to the wood normally used in domestic fires, even though it might be contaminated.
15. In fact, the figures reported in the Strategic Plan for the Management of Industrial Waste (PESGRI) eventually demonstrated that, in this respect, almost everything still remained to be dealt with. From the enquiry sent out by the government to all registered industrial establishments, it was only possible to gather data relating to 1.3 per cent of the total number of companies, since the rest had not filled in and returned their forms. Even given that those who replied represented the largest companies in the country, the limitations of these figures are quite obvious.
16. Owing to the lack of any concrete data on the Portuguese situation, several sources, including the report submitted by the Independent Scientific Commission, estimate that the waste destined for burning represents only about 2 per cent of the total waste produced in Portugal and about 10 per cent of the total dangerous industrial waste.
17. Ironically, the government actually ended up deciding that air filters – instruments which significantly reduce the dangers associated with atmospheric emissions and which can be used in any cement factory in the country – would only be installed in cement works in the areas which had been 'awarded' co-incineration.
18. The government followed up this opinion with Resolutions no. 91 and 92/2000. Although establishing co-incineration as the method to be adopted for the treatment of dangerous industrial waste, it is also significant that, within the legislative text itself, they advanced the proposal that only waste that could not be treated by any other method should be burned.
19. The results presented by the CLCC served as a basis for the closer involvement of the Coimbra School of Medicine, which, in partnership with the ADAS, began to develop epidemiological studies in the areas affected by the cement works. It has had the total support of the local population.

REFERENCES

Barros, H., S. Germano Sousa, N. Grande, S. Massano Cardoso, J. Pereira Miguel and J. Torgal (2000): *Relatório do Grupo de Trabalho Médico*, http://www.fe.up.pt/ ~ jotace/.

Brown, P., *et al.* (2000): 'Popular Epidemiology and Toxic Waste Contamination: Lay and Professional Ways of Knowing', in S. Kroll-Smith, *et al.* (eds.), *Illness and the Environment: a Reader in Contested Medicine*, New York: New York University Press, pp.364–83.

Clark, J. and J. Murdoch (1997): 'Local Knowledge and the Precarious Extension of Scientific Networks: a Reflexion on Three Case Studies', *Sociologia Ruralis* 37/1.
Comissão de Luta Contra a Co-incineração (2001): *Parecer sobre o estado de saúde da população de Souselas*, http://www.co-incineracao.online.pt/Souselas.pdf.
Ezrahi, Y. (1996): 'A ciência e a ilusão da fuga à política', in Maria Eduarda Gonçalves (ed.), *Ciência e Democracia*, Venda Nova: Bertrand Editora, pp.21–9.
Fixdal, J. (1997): 'Consensus Conferences as extended peer groups', *Science and Public Policy* 24/6, pp.366–76.
Font, N. (1998): *New Instruments of Citizen Participation.*, Barcelona: Institut de Ciènces Polítiques y Socials.
Formosinho, S., C. Pio, H. Barros and J. Cavalheiro (2000): *Parecer relativo ao tratamento de resíduos industriais perigosos*, http://www.fe.up.pt/ ~ jotace/.
Gonçalves, M.E. (1996): 'Ciência e política em Portugal: O caso da "doença das vacas loucas"', in M.E. Gonçalves (ed.), *Ciência e Democracia*, Venda Nova: Bertrand Editora, pp.121–39.
Gonçalves, M.E. (2000): 'Ciência, política e participação: O caso de Foz Côa', in M.E. Gonçalves (ed.), *Cultura científica e participação pública*, Oeiras: Celta Editora, pp.201–30.
Gusterson, H. (2000): 'How not to Construct a Radioactive Waste Incinerator', *Science, Technology and Human Values* 25/3, pp.332–51.
Irwin, A. (1996): *Citizen Science: A Study of People, Expertise and Sustainable Development*, London: Routledge.
Jamison, A. and B. Wynne (1998): 'Sustainable Development and the Problem of Public Participation', in A. Jamison (ed.), *Technology Policy Meets the Public. Pesto Papers 2*, Aalborg: Aalborg University Press.
Kleinman, D. (2000): 'Democratizations of Science and Technology', in Daniel Kleinman (ed.), *Science, Technology and Democracy*, Albany: State University of New York Press, pp.139–65.
McAdam, D., S. Tarrow and C. Tilly (2001): *Dynamics of Contention*, Cambridge: Cambridge University Press.
Nunes, J.A. (1999): 'Para além das duas culturas: tecnociências, tecnoculturas e teoria crítica', *Revista Crítica de Ciências Sociais* 52/53, pp.15–60.
Petts, J. (2000): 'Processos de formação de consensos na gestão de resíduos: Os peritos, a ciência e o público', in M.E. Gonçalves (ed.), *Cultura científica e participação pública*, Oeiras: Celta Editora, pp.161–81.
Rodrigues, M.E. (1995): *Os novos movimentos sociais e o associativismo ambientalista em Portugal*, Oficina do CES, p.60.
Rodrigues, M.E. (2000): 'Globalizacão e ambientalismo: Actores e processos no caso da incineradora de Estarrejo', Master's Thesis in Sociology, School of Economics, University of Coimbra.
Ross, A. (ed.) (1996): *Science Wars*, Durham: Duke University Press.
Rowe, G. and F. Lynn (2000): 'Public Participation Methods: A Framework for Evaluation', *Science, Technology and Human Values* 25/1, pp.3–29.
Santos, B. de S. (1990): *O Estado e a sociedade em Portugal (1974–88)*, Porto: Edições Afrontamento.
Santos, B. de S. (1993): 'O Estado, as relações salariais e o bem-estar social na semiperiferia: o caso português', in B. de S. Santos (ed.), *Portugal: um retrato singular*, Porto: Edições Afrontamento, pp.17–56.
Santos, B. de S. (1994): *Pela mão de Alice: O social e o político na pós-modernidade*, Porto: Edições Afrontamento.
Santos, B. de S. (1995): *Toward a New Common Sense: Law, Science and Politics in the Paradigmatic Transition*, New York: Routledge.
Santos, B. de S. (1996): *Introdução a uma ciência pós-moderna*, Porto: Edições Afrontamento.
Santos, B. de S. (1998): *Reinventar a democracia*, Colecção Fundação Mário Soares, Cadernos Democráticos, 4, Lisboa: Gradiva Publicações.

Santos, B. de S. (2000): *A crítica da razão indolente – contra o desperdício da experiência*, Porto: Edições Afrontamento.
Scott, J. (1998): *Seeing Like a State: How Certain Schemes to Improve the Human Condition Have Failed*, New Haven and London: Yale University Press.
Szerszynski, B., S. Lash and B. Wynne (1996): 'Ecology, Realism and the Social Sciences', in S. Lash, B. Szerszynski and B. Wynne (eds.), *Risk, Environment and Modernity. Towards a New Ecology*, London: Sage, pp.1–24.
Yearley, S. (1993): 'Standing in for Nature: The Practicalities of Environmental Organizations use of Science', in K. Milton (ed.), *Environmentalism: The View from Anthropology*, London: Routledge, pp.59–72.
Yearley, S. (1996): 'Nature's Advocates, Putting Science to Work in Environmental Organizations', in Alan Irwin and Brian Wynne (eds.), *Misunderstanding Science? The Public Reconstruction of Science and Technology*, Cambridge: Cambridge University Press, pp.172–90.

Sexual Orientation in Portugal: Towards Emancipation

ANA CRISTINA SANTOS

In a context of hegemonic globalization, minorities constitute counter-powers whose potential for resistance and subversion may effectively result in a renegotiation of the rules of the game. In this context, the complex, heterogeneous and often diffuse lesbian–gay–bisexual–transsexual movement (LGBT)[1] offers an important challenge to contemporary sociological thought (Stein and Plummer 1996; Hawkes 1996; Seidman 1997). There are two central aspects to the debate about the LGBT movement within the wider reflection upon alternative forms of social emancipation. First, there is voluminous historical evidence of the oppression of homosexual, bisexual and transsexual men and women throughout the centuries by the 'compulsive heterosexuality' (Rich 1993) and, since the Inquisition, there have been many cases of persecution, torture and murder of people because of their sexual orientation, acts still legally permitted in some countries (Mott 1987; Richards 1990; Amnesty International 1997; and Rosenbloom 1996). But, rather than simply repeat well-known facts, there is a need to question whether this form of oppression necessarily contains potential for emancipation. In other words, is the social oppression of a particular minority group enough to turn it into a counterhegemonic force?

The second important aspect is the so-called 'pink industry', which, since the 1980s has become a visibly lucrative trade, resulting in the design and production of cultural products specifically targeted towards this sector of the market. It includes its own press, bars, discotheques, saunas, hotels, sex shops, among others, as well as the growth of

---

The author would like to thank Boaventura de Sousa Santos and João Arriscado Nunes for their constructive criticism of the various versions of this essay. Thanks also to Fernando Fontes and Sílvia Ferreira for their careful reading of the text, constant availability and comments, and to the authors of the other essays in this volume with whom I had the privilege of working during the Symposium 'The Reinvention of Social Emancipation', held in Coimbra from 23 to 26 November 2000.

the international gay tourist circuit. The expansion of this specifically gay market has been largely due to the forces of globalization, which have made available a wide range of 'pink' products for consumption by male homosexuals. Factors such as an allegedly better social and economic status, and successful publicity campaigns specifically directed at the gay consumer, have obviously played an important part. Lastly, the growing public visibility of homosexuality, evident in the frequency of debates and demonstrations, for example, reflects the benefits that the LGBT movement has reaped from globalization, particularly by means of electronic information networks and tourism.

This essay is divided into four sections. It begins with a theoretical reflection on the concepts of equality and difference, leading to the question of the conditions and possibilities provided by capitalism to the struggle for sexual emancipation. This is followed by an analysis of the specific nature of contemporary Portuguese society, considering questions such as its semiperipheral location, the fragility of civil society and the predominance of Judaeo-Christian ethics. Then, I will move to a more empiricial reflection on the strategies, alliances and socio-political aims of the Portuguese LGBT organizations, within the international context of the globalization of the LGBT movement. This involves the examination of documents, internal literature, and other theoretical and empirical studies on this subject, with priority given to the direct observation of recent public events organized by this movement such as the Gay Pride March (June 2000), the Gay Pride Fest (*Arraial Gay*) (1999 and 2000), and the Gay and Lesbian Film Festival (1999 and 2000). Finally, I will attempt to assess the counterhegemonic potential of the struggle for sexual emancipation, based on the involvement of the Portuguese LGBT movement in other struggles for the right to difference and non-discrimination.

CONSTRUCTING EQUALITY AND DIFFERENCE

The systems of inequality and exclusion surrounding us and affecting our daily lives result from a complex interplay of powers, by means of which hegemonic groups construct and impose languages, ideologies and beliefs which lead to the rejection, marginalization, or silencing of all who oppose them. This is a historical process of hierarchization, according to which a culture, by means of a discourse of truth, creates proscriptions and thus defines the boundary beyond which all is transgression. With these rules, all groups affected by social proscriptions (such as the insane, criminals, gypsies, homosexuals, etc.) are pushed into the margin of the heterotopia (Santos 1999). In speaking of equality and difference, we are necessarily conditioned by a context that is by no means neutral.

The right to difference is not the same as equal rights for all. The right to difference means that specific characteristics are not devalued, and that there are alternatives that do not lead to scapegoating. It means the rigorous application of a categorical imperative that could be phrased thus: the right to be equal whenever difference makes us inferior; the right to be different whenever equality decharacterizes us (Santos 1999: 45). Therefore, I propose the concept of 'useful universalism' to define a politics involving the diffusion of universal principles of non-discrimination while retaining the constitutive aspects of the identity of subcultures valued by the individuals involved. Thus, it becomes possible to defend the general application of laws and, simultaneously, the legal protection of groups likely to be excluded. This seems to have been the double concern of the Portuguese state when, on 15 March 2001, its Parliament approved bills on so-called joint or common economies (law 6/2001, of 11 May) and common-law partnerships (law 7/2001 of 11 May), irrespective of gender. The passing of both bills made clear the need for positive discrimination for homosexual citizens. For, while there is nothing that prevents a homosexual couple from benefiting from the legal protection provided by the law on common economies, this was considered insufficient by Portuguese LGBT associations, since it removes the affective component from the LGBT family relationship, reducing it to a merely economic concern.[2] This was why, during the street demonstration in front of the Sixth Civil Registry Office on 6 February 2000, several lesbian and gay couples kissed each other while waving placards bearing the words 'This is common economy!' By explicitly stipulating in Article 1 that it applies to 'any two people, regardless of gender', the law on common-law partnerships thus provides against narrower interpretations of the protection in question.

Thus, it may be concluded that the route to a more inclusive society passes through stages in which it is neither useful nor just to promote an essentialist universalism that does not take into account the specifics of the context. Useful universalism should lead to policies of equality, while avoiding homogenization, which is always carried out by those at the top of the pyramid. It is because of this risk of homogenization that some LGBT activists have strongly criticized the discourse of equality, arguing that 'equal rights' ultimately aim at the annulment of diversity within the LGBT movement itself. In fact, recognition of the rights of LGBT couples may be interpreted as an incentive or reward for adhering to a model of sexual behaviour very close to that of conventional heterosexuality, namely a stable, monogamous relationship[3] (Tatchell 2001).

Reflection upon equality and difference should be viewed within the context of neoliberalism, where these poles intersect, approximate and diverge, forming complex dynamic networks that are not always easy to disentangle. The relation between the Portuguese LGBT movement and the capitalist system is permeated by contradictions that derive from this complexity as well as from the need to constantly articulate the resources available to groups which, while struggling for equal rights, wave the banner of pride in difference.

The following is a brief analysis of the conditions imposed by the dominant system on the struggle for sexual emancipation, in an attempt to understand the extent to which this may be successful in the context of a capitalist society.

(In)Equality in the Capitalist System

Clearly, situations of extreme poverty, involving a constant struggle for survival, do not leave much space, or energy, to the struggle for other causes apparently less crucial. However, when objective conditions of existence improve, then the spectrum of social claims and complaints broadens, since it is at this point that other needs, such as freedom of expression or of self-determination of the body, become visible. It is in this sense that the capitalist system has provided some of the essential conditions for the emergence of the homosexual movement, amongst which the most important are the monthly salary and the manufacture of products for consumption.

In a frequently quoted article, D'Emilio (1996) argues that:

> It has been the historical development of capitalism – more specifically, its free-labor system – that has allowed large numbers of men and women in the late twentieth century to call themselves gay, to see themselves as part of a community of similar men and women, and to organize politically on the basis of that identity (1996: 264).

In fact, by removing from the family unit its traditional role of economic producer, the capitalist system converted it into a space for the establishment and strengthening of affective relations, which would permit the worker to maintain the high level of performance required by the system. What was unexpected in this process was that the nuclear family was transformed into a space for well-being and happiness where feelings were given priority over obligations. Thus, the way was opened for new family models which transcend traditional blood ties. On 24 March 2000, a paper presented by ILGA-Portugal at the Alternative Summit defined the family for the LGBT organization as follows:

> Many of us are in common-law partnerships, therefore we are in favour of the family, understood as the privileged place for

affections, and not as a legal transaction. For us, the family is not only the old family that we have inherited, which in many cases is in grave crisis, but also our new families, involving same-sex couples, single mothers, lesbian mothers, single fathers, widows and widowers, gays, bisexuals, transsexuals, families with adopted children, and with children resulting from artificial insemination, all who feel themselves to be in a family in the home where they are brought up, cared for, looked after and loved (Rodrigues 2000).

This transformation has affected the heterosexual family itself. The number of children per couple, for example, has dropped dramatically, now that children are no longer needed as workers contributing to the household economy, but are instead desired for affective reasons.

Furthermore, the development of markets has led to a greater circulation of people and goods, which stimulates an exchange of information and experience that would otherwize have remained unknown. António Serzedelo, president of Opus Gay, argues that policies for economic growth:

have given Portugal good roads and bridges, which bring things into the country – or don't, but that is another question – and these roads have also brought into the country many European ideas dear to the urban bourgeoisie. A side-effect, certainly not anticipated, is that with this have come, on aeroplanes, buses and trains, liberalizing ideas which are the consequence of the liberalization of capital (Santos and Fontes 1999).

In fact, the decade of the 1990s saw the beginning of a Portuguese LGBT market, consisting mostly of night spots, such as bars and discotheques, but also including saunas, an estate agency, a hotel, a travel agency, a bookshop and the magazine *Korpus* (the only gay periodical since 1996), in addition to the different services provided by the associations themselves. Therefore, there seems already to be a perception that homosexuals are also consumers whose purchasing power may be attracted commercially, although in Portugal this market is still a long way from the 'pink' industries of the United States, the United Kingdom or even Spain. In any case, the increasing socio-economic power of this group has led to a greater capacity for the negotiation of social and political rights, as well as to a growth in the public visibility of homosexuality. According to Santos, 'many social groups which are "different", such as ethnic minorities and others, have begun to have sufficient organizational resources to enable their specific needs and aspirations to be placed on the political agenda' (1999: 23).

The other side of the coin is that capitalist ideology is at the origin of sexual oppression, an aspect which is considered below. Some studies have identified the bourgeois nuclear family (defined as the economic institutionalization of personal relations in the context of the capitalist system) as the main justification for homophobia.[4] This oppression dates back to the period when the bourgeois family model began to be instituted, incorporating an 'economically useful and politically conservative sexuality' in the words of Foucault (1994: 41). It was with this family model that the sexual division of labour was introduced, according to which women were responsible for maintaining the stability of the home, taking care of clothes, meals, cleaning and children. Although this role amply served the needs of the economic system, it did not result in social recognition, and women were relegated to routine tasks considered unimportant. This means that, although women had been oppressed and exploited long before this time, the bourgeois nuclear family model contributed to reinforcing the inequalities in which women were caught. Even though the labour market gradually began to absorb women into the work force, after the industrial revolution, the traditional role of women in the home did not change greatly (Ferreira 1981). Indeed, capitalist ideology constructed and disseminated a strong sexual dichotomy which assigns different and frequently opposed roles to men and women (Joaquim 1998; Müller 1998; Osório 2002). Homophobia is one of the facets of this patriarchal ideology, since individuals, whether men or women, who consider themselves equal and fight for the right to difference, constitute a real threat to a system whose construction has been based on dichotomies that also pertain to gender. In other words, the bourgeoisie:

> terrified by the communist spectre of the equality of women and men, labels sexual equality as unnatural. Gayness is also labeled 'unnatural' and therefore a threat to bourgeois domination, precisely because it rejects the 'natural' bourgeois society as reflected in the 'natural' bourgeois/proletarian relationship of the nuclear family (LARG 1996: 350).

Even these days, homosexual workers are frequently dismissed or have their career advancement blocked (in slang, to be 'shelved') for motives that have less to do with work performance than with their sexual orientation, inferred or assumed.[5] Knowledge of this type of discrimination affecting LGBT workers led to the approval of a motion supporting the claims of the Gay, Lesbian and Transvestite Movement at the Sixth

National Congress of the Brazilian union federation Central Única de Trabalhadores, in São Paulo, in August 1997:

> The 6th CONCUT resolves: ... to fight homophobia within trade unions and at the workplace, by developing a policy designed to suppress discrimination against gays, lesbians and transvestite workers in unions and in society at large, in general agreement with entities that are already struggling against this prejudice (CUT 1997: 61).

Outside the sphere of work, whenever a homosexual parent is refused child custody, whenever a LGBT couple avoids affectionate behaviour in public, or whenever a gay is beaten up for not being heterosexual, there is a subjugation of difference to the heterosexual hegemony, which also serves the interests of bourgeois capitalism. The fact that this oppression operates on the basis of sexuality – seen equally in regard to race, class or gender – reveals how powerful the weapons of capitalism are in depriving individuals of their power of resistance, condemning them to isolation and invisibility for the most diverse of reasons.

In addition to these more direct forms of exclusion due to homophobia, the allegedly high economic status of homosexuals is not enough to emancipate them. In a message distributed by e-mail in August 2000, the Australian organization Queers United to Eradicate Economic Rationalism (QUEERS) warned about the false acceptance that homosexuals were apparently enjoying as a distinct market niche, as a result of their spending power. In this message, the group rejected this claim to acceptance, arguing that 'our rightful place in society must not be bought. Freedom does not come from consumption' (QUEERS 2000). This rejection of an LGBT lifestyle characterized by a high level of consumption is at the basis of 'Queeruption', a celebration of alternative gay pride, ostensibly non-commercial and strongly politicized, planned for London and San Francisco, in an attempt to overcome the image of gay identity as 'having less to do with sexual orientation than with the make of beer that you drink, the car you drive or how you decorate your house' (Fox 2001).

The Madrid neighbourhood of Chueca is another example. Although this area is apparently receptive to the LGBT community, where trade and industry have developed with the gay consumer in mind,[6] the truth is that Chueca is no more than a commercial ghetto, around which a certain LGBT lifestyle has developed. That is to say, it is a community with buying power, which takes care of the body but is diluted, without many concerns for its identity, within a society that continues to be patriarchal and heterosexist. Once again, consumption has not resulted in the actual inclusion of gays as citizens, but only in the appropriation of a circumscribed area of the city. One of the greatest risks of 'pink consumption' is the subversion of the emancipatory objectives of LGBT organizations, as Eugeni Rodriguez (2000) of the Gay Liberation Front of Catalonia has pointed out:

> The construction of this network effectively ridicules, marginalizes and criminalizes the gay liberation movement ... The union of gay entrepreneurs with politicians, eager to normalize homosexuality, is behind this lobby. The rights of gays no longer require confrontation, but rather their insertion into consumer society and their restriction to specific neighbourhoods and timetables.

In Portugal, Vitorino (2000) has warned of the danger of confusing the role of the associations, as a network for support and integration of LGBT youth, with the role of the commercial establishments, oriented towards entertainment, consumption and maximum profit.[7] One obvious difference between the two is the fact that a poor homosexual, living in a rural region and terrified at the possibility that his sexual orientation might be socially exposed, is a very different case from one whose economic power allows him to frequent the circuits of gay tourism, participate in private parties or go regularly to the saunas and night bars in the capital.

SPECIFIC LEGAL, SOCIAL AND RELIGIOUS CONDITIONS IN PORTUGAL

In order to understand the emergence of the LGBT movement in Portugal, it is necessary to contextualize it in space and time, and take into consideration the specific situation resulting from the country's semiperipheral position in the world system. In effect, Portuguese society has some features that are similar to those of core countries, together with others that have more in common with peripheral countries (Santos 1992: 105). Its gradual approximation to the rest of Europe, culminating in its joining the European Union in 1986, has meant an effort to bring the Portuguese legal system up to the level of the constitutions and legal codes of other European countries.

Eight years after the democratic revolution of 1974, the Portuguese Penal Code was revized, in the wake of the policy of approximation to the rest of Europe. Asserting the principle that its task was to protect freedom of determination and the authenticity of sexual expression, and not to control sexual morality, the new penal code decriminalized sexual acts practised by consenting adults in private. These included adultery, incest, prostitution and homosexuality, which had figured in previous penal codes (including the reform project of 1966) as 'crimes against decency' or 'crimes against custom'. Only 'sexual crimes' such as rape, indecent assault, public offence to modesty or the assault of minors are now punishable. This is why the new penal code only punishes homosexuality in cases involving children under 16 (Article 207). With the alterations introduced in 1995, homosexual relations with an adolescent between 14 and 16 years of age continue to be punished, a situation which may be contrasted with heterosexual relations in the same circumstances, for which legislation allows the possibility of the minor's informed consent (Articles 174 and 175).

One feature specific to Portugal is the frequent inconsistency between the formal law and its effective application. This affects the way in which sexuality is experienced, permitting the persistence of attitudes and behaviour that are inconsistent with the progressive legal system being asserted. This lack of coherence may operate in different ways: through an excessive time lapse between the approval of the law and its implementation; failure to enforce the law or selective enforcement; and the instrumental use of the law (Santos 1992: 135 ff.).[8]

Since the last quarter of the twentieth century, Portuguese civil society has been showing a greater capacity to voice demands, with the emergence and action of many different social movements, the most recent of which is the LGBT movement. However, half a century of dictatorship and the persistence of a strong Catholic morality (which will be analyzed below) have meant that intervention in the public sphere has been meagre and that existing social movements are frail.[9] Unlike many core countries, Portugal has not had any strong social movements, although there are associations active in the field of women's rights, workers' rights,[10] the fight against racism, and, more recently, environmental protection. If we relate Portuguese civil society's weak level of intervention with the characteristics of its social basis of support, we can infer that 'the weakness of protest groups is due to the reduced importance of the new middle classes and, consequently, to the fact that the (rural) populations only mobilize when their immediate material interests are at stake' (Rodrigues 1995: 7).[11]

The fragility of civil participation is counterbalanced by moments of strong activism and the mobilization of certain sectors of the population around issues that affect and/or directly threaten their daily lives. That was what happened in 1998 when the country witnessed the sudden appearance of citizen groups, organized in two months, to campaign in the period before the referendum about the decriminalization of abortion.[12] In a country where issues of sexual politics and reproductive rights have no deep-rooted tradition, there was an ardent public debate about sexuality, in which an active part was played by common citizens as well as by experts. This participation around the time of the campaign was not, however, reflected in the percentage of votes at the referendum, which was only 31.94 per cent.

The (lack of) civic participation by the Portuguese in debates or movements about social issues is to a large extent influenced by the stance of the Catholic Church in relation to some of the issues in question. Indeed, the Portugese clergy has shown that it has considerable powers of social intervention, both in blocking initiatives and in mobilizing people, often determining the direction taken by political decisions. Given the central role of religion in Portugal, particularly incisive in questions of sexuality, it is worth taking a closer look at some of the issues raised by this situation.

Catholicism in Portugal

Portuguese society has been profoundly influenced by Judaean-Christian morality, reinforced by the frequent interventions of the Catholic Church in matters concerning sexuality. In fact, the Portuguese Catholic Church has long played a central role in defining the boundaries between what is socially desirable and what is morally wrong, and it is between these two poles that the game of sexual emancipation is played out. As we shall see, the Catholic Church has blocked both women's emancipation (systematically condemning the use of contraceptives, abortion, and the right of women to enter the priesthood), and the emancipation of LGBT rights (issuing public statements against common-law partnerships between homosexuals).

As regards contraception, in March 1996, a television advertisement prepared by an NGO involved in the struggle against AIDS showed a priest handing a condom to a young couple in front of a church. The Catholic Church reacted violently, by declaring the advertisement to be complete nonsense and in bad taste (*Expresso* 30 March 1996).

In 1998, concerning the referendum on the decriminalization of abortion, the clergy also clearly influenced the results obtained. On 3 February 1998, following a meeting of the Portuguese Episcopal Council, a pastoral letter was published asserting that 'in the referendum, Catholics and other citizens should not stray, having a clear duty to declare themselves in favour of life' (*Público* 21 February 1998). In the week of the referendum, the cathedral of Braga, in the north, displayed two posters with the words: 'With intelligence and conscience, say no to abortion' (Praça 1998: 8). Another example, amongst many others, was the strategy followed by the parish of Nossa Senhora de Lourdes in Coimbra, which included in its weekly newsletter articles and comments invariably opposed to decriminalization. In fact, the Church made use of multiple mechanisms to sway the vote against decriminalization of abortion. It was in the light of this potential for social mobilization by the Portuguese Catholic Church that political and social analysts interpreted the results of the referendum, held on 28 June 1988, as representing a clear division between the conservative Catholic North and the secular liberal South (Moreira 1998; Santos 2001).

These examples, based upon the public position of the Catholic Church relative to issues of contraception and abortion, clearly illustrate a profoundly conservative attitude in matters of sexuality, as well as an attempt to maintain a strong power of moral regulation. It is this power which the Catholic Church also seeks to use in the field of sexual orientation. That is why its public interventions on matters of homosexuality usually take place at times when political decisions are being made in respect to LGBT rights in the country. Regarding the power of the Catholic Church to exercise regulation over issues related to sexual orientation in Mexico, Mejía states that:

> the Church was the true moral author, through its medieval understanding of homosexuality, of the oppressive environment of the not very distant past ... and of anti-gay prejudice ... The state's written and unwritten rules aimed at safeguarding Mexican morals and public decency were copied from the Church's teachings. (2000: 53)

In Portugal also, religious intervention is partly responsible for the systematic blocking of progressive social and legal efforts, promoting concepts such as sin and normality, diffusing fear, and instigating disapproval and rejection. Among many others, we can cite the following example: in 1994, a national newspaper made a front page story out of the intention by the Socialist Youth to legalize common-law partnerships between homosexuals (*Expresso* 13 June 1994). This news aroused hard commentaries of a homophobic nature from the then archbishop of Braga, D. Eurico Dias Nogueira:

> The state will soon be the first victim, because a state that is not based upon properly constituted families is a fragile state. ... The fall of the Roman Empire was not due to barbarian attacks but to the break-up of the family unit (*Expresso* 13 June 1994).

Some time later, the same archbishop once again stated his opposition to the legalization of common-law partnerships between homosexuals in the same newspaper:

> To classify a homosexual union as a family is an abuse, it is nonsense. I do not question the existence of people who have chosen these paths, or their rights; the problem is that they want to call a family something that cannot in any way be considered one (Rodrigues 1994: 19).

In a pastoral letter entitled 'The Church in Democratic Society', published in 2000, the Portuguese Episcopal Council (CEP) openly rejected the 16 March recommendation of the European Parliament to its Member States to extend to single-parent families and common-law partnerships the same rights as enjoyed by married couples. Rejecting any equivalence between the concepts of 'common law partnership' and 'family', the CEP placed itself clearly on the side of the Pontifical Council for the Family, which, in its document 'Family, Matrimony and Common-law Partnerships', dated November 2000, asserted that common-law partnerships between homosexuals 'are a deplorable distortion of what ought to be a communion of love and life between a man and a woman, who are committed to each other and to the generation of life'.

On 26 April 2001, the Portuguese Episcopal Council published a document entitled 'Crisis of Society – Crisis of Civilization', in which it analyzed the legislative recognition extended the previous month by the Portuguese parliament to common law partnerships between people of the same sex, accusing legislators of undermining the 'dignity of the family'. In the opinion of the Portuguese bishops, the approval of the law on common-law partnerships reveals 'the intentions of certain groups to cause ruptures in the structure of traditional Portuguese culture, or even in what concerns the influence of Church doctrine upon society', concluding that cultural change of this kind heralds a crisis of civilization. This public position of the Catholic Church, which was contested by some political and social sectors and praised by others, effectively reaffirmed the Church's power of contestation and intervention on matters of sexual morality.

Comparing the ecclesiastical perspective with the beliefs and attitudes of the Portuguese people, there is evidence of a strong rejection of male and female homosexuality amongst practising Catholics. Although the number of non-believers who accept sexual relations of gays and lesbians is 22.6 per cent and 24.1 per cent respectively, this figure drops to 5.5 per cent amongst practising Catholics and followers of other religions (Pais 1998: 442). Therefore, if we consider that 89 per cent of Portuguese people consider themselves to be religious, and that 97 per cent of those are Catholic (Vala *et al.* 2003), it is clear that Catholic morality exercises a massive influence upon political decisions directly affecting LGBT citizens, and also upon the emergence and consolidation of the LGBT movement in Portugal. It is this process that will be the concern of the next section.

THE EMERGENCE OF THE LGBT MOVEMENT IN PORTUGAL

The achievement of democracy after the political–military revolution in April 1974 generated a climate of ideological openness, apparently propitious to the acceptance of perspectives that had been silenced for almost half a century by the Salazar regime. Throughout the revolutionary period, there were some manifestations of homosexual mobilization in the country. In 1974, during the 1 May celebrations in Oporto, a placard appeared bearing the words 'Freedom for Homosexuals'. On 13 May of the same year, the *Diário de Lisboa* published the manifesto of the Revolutionary Homosexual Action Movement (*Movimento de Acção Homossexual Revolucionária* – MAHR), entitled 'Freedom for Sexual Minorities'.[13] Six years later, on 25 October 1980, the Revolutionary Homosexual Collective (CHOR) was established. Despite the importance of this movement as the first dynamo of collective action for Portuguese homosexuals, CHOR disappeared two years later. During the 1980s, there were two other events that directly affected the Portuguese gay/lesbian scene: first, the cycle of debates 'To Be (Homo)sexual', which took place in 1982 at the National Centre for Culture, considered to be the first large-scale public debate on the theme; then, the First and Second National Congresses of Sexology, held in 1984 and 1987, in which the topic of homosexuality was discussed by a panel.

With the exception of these movements, the 1980s were disappointing for many as regards what was achieved in this area, especially given the situation in countries like Great Britain, France and the United States.[14] But while this decade was perhaps characterized by a series of small dispersed events, such as debates, the 1990s were marked by the emergence of different LGBT organizations and by various actions organized by them. Therefore, it seems appropriate to describe some of the principal organizations which have been working in the field for more than a decade.

In 1990, the journal *Organa* was launched by a group of lesbian women with the objective of debating issues related to homosexuality and fighting the isolation of many lesbian women outside the urban centres.

A year later, the Homosexual Working Group (*Grupo de Trabalho Homossexual* – GTH) was established within the Revolutionary Socialist Party, with the aim of 'raising the consciousness of Portuguese society as regards the repression and discrimination practised by the dominant sexual morality' (GTH 1991). This group, which presently has 30 members, organizes mostly street demonstrations and other activities to expose attitudes of homophobia,[15] and has been directly involved in struggles to alter legislation to provide more legal protection against discrimination. The most important of these was the demand for the approval of the law on common-law partnerships between people of the same sex and the inclusion of non-discrimination on the basis of sexual orientation in Article 13 of the Constitution of the Republic where the principle of equality between citizens is defined.

In 1993, *Organa* was replaced by *Lilás*, a triannual magazine for the dissemination of information and the defence of lesbian rights, which has gradually become an association, organizing meetings, poetry sessions, discussions about literature and film, and gatherings for collective reflection. One of the main objectives of the Lilás Group has been to distribute information to lesbians in rural parts of the country.

In 1995, the Portuguese delegation of the International Lesbian and Gay Association (ILGA-Portugal) began operations, gaining official recognition in November 1997 with the inauguration of the new Gay and Lesbian Community Centre in a building provided by the Lisbon City Council. This organization has a documentation centre and a bar, provides weekly psychological and legal consultations, and frequently stages plays, poetry sessions or thematic festivals. It is currently the largest lesbigay association in Portugal, both as regards the number of members (estimated betwen 500 and 600), and the amount of initiatives it organizes.

In January 1996, the Sappho Club was formed by three friends, and although it still does not have premises or formal statutes, it now has 100 members and sympathizers, who hold meetings, New Year's Eve parties, sports activities, and an annual Sapphic camp. Since September 1997, it has published the bi-monthly newsletter *Zona Livre*, for the propagation of information about lesbian issues, with a growing capacity to fight against discrimination.

The magazine *Korpus*, the first and, until now, only male homosexual periodical, was launched in September 1996 by Isidro Sousa. Covering a wide range of LGBT issues, it has approximately 200 regular subscribers and is sold all over the country.

Opus Gay appeared in 1997, with the aim of working in the area of LGBT human rights. Based in Lisbon since September 1998, this organization has 80 members, with informal delegations in Oporto and Coimbra. Amongst its activities, the most important was the commemoration of Gay Pride Day, on 19 June 1999, which took place outside the capital, in Oporto. It has also prepared the first anthology of homoerotic literature in Portuguese, bringing together texts in prose and poetry by Portuguese authors. It also provides a series of services for the LGBT community, including 'dog and cat sitters', a home cleaning service, legal, medical and psychological advice, tarot sessions, and a philately club. It also publishes a monthly newsletter, with useful contacts, forthcoming events, national and foreign news, as well as sections for poems, reading suggestions and personal messages.

In May 1998, the women of ILGA-Portugal formed the Women's Group (*Grupo de Mulheres* – GM). With its own issues and manifesto, this group has made a mark on the lesbian scene through its organization of debates, lunches, excursions and other entertainments. In 1999, it organized a Cycle of Lesbian Films, shown on Saturdays at the ILGA-Portugal headquarters to an audience composed almost exclusively of women. During the preparation of the Third Gay and Lesbian Film Festival, this group played an important part in the selection and subtitling of the films for women.

In May 2000, the group NÓS appeared, a self-designated university movement for sexual freedom, based at the University of Oporto. In a communiqué, it asserted its aim to 'confront the viewpoints of the hegemonic (heterosexual, homophobic, macho) tradition with all the other existing truths'. It also organized most of the activities of the First LGBT Pride Week in Oporto, in 2001, such as debates, film showings, poetry sessions and awareness campaigns aimed toward the general public.

In September 2000, the Group Gay West was set up by Simão Mateus, with the main aim of including in the LGBT community gays living in the western part of the country. This group organizes discussion sessions about discrimination and homosexuality, and aims to set up spaces where gays can socialize.

Finally, in November 2001, the association 'don't deprive yourself [*não te prives*] – Group for the Defence of Sexual Rights' appeared in Coimbra. Although it is not an exclusively LGBT association, it has a strong nucleus of work in this field as well as in women's rights, holding that 'the rights to the body, to sexuality and to equal opportunities between women and men, regardless of their sexual orientation, are human rights' (*não te prives* 2001).

In the history of the Portuguese LGBT movement, two years are particularly significant. The first was 1997, the year when the Gay and

Lesbian Community Centre in Lisbon was inaugurated, under the responsibility of the International Gay and Lesbian Association (ILGA-Portugal). The year of the first homosexual pride celebration in the country (called '*Arraial Gay*'[16]) and the first Gay and Lesbian Film Festival also both took place in Lisbon in 1997. The second year was 2000, when the First Homosexual Pride March was organized, attracting around 500 participants. Also that year, the Gay Fest was jointly organized by the main homosexual groups, and thus ceased to be the exclusive responsibility of ILGA-Portugal, as had been the case until then. In addition to the customary Lisbon Mayor's communiqué, the *Arraial 2000* began with reflections by the leaders of the LGBT organizations involved upon the importance of that day in the process of sexual emancipation, stressing the need to extend the struggle to the interior of the country, to those who are isolated, and to the whole of society.

Constructing Networks with Other Discriminated Groups

The year 2000 has been a year of great public visibility for the Portuguese LGBT movement. What is its ideological framework and who are its allies in different sectors of civil society? One response will answer both questions: the democratic left.[17] However, closer analysis of the practices and discourse of the LGBT movement reveals that the identification of strategies and of potential allies is a more complex matter.

On 30 June 2000, a debate was held at the headquarters of ILGA-Portugal about the various forms of struggle used by the LGBT movement. It involved representatives of the GTH, the Sappho Club and ILGA itself, and was an occasion for the examination of the aims, strategies and alliances of the movement. From the point of view of the associations present, the main objectives and strategies were: intervention in schools and amongst the medical profession, through the dissemination of information, participation in debates, and so on.; continuation of the struggle against homophobia, by writing communiqués and letters to the press, etc.; the creation of visibility (through street demonstrations, and so on); and the decentralization of the movement itself. Favourite allies in the struggle for sexual emancipation included human rights groups, women's groups and the so-called 'friendly straights', which include some journalists and students.[18]

The manifesto published by the movement during the 2000 March identified new interlocutors in civil society:

> Because we are discriminated against, we cannot abandon the struggle for human rights, for a society in which sexual orientation, gender identity, the colour of the skin, handicap, nationality,

economic means and sex are not a pretext for exclusion or violence against any human being ... a multicultural country based upon solidarity. We want the legalization of immigrants that live and work in Portugal. We want more sympathetic asylum laws. ... We want social rights at work and in the healthcare system. We want the end of employment insecurity. ... We are against violence to women, particularly handicapped women. We want the right to decide about our own bodies.

Among the different organizations subscribing to this manifesto were the Portuguese Handicapped Association, the Anti-Racism Network, SOS-Racism and the General Union of Workers (UGT). Therefore, in addition to the expected alliance with the feminist movement, shown by the presence of organizations like the Democratic Women's Movement (MDM) and the Alternative and Response Women's Union (UMAR), the Portuguese LGBT movement has been able to muster support amongst workers, ethnic minorities and handicapped people, by means of platforms of common interest and understanding.

The concerns which have marked the development of the Portuguese feminist movement have intersected with many of the issues of the LGBT movement, and thus their struggles have converged at different moments. The system of oppression, patriarchy, is of course common to both, in that it imposes stereotypical models of man and woman and assigns them predetermined social roles.[19] Two of the many different partnerships may be cited. During the Women's World March, in October 2000, different lesbian organizations promoted the active participation of the community, and the final document, signed by all associations involved in the event, contained special demands for lesbians. More recently, the Homosexual Working Group issued a public complaint about a television programme called *Mulher Não Entra* (Women Not Allowed), which it called 'misogynist, macho and sexist' for reducing women to 'mere objects of male desire, despising them and diminishing their identities and their social, cultural and political role' (*Público* 21 April 2001). This public defence of women's dignity by an LGBT organization, regardless of their sexual orientation, would seem to illustrate clearly the similarities between the LGBT and feminist movements.

Another old alliance has been with groups campaigning around AIDS, particularly Abraço, an association which later came to head the LGBT movement in Portugal (Santos 2002). Indeed, the first president of ILGA-Portugal, Gonçalo Diniz, began his work at Abraço, deciding some years later to found the group which has become the largest Portuguese lesbigay organization. Since 1997, ILGA has organized an annual March in

Memory of and Solidarity with Victims of HIV-AIDS. As regards the first march, held on 4 May 1997, Almeida (1997: 98) wrote:

> Never have so many people been mobilized to take part in street demonstrations about sexual politics, except for the issue of abortion. ... Everyone knows that the struggle against AIDS is not and never has been a 'normal' movement of solidarity with victims or a request for funds for healthcare. It has never been just this. It has always been (particularly in this country) a catalyst, an opportunity and a motivation for the assertion of citizenship and sexual politics and lifestyles.

Political allies, operating under banners not always directly connected to the homosexual cause, are mostly found amongst parties of the left. Thus, in 1997, the Socialist Youth proposed a bill aimed at legalizing common-law partnerships between homosexuals. This was supported by the Green Party, but aroused the opposition of right-wing parties, seconded by the Catholic Church. Since 1999, LGBT rights have been particularly defended by the recently formed Left Bloc (*Bloco de Esquerda*), whose party leaders participated in the First Gay Pride March, in Lisbon in 2000. Indeed, since its formation, the Left Bloc has included on its political agenda the struggle against discrimination due to sexual orientation, presumably as a result of the existence of the Homosexual Working Group within the Revolutionary Socialist Party, one of the members of the Left Bloc. In March 2001, left-wing parties, namely the Portuguese Communist Party, the Greens, the Left Bloc and the Socialist Party, joined forces and managed to get the bill on common-law partnerships between homosexuals approved.

The relationship between the homosexual movement and the left has emerged from a common ideology based on the defence of freedom and the right to difference, essentially a struggle against all forms of oppression and exploitation. As Vitorino argues:

> to support left-wing politics requires the courage to fight for all policies that are just, even the most complicated, and to break with all institutionalized injustices because we are fighting for a profound change in the unjust society in which we live. ... The LGBT movement is therefore as subversive of the present order as the ideas of the left. The emancipation of all the oppressed, including LGBT individuals, is the Left's cause (1999: 6).

This linking of the Portuguese LGBT movement with other associations or social movements is consistent with the new social movements of the South, particularly in Latin America, where the creation of networks between movements is common (Santos 1995b: 226). In Mexico, for example, the 1968 student uprisings have been identified as the precursor of LGBT liberation in that country, as it was the student movement that first introduced onto the political agenda demands relating to sexual autonomy from the government and the family. When the LBGT movement emerged in Mexico in 1978, it was characterized by its solidarity with other socially oppressed groups, such as prisoners, workers, and peasants. These connections later attracted the support of the feminist movement and intellectuals (Mejía 2000: 49–50). In Brazil, too, in 1978, the first LGBT organization of the country, called SOMOS: Group for Homosexual Assertion, became actively involved in struggles against racism and misogyny (Green 2000: 59ff.). More recently, the document prepared for the 10th National Plenary Meeting of the Brazilian labour federation CUT, held from 4 to 7 December 2001 in São Paulo, included a statement by the secretariat of social policy recommending the strengthening of:

> trade union action oriented towards discussion, and the training, organization and mobilization of workers, in order to raise their awareness about homosexual rights and promote respect for different sexual orientations, as well as [the establishment of] partnerships with homosexual organizations, in order to achieve unity of action (CUT 2001: 35).

ALTERNATIVE OR GLOBALIZED EMANCIPATIONS?

The Portuguese LGBT movement is constructed between two different poles, just as happens internationally.[20] On the one hand, there is the gay subculture, or the so-called 'pink industry', involving the consumption of homoerotic products manufactured and diffused through the globalization of supply and demand markets (for example, night entertainment, saunas and tourism).[21] On the other, there is the political movement, which organizes campaigns to end discrimination, promote diversity and defend the right to difference and to the body, among other issues. This fight against discrimination is frequently linked to the struggles of other socially oppressed groups. An example of this is the launch of the project 'Office against Discrimination', in June 1999, proposed by Opus Gay and supported by the Portuguese Deaf Association, amongst others.

Between the two poles, public demonstrations of the LGBT community, on occasions such as the marches, fairs, or film festivals, overflow with symbols which, though globally commercialized, are indissociable from the struggle against discrimination.

How can we thus evaluate the emancipatory potential of this movement with some measure of reliability, dissolved as it is in spaces of consumption and leisure and at the same time involved in struggles for the recognition of rights? In the final part of this essay, I attempt to reply to this question by discussing two key ideas:

(a) within the counterhegemony itself, sexual emancipation, as proposed by the international LGBT movement, is an alternative;
(b) the Portuguese LGBT movement presents socio-historical specificities which distinguish it from the globalized LGBT movement.

Let us first consider the concept of emancipation. The idea of emancipation presupposes the existence of unequal power relations, since, if power were not exercised in an exclusionary way, there would be no need to fight for equal opportunities and rights, for the right to difference or for inclusion. In other words, inequality and exclusion create the necessary conditions (subjection and exploitation) for the emergence of the will for emancipation. This view of sexual emancipation is based on the understanding that 'emancipatory relationships develop within relationships of power, not as the automatic outcome of any essential contradiction, but as created and creative outcomes of created and creative contradictions' (Santos 1995a: 409). This is to say, rather than seek some essence of emancipation, it is necessary to identify paths, seeds, diverse forms and alternatives for the emancipation of individuals and for their empowerment in the struggle against exclusion. Above all, it is important to understand that there is not one but many forms of emancipation and domination. Just as hegemony has many facets, so resistance requires multiple agencies and structures. As Weeks argues (1999: 47):

> These new stories of the 'self', about sexuality and gender, are the context for the emergence of the sexual citizen, because these stories telling of exclusion, through gender, sexuality, race, bodily appearance or function, have as their corollary the demand for inclusion: for equal rights under the law, in politics, in economics, in social matters and in sexual matters.

Movements operating in the area of sexual orientation may, and frequently do, form alliances with other socially discriminated groups in the struggle for racial, political or sexual freedom (Diniz 2001). But individually, each one of these struggles has its specific ambit of oppression and resistance, according to which it defines its goals, strategies, allies and enemies. In the case of the LGBT movement, the struggle is waged against the imposition of the heterosexual model as a norm, which systematically silences and marginalizes thousands of gays, lesbians, transsexuals and bisexuals.

Using the map of structural spaces in contemporary societies proposed by Santos (2000), we can see that the struggle operates on many different fronts. In the domestic sphere, it involves fighting against a patriarchal ideology that constructs and nourishes historically dichotomized stereotypes of male and female roles, which is the basis for the subjection of homosexuality in relation to heterosexuality. The demand for recognition of common-law partnerships, formulated in 1997 by the Portuguese LGBT movement, is related to the need to democratize the domestic space, opening it up to alternative family models.

In the space of production, there is a need to prevent dismissals or the blocking of career advancement because of sexual orientation; a good example of this are the conversations begun in 1999 between the Homosexual Platform (consisting of Opus Gay, ILGA-Portugal, the Women's Group, GTH and the Sappho Club) and the General Confederation of Portuguese Workers (CGTP), the General Union of Workers (UGT) and the Unitary Workers Front, in order to ensure the protection of workers who may be discriminated against because of their sexual orientation.[22]

As regards the market, there is a need to promote spaces for LGBT entertainment, beyond the promotion of the pink industry, and for the diffusion of LGBT symbols such as the pins showing an inverted triangle or rainbow coloured flags. Indeed, this is the only space where awareness of oppression sometimes gives way before the pressure of consumption and mass culture. It should be stressed that the consumption of LGBT products may also be a way of achieving visibility (Bell and Binnie 2000). Therefore, the development of the LGBT market may be a way of deepening political consciousness of oppression and discrimination, without necessarily resulting in alienation from these issues. This is one of the alternative aspects of sexual emancipation within the wider context of counterhegemonic struggle.

Within the community, it involves investing in the maximization of identity and in its legitimation, going against the dominant Judaeo-Christian morality by resisting notions of sin and guilt, and exposing homophobic attitudes amongst the clergy, politicians, and civil society.

The space of citizenship constitutes the legal arena par excellence, where the struggle against discrimination and for legal protection take place. This has been the space privileged by the Portuguese LGBT movement up to now, culminating in March 2001 with parliamentary approval of common-law partnerships between homosexuals.

Finally, there is what Santos calls the worldplace (1995a: 417), where the epistomological form of global culture, human rights and global models of homosexuality are valorized; it is at this level that international LGBT organizations (such as ILGA-Europe, ILGA-World, International Gay and Lesbian Human Rights Commission, and so on) tacitly or explicitly define their symbolic resources and political strategies.

In this global process for sexual emancipation, the main allies have historically been the feminist movement and the black movement: the first because it is the oldest and best organized of the social movements against sexual oppression, and the second because it brings together a group of people who have always been deprived of access to the most basic rights in democracy. In the words of Hugo (1998), a GTH activist, racism and homophobia are two sides of the same coin:

> Gays, lesbians, bisexuals and transsexuals continue to be segregated for challenging the bourgeois model of the family, necessary for the survival of capitalism for the reproduction of the work force; ethnic minorities continue to be exploited as cheap labour with no rights by that same bourgeoisie. In fact, we are all excluded and we have common enemies: the state, which does not recognize our rights, and the extreme right, which preaches against ethnic minorities as much as against homosexuals...

However, despite the collaboration of the three movements (LGBT, feminists and ethnic minorities), the participation of gays and lesbians in feminist and anti-racist organizations has not always been peaceful. In truth, many Portuguese lesbians have accused the feminist movement of using them to fill the rows of the struggle against discrimination at work or for the right to abortion, and sidelining other demands more directly related to the lesbian condition (GM, 1999: 7). In Portuguese lesbigay organizations, there is also the perception that there is a great deal of homophobia amongst ethnic minorities, just as there may be racism within the LGBT community (Hugo, 1998: 6). However, if we compare the LGBT movement with, firstly, the feminist one, and, secondly, with the anti-racist one, it would seem that there is a stronger connection between the homosexual and anti-racist struggles, proved, for example, by the constant presence of the association SOS-Racism at all the Gay Parades held in the country. However, recent initiatives on the part of women's organizations, such as the Women's World March, represent a qualitative leap in the defence of a set of demands shared by Portuguese feminists and lesbians. The participation of feminists in debates organized by lesbigay associations has also increased, as has the joint organization of discussion panels on subjects relating to the body and to gender.

To return to the previously mentioned key notion that, within the counterhegemony itself, the sexual emancipation proposed by the international LGBT movement is an alternative, we can see that its difference resides particularly in the use made of tools supplied by hegemonic globalization (such as the press and internet) and in the maximization of the 'pink' industry and trade as a way of making visible a minority movement. This has been the strategy adopted mainly by LGBT movements in core countries such as the United Kingdom and the United States.

The second key notion has to do with the idiosyncrasies of the Portuguese homosexual movement. If we remember that for almost half a century, Portugal was under a dictatorial regime, which even prohibited the importation of consumer products like Coca Cola, it is easy to understand that the LGBT movement in Portugal, which has only manifested its presence publicly since the 1990s, does not have a wide range of homoerotic products for consumption, since these require a developed market. In truth, the Portuguese pink market, as well as being a very recent phenomenon, is restricted to a few entertainment places (bars, discotheques and saunas, most of which are situated in Lisbon), a bookshop, a hotel, a travel agency, and services supplied by the associations. In addition to circumstances imposed by this recent political past, the Portuguese LGBT movement itself is strongly influenced by the oldest homosexual organization in the country, the Homosexual Working Group (GTH) of the Revolutionary Socialist Party. The GTH, which has been operating since 1991, supports an ideology of liberation traditionally associated with the left, defending racial, sexual and gender equality, and this is reflected in all their public interventions (protests, marches, media interviews, and so on). In an interview given in 1999, Sérgio Vitorino, president of the GTH, stated, on the subject of right-wing homosexual organizations:

> I think these right-wing movements are wrong, and are contradictory, because a right-wing homosexual movement is against the homosexual movement; in my opinion, it defends ideas that prevent us from achieving emancipation. They may be in perfect agreement with us as regards a series of legal discriminations, but they will not agree with us about the reduction of differences between genders, between masculine and feminine, about social inequality between men and women... when we speak of sexual freedom, when we demand sexual education in the schools... (Santos and Fontes 1999).

As Roberts argues, 'gay identity implies legal, civil and human rights, so that one can live one's homosexuality openly, enjoying the same rights of association and relationship as other men and women' (1995: 250). In other words, the right to choose and express a sexual orientation presupposes other rights and freedoms, which in turn lead to others.

The historical development of the LGBT movement shows that, although it began as a minority struggle, it has managed to transform itself into a large-scale expression of the claim to the right to the body and to sexual self-determination. In addition to obtaining rights and protection against discrimination, the Portuguese LGBT movement has frequently been an important ally in campaigns for the liberalization of abortion[23] and in struggles for the introduction of sexual education in schools, against domestic violence and for equality of gender. These alliances reveal the most emancipatory aspect of this fight, since the spectrum of claims encompasses both feminists and anti-racism groups. Thus, it is reasonable to assert that the LGBT cause actively seeks to enlarge human potential, freeing it from the prejudice and oppression that reduce it to a homogeneous model. It is, in sum, a struggle for diversity and, therefore, becomes most effective when it is undertaken by different groups in different circumstances of oppression and exploitation based on gender, race, ethnicity, class, status or sexual orientation. In the words of Serzedelo (2001), president of Opus Gay, 'this struggle is a struggle for democracy, a civic struggle, a moral struggle and a struggle for freedom: freedom for homosexuals and for heterosexuals, because where there are oppressed there are also oppressors'. Sexual emancipation thus bridges the gap with other forms of expansion of rights and liberties, empowering individuals to defend the right to difference without this being equivalent to inferiority. As D'Emilio argues, homosexuals have an important role to play in this respect:

> Already excluded from families as most of us are, we have had to create, for our survival, networks of support that do not depend on the bonds of blood or the licence of the state, but that are freely chosen and nurtured. The building of an 'affectional community' must be as much a part of our political movement, as are campaigns for civil rights. In this way, we may prefigure the shape of personal relationships in a society grounded in equality and justice rather than exploitation and oppression, a society where autonomy and security do not preclude each other but coexist (1996: 270).

The need to collaborate with other exploited and oppressed groups, exposing injustices and inequalities, is in fact the goal of many LGBT organizations at the international level. In 1995, in the context of the vote for Proposition 187, which defended the denial of healthcare, education and social security to illegal immigrants in the United States of America, the National Gay and Lesbian Taskforce publicized its position:

> The current battles against gay rights and immigrants pose a critical question about our country: will our democracy expand to provide rights to an increasingly diverse population, or will it contract to limit rights to only a few? Gay, lesbian, bisexual and transgendered communities must work in alliance with immigrant communities, communities of colour, and other groups to expose the broader agenda of the right, an agenda that attacks basic civil, human, labour, economic and reproductive rights. We must build a solid united front against intolerance to fight for a more inclusive democracy for all (Timoner 1995).

The joint struggle against oppression which discriminates on the basis of sex, ethnicity or sexual orientation is only one of the aspects which brings national LGBT organizations closer to other organizations at the international level. Work carried out collectively by Portuguese LGBT organizations and international NGOs is evident in the case of Amnesty International, for example. Not only did this organization participate in the Homosexual Pride March of 2001, it also set up an LGBT working group in the Portuguese section of Amnesty International, in July of that same year, similar to situations existing in other countries.

As regards the joint work of international and Portuguese LGBT associations, contacts have been made especially at the European level. From 4 to 8 October 2000, at the ILGA-Europe Conference in Bucharest, Romania, representatives from the Portuguese associations ILGA-Portugal and Opus Gay were present. On that occasion, the 2002 ILGA-Europe Conference was scheduled, which will be hosted by Portugal. Branco (2000) has praised the participation of the Portuguese in international discussion forums, emphasizing the importance of the European framework as a source of power vis-à-vis the Portuguese government:

> It is clearly important that Portuguese associations, in liaison with ILGA-Europe and other organizations, create pressure groups operating on the Portuguese state in order to achieve once and for all material equality; that is to say, so all of us can enjoy the same rights without any kind of discrimination, and so that we have a Community of People, a true Social Community.

In March 2000, Kurt Krickler, president of ILGA-Europe, was in Portugal and, in an interview with the magazine *Korpus*, mentioned the importance of the relationship between national and international

LGBT organizations. According to him, the success of LGBT demands at the European level:

> depends upon the strength of the organizations within each individual country, because, in Brussels, it is still the governments of the member states of the European Union that make decisions. If the various national organizations are not strong in their own countries, they will not manage to do anything in Brussels. The success of ILGA-Europe depends upon the success of its national counterparts (Sousa and Mailänder 2000).

The internet homepages of the different national LGBT associations represent another mechanism for the diffusion of activities organized by the LGBT movement in other countries or among international bodies such as the United Nations, the European Union or the European Parliament.[24] This information is also available through *Euroletter*, the monthly electronic newsletter of ILGA-Europe, which publishes news about the development of the legal situation of gays, lesbians, bisexuals and transsexuals in Portugal (http://www.steff.suite.dk/eurolet.htm).

CONCLUSION

The groups and associations that make up the LGBT movement in Portugal have similar goals: the recognition of the civil rights of LGBT people and effective protection against all forms of exclusion. This is why I consider the LGBT struggle to be manifestly counterhegemonic, since exclusion is understood to be an arbitrary process, a result of the hegemonization of a truth discourse, which credibilizes the 'we' through the demonization of the 'other' (Santos 1999). But there are other reasons why it may be considered counterhegemonic, the most obvious of which is the fact that it asserts a sexual orientation that is not shared by the majority, nor defended by the dominant religious, social and political powers.

As I have tried to show, the strategies adopted by the LGBT movement in international and national contexts offer alternatives within the counterhegemonic current itself. In fact, in the struggle for sexual emancipation, the LGBT movement has managed to use the resources made available by globalization to disseminate its ideals, symbols and products.

However, despite the fact that the LBGT culture seems to benefit from the conditions created by the capitalist system, sexual politics operates within the context of a 'bottom-up' form of globalization. In other words, the work undertaken by national LGBT associations is characterized by the establishment of:

> transnational coalitions of social groups victimized by the systems of inequality and exclusion, establishing networks between local, national and transnational associations as the most efficient way of struggling for equality and identity against the logic of capitalist globalization (Santos 1999: 59).

In order for the Portuguese LGBT movement to assume a posture of political and ideological rupture with the heterosexual hegemony, thus constituting an alternative for sexual emancipation, a list of important measures has been drawn up, some of which are already on the national LGBT agenda:

(a) the creation, development and strengthening of networks with other NGOs and social movements;
(b) the preparation of material for training workshops on equality aimed at the sectors of banking, real estate, journalism, law, etc.;
(c) awareness and social information campaigns;
(d) active defence of other subjects, such as sexual education in schools, the right to abortion and the end to domestic violence;
(e) public exposure of cases of discrimination due to sexual orientation;
(f) decentralization of actions in order to fight the isolation of LGBT citizens in rural parts of the country;
(g) assessment studies on the use and application of the law on common-law partnerships and its social impact.

As may be inferred, the LGBT agenda for the next decades must necessarily go beyond merely legal demands, since homophobic attitudes and discrimination do not change by decree.

Given the conservative political trends that have characterized Portuguese society in the last decades, and considering the enduring strength of the Catholic Church, one might wonder how the LGBT movement managed to achieve its (however small) victories, namely the legal approval of the common-law partnerships in 2001. In fact, as I have tried to stress throughout this essay, that represented one single moment of public recognition, and even so it had little impact on the everyday life of the non-heterosexual person, since that law is still awaiting implementation. Nevertheless, it was a highly celebrated achievement and one can only attempt to explain it by linking it to two main factors: on the one hand, the insertion of Portugal into a broader political framework, namely the EU and the Council of Europe, among other European institutions; on the other hand, the strategy of the LGBT movement towards a more diversified and inclusive visibility, which allows for networking and coalition building among several other social struggles. By doing so, the Portuguese LGBT movement found a way out of its inherited lack of social legitimation, and at the same time it mobilized more activists to defend LGBT rights as human rights.

For reasons given above, we may conclude that, while the globalized LGBT movement frequently makes use of the capitalist tools of industry and commerce in order to achieve greater social visibility, Portugal is the stage for an emancipatory and counterhegemonic LGBT movement which has not allied itself to the expansionist and predatory logic of the global gay market. On the contrary, the agenda of the Portuguese LGBT movement includes demands that reflect the need for transversal liberation and self-determination for the whole of society, permitting the creation of links between very diverse associations and movements. Thus, Portuguese LGBT associations have been distinguished by a discourse that actively defends human rights, and which is expressed in practice in the struggle towards a social system that values diversity, in which difference does not mean exclusion and in which the civic participation of gays, lesbians, bisexuals, transsexuals, ethnic minorities and women (the sectors of the population which have most suffered from discrimination in the past) is considered a factor for social, political and cultural enrichment.

NOTES

1. Since the concept 'homosexual' refers to a very restricted universe that does not correspond to the diversity of sexual orientations within the movement, throughout the text I will use the initials LGBT to refer to 'lesbian/gay/bisexual/transgender'.
2. Sérgio Vitorino, president of the Homosexual Working Group (*Grupo de Trabalho Homossexual* – GTH), claimed that 'the relationship between homosexuals is much more than just an economic and financial issue', arguing that common-law partnerships 'presuppose a family setting that a *common economy* does not alone imply' (*Korpus* 14).
3. It is important to remember that the conventional heterosexual model is a cultural product that has been skilfully constructed in order to serve the economic interests of the capitalist system. As Greenberg and Bystrin remind us, 'the resulting ideology of the family called for monogamy, linked sex inextricably with love and procreation, asserted the sexual innocence of children despite prolonged adolescence, and endorsed a sharp sexual division of labour' (1996: 88).
4. See, amongst others, LARG, 1996. Greenberg and Bystrin (1996) identify five factors that relate the advent of the capitalist order with the stigmatization of homosexuality: (a) the intensification of competitiveness at work; (b) the development of an ethos of self-restraint contrary to the expression of sexuality; (c) a sharper sexual division of labour; (d) the strengthening of the ideology of the family; (e) the medical interpretation of deviance.
5. A report on homosexuality in Portugal, carried out in 1998, gives some examples of stories with a less than happy ending. See *Visão*, 24–30 September 1998: 73.

6. Recently posters could be seen on the streets of Chueca with the words 'Assert yourself, consume Gay!'
7. In the same vein, Quiroga (1997: 147) asserts: 'The consumers of capitalist sex are becoming isolated members of a tribal category where sexuality is commercialized in saunas, where the simulacrum of sex leads to alienation'.
8. For a similar phenomenon in the Colombian context, see Villegas and Uprimny (2002).
9. As Rodrigues asserts, 'as conflict and dissatisfaction are inherent to the whole of society, the formation of social movements does not depend upon this type of factors, but upon the material and human resources indispensable for the channelling of discontent and the pursuit of collective aims' (1995: 3–4).
10. Contrary to what is commonly supposed, particularly by outsiders, the revolution for democracy in 1974 did not entail an explosion of a strong workers' movement. In fact, as Estanque notes, Portugal witnessed the emergence of several social movements characterized by their heterogeneity, local dimension, fragmentation, high media visibility and ephemerality (see Estanque 1999).
11. In different contexts, other factors explain the absence of a strong tradition of social movements. In Colombia, for example, violence plays a central role. See Villegas and Uprimny (2002).
12. By 14 May 1998, the deadline for groups of citizens to register with the National Election Committee in order to be entitled to radio and TV spots during the campaign, eight groups had done so: three in favour of decriminalization and five against.
13. This manifesto was characterized by a strong political consciousness identified with the revolutionary left, and it appealed to all citizens to join the struggle against sexual repression, while demanding the introduction of sexual education in schools and the decriminalization of homosexual practice.
14. The 1970s was of course a period of homosexual liberation in the United States of America, which became the stage for a growing sexual diversity, increasingly more public and politicized, and the consolidation of homoerotic culture. It was during this decade that the American Psychiatric Association withdrew homosexuality from its list of mental illnesses, an important moment in the struggle against discrimination.
15. An example were the demonstrations in 1996 against the definition of the terms 'homosexuality' and 'lesbianism' supplied by the *Dictionary of the Portuguese Language* (Porto Editora), or, more recently, the inclusion of homosexuality in the National Classification of Disorders, published in the *Diário da República* (II^{a} Série), on 6 January 1999.
16. In June 1969, a group of police officers invaded the New York bar Stonewall Inn and beat up homosexuals who, for the first time, resisted, which led to a riot. This was the event that kindled the struggle for the homosexual cause in the United States, and since then, 28 June has been marked as the day for the celebration of gay pride worldwide, with marches, candlelit processions, festivals and shows promoting the LGBT movement.
17. On the relationship between the LGBT movements and the political left, see Green (2000). This author has studied the establishment of alliances between the Brazilian LGBT movement, on the one hand, and the trade unions and some sections of the left, on the other, and points out that this relationship was the result of a long process of negotiation that lasted for more than two decades.
18. It is interesting to explore the possibility of an alliance between homo- and heterosexuals within a society that includes all. This is the intention of 'Gay and Straight Alliances', groups of North American public school students, who have, since 1988, joined together to fight against all forms of homophobia (Roxo 2000: 10).
19. On this subject, Santos (1995b: 233) states: 'Obviously, sexual discrimination is not limited to the domestic sphere, nor is it always the result of the exercise of patriarchal power; but it sets, as it were, the matrix that legitimizes other forms of power that produce sexual discrimination'.

20. Thanks to Joan Tronto for drawing my attention to this double aspect.
21. Concerning the growing commercialization of the annual LGBT pride celebrations in the US, Fox (2001) states: 'With the passing of years, the pride celebrations in the country have become more and more commercialized, and are now marketing opportunities for companies that wish to make a profit out of gay consumers'.
22. This dialogue is still in an experimental phase, with as yet no visible alterations on the agendas of these trade union confederations, a fact which has frequently been criticized by the LGBT movement in Portugal. According to Santos (1995b: 222), 'the exposure of new forms of oppression implies the denunciation of emancipatory theories and movements which have ignored, neglected, or even sanctioned them. This implies, therefore, a criticism of Marxism and of the traditional labour movement'.
23. In May 1998, in the newsletter *Zona Livre*, Fabíola Cardoso stated: 'I am a lesbian, but the issue of abortion concerns me directly. It concerns me because I am a woman, and because I would like to see the sun rise on the day when women reclaim some of the rights lost by their ancestors at a dark moment of history' (*Zona Livre*, 5).
24. The sites of ILGA-Portugal, Opus Gay and the Sappho Club are, respectively, http://www.ilga-portugal.org/mapasite.html, http://www.opusgayassociation.com/, and http://www.clubesafo.com.

REFERENCES

Amnesty International (1997): *Breaking the Silence. Human Rights Violations Based on Sexual Orientation*, London: Amnesty International.
Almeida, M.V. de (1997): '*Pontapés na Bola Precizam-se*', *Visão*, 22/05/1997, 98.
Bell, D. and J. Binnie (2000): 'The Love that Dares Not Forget Its Brand Name', in D. Bell and J. Binnie (eds.), *The Sexual Citizen. Queer Politics and Beyond*, Cambridge: Polity Press, pp.97–107.
Branco, L. (2000): 'A União Europeia Social e a Orientação Sexual', *Korpus* 11, p.21.
Central Única de Trabalhadores – CUT (1997): *6° CONCUT: Resoluções e Registros*, São Paulo: Coordenação Nacional do 6° CONCUT.
Central Única de Trabalhadores – CUT (2001): *10ª CUT Plenária Nacional. Texto Base*, 10, São Paulo: Coordenação Nacional da CUT.
D'Emilio, J. (1996): 'Capitalism and Gay Identity', in D. Morton (ed.), *The Material Queer. A LesBiGay Cultural Studies Reader*, Oxford: Westview Press, pp.263–71.
Diniz, G. (2001): 'Um Movimento Aberto', newsletter *Sem Medos!* 9, p.19.
Estanque, E. (1999): 'Acção Colectiva, Comunidade e Movimentos Sociais', *Revista Crítica de Ciências Sociais* 55, pp.85–111.
Ferreira, V. (1981): 'Mulheres, Família e Trabalho Doméstico no Capitalismo', *Revista Crítica de Ciências Sociais* 6, pp.47–86.
Foucault, M. (1994): *A História da Sexualidade – A Vontade de Saber*, Lisbon: Relógio D'Água.
Fox, C. (2001): 'We're Here, We're Queer, We Drink Coors Beer', *The Rocky Mountain Bullhorn Online*, http://www.rockymountainbullhorn.com/PrideFest.html, June 2001.
França, L. (ed.) (1993): *Portugal, Valores Europeus, Identidade Cultural*, Lisbon: Instituto de Estudos para o Desenvolvimento.
Green, J.N. (2000): 'Desire and Militancy: Lesbians, Gays and the Brazilian Workers Party', in P. Drucker (ed.), *Different Rainbows*, London: Gay Men's Press, pp.57–70.
Greenberg, D. and M.H. Bystryn (1996): 'Capitalism, Bureaucracy, Homosexuality', in S. Seidman (ed.), *Queer Theory/Sociology*, Oxford: Blackwell, pp.83–110.
GM – *Grupo de Mulheres* (1999): 'Feminismo e Lesbianismo em Portugal: Uma Luta à Parte?', *Sem Medos!* 4, p.7.
GTH – *Grupo de Trabalho Homossexual* (1991): *Manifesto de Fundação do Grupo de Trabalho Homossexual do Partido Socialista Revolucionário*, Lisbon: GTH/PSR.

Hawkes, G. (1996): *A Sociology of Sex and Sexuality*, Buckingham: Open University Press.
Hugo, (1998): '*As moedas têm duas faces*', *Sem Medos!*, 2, 6.
Joaquim, T. (1998): 'Social Citizenship and Motherhood', in V. Ferreira, T. Tavares and S. Portugal (eds.), *Shifting Bonds, Shifting Bounds. Women, Mobility and Citizenship in Europe*, Oeiras: Celta, pp.77-84.
LARG - Los Angeles Research Group (1996): 'Material Oppression', in D. Morton (ed.), *The Material Queer. A LesBiGay Cultural Studies Reader*, Oxford: Westview Press, pp.349-51.
Mejía, M. (2000): 'Mexican Pink', in P. Drucker (ed.), *Different Rainbows*, London: Gay Men's Press, pp.43-56.
Moreira, V. (1998): '*Lições do Primeiro Referendo*', *Público*, 30/06/1998, 10.
Mott, L. (1987): *Inquisição e Homossexualidade, I Congresso Luso-Brasileiro sobre Inquisição*, Lisbon: Universitária Editora.
Müller, U. (1998): 'The Micropolitics of Gender Difference in Family Life', in V. Ferreira, T. Tavares and S. Portugal (eds.), *Shifting Bonds, Shifting Bounds. Women, Mobility and Citizenship in Europe*, Oeiras: Celta, pp.329-44.
não te prives (2002): *Manifesto*. (*mimeo*). Available upon request to naoteprives@yahoo.com
Osório, C. (2002): 'Poder político e protagonismo feminino', in B.S. Santos (ed.), *Democratizar a Democracia. Os Caminhos da Democracia Participativa*, Rio de Janeiro: Civilização Brasileira, pp.419-51.
Pais, J.M. (ed.) (1998): *Gerações e Valores na Sociedade Portuguesa Contemporânea*, Lisbon: Secretaria de Estado da Juventude.
Praça, A. (1998): '*Cónego Melo Apelo ao Voto*', *Público*, 29 June 1998, 8.
QUEERS, E-mail sent to author in August 2000.
Quiroga, J. (1997): 'Homosexualities in the Tropic of Revolution', in D. Balderston and D.J. Guy (eds.), *Sex and Sexuality in Latin America*, New York: New York University Press, pp.133-51.
Rich, A. (1993): 'Compulsory Heterosexuality and Lesbian Existence', in H. Abelove, M.A. Barale and D.M. Halperin (eds.), *The Lesbian and Gay Studies Reader*, London: Routledge, pp.227-54.
Richards, J. (1990): *Sexo, Desvio e Danação. As Minorias na Idade Média*, Rio de Janeiro: Jorge Zahar Editor.
Roberts, M.W. (1995): 'Emergence of Gay Identity and Gay Social Movements in Developing Countries: The AIDS Crisis as Catalyst', *Alternatives* 20, pp.243-64.
Rodrigues, E. (1995): 'Os Novos Movimentos Sociais e o Associativismo Ambientalista em Portugal', *Oficina do CES*, p.60.
Rodrigues, L.P. (1994): '*Uniões de Facto são Marginais*', *Expresso*, 26/07/1994, 19.
Rodrigues, R. (2000): 'Numa Europa Social os Trabalhadores Não São Só Trabalhadores', paper presented at the *Alternative Summit*, Lisbon, 24 March 2000.
Rodriguez, E. (2000): 'A peseta rosa', *Sem Medos!* 6, pp.8-9.
Rosebloom, R. (1996): *Unspoken Rules*, London: Cassell.
Roxo, J. (2000): 'Alianças Gay-Hetero Contra a Homofobia', *Sem Medos!* 6, p.10.
Santos, A.C. and F. Fontes (1999): 'Descobrindo o Arco-Íris: Identidades Homossexuais em Portugal', BA thesis in Sociology, Faculty of Economics, University of Coimbra.
Santos, A.C. (2002): '*Sexualidades politizadas: o activismo nas áreas da sida e da homossexualidade em Portugal*', *Cadernos de Saúde Pública*. Ministério da Saúde, Brasil. vol. 18, n. 3 (mai-jun 2002): 595-611.
Santos, B. de S. (1992): *O Estado e a Sociedade em Portugal (1974-1988)*, Oporto: Afrontamento.
Santos, B. de S. (1995a): *Towards a New Common Sense. Law, Science and Politics in the Paradigmatic Transition*, London: Routledge.
Santos, B. de S. (1995b): *Pela Mão de Alice. O Social e o Político na Pós-Modernidade*, Oporto: Afrontamento.

Santos, B. de S. (1999): 'A Construção Multicultural da Igualdade e da Diferença', *Oficina do CES*, p.135.
Santos, B. de S. (2000): *A Crítica da Razão Indolente*, Oporto: Afrontamento.
Santos, B. de S. (2001): *A Cor do Tempo Quando Foge*, Oporto: Afrontamento.
Seidman, S. (1997): *Difference Troubles. Queering Social Theory and Sexual Politics*, Cambridge: Cambridge University Press.
Serzedelo, A. and J.M. Cunha (2001): '*Direitos Humanos e Cidadania*', http://www.opusgayassociation.com, April 2001.
Sousa, I. and M. Mailänder (2000): 'Entrevista com o Presidente da ILGA-Europe', *Korpus* 11, pp.20–2.
Stein, A. and K. Plummer (1996): '"I Can't Even Think Straight": "Queer" Theory and the Missing Sexual revolution in Sociology', in S. Seidman (ed.), *Queer Theory/Sociology*, Oxford: Blackwell, pp.129–44.
Tatchell, P. (2001): paper presented at the conference *Encontro Internacional Lutar Amando, Amar Lutando*. Lisbon: GTH, 12–13 May 2001.
Timoner, R. (1995): 'The Costs of Scapegoating: Anti-Immigrant Backlash', *National Gay and Lesbian Taskforce*. http://www.ngltf.org/library/archive.cfm, Nov. 1999.
Uprimny, R. and M.G. Villegas (2002): 'Corte Constitucional y Emancipación Social en Colombia', in B.S. Santos (ed.), *Democratizar a Democracia. Os Caminhos da Democracia Participativa*, Rio de Janeiro: Civilização Brasileira, pp.297–339.
Vala, J., M.V. Cabral and A. Ramos (eds.) (2003): *Valores Sociais: Mudanças e Contrastes em Portugal e na Europa*, Lisbon: Imprensa de Ciências Sociais.
Vitorino, S. (1999): 'A Homossexualidade e a Esquerda – Que Esquerda?', *Sem Medos!*, p.4.
Vitorino, S. (2000): *Intervention in the Debate Formas de Luta do Movimento LGBT*, Lisbon: ILGA-Portugal.
Weeks, J. (1999): 'The Sexual Citizen', in M. Featherstone (ed.), *Love and Eroticism*, London: Sage, pp.35–52.

Who Saved East Timor? New References for International Solidarity

JOSÉ MANUEL PUREZA

All emancipatory struggles begin as struggles for the impossible. The struggle of the Timorese for their self-determination was undoubtedly so. Writing in August 1979, Noam Chomsky stated that:

> the people of East Timor are among the victims of the current phase of Western ideology and practice.... Citizens of the Western democracies may prefer to avert their eyes, permitting their governments to make their essential contribution to the slaughter that continues as Indonesia attempts to reduce what is left of Timor and its people to submission. They also have it within their power to bring these horrifying crimes to a halt (Kohen and Taylor 1979: 11).

The referendum organized by the United Nations in August 1999, in which an overwhelming majority of the Timorese voted for independence, was a very clear sign that sometimes the impossible happens.

This reversal of what seemed to be a definite fate of that insignificant people poses fundamental questions to the dominant readings of international reality. Above all, two crucial questions must be answered. First, is the case of East Timor evidence of such a deep change in the role played by international solidarity that it turns it into a fundamental element within the framework of counterhegemonic globalization? Secondly, has the triumph of this 'impossible' struggle for self-determination established a break with the stabilized legacies of the past, namely the positivist–realist common sense? In order to answer these questions, I shall first analyze the contents of such hegemonic legacies and of the counterhegemonic

---

I would like to thank Alfreda Fonseca, António Barbedo de Magalhães, António Ramos, Boaventura de Sousa Santos, Carlos Gaspar, Fernando Reino, Francisco Louçã, João Gomes Cravinho, Luísa França and Zito Soares for their comments on the preliminary versions of this text, as well as their commitment to the international solidarity movement on behalf of East Timor. I would also like to thank Mónica Rafael for her help in the preparation of this version.

proposals conveyed by alternative discourses at both the legal and political levels. Subsequently, and within this theoretical framework, I will focus on some specific features of the East Timorese case and ask whether it can be taken as evidence of such a paradigmatic shift.

WESTPHALIA AND BEYOND

Richard Falk has called our attention to the fact that the current change in the world order is, in a certain way, symmetrical to the one created by the Westphalia Peace Treaties of 1648. 'The seventeenth century completed a long process of historical movement from nonterritorial guidance toward territorial decentralization, whereas the contemporary transition process seems headed back toward nonterritorial central guidance' (1999: 5). According to the author, the contemporary crisis of that fragmented political and institutional system and the emergence of new forms of transnational authority are evidence of such a symmetry.

Westphalia brought a principle of decentralization to the world institutional order, with its internal and external dimensions. First of all, Westphalia represented the definition of a political structure for each national community. Such dynamic was based on the differentiation between public and private spheres and it has been mainly expressed through the progressive monopolization of the legitimate use of force by central authorities.

The external aspect of the Westphalian legacy is the other side of the coin of imagined national communities. Sovereignty, conceived by Bodin as *summa in cives ac subditos legibusque potestas*, brought with it the idea of a clear contrast between internal and external: monopolization of force by the state within its territory, legitimization of the use of force between states; order and contractual relations within a state, anarchy and war of all against all outside the borders. In order for the national community to be an imagined community, the international community had to be, by definition, unimaginable (Pureza 1998: 35). Within this context, the legacy of Westphalia has essentially been 'a historically specific form of political space: distinct, disjoint and mutually exclusive territorial formations' (Ruggie 1998: 172).

We are now at the heart of a reversal of this Westphalian state-centricity. The so-called post-Westphalian age is essentially a very strong movement (a return?) towards a global nonterritorial political guidance. But the fact that this guidance overcomes the traditional identification of politics with national state boundaries is contradictory.

On the one hand, a new hegemonic combination between the principles of the market and of the state is taking place. Neoliberal globalization is operating through facilitating states, whose main role is to guarantee liberalization, privatization, minimal economic regulation, welfare cuts, reduced expenditures on public goods, tightened fiscal discipline, freer flows of capital, strict controls on organized labour, tax reductions, and unrestricted currency repatriation (Falk 1999: 1). So, the true reality of facilitating states is not so much that of a complete absence of regulatory power, but rather a reorientation of their priorities and a selectively conducted institutional destruction.

On the other hand, an alternative, counterhegemonic, reading of the post-Westphalian order is under construction. I suggest that such an alternative lies in a new strategic mix between a radical cut with state centrism and a reconstruction of the nation states' role. International solidarity has to be reinvented in a way that corresponds to the demands of a contemporary ethos of cosmopolitan democracy. The metaphor of the citizen–pilgrim, used by Richard Falk (1995: 95; 1999: 153), is perhaps the best anticipation of this reinvention. It underlines the major foundation of global citizenship as the contemporary formula of cosmopolitan internationalism: a notion of citizenship based upon the primacy of shared responsibility over individual autonomy and a situated stewardship ethic over an ethic of abstract principles.

Together with the citizen–pilgrim, the militant state is the other metaphor of a counterhegemonic reading of the post-Westphalian era. With this metaphor I wish to illustrate the transfiguration of the traditional concept of sovereignty into the offer of the state as a vehicle of support for some crucial emancipatory struggles taking place in global civil society and led by transnational NGO coalitions. The militant state can be seen as a post-modern sequel to modern compassionate states: 'Post-modern compassionate states would align themselves with progressive social forces in various specific settings and refuse to endorse the discipline of global capital if the results were to produce social, environmental, and spiritual harm' (Falk 1999: 6).

POSITIVISM AND BEYOND

The Westphalian image of the world has been transformed into common sense by the realist discourse on international relations. Realism is a form of positivism, since it assumes an absolute distinction between facts and values, granting absolute primacy to the former over the latter – a 'bias towards objective explanation', according to Frost (1996: 12).

Two main corollaries emerge from this basic equivalence between empirical regularities and normative demands. The first one is the understanding of international politics as mere power politics.

Realism has reduced all intellectual representations of international politics to problem-solving procedures, which means that it accepts the world as it is (and intends to keep it that way), and assumes the existent forms of social relations and power as a pre-established (and untouchable) framework. For realists, the international political landscape is nothing but a struggle amongst different 'national interests': this state-centric obsession of realism condemns the world to remain in an eternal state of nature, each state living in permanent suspicion of all others, with no institutional forms for the monopolization of the use of force (*ni législateur, ni juge, ni gendarme*).

The second corollary is a consequence of this reasoning: all regulation is self-regulation (Starr 1995) and there is no place for a true international law. The denial of a truly effective legal character to international norms results from the positivist belief in a single kind of legal norm: the one that emanates from the state, having the use of *jus imperium* as a final enforcing mechanism. The only kind of legal discourse recognizable for realism is what Austin called 'the sovereign order', meaning a system of prohibitions and sanctions, supported by state coercion.

Since it does not have this guarantee, international law is limited to the role of a contractual basis amongst states – a bric-a-brac, according to Combacau (1986: 86) – and its only use is the legitimization of inter-state practice. That is why Martti Koskenniemi (1989: 40) asserts the primacy of an 'ascending pattern of justification' within the positivist–realist perspective of international law: in fact, order and obligation in international affairs are seen as based upon state behaviour and not upon justice, common interests or any other values.

At this point, the question to be asked is obviously the following: what is the impact of the changes that took place in the Westphalian order on this double legacy of realism–positivism? Most of all, the emergence of a post-Westphalian scenario brings with it the perception of a dualism in international law: power politics and empirical effectiveness are not total realities. International law is also founded upon a 'descending pattern of justification', that is, 'upon justice, common interests, progress, nature of the world community or other similar ideas to which it is common that they are anterior, or superior, to state behaviour, will or interest' (Koskenniemi 1989: 40–41). This means that the post-Westphalian paradigmatic transition in international law is made of two main building blocks: a stronger emphasis on the utopian (counterhegemonic) dimensions of the international legal discourse (mostly visible in areas like the common heritage of humankind, or human rights and peoples' rights), and a break with a narrow vision of legal effectiveness, reinforcing international law's value of symbolic efficacy. Beyond the traditional system of rules, prohibitions and sanctions, there is a post-Westphalian international law whose fundamental feature is the centrality of emancipation of individuals, groups, nations and humankind as a whole.

EAST TIMOR: A POST-POSITIVIST STRUGGLE

The case of East Timor can be analyzed, first of all, as a shift operated in the hegemonic answers given to three main tensions: between *fait accompli* and legitimacy, between geopolitics and legal order and between efficiency and multilateralism. A fundamental legacy of the Timorese struggle for independence is that it has added something to the counterhegemonic elements of these three tensions: legitimacy against *fait accompli*, legal order against geopolitics, and multilateralism against efficiency.

Fait Accompli and Legitimacy

This first tension was experienced within two different historical contexts. The first was that of Portuguese colonial rule. East Timor became a Portuguese colony at the beginning of the sixteenth century. Treaties signed in 1859 and 1904 set the borders between the eastern and western parts of the island, the latter being under Dutch rule and, after its independence in 1949, under Indonesian rule. Having become a member of the United Nations in 1955, Portugal was confronted with the applicability of the UN Charter to its colonial territories (Galvão Teles 1997: 195). Against the establishment of a new standard of international legitimacy founded upon the progressive dynamics of the UN in favour of the self-determination of colonial peoples (the UN General Assembly adopted crucial resolutions concerning this issue at least as early as 1960), the Portuguese colonialist regime claimed alleged historical rights and refused to accept the legal duties resulting from the UN Charter, namely the duty to report on the progress of those territories towards self-determination.

> The argument invoked by the Portuguese government in its defence ... was that Portugal was a multi-continental state to which one could not logically apply Chapter XI of the UN Charter, which recognizes the right to self-determination of colonized peoples. On the other hand, Indonesia, with its policy of non-alignment, had always supported the right to self-determination of the people of East Timor and renounced any claim to the territory (Escarameia 1993: 47).

Having found itself fighting against history, the Portuguese government tried to use effectiveness and time as its main allies.

The Portuguese democratic revolution of 1974 led to a radical change in this strategy. Portugal not only formally adopted the legal doctrine of the United Nations, but in fact embraced the ideology of international public service as a new element of its identity within the international system. The fundamental relevance of anti-colonialism in the struggle against fascism in Portugal explains how naturally this shift was placed at the heart of the new democratic regime. Specifically regarding East Timor, Portugal adopted a law in July 1975 (Law 7/75) that established a decolonization programme for the territory, to be pursued through popular ballot and, in line with the United Nations legal doctrine, offering three choices: independence, integration or free association with a third state. Thus, since then, Portugal has seen itself as having a fresh and genuine legitimacy to demand compliance with the self-determination principle, wherever it was disputed, and most of all (obviously) when referring to its former colonies.

The second historical setting for the above-mentioned tension was the Cold War. Bipolar rivalry was responsible for the acceptance of the Indonesian invasion and occupation of the territory, and of the genocide suffered by the Timorese people. In fact, the illegitimacy of the Indonesian attitude was accepted as a reasonable price to pay for the protection of western interests in the region: the fight against communism in southeast Asia, the passage of nuclear submarines between the Pacific and Indian waters, the vast oil reserves of the Timor Sea, safeguarding the Catholic minority in the world's most populated Muslim state, and so on. (Barbedo Magalhães 1992: 23; Kohen and Taylor 1979: 95). To a large extent, the forgetting of the Timorese question in the Security Council's agenda since 1976 – meaning its absence from the working agenda of the Council since the approval of resolution 389/76, in April of that year – is an obvious sign of such acceptance. Indeed, the Council's 'art of indecision' (Monteiro 2001: 7) for 23 years resulted from a clear consensus between the five permanent members of the Security Council on the strategic interest of a regional power such as Indonesia. The United States formally demonstrated such a priority as early as 1976, when it abstained from voting on the above-mentioned resolution ('a practical veto', as pointed out by António Monteiro). The perception of Indonesia's geopolitical relevance in the fight against communist expansion in the region – one must bear in mind the relevant role that the so-called 'domino theory' played in the analysis of the powers' dynamics in the Cold War scenario – granted it clear support by the United States, the United Kingdom and France.[1] Likewise, the Popular Republic of China did not envisage any attitude that could affront such a relevant Asian ally, especially if that meant supporting the claim of the former European colonizer. Finally, the Soviet Union – despite the fact that Suharto's regime resulted from the violent defeat of the pro-Communist government of Sukarno – acted according to realpolitik's pragmatism: 'Indonesia was (and is) too important within the developing world to be considered an "enemy to be shot"' (Monteiro 2001: 8).

With this tactical forgetting of legitimacy by the international community as a background, Indonesia felt free to use *fait accompli* as its main argument. Benedict Anderson (2000: 5) illustrates this point by sharing some information given to him by a personal friend from the Indonesian intelligence on the eve of the invasion: 'Don't worry. In a few weeks, everything will be over...Besides, time is on our side'. According to Anderson, 'the international community's belief was that sooner or later the Timorese Resistance would be destroyed and the world would accept its annexation by Indonesia, as it had accepted Goa's integration in Nehru's India, 20 years before'. Therefore, according to him, the fundamental question posed by the Timorese case is 'when and why has time moved to the Timorese side?' (Anderson 2000: 6). As such, and although the UN always regarded this annexation as illegal, condemning it in successive resolutions, Suharto's government always resorted to the international community's alleged acquiescence with East Timor's annexation as Indonesia's 27th province.

Against this strategy, the East Timorese struggle for self-determination was always founded on the central role of legitimacy in international relations. Principles and values such as the prohibition of the use of force, the non-recognition of occupation as legitimate grounds for sovereignty, the illegality of colonialism and the right to self-determination were the major axes of the international Resistance and of the mobilization of both non-governmental and diplomatic allies.

Portugal, the United Nations and international solidarity groups always argued that East Timor remained a non-self-governing territory, according to Chapter XI of the UN Charter. This implied that Portugal continued to be the territory's administrative power until Timorese self-determination. Such a stance contested the (weak) Indonesian argument that annexation had been requested by a popular assembly composed by two representatives from each of the 13 Timorese districts (with the exception of Dili, which had three representatives) and by ten leaders appointed by the interim government. The legal legitimacy argument against the *fait accompli* also played a major role in condemning Indonesia's annexation. Most of the authors (Clark 1980; Hannikainen 1988; Cassese 1995) denounced both the non-representativeness of such an assembly and the blatant violation of the Declaration on the Granting of Independence to Colonial Countries and Peoples (Resolution 1541 [XV], 1961), where it is established that integration 'should be the result of the freely expressed wishes of the territory's peoples acting with full knowledge of the change in their status, their wishes having been expressed through informed and democratic processes, impartially conducted and based on universal adult suffrage'. Notwithstanding this, it should be noted that political and diplomatic action followed instead the dictates of realpolitik. In this context, Portugal's sustained effort for self-determination was frequently seen as too strict a policy, incapable of coping with the attempts for a peaceful solution to relieve the Timorese from suffering (Neves 2000: 29). Such arguments found support among some Portuguese political leaders and actually guided the process's diplomatic course of action during the 1980s, as I will discuss below.

The tension between legitimacy and *fait accompli* also explains the contrast between silence and media visibility as fundamental tools for the respective strategies of Indonesia and the Resistance: silence was considered a necessary condition for the successful creation of a *fait accompli*, and led to the closure of the territory to journalists, NGOs and humanitarian aid until 1988–89, as if it were one gigantic concentration camp; the media, as an instrument for raising public awareness on the illegitimate situation in East Timor, was an utmost priority of both the internal Resistance and the solidarity movements. Clearly, both sides tried strategically to convey the idea that knowledge is a form of (non) power.

Geopolitics and Legal Order

East Timor should be considered as one of those 'hard cases' that test the validity of certain theoretical readings of international reality. Against a superficial antagonistic perspective between pragmatism and idealism, the East Timor case has proved that realist cynicism (exclusively based on the rawness of geopolitics, expressed either by indifference towards human suffering or by over-interventionism) and naive legalism (which over-emphasizes the constructive role of formal obligations) are not the only ways to interpret the flow of history (Falk 1998: 81).

Realpolitik and power politics are the major categories of the realist common sense. Within this framework, there can be no case for a 'superfluous people' that inhabits half an island of 19,000 square kilometres in extremely poor conditions. In its turn, the legalistic reading of international politics tends to highlight a formal representation of reality (legal versus illegal) without attending to the facts and realities of power. According to this view, East Timor should be seen as an obvious 'black and white' case of clear non-fulfilment of the basic principles of international law. It should be underlined that there is no inherent conflict between geopolitics and a respect for international law. Falk has clarified this:

> When international law reinforces the political will of dominant states, it is likely to be invoked to support global policy initiatives ... But when a reasonable interpretation of international law inhibits the preferred policies of strong states on matters of high priority, then the law will tend to be cast aside or ignored by its violators (1998: 58).

East Timor brought something new to this traditional understanding: an alternative use of international rules and of geopolitical factors. International law played a crucial role in the emancipation of the Timorese people. Both the already mentioned primary rules and secondary rules (namely the UN resolutions from 1975 to 1982) froze the Indonesian pretensions and kept alive the legal understanding that Portugal would remain as an administrative power until a legitimate act of self-determination had taken place. International norms concerning armed aggression, annexation and military occupation, genocide, torture, basic human rights and sovereignty over natural resources played a major role in denouncing the situation (IPJET 1995). Both the Resistance and the solidarity movements often used such rules as basic instruments for asking the international community to take a position that would be consistent with its ideological discourse on principles and decency. Indeed, it should be emphasized that normative arguments became a truly global discourse on East Timor. As Escarameia (1993: 95) showed, the quest for legal legitimacy was a permanent concern in the UN treatment of the case. Hence, the resolutions approved on this matter either expressly invoke or implicitly place authoritative documents (particularly fundamental declarations or previous resolutions) in a position of hierarchical superiority. This has the effect of associating each decision with some other decision considered to be 'more fundamental', and thus giving added historical and moral legitimacy to each legal step.

But despite the importance of the legal dimension of the case, the truth is that geopolitical factors, broadly speaking, were essential not only to the strategy of Indonesia (as I have mentioned before) but also to the shift from fate to freedom. Portugal's integration into the European Community in 1986, the 'CNN effect' of the Santa Cruz massacre (1991) and the Nobel Peace Prize awarded to José Ramos Horta and Bishop Belo (1996), as well as the combined effect of the democratic transition in Indonesia and the economic crisis of the 'Asian dragons' (from 1997 onwards) were historical opportunities without which legal and political progress would never have occurred. António Monteiro (2001): 5) points out that

> as in similar cases, only the removal of the principal obstacle to any solution different from the mere consecration of the status quo, that is, the fall of the dictator Suharto, opened real perspectives for a solution of that type [a fair, global and internationally acceptable solution for the East Timor case]. Even so, the fact that the possibility of a referendum over independence came so quickly was surprising. Such a fact was only possible due to the sudden change of heart of Suharto's successor in that direction.

Perhaps the major symbol of this alternative use of geopolitical forces was the pressure put on superpowers and international financial institutions (like the International Monetary Fund and the World Bank) to obtain a halt in the destruction of East Timor and the massive killings of its people by the Indonesian army and militias in September 1999, after the public announcement of the referendum results. As John Taylor (1999: 222) summarized it:

> actually it was the whole combination of strategies designed to suspend the sale of arms, associated with the threat of specific economical sanctions, directed towards the restructuring of banking and the debts of the big groups that, in the long run, seems to have pursuaded Habibie, his Cabinet, and the majority of his principal military personalities to accept the entry of a peacekeeping force.

Efficiency and Multilateralism

The legacy of the East Timor case also includes a critique of the recent tendencies towards over-emphasizing efficiency as a criterion for international intervention.

Hopes for a multilateral consolidation of the political and conceptual approaches proposed by Boutros Ghali's *Agenda for Peace* seem to have been totally withered by the latest geopolitical shifts of power, the new security challenges and the impetuous force of neoliberal globalization. What seemed to be a return of the United Nations to its main role in preventing, managing and resolving international conflicts, ended up in the discrediting of the organization's political, financial and operational activities, creating the conditions for unilateralism to take place (Debiel 2000).

The debate on the alleged right to humanitarian intervention is a clear sign of this tendency (Lyons and Mastanduno 1995). Those favouring this 'right' invoke the failure of the classical principle of non-intervention and its gradual replacement by a post-Westphalian right to enforce the accomplishment of basic human rights wherever gross violations occur and the right to use force if needed. Is there anything really new in this proposal? Richard Falk (1998: 87) has expressed this doubt in question form: 'are we dealing mainly with a change in discursive reality such that what has mainly changed is language, not behaviour, with major states still retaining on a behavioural level a discretionary option to use force?' The dynamics created after the end of the Cold War has motivated this suspicion: instead of a move towards collective and institutionalized action, the 1990s have shown 'that the UN will be used ... only when geopolitically useful, especially to provide a 'law-laundering' service, that is, to provide a kind of legitimizing mandate for what is, in its essence, a unilateral, or at best a use of force by a coalition of likeminded states' (Falk 1998: 66).

Now, it should be remembered that this selectivity has been confirmed in several conflicts during the occupation of East Timor by Indonesia. And it should also be underlined that a few months before the dramatic destruction and massacre that followed the referendum, in September 1999, there had been a crucial step in the unilateralist direction: NATO's intervention in former Yugoslavia without any kind of mandate from the Security Council during the Kosovo crisis.

Within this context, the concrete procedure adopted for the creation of an international peace-enforcing force (INTERFET) (Security Council Resolution 1264, 15 September 1999) gave back the primacy to multilateral decision-making structures, introducing a detour in the dominant tendency of the 1990s.

The political price to pay for this option (or imposition?) was undoubtedly very high – although one must always add, as Fernando Neves (2000: 38) reminds us, that 'the price for Indonesian occupation was, and would continue to be, much more intolerable: the destruction of an entire people'. In line with the 5 May Agreement, which incongruously granted complete control of the territory's security to Indonesia, the Security Council immorally stood still after the referendum results were announced and the slaughter of the Timorese by Indonesian military and militia proceeded. The Security Council not only followed unclear formal procedures – promoting informal meetings instead of public debate (Monteiro 2001: 19) – but was also continuously determined not to affront Indonesia. Constantly attempting to persuade Indonesian authorities to act, the Security Council avoided until the last minute the adoption of strong and adequate measures (already suggested by Portugal, Australia, and the Secretary-General himself) to deal with the terrible situation in the field. Supporting this idea, on 2 September 1999, the *Times* quoted a UN spokesman: 'This is an operation on Indonesian soil where Indonesia is fully responsible for security. There is no intention at this time to ask for a change in that. Rather, what we are doing is pressing Indonesia to work harder on securing the environment'.

Whilst passionately describing the 'heated days' of the Timorese issue in the United Nations, António Monteiro unsurprisingly quotes the answer from a member of the US permanent mission with the UN when questioned, in August 1999 on what would be done by Washington and the Security Council if bloodshed were to take place in East Timor: 'Nothing, I'm afraid' (2001: 27). Such confidence was a tragic premonition of what happened in 1999. It seems indisputable today that at the same time that the Indonesian leaders signed the 5 May Agreement, branches of their military – through militia groups like *Besi Merah Puti*, *Aitarak* or *Darah Merah* – started to implement the secret plan *Operasi Sapu Jagad* (Global Clean-up). This operation's objectives were 'to portray East Timor as a territory shattered by civil war, and therefore incapable of self-rule, to sabotage the referendum, and to eliminate the local members of the independence movement' (Taylor 1999: 204). Likewise, it is irrefutable that the systematic killings and destruction perpetrated during the referendum were facilitated both by the security regime set by the New York Agreements and by UNAMET's frailty (241 UN international staff members, 420 volunteers, 280 policemen and 50 military).

The unequivocal results of the popular ballot on 30 August (78.5 per cent for independence) led to the killing of independence supporters from all sectors of the Timorese society, attacks on Catholic Church members and installations, destruction of archives and documents, forced deportation of thousands of Timorese, and the looting and destruction of the territory. As militia leader Eurico Guterres threatened, if the people chose independence, East Timor would become a 'sea of fire'.

In such a situation, similar to ethnic cleansing scenarios in Kosovo or Rwanda, the option for an intervention outside multilateral institutionalism, namely a multinational regional force outside the UN, would have followed the unilateralist actions of the 1990s. In this sense, the legacy of the East Timor case can be seen as encouraging 'a more constitutionally oriented approach to the activities of the Security Council, thereby softening the current impression of its services as a geopolitical rubber-stamp' (Falk 1998: 68). It must be underlined that INTERFET's creation was equally relevant in a substantive way, since it constituted a new step in the international community's new tasks in post-conflict social reconstruction, rather than just a traditional peace-keeping or peace-enforcing operation.

EAST TIMOR: A POST-WESTPHALIAN STRUGGLE

The Timorese struggle for self-determination must be perceived as an important precedent of a post-Westphalian combat for two main reasons: first, East Timor has remained as a topic of the international agenda due to the work of solidarity movements, much more than to the diplomatic initiatives of states and intergovernmental agencies – in this sense, *Timor LoroSae* is a product of pilgrim citizenship; second, the role played by Portugal, the former colonial power, as an ally of the Timorese people and of the solidarity movements, and the articulation between Portuguese diplomacy and these non-governmental actors in crucial areas of this process (human rights diplomacy, Security Council decisions, regional multilateral organizations, Decolonization Committee) raise the question of the applicability of the militant state metaphor to Portugal in this specific case.

The Role of Pilgrim Citizenship

There is nothing new in the use of non-governmental instruments or the establishment of tactical alliances with non-governmental entities for the support of states' interests. Portugal itself had previous experiences in this domain: for example, the use of the Atlanticist lobby in the United States against the policy of Kennedy's administration concerning Portuguese colonialism. Besides, the concrete structure of the solidarity movement in the East Timor case echoed some previous international references, such as the anti-apartheid movement or even the frontist experiences of anti-fascist solidarity and humanitarian assistance movements, and the way these movements took advantage of the growing importance of the media.

But, despite these continuities, there is a major difference: in the case of East Timor, solidarity movements did not play a merely defensive role. On the contrary, they became the most prominent strategic ally of the Resistance, controlling, with the Timorese leaders, the flow and content of information placed on the agenda of the international media and of the worldwide information networks.

There were two different stages in the formation of the movement of solidarity with East Timor. During the first stage, until the end of the 1980s, non-governmental solidarity was fragile, since it faced the indifference of governments and politicians, and was restricted to a few local committees or even to individual initiatives. In Australia, for example, some individual activists – like James Dunn, Robert Wesley Smith or David Scott – were decisive during this period. Apart from Australia, the Portuguese solidarity movement had a crucial importance during this decade, since it served as an intermediary between the local Resistance and the outside world, and simultaneously prevented the Portuguese government from accepting any kind of deal with the Indonesian authorities, as well as from abdicating its responsibilities as an administrative power (see below). In the front line of the Portuguese movements, and in addition to the creation of several committees of support to the RDTL (Democratic Republic of East Timor, unilaterally proclaimed by Fretilin in November 1975), CDPM (Maubere People's Rights Commission) emerged as a leading entity. This Commission was formed to organize a session of the Permanent Tribunal of Peoples, which took place in Lisbon, in June 1980.[2] Its leader, Luísa Teotónio Pereira, had been involved in the activities of CIDAC (Anti-Colonialist Information and Documentation Centre) for a long time. During the 1980s, CDPM served as a privileged (and often exclusive) information platform, bringing information on the factual developments inside the territory (silenced by the closure imposed by Indonesia) to the most important international fora, like the UN and its agencies and human rights organizations. A small example of the importance of this role: in one of the negotiation rounds between Portugal and Indonesia under the auspices of the UN Secretary-General, the Portuguese government, using information provided by CDPM, presented a detailed list of Timorese political prisoners, thus embarrassing the Indonesian representatives, whose report was significantly less detailed.

A second group of initial supporters of the Timorese cause was connected with Christian churches, and especially the Catholic Church. The latter has been the centre of a multiplicity of humanitarian and material aid structures. Having emerged as the only 'official' local institution that defended Timorese cultural specificity and as a pillar of day-to-day resistance to the occupation, the church itself became an organizational structure of the political Resistance. 'The church, the priests and religious people are the three elements that threaten East Timor's integration into Indonesia', peremptorily stated Major Prabowo, Suharto's son-in-law and one of the occupation's military leaders (quoted in Taylor 1993: 300). Indeed, notwithstanding the Vatican's systematic ambiguity – although it has kept Dili's apostolic administration outside the Bishops' conference of Indonesia, it always gave clear priority to the protection of the Indonesian Catholic community, often to the detriment of the Timorese Catholics – the Timorese Church was always at the front line in denouncing human rights violations, demanding a self-determination referendum and preserving the people's identity. Thus, the international solidarity movement had a Catholic (or Christian) dimension, founded both on Christian solidarity and on the commitment of progressive groups to the struggle for human rights. This religious part of the solidarity movement included both small ad hoc groups (like '*A Paz é Possível em Timor Leste*', from Lisbon), national Catholic institutions (like the Catholic Institute of International Relations, from the United Kingdom) and institutionalized international Catholic movements (Pax Christi, Catholic Relief Service or Justice and Peace Commissions, for example).

Finally, a third component of this first stage was that of movements fighting against the Indonesian dictatorship in general terms. Having the public denunciation of massive violations of human rights as one of their priorities, those groups saw in the Timorese situation a concrete expression of the dictatorial and militaristic nature of the Indonesian state. At the top of this last group, we find TAPOL, a permanent body campaigning for the release of Indonesian political prisoners (TAPOL is a contraction of *tahanan politik*, political prisoner). TAPOL was at the root of specialized solidarity movements that emerged in the second stage (from 1991 onwards), like 'Parliamentarians for East Timor', established by Lord Eric Avebury and Ann Clwyd, supporters of TAPOL. Subsequently, Solidamor also acquired much relevance within this third group.

The second stage of the solidarity movement began at the end of the 1980s. The departure point was the Santa Cruz massacre, whose coverage by international media can be considered a turning point in the internationalization of the case. This second stage had three fundamental characteristics. The first was a stronger emphasis on the connection between the Timorese struggle for independence and the domestic struggle of Indonesians for democracy. This factor pushed the solidarity movement towards Asia, namely in countries like the Philippines or Japan. The second characteristic was the worldwide enlargement of the movement, with strong emphasis on the United States, Australia and Japan. Both generalist and specialized groups adopted as their strategy the inclusion of members from all over the world. One example: the International Platform of Jurists for East Timor, founded in Lisbon in November 1991, was directed by an international executive council with members from the Netherlands, Portugal, the United States, Australia, India, Mozambique and Brazil. The third characteristic was the dynamics of coordination between the solidarity groups. This gave rise to several federations of NGOs which focused on the decolonization process of East Timor, human rights and other aspects of life of the people in and from the territory. Two important examples of this tendency are the International Federation for East Timor (IFET) and the Asia Pacific Coalition for East Timor (APCET), itself a member of IFET.

In 1999, IFET had 36 member groups from 21 different countries, like Australia, Canada, Fiji, Sweden, Portugal and the United States. APCET had 23 member groups from 15 countries of that region. This coordination effort went hand in hand with the deepening of the networking methodology of the solidarity movement, at both the international and the national levels (for example, the East Timor Action Network/US), and its global scope was improved by the growing use of e-mail and the internet. It must be stressed that this sudden growth of the solidarity movement, from the 1990s onwards, was anticipated by a fundamental political shift within the Timorese Resistance, which happened between 1983 and 1987. This shift consisted of the gradual replacement of an adversarial understanding of the relations between the different Timorese political factions and parties (like Fretilin and UDT) with the creation of a nationalist unitary front ('*Convergência Nacionalista*', which later became the Timorese Resistance National Council, CNRT), the end of Fretilin as a Marxist–Leninist party and the emergence of Xanana Gusmão as a consensual leader. This led to an increasing support all around the world, from diplomatic channels, states and intergovernmental agencies.

Portugal: A Militant State?

Can a state commit itself to a non-governmental emancipatory struggle? Can a government be an agent of international solidarity in a cause that is not related with strategic geopolitical interests? In other words, can a state be motivated only by genuine solidarity? Does a small state have some 'comparative advantages' concerning this domain when compared to the major powers?

The role played by Portugal in the international solidarity movement with East Timor was fundamental. In fact, for better and for worse, Portugal was the diplomatic vehicle of the Timorese people's will to be self-determined. From the moment of the invasion in 1975 until the referendum in 1999, Portugal led diplomatic efforts to reach a fair and legal solution to the case, denouncing the occupation, the gross and massive violations of basic human rights, and the illegal appropriation of Timorese natural resources.[3] The truth is, however, that the effective involvement of the Portuguese state until 1982 was extremely slight, increasing only in the following years, and becoming progressively stronger from 1986 onwards. John Taylor, one of the most respectable experts of the Timorese case, bluntly affirms that:

> globally, Portuguese foreign policy gave too little, too late. The government's international actions to publicize the situation

in East Timor were usually rhetorical statements, or small thorns in the side of Indonesian diplomacy.... In the years immediately after the invasion, the Portuguese government attempted to renounce its responsibility for political convenience, whilst trying to bury the Timorese case. When this failed, it tried to find an 'honourable solution'. However, it found several difficulties in defending its 'national honour', due to its past actions, its contradictory approach and its 'flexibility' in key areas like self-determination and elections (1993: 329).

Notwithstanding this obvious truth, it is also a fact that the Portuguese position evolved a lot, and that the main forces responsible for this change were both the internal Resistance of the Timorese and the non-governmental solidarity movement. This evolution can be analyzed in four different phases.

The first took place between 1975 and 1982. We could perhaps call it the phase of 'multilateralism as the only way'. The philosophy adopted by Portugal was that the Timorese case did not pit Portugal against Indonesia, but Indonesia against the international community; being so, the United Nations should be confronted with its responsibilities in the case. The truth is that in fact the real actors in the diplomatic arena came to be the African Portuguese-speaking countries (especially Mozambique), which kept the question alive in intergovernmental organizations. José Ramos Horta (1994: 180) is very clear on this matter:

> The five African Portuguese-speaking countries were, from 1975 onwards, the diplomatic back-up of our struggle. Despite their weaknesses and material limitations, they have never denied support to Fretilin .... Without that support, the East Timor issue would have been dropped out of the United Nation's agenda shortly after the invasion.

He underlines the fact that 'between 1976 and 1982, the Portuguese Mission within the United Nations had no input into the drafting of the problem-solving projects for East Timor .... The Portuguese mission was a disinterested, neutral observer. At least, so it seemed' (Horta 1994: 218). The only exception to the Portuguese passivity was Maria de Lourdes Pintasilgo's interventions in the General Assembly, first as prime minister and, later, as special advisor of the Presidency for the Timorese issue, in the beginning of the 1980s.

From 1975 to 1981, the resolutions passed by the UN General Assembly on East Timor showed a growing lack of international political support.[4] As early as 1975, the voting of the resolution led to a strong pessimism: a separate vote on the paragraph stating that it 'strongly condemns the Indonesian military intervention in Portuguese Timor' was demanded, and the result was 59 in favour, 11 against and 55 abstentions. These abstentions came from Arab and western countries, and this, according to Ramos Horta (1994: 184), was interpreted in Jakarta as a 'carte blanche' to continue the process of East Timor's annexation. This means that multilateralization was merely passive, since Portugal showed almost complete lack of capacity for influencing the decisions of the UN.

Having actively participated in the UN follow-up of the Timorese file, António Monteiro describes this phase as follows:

> Indonesia had all the interests on its side and was supported by the most influential members of the international community, who were ready to safeguard their political and economic gains; Portugal (and East Timor) had the principles on their side .... It was a 'stable balance' that in no way burdened the international community. Typical in such situations, the first one to break the balance could be 'punished'. Only this circumstance justified Jakarta's tactic: defending itself from an annual resolution, whilst trying to attract new allies so that with time the issue could be forgotten (2001: 10).

The granting of a mediation mandate to the UN Secretary-General (Resolution 37/30, from 1982) – promoted by Vasco Futscher Pereira, Permanent Portuguese Representative at the UN at this time – is a crucial landmark in the international legal and political battle (Neves 2000: 32). This is even more so if one considers the Security Council's apathy towards the issue, as well as the impossibility of having a consultative opinion from the International Court of Justice on the legality of the Balibó Declaration as an alleged act of self-determination (Horta 1994: 227).

The second phase, from 1982 to 1986, could have 'let's talk' as its motto. Its basic assumption was that Portugal should safeguard a minimal core of values: respect for the fundamental human rights of the Timorese, the presence of Portuguese culture in the territory and the religious identity of the Timorese. The official rhetoric of the Portuguese authorities during this period was that, since humanitarian talks were taking place between Portugal and Indonesia, no external initiatives should disturb them. So, an accord between Indonesia and the Secretary-General established that, from 1983 onwards, the Timorese question was no longer on the agenda of the Fourth UNGA Commission. The consequence was an effective tendency to legitimize the status quo created by Indonesia in the territory.

Meanwhile, a significant victory of the non-governmental solidarity movement had been the creation by the Portuguese Parliament, in 1981, of a Parliamentary Commission on East Timor. A visit of the members of this Commission to Australia and the United Nations helped publicize the fact that Portugal was not fulfilling its responsibilities as the administrative power of East Timor – it was not taking initiatives to support the cause of self-determination and it was not even presenting reports on the situation of the territory to the UN competent bodies. The year of 1986 was decisive in what concerns this gradual acceptance of a *de facto* Indonesian sovereignty in East Timor. In March, Deputy Secretary General Reffendin Ahmed presented a plan by which Portugal would withdraw East Timor from the record of non-autonomous territories in exchange for a set of guarantees by Indonesia concerning the above-mentioned relevant points. In July, the Portuguese State Council rejected this plan, though not without divergent positions. This was not the first time that at the highest level of the Portuguese state an abandonment solution had been considered. In 1983, a government memorandum recommended that a parliamentary mission be sent to East Timor, in order to invoke at a later date the economic development promoted by the occupier as a means to smooth diplomatic relations with Indonesia and accept the annexation (Horta 1994: 277). With the shift in the Portuguese policy regarding East Timor from 1986 onwards, the possibility of making a parliamentary visit was based on very different aims, until it failed in 1991.

The third phase (1986–97) had as its main reference Portugal's *dédoublement fonctionnel*. Portugal became a member of the European Community in 1986 and, under the pressure of the NGO solidarity movement, its new status was used to internationalize, in a sustained manner, the Timorese problem. Regarding this, Anderson (2000: 6) affirms that 'time started to shift from the Indonesian to the Timorese side when Portugal joined the European Community'. According to the author, until then only courtesy explained why the European powers did not recognize the *de jure* Indonesian sovereignty over East Timor. Such a frail motivation allowed these countries, especially the United Kingdom, to promote extremely important arms trade exports and to channel considerable resources into Indonesia. So, 'it was a matter of how long such courtesy would last'. Portugal's accession to the European Community granted it a permanent legal veto against any European attempt to recognize annexation. This was extremely relevant, especially if one considers the other Member States' 'impatience and incomprehension', or even the European Commission's 'vigorous hostility' towards Portuguese stances (Neves 2000: 32).

A significant expression of this new possibility was the common position assumed by the European Union in 1996, acknowledging that whichever solution was found should respect 'the legitimate interests and aspirations of the Timorese people'. This common standpoint, not only joined European countries in a united official perspective regarding the Timorese problem, but also set the basis for the Union's political and negotiating course of action in international fora, such as the UN (Neves 2000: 34).

Portuguese diplomacy – with Rui Quartin-Santos as coordinator of the Timorese file, Fernando Reino as Permanent Representative in New York, advised by Ana Gomes, Francisco Ribeiro Teles and José Júlio Pereira Gomes, Costa Lobo's continuing presence in Geneva, and António Monteiro as coordinator of political foreign affairs – was pushed by the facts to keep on implementing such internationalization strategy: the Pope's visit to the territory (1989), the Santa Cruz massacre (1991), the occupation of the American embassy in Jakarta by Timorese students as President Bill Clinton arrived for the annual APEC meeting (1995), and the Nobel Peace Price awarded to Bishop Belo and Ramos Horta were viewed as challenges to an improved strategic alliance between Portugal and the NGOs. The concrete results were an increased material support to some NGO initiatives and to the diplomatic component of the Timorese Resistance,[5] as well as a better articulation between diplomacy and solidarity (for example, in the Human Rights Commission sessions in Geneva[6]).

This reinforcement of the militant character of Portuguese diplomacy did not merely result in the growing international affirmation of the struggle for independence promoted by the Resistance and by international solidarity. It also meant an intensification of the Indonesian forces' control over and repression inside the territory. The arrest and trial of Xanana Gusmão, in 1992, was the first step in an operation led by 'ninja' groups and the Indonesian military special forces (Kopassus) to identify and 'cleanse' those in favour of independence (Taylor 1999: 197). Hence, the years that followed the Santa Cruz massacre witnessed a radical intensification of positions, and it is within this context that the intensification of Portugal's diplomatic work must be seen.

Finally, the last phase is 'the end of the dragon'. The dramatic financial crisis faced by Indonesia since 1997 and the inherent contradictions of the beginning of a democratic transition process were seized by Portuguese diplomacy as a unique historical opportunity to bind the Indonesian state to a legal compromise, under the auspices of the UN. As Barbedo de Magalhães underlined, 'East Timor has become the major crossroads of the Indonesian transition' (1999: 174).

East Timor's strategic relevance in Indonesian political change was visible both in initiatives from leading Indonesian authorities and in the UN's handling of the process. Indonesian leadership, aware of that relevance, was forced to take the 'impossible step': in January 1999, President Habibie, faced with the international rejection of his proposal for a special autonomous regime for East Timor, announced the invader's willingness to withdraw: 'I shall prove to the world that I can make an important contribution to world peace.... It will roll like a snowball and no one will be able to stop it'. Dewi Fortuna Anwar, presidential advisor for external policy, was even more clear: 'Why should we keep East Timor if it is harming us and the Timorese are miserable with the situation?' (Taylor 1999: 201). On the other hand, talks between Indonesia and Portugal under the auspices of the UN Secretary-General, which since 1983 had been limited to small measures to rebuild trust between the parties (namely, the conducting of humanitarian operations by the International Committee of the Red Cross, the repatriation of some Portuguese nationals, former functionaries of the colonial administration who were still in Timor, and the family reunification of those who had already left the territory), gained a clear momentum from 1997 onwards, with Kofi Annan's appointment as United Nations Secretary-General. Having announced early on his willingness to take an active stance in this matter, Annan quickly nominated a personal representative (Jamsheed Marker from Pakistan) for the East Timor problem. This scenario slowly evolved with the opening of Portuguese and Indonesian interests sections in other countries' diplomatic missions, as well as with the preparatory dynamics for the negotiation of the New York Agreements. Since a rapid transition to independence was already close at hand, in early 1999 Kofi Annan created a contact group to oversee the mediation process, composed of the United States, Japan, Australia, New Zealand, the United Kingdom and Canada.

The New York Agreements,[7] signed on 5 May 1999, were not the object of a consensual evaluation. Above all, it was the frailty (and illegitimacy) of granting Indonesia the exclusive responsibility of guaranteeing security during and after the popular ballot that was denounced as a strategic error. Despite the obvious problems that this solution implied, I stand by Patrícia Galvão Teles's opinion that 'maybe this was the only possible compromise at the time', and that the agreements were 'the fundamental tool that allowed the Timorese to exercise their right to self-determination, even though the price was too high' (1999: 393). Ian Martin, Special Representative of the Secretary-General for the supervision of the popular ballot and Head of the UN Administrative Mission in East Timor, has a similar opinion:

> There is no doubt that the East Timorese people would have been spared another cycle of violence if the popular ballot had taken

place with an international military force mandated to guarantee their security, and the agreements have been criticized for giving the Indonesian police the responsibility of guaranteeing security. But there is also no doubt that any attempt to demand an international security presence would have meant the non-existence of an agreement. A stronger position, from key governments, in the East Timor case, might have, with time, changed such a reality, but the negotiators worked with the prevailing reality at the start of 1999. What is striking is not that the agreements did not contain stronger security measures, but that they were signed at all: the truth is that President Habibie's will to accept the choice of independence had little support, within and outside his own government, and even less within the TNI [the Indonesian armed forces] (Martin 2000: 28).

Once again, Portugal assumed this deal as a reasonable outcome, trusting that, in any event, the international community would act to enforce the fulfilment of the agreement and to ensure respect for the results of the referendum. The massacres of September 1999 challenged this understanding. And, more than ever before, the articulation between the three fundamental pillars of this struggle – the Timorese Resistance, Portuguese diplomacy and the international solidarity movement – was subjected to a crucial test. The fascinating strength of this articulation was globalized by the channels of the global village: the media, information networks, global civil society, and so on. Perhaps better than any academic reasoning, a true and very amusing episode of that September 1999 may metaphorically summarize the importance that this triangle (Resistance, Portugal, NGOs) had in the saving of East Timor. In a massive demonstration before the United States embassy in Lisbon, the Ambassador told the representatives of the demonstrators that the US Administration was ready to assume its responsibilities in favour of the people of East Timor. The reason was the immense mobilization of public opinion all around the world. The Lisbon demonstration was an example of what he was saying, since he had already seen it ... on CNN (and not through the window of the Embassy).

CONCLUSION: WHO WAS SAVED AFTER ALL?*

After 24 years of oppression and ordeal, the people of East Timor were at last able to exercise their right to self-determination. Until independence was formally declared, Timor would remain a non-autonomous territory, since the administrative power of the territory was transferred from Portugal (*de jure* authority) and Indonesia (*de facto* authority) to the United Nations – which created the United Nations Transitory Administration in

East Timor. UNTAET had three main responsibilities: government and public administration, humanitarian and emergency rehabilitation, and military. It had a very wide mandate, including the provision of security and the maintenance of law and order throughout the territory, assistance in the development of civil and social services, as well as ensuring the coordination of humanitarian aid and the support of capacity building for self-government, whilst promoting the establishment of conditions leading to a future sustainable development (Galvão Teles 1999: 420).

Legally speaking, the United Nations had mere non-sovereign administration powers, such as in Western Iran (UNTEA), Cambodia (UNTAC), Eastern Slavonia (UNTAES) or in Kosovo (UNMIK). But the uniqueness of the Timorese contribution to the historical patrimony of international solidarity can also be found in the several questions raised by the mandate's breadth, namely in the question of whether this constituted a crucial precedent in what concerns the United Nations' new tasks in the contemporary world.

Significantly, James Traub qualified UNTAET's mission as 'an exercise in benevolent colonialism' (2000: 75). This sustains Edward Luttwak's provocative hypothesis that, in most cases, UN multilateral interventions aiming at putting a halt to the systematic and massive violation of fundamental human rights 'cannot be mere raids or visitations à la Somalia', but 'must instead lead to the establishment of UN protectorates that can build infrastructures, provide education, and administer all the necessary functions of civil government. Of necessity the duration of these protectorates is more likely to be measured in decades rather than in years' (2000: 62).

Timor can thus be seen as a small-scale rehearsal of new UN tasks, which bring together post-Westphalian motivations (universal protection of human rights) and typically Westphalian views (building the nation-state out of administrative and civil chaos).

This immediately raises two kinds of problems and concerns. First, despite being called benevolent, the colonial attitude is the opposite of emancipatory practice. Testimonies of UNTAET members confirm this reservation. Pedro Bacelar de Vasconcelos, from UNTAET's Political, Constitutional and Electoral Affairs Department, points out that 'the vaguely neocolonial approach, resulting from the marriage between the politically correct American academic and an Indiana Jones attitude in exotic scenarios, gives rise to a gaping inability to understand the Timorese, to get on with them, and to understand what is important for this last lap of transition to independence' (interview in *Público*, 26 December 2000). Another UNTAET high official, Jarat Chopra, asserts that 'the United Nations, in the field, works as if it were in New York. ... Keeping them [the Timorese] from entering the administration was a deliberate strategy of those who wanted to concentrate the maximum number of UN officials in their teams in order to increase their power within the system. Because they think that, if they fail in their mission, that will harm their curriculum. When this becomes the only reason to act, it starts to affect the chain of events' (interview in *Expresso*, 7 July 2001).

There is yet another problem. The increase and time span of UN tasks makes it even more dependent on the financing of states, as well as on their political will to commit to long-term and potentially unproductive expenditures. Now that independence has been formalized, it is quite probable that the principal contributory states of the UN – the ones who have repeatedly expressed their non-availability for the responsibilities in the 'business' of building countries – may demand that the organization's actions be supported by voluntary contributions from (other) interested Member States (Australia and Portugal, in particular) and not by the general budget.

Within this context, a worrying scenario arises: 'There is little constructed capacity. There will be a vacuum between what the Timorese will need and what the Mission will leave them.... The UN will set the elections without having created capacity in East Timor – and then it will leave, leaving disaster behind it' (Jarat Chopra in *Expresso*, 7 July 2001). Who was saved after all?

The Timorese struggle for self-determination added valuable elements to history as an emancipatory narrative. This was at first seen as impossible, then as unlikely and, finally, it happened. Or began to happen. Because emancipation is never a moment, but always a process. Xanana Gusmão, leader of the Timorese Resistance, speaks for this always unachieved ambition:

> The people of East Timor did not simply wish for independence, did not simply fight to have a flag, a hymn, a president and a government. The Timorese people cherished other dreams that they knew could only happen through independence. Only independence would make them active subjects of their own development, both at the collective level and at the level of individual freedoms and citizenship rights. (2000: 39).

NOTES

1. Richard Holbrooke, then deputy Secretary of State for Asia and the Pacific, was, in 1980, a forceful spokesperson for that pragmatic support of Indonesia: 'Indonesia, with a population of 150 million inhabitants, is the fifth most populated nation in the world. It has the largest Muslim population in the world, it is a moderate member of the Non-Aligned Movement – it has a moderate role in OPEC – and occupies a strategic

position along the maritime routes between the Pacific and Indian Oceans. President Suharto and other prominent Indonesian leaders have publicly demanded the liberation of our hostages in Iran. The position of Indonesia in ASEAN is also important and it has played a central role in the support of Thailand ... in the face of Vietnamese destabilization actions in Indochina .... Indonesia is, without any doubt, important for our key allies in the region, especially Japan and Australia. We highly value our relationship of cooperation with Indonesia' (quoted in Horta, 1994: 162). The then Permanent Representative of the US in the UN, Daniel Moynihan, wrote the following on his action concerning East Timor: 'The United States wanted things to run the way they did, and acted in conformity. The State Department wanted the UN to be totally inefficient in whatever action it would take. I have been given this mission and I accomplished it with notable success' (1978: 247).
2. The Permanent Tribunal of Peoples is a non-governmental organization established in 1979 and based on the model of the Bertrand Russell Tribunal on Vietnam and of the 2nd Bertrand Russell Tribunal on Latin America. It has rendered sentences on several cases, namely the Western Sahara (1979) and East Timor (21 June 1980). The latter was the seventh decision or advisory opinion delivered by the Tribunal.
3. Portugal presented a claim against Australia in the International Court of Justice in February 1991, concerning an agreement signed by Australia and Indonesia for the prospecting and exploration of oil deposits in the Timor Sea. In the final decision, delivered in June 1995, the Court declared it lacked the competence to decide on the substantive questions raised by the Portuguese claim.
4. Resolution 3485 (1975): 72 in favour, ten against and 43 abstentions; Resolution 3153 (1976): 68 in favour, 20 against and 49 abstentions; Resolution 3234 (1977): 67 in favour, 26 against and 47 abstentions; Resolution 3339 (1978): 59 in favour, 31 against and 44 abstentions; Resolution 3452 (1979): 62 in favour, 31 against and 45 abstentions; Resolution 3527 (1980): 58 in favour, 35 against and 46 abstentions; Resolution 3650 (1981): 54 in favour, 42 against and 46 abstentions. The final resolution passed by the General Assembly (Resolution 37/30, from 1982) had 50 votes in favour, 46 against and 50 abstentions.
5. Such articulation was not, however, free from serious gaps and omissions. Referring to 1993, José Ramos Horta (1994: 168–9) exemplifies how his appeals for support from the Portuguese state to employ Bruce Cameron, a lobbying specialist in Washington, were ignored by Lisbon. It was the international solidarity movement (*Galeria Nazoni*, *Cooperativa Árvore* and Maubere People's Rights Commission) that paid for such a crucial initiative.
6. The Resistance, both inside the country and outside, had early realized the strategic relevance of international human rights fora for the Timorese fight. It is thus particularly important that the Santa Cruz massacre, in November 1991, happened precisely when the UN Human Rights Commission's representative was in Dili, engaging in dialogue with local authorities.
7. On 5 May 1999, three agreements were signed between Portugal and Indonesia. The first and main one had the fundamental aim of creating a framework so that a genuine act of self-determination could happen in East Timor, through a popular ballot on the status of special autonomy. The second agreement regulated the key aspects of the electoral process (date, calendar, electoral capacity, and so on.). Finally, the agreement on security aimed at defining obligations, mainly on the part of Indonesia, with respect to the guarantee of order during and after the referendum.
* This version was finished in 2001 and therefore did not include several important developments concerning the UN administration of East Timor beyond UNTAET.

REFERENCES

Anderson, B. (2000): 'O tempo está do nosso lado. O colapso do colonialismo indonésio em Timor Leste', *Política Internacional* 3/21, pp.5–16.
Barbedo de Magalhães, A. (1992): *East Timor: Indonesian Occupation and Genocide*, Oporto: Universidade do Porto.
Barbedo de Magalhães, A. (1999): *Timor Leste na encruzilhada da transição indonésia*, Lisbon: Gradiva/Fundação Mário Soares.
Camilleri and J. Falk (1992): *The End of Sovereignty? The Politics of a Shrinking Fragmented World*, Aldershot: Edward Elgar Publishers.
Cassese, A. (1995): *Self-determination of Peoples. A Legal Reappraisal*, Cambridge: Cambridge University Press.
Clark, R. (1980): 'The "Decolonization" of East Timor and the United Nations Norms on Self-determination and Aggression', *Yale Journal of World Public Order* 7, pp.2–44.
Combacau, J. (1986): 'Le droit international: bric-a-brac ou système?', *Annuaire de Philosophie du Droit*.
Commission on Global Governance (1995): *Our Global Neighbourhood*, Oxford: Oxford University Press.
Debiel, T. (2000): 'Strenghtening the United Nations as an Effective World Authority: Cooperative Security versus Hegemonic Crisis Management', *Global Governance* 6, pp.25–41.
Escarameia, P. (1993): *Formation of Concepts in International Law. Subsumption under Self-determination in the Case of East Timor*, Lisboa: Fundação Oriente.
Falk, R. (1989): *Revitalizing International Law*, Ames: Iowa State University Press.
Falk, R. (1995): *On Humane Governance. Toward a New Global Politics*, Pennsylvania: The Pennsylvania State University Press.
Falk, R. (1998): *Law in an Emerging Global Village. A Post-Westphalian Perspective*, Ardsley: Transnational Publishers.
Falk, R. (1999): *Predatory Globalisation. A Critique*, Cambridge: Polity Press.
Frost, M. (1996): *Ethics in International Relations. A Constitutive Theory*, Cambridge: Cambridge University Press.
Galvão Teles, M. (1999): 'As Nações Unidas e a questão de Timor Leste', *Política Internacional* 3/20, 177–91.
Galvão Teles, P. (1997): 'O estatuto jurídico de Timor-Leste: um case-study sobre as relações entre os conceitos de autodeterminação e soberania', *Política Internacional* 1/15/16, pp.193–248.
Galvão Teles, P. (1999): 'Autodeterminação em Timor-Leste: dos acordos de Nova Iorque à consulta popular de 30 de Agosto de 1999', *Documentação & Direito Comparado* 79/80, pp.379–454.
Gusmão, X. (2000): 'O presente e o futuro de Timor-Leste', *Política Internacional* 3/21, pp.39–48.
Hannikainen, L. (1988): *Peremptory Norms (jus cogens) in International Law. Historical Development, Criteria, Present Status*, Helsinki: Lakimiesliiton Kustannus.
Horta, J.R. (1994): *Timor Leste: amanhã em Dili*, Lisboa: Dom Quixote.
IPJET (International Platform of Jurists for East Timor) (1995): *International Law and the Question of East Timor*, London: CIIR/IPJET.
Kohen, A. and J. Taylor (1979): *An Act of Genocide: Indonesia's Invasion of East Timor*, London: Tapol.
Koskenniemi, M. (1989): *From Apology to Utopia. The Structure of International Legal Argument*, Helsínquia: Lakimiesliiton Kustannus.
Lyons, G. and M. Mastanduno (1995): *Beyond Westphalia? State Sovereignty and International Intervention*, Baltimore and London.
Luttwak, E. (2000): 'A regra de Kofi: intervenção humanitária e neocolonialismo', *Política Internacional* 3/21, pp.59–67.

Martin, I. (2000): 'A consulta popular e a Missão das Nações Unidas em Timor Leste', *Primeiras reflexões, Política Internacional* 3/21, pp.17-28.
Monteiro, A. (2001): 'O Conselho de Segurança e a libertação de Timor Leste', *Negócios Estrangeiros* 1, pp.5-39.
Moynihan, D. (1978): *A Dangerous Place*, Boston: Little, Brown and Co.
Neves, F. (2000): 'Timor Leste: processo diplomático', *Política Internacional* 3/21, pp.29-38.
Pureza, J.M. (1998): 'Eternalizing Westphalia? International Law in a Period of Turbulence', *Nação & Defesa* 87, pp.31-48.
Ruggie, J.G. (1998): *Constructing the World Polity. Essays on International Institutionalisation*, London and New York: Routledge.
Starr, H. (1995): 'International Law and International Order', in C. Kegley, Jr. (ed.), *Controversies in International Relations Theory*, New York: St. Martin's Press, pp.299-315.
Taylor, J. (1993): *Timor, a história oculta*, Lisboa: Bertrand Editora.
Taylor, J. (1999): 'A Indonésia e a Transição para a Independência em Timor Leste', *Política Internacional* 3/20, pp.193-225.
Traub, J. (2000): 'Inventing East Timor', *Foreign Affairs* 79/4, pp.74-89.

Portuguese Trade Unionism vis-à-vis the European Works Councils

HERMES AUGUSTO COSTA

INTRODUCTION

Ten years have passed since Council Directive 94/45/EC came into force. On 22 September 1994, this Community law created effective conditions for both the establishment of European Works Councils (EWCs) and the creation of mechanisms for information and consultation of employees in Community-scale companies or groups of companies, that is, companies with at least 1,000 employees within the European Economic Area where at least two different Member States employ a minimum of 150 employees in each of them. This was the first legal mechanism that was passed within the framework of the Protocol on Social Policy to comply with the Agreement on Social Policy, both signed at Maastricht (1992), although the discussions on employees' rights to information and consultation in multinational companies had started in the 1970s and continued during the following decades.[1]

My aim in this text is to present an account of the way the EWCs have been functioning and address especially the question of the participation of Portuguese trade union organizations in this process. I will try to emphasize the potentially emancipatory aspects of the theme under discussion from the social point of view, rather than provide an in-depth discussion of either the articles of the Directive or the contents of the various agreements that have been signed.[2] The first part of this text briefly reviews some of the literature on the relationship between globalization and labour in order to provide a framework for the discussion on the role of the EWCs. The second part highlights the principal emancipatory objectives of the EWCs, although it also identifies

---

I would like to thank Professor Boaventura de Sousa Santos, the director of the project *Reinventing Social Emancipation*, for his insightful comments and suggestions concerning an earlier version of this text. I would also like to thank my colleagues in the project's 'New Labour Internationalism' working group, especially Roberto Véras and Leonardo Mello e Silva, for making our permanent and fruitful dialogue possible.

some of the difficulties associated to them. The third part presents a deeper analysis of the case of Portugal, where EWCs are taking their first steps. On the one hand, I discuss the position of trade union confederations regarding this matter. On the other hand, and based on my fieldwork,[3] I shall argue that the ability to identify obstacles both to the establishment and the operation of EWCs is the first condition for overcoming those same obstacles.

SOME BRIEF COMMENTS ON GLOBALIZATION AND COUNTERHEGEMONIES

One of the questions that can be raised within the context of globalization is the following: Is globalization (especially in its economic dimension) inherently repressive to labour and trade unionism, or, on the contrary, does it contain antirepressive and emancipatory discourses and practices in what concerns trade unionism?

My belief is that both possibilities obtain. On one hand, the multiple destructuring impacts of economic globalization on labour are well known: the destruction of the equilibrium between the production and reproduction of the workforce, the deregulation of the labour markets, the rise in unemployment and job insecurity, the proliferation of precarious employment and employment in the informal sector, the relocation of production, the crisis in trade unionism and the weakening of the bargaining power of unions, and so forth.[4] But, on the other hand, there has been an increase in the number of studies made on the labour movement's strategies of resistance and on transnational responses to this scenario.[5] It is true that, as Munck argues (1999: 20), the 'recognition of the processes and impact of globalization does not lead automatically to a new labour internationalism'. However, globalization provides emancipatory forces with an overall view of the world, thus allowing them to have a better understanding of the connections between civilization and barbarism, and to aspire to the construction of strategies geared towards a civilization of the global society (Waterman 2000a: 136). In addition to highlighting the crisis in the labour movement, globalization 'forces reconsideration of the questions of union identity and the terms of inclusion and exclusion' (DeMartino 1999: 84); furthermore, in the face of the siege on union rights, it provides reasons for doing something, for reacting in an organized and collectively responsible manner (Ewing 2000: 20; Mazur 2000: 86).

It is in this sense that the EWCs point the way towards possible transnational responses by the trade union movement. During its 9th Congress, held in Helsinki, 1999, the largest European trade union organization, the European Trade Union Confederation (ETUC), considered the EWCs as being a 'central element of industrial relations' (CES 1999: 69) and defended the extension of the right to information and to consultation both to employees in all companies, irrespective of their size, and to the public sector (CES 1999: 51). This discourse of struggle for a balance of power between capital and labour reveals a need that is constantly pursued by European trade unions: that of asserting themselves as a counterpower, and as an alternative to the (dominant) power of employers.

According to the ETUC, the 'Europeanization' of industrial relations thus presupposes an 'Europeanization' of trade unionism. Only by means of a strong, independent trade unionism will workers' interests be effectively defended and, as such, will a European system of industrial relations be constructed. The following are some of the steps that should lead towards the attainment of these objectives: a policy of collective bargaining at the European level; the modernization and consolidation of national trade union structures; a progressive 'Europeanization' of trade unions through such measures as the transnational recognition of trade union membership and of the right to protection and services (an aspect which some trade unions have already been able to achieve, namely as a response to the needs of the cross-border mobility of workers). It is especially considering this last objective that the ETUC proposes to create a charter of transnational (mutual) recognition of trade union protection for European workers, whatever their national origin and organization. The mutual recognition of trade union membership among the organizations affiliated to the ETUC would therefore constitute a contribution towards the construction of a European trade union identity (CES 1999 : 71).

These passages of the ETUC discourse – which were reinforced at its 10th Congress, held in Prague, 2003 (ETUC, 2003) – show that there are multiple emancipatory options for European trade unions, as well as other workers' organizations.[6] Therefore, if it is possible to argue, as Santos does (1995: 262–5; 1997: 14–18; 2001), that there is not only one (hegemonic or dominant) globalization, but, rather, globalizations (since there is a whole complex web of economic, social, political, cultural, legal and other processes which cross through each other and are overcrossed by contradictions and unequal evolutions), when one wants to give voice to counter-discourses and one takes the weakest party as the point of reference (as is the case of trade unionism in its relationship with employers), it will also make sense to talk not just about one form of emancipation, but rather of 'emancipations', or distinctive dimensions of emancipation (Laclau 1996: 1–19). Discussing the concept of ideology associated with trade union action, Pasture (1996: 393) argues that trade unionism is faced with the difficulty of producing a counter-discourse that is adequate, efficient and, it is worth adding, singular. Thus, in my view, he is also suggesting the existence of several 'emancipations'. Maybe it would be more correct to talk about different ways of producing emancipation – which derive from the existence of different national traditions of representing workers at the level of the company (be they, for instance, workers' organizations, trade union organizations, or organizations combining joint interests with representatives of the employers) – or even different ways of conceiving emancipation.

There are different ways of organizing emancipatory solutions, and, therefore, the emancipatory priorities of workers' organizations are also different, which makes it difficult to construct linear counterhegemonic discourses and practices. As Santos argues (2001: 75), the progressive and counterhegemonic character of cosmopolitan coalitions is 'intrinsically unstable and problematic'.[7] In fact, the nationality of the parent company (that is, the head company where the EWC is going to be set up) influences the access to information by citizens of other countries (who work in the company's subsidiaries), and can therefore influence and distinguish between the answering capacities of trade unions or workers' organizations in a given multinational.

As I see it, EWCs have both a regulatory aspect and an emancipatory one. They are, on the one hand, the result of a Community piece of legislation and in this sense they can be seen as heirs to a top-down regulation (Miller 1999: 346) which aims to create a transnational information system that is adequate to the transnational structure of Community-scale companies or groups of companies. One could therefore talk about a globalized localism, according to the classification Santos proposes (1995: 263; 1997: 16; 2001: 71), which can be observed in the way a multinational company is in a position that enables it to extend its activities beyond a merely local or national scope. On the other hand, behind the establishment of the EWCs there was also the need to create the possibility of bottom-up action, which leads us back to what the same author calls cosmopolitanism – a term used to describe practices and discourses of resistance (Santos 1995: 246; 1997: 17; 2000: 47–8). Thus, it would be theoretically possible to create the conditions for the existence of a transnational labour organization based on an articulation of actions as a result of the sharing of problems that are common to workers of the same company, even if they are of different nationalities. I believe that this emancipatory feature is the most promising in terms of the possibility of imagining a new labour internationalism (Waterman 1998; 2000b; 2002), especially if it leads to the reassertion of 'social as against individual emancipation, and social being in contrast to an instrumental economic being' (Lambert and Webster 2004: 7, *mimeo*).

The identification and exposure of obstacles to the constitution and operation of EWCs presupposes the existence of a critical standpoint, which leads to processes of collective resistance involving joint labour actions which aim at solving problems reactively – that is why EWCs can be defined as 'reactive institutions of industrial relations' (Miller 1999: 347). Resistance is, thus, the first step to set labour resignation free from the Weberian 'iron cage', that is, from the employers' oppression in which it is often entangled. The corollary of the consolidation of that resistance is the rewards or achievements that may eventually benefit the relations between capital and labour (the central relational axis in the EWC Directive), or the relations between workers and their representative structures within the company. A reflex of problem solving, proposing alternatives can also help anticipate problems, and the Directive does in fact consider the possibility that the workers of a multinational company may have an influence on a decision of the company's central management during the discussion phase preceding the implementation of that same decision. This means, *a priori*, that strategies of anticipation can be collectively designed to maximize the position of those workers and their working conditions within the company, thereby seeking to convert usually defensive practices into active, initiative-taking behaviours.

EWCS: MAIN EMANCIPATORY VIRTUES AND DIFFICULTIES TO BE OVERCOME

The main objective of the Directive is 'to improve the right to information and to consultation of employees in Community-scale undertakings and Community-scale groups of undertakings' (Article 1, no. 1), by putting them in contact with one another (Bushack 1999a: 386). As I mentioned above, this objective applies to all companies within the European Economic Area (EEA) with at least 1,000 employees where at least two different Member States employ a minimum of 150 employees in each of them.[8] Moreover, it also applies to American, Japanese, Australian, South African, or other companies, provided they are situated in the EEA.[9] Table 1 shows how significant is the number of companies covered by Directive by country of ownership: 1,865.

The emerging opportunities offered by the Directive include a policy of granting the right to information – regarding 'transnational questions which significantly affect workers' interests' (Article 6.3 paragraph 3) – and to consultation – 'the exchange of views and establishment of dialogue between employees' representatives and central management or

TABLE 1
EWCS: NUMBER OF COMPANIES COVERED BY DIRECTIVE BY COUNTRY OF OWNERSHIP

Countries	Number
Austria	39
Belgium	57
Denmark	53
Finland	47
France	185
Germany	398
Iceland	
Ireland	40
Italy	57
Liechtenstein	2
Luxembourg	2
Netherlands	122
Norway	19
Portugal	7
Spain	38
Sweden	100
UK	232
Australia	8
Bahrein	1
Switzerland	95
Canada	15
Hong Kong	2
Japan	49
Kuwait	1
Malasia	2
Singapore	2
South Africa	3
South Korea	3
USA	286
TOTAL	**1,865**

Source: Kerckhofs (2002: 33).

any more appropriate level of management' (Article 2.1.f.) – with consultation presupposing more than a mere exchange of opinions or of points of view and more than a mere acquisition of information on decisions that have already been made from 'top-down'. That is, as I mentioned before, the Directive also opens up the possibility of workers influencing a decision of the central management that has not yet been made and is therefore under discussion. One of the examples mentioned by Lecher (1999: 285) illustrates this quite well:

> Group management was planning a clear production relocation of white cap seals production from Hanover to Italy, a move that would have meant making 120 employees in Hanover redundant.

> In the Italian plant involved, which lacked the capacity to step up production and did not plan further investments, this would have made working conditions worse by expanding the third shift and introducing Saturday and Sunday work. When the EWC got wind of this, it sat down with the staff representatives of the firms involved. They formed a working group – one that did not consist of EWC representatives – which embarked on negotiations with group management. These enabled the planned measures to be softened: production in Hanover was reduced by only 10 per cent, and weekend work was prevented in Italy

This example also shows that we are facing what Buschak (1995: 134–5) considers a decisive step towards 'industrial democracy', since the setting up of the EWCs or the creation of an employee information and consultation procedure – with the previous establishment of a 'special negotiating body' (SNB, which defines the EWC's competencies and working conditions) to negotiate with central management – can lead to a different relocation policy (one that avoids confrontation between workers), an active information policy, a strengthening of contacts between the employees' representatives from different companies and the development of social dialogue within the company.

EWCs are the result of an option taken for a model of change and innovation based on social dialogue (Bushack 1996: 3). According to the Directive itself, negotiations between the company's central management and the SNB on the rules governing the setting up of information and consultation procedures should be undertaken 'in a spirit of cooperation' (Article 6.1); the same is true regarding the contacts between central management and the EWC and central management and the employees' representatives within the operation of the EWC and the information and consultation procedure for workers (Article 9). This 'spirit of cooperation' can be understood as an 'expression of political will and not of a legally enforceable obligation' (Simões 1996: 22), although it should also be mentioned that 'Member States shall provide for appropriate measures in the event of failure to comply with this Directive; in particular, they shall ensure that adequate administrative or judicial procedures are available to enable the obligations deriving from this Directive to be enforced' (Article 11.3).

In this respect, I should also mention that Article 7 of the Directive ('Subsidiary Requirements') includes a set of subsidiary prescriptions to be automatically applied regarding the establishment and working of an EWC whenever the negotiations between the SNB and central management are not successful. This article includes a detailed description of the situations in which one may resort to the above-mentioned requirements (Annex of the Directive), while item 2 of the same provisions lays down the following group of questions to which information and consultation may relate; these questions therefore highlight the emancipatory potential of the Directive:

(a) the company's structure;
(b) its economic and financial situation;
(c) the probable development of the business, production, and sales;
(d) the situation and probable trend of employment;
(e) the question of investments;
(f) substantial changes concerning organization;
(g) introduction of new working methods or new production processes;
(h) transfers of production;
(i) mergers, cutbacks or closures of companies, establishments or important parts of establishments;
(j) collective redundancies.

On the other hand, the EWC has a right to be informed of any 'exceptional circumstances affecting the employees' interests to a considerable extent, particularly in the event of relocations, the closure of establishments or undertakings or collective redundancies' (item 3 of the Annex of the Directive).

An important lever for the Directive which has helped put EWCs in motion was provided by the voluntary agreements signed before 22 September 1996, a date after which the negotiation of agreements between the parties became legally established (Article 14). These voluntary agreements allowed workers in multinational companies to gradually become aware of the fact that they were part of a wider and more complex group of companies than that in which they were working; this had the potential of bringing about a deeper involvement of workers in their company's life, as well as a better management of human resources (Savoini, 1995: 247). The fact that some multinational companies had promoted and concluded information and consultation procedures before September 1996 may, after all, have helped to make the relations between labour and management less 'rigid' and, therefore, more adequate to the specificities of the Community-scale company or group of companies concerned. Indeed, the Directive itself encourages 'social partners' to start direct negotiations at company level so as to make the EWC an adequate procedure,[10] and that is the reason why voluntary agreements did not lose their importance after the Directive came into force, although, according to its Article 13, they are not affected by it. It should therefore be remembered that in companies or groups of companies where those agreements are signed, the respective national law regarding their transposition into national legislation does not apply – what is valid is the system stipulated by the agreement, which, to a smaller or greater degree, does not have to comply with the provisions of the Directive.

Although these voluntary agreements are markedly diverse, given the inevitable differences between countries, between sectors of activity, between the size of the workforce, between the dates when the agreements were signed, between the types of trade union intervention, and so on, some recent analyzes (Marginson, Gilman, Jacobi and Krieger 1998; Marginson 1999) of 386 voluntary agreements arrange them according to a standard frame, analyzing such characteristics as the following: the nature of the agreement (date of agreement; employee-side signatories; national law applicable); the form and scope of the EWCs (composition; geographical scope; business structure covered); the role and functions of the EWC; the composition of the EWC (the number and geographical distribution of employee representatives; allocation of seats; selection of employee representatives; external participants); the type of existing select committee; the analysis of EWC meetings; equipment and experts available for the employee side.

In Marginson's view (1999: 265), 'EWCs offer the potential to organize and coordinate employee representatives across different countries around common positions in the face of the growing international integration of production, and accompanying restructuring and rationalization, and eventually to forge common bargaining positions'. What this involves, in fact, as Jane Wills argues (2001: 180), is the creation of transnational horizontal networks of communication among workers, from which trade union responses can be activated and solidarity mechanisms can be implemented. Based on the above-mentioned 386 voluntary agreements,[11]; Lecher (1999: 299), Marginson (1999: 266) and Bushack (1999a: 388; 2000: 169) believe that trade unions seem to be taking advantage of that potential, for they have participated in the process, either as co-signatories or as active elements in the negotiations leading to the conclusion of the agreements in about 75 per cent of the cases. This also reveals the importance 'of the freedom given to social partners in the choice of forms and structures of employee co-determination' (Blanke 1999a: 49).

Table 2 indicates the number of companies that have set up EWCs by countries of ownership. In spite of the fact that the number of EWCs has been growing in the last few years,[12] more than 1,200 still need to be set up in order to reach the number of 1,865 covered by the Directive (according to Table 1). If it is true that 639 companies have set up EWCs

TABLE 2
COMPANIES THAT HAVE SET UP EWCS BY COUNTRY OF OWNERSHIP

Countries	Number
Austria	14
Belgium	28
Denmark	19
Finland	20
France	65
Germany	100
Iceland	
Ireland	5
Italy	20
Liechtenstein	
Luxembourg	2
Netherlands	47
Norway	14
Portugal	
Spain	2
Sweden	43
UK	93
Australia	3
Bahrein	
Switzerland	37
Canada	3
Hong Kong	
Japan	21
Kuwait	
Malasia	
Singapore	
South Africa	1
South Korea	1
USA	101
TOTAL	639

Source: Kerckhofs (2002: 33).

which 'represent over eleven million workers', it is no less true that 'if all the 1,865 firms falling within the scope of the Directive were to comply with provisions, then a further six million workers would be able to exert cross-border influence on the decisions taken by multinationals' (ETUI 2003: 1).

These observations suggest the persistence of some problems regarding the establishment of EWCs. Among the main limitations usually mentioned, the following should be highlighted. Despite the fact that trade unions are ensured a role in many EWCs, there are significant differences regarding the formal capacity of workers' representatives to carry out their roles and build an active European structure (Marginson 1999: 257). The status of EWCs within companies is bound to vary significantly between countries (Streeck 1998: 445), which also explains the fact that the impact of the EWCs is not the same in every country (Pedersini 1998: 16–17; Waddington 2002: 187). EWCs are not truly European institutions, but rather extensions of different national structures for worker information and consultation (Streeck 1998: 445; Miller 1999: 346; 347–8; 351). The voluntary nature of many agreements (signed prior to the deadline laid down in the Directive for the formal establishment of EWCs) has meant that there has not always been room in some of them for renegotiation.[13] The right to training of workers who are members of the EWC has not been duly provided for (Miller and Stirling 1998; Lecher 1999: 299; Bushack 1999a: 389). Although stipulated in the Directive's subsidiary requirements, the rights to information on transfers of production, mergers, acquisitions/takeovers, or collective redundancies are relatively weak (Edwards 1999: 338). Consultation (which presupposes dialogue and the exchange of views between capital and labour) should take place before decision making, although many entrepreneurs do not seem to take it seriously, considering EWCs 'merely as a body that can be used to legitimize decisions that have already been made' (Bushack 1999a: 386–7). The absence or ineffectiveness of consultation may be due 'not only to management unwillingness to consult' workers but also to the 'passive attitude of some EWCs and conflicts of interest between EWC members and between EWCs and national/local consultation processes' (Hall 2003: 6). Beyond merely formal meetings, there are very few meetings of workers' representatives (Wills 2001: 192); the transposition of the Directive into the legislation of the countries to which it applies was made at unequal rhythms (Kerckhofs 1999: 441). Insufficient attention has been devoted to developing the agenda of those EWCs that are in place (Waddington and Kerckhofs 2003: 324). Generally, as a consequence of the EWC's limited scope of action, the 'grail for the international labour movement' – multinational collective bargaining – is surrounded by obstacles (Ramsay 1997: 520–21; 1999: 212).

These difficulties imply the immediate need to review some of the items of the Directive, as is in fact laid down in Article 15. Among the items mentioned by authors who have studied the question as justifying the revision of the Directive and the resultant improvement of its procedures, I would highlight those which reflect trade union concerns: to ensure that information is passed on to employees as early as possible, regularly and in written form; to ensure that the consultation of workers is always carried out early on; to explicitly mention European Industrial Federations (EIFs) as a party to be informed of the composition of the SNB; to ensure that the SNB can be assisted by experts of its choice and that they participate in the negotiations with central management; to introduce effective sanctions in the case of infringement of EWC agreements by the company; to shorten the term of agreement negotiations to a maximum of one year; to give a greater general efficacy to the training of the workers' representatives; to reduce the Directive threshold from 1,000 to 500 workers.[14]

THE PORTUGUESE LEARNING PROCESS

According to Kerchofs (2002: 33), although there are seven companies with central management in Portugal which comply with the Directive's requirements (Table 1), none of them has set up an EWC (Table 2) (interview, CGTP leader, 6 June 2002, p.3), notwithstanding the transposition of the Directive into Portuguese national legislation (Law 40/99, 9 June). According to available CGTP information regarding multinational companies with subsidiaries in Portugal which comply with the Directive's requirements (not including the Portuguese 'parent companies' where there are no EWCs yet), there are 133 such companies, distributed as follows: 13 in food; one in banking; seven in cellulose; one in ceramics; two in commerce; eight in hotels; 18 in electrical industries; 25 in metalwork; 22 in chemicals; 36 in textiles, clothing and footwear. But if we deduct from these 133 companies those where there is no indication of the number of workers (28), as well as the situations where the number of workers is fewer than 150 (11), the total number of EWCs established or in the process of being set up comes to 94 (CGTP 1999a). However, according to the ETUI's European Works Councils Multinationals Database of October 2002, the estimate might be a bit more 'generous'. Thus, from the 1,865 companies covered by the Directive, 366 operate in Portugal, of which 176 set up EWCs (Kerckhofs 2002: 35).

On the other hand, only slightly 'over one hundred workers were elected by the two Portuguese trade union confederations to be members of the EWCs' (*Público* newspaper, 3 August 2000; interview, CGTP leader, 6 June 2002, pp.21–2). Furthermore, Portuguese workers were not called to participate in most of the SNBs which implemented EWC agreements in companies with subsidiaries in Portugal; in fact, they were even excluded from some of the EWCs in operation (Cruz 1999: 38). Thus, it would not be wrong to say that, in Portugal, the institution is still taking its first steps, which gives the Portuguese experience the form of a learning process or, as Lecher (1999: 294) would put it, of a 'still-embryonic condition'. Most of the examples mentioned below refer therefore to an early stage of the establishment of EWCs in Portugal.

The Positioning of the Trade Union Confederations

In my opinion, the position of the main Portuguese trade union confederations – General Confederation of Portuguese Workers (CGTP) and the General Workers' Union (UGT) – regarding the EWCs has, from the beginning, been influenced by three factors:

(a) a fear that delays in transposing the Directive into Portuguese law could become (as it did) a source of problems (Costa 1996: 64–6);
(b) the existence of different trade union policies which reflect, at the transnational level, the historical divergences of these two confederations at the national level (Costa 1999: 11), and, in the end, also influence their opinion regarding the EWCs;
(c) the dilemma between maximizing national representativeness or valorizing transnational affiliation.

I will deal especially with the second and the third factors, not only because there is a close relation between them, but also because they have become particularly important in the Portuguese context.

Concerning the second factor – the existence of some nuances in the CGTP's and UGT's interpretation of EWCs – it should also be mentioned that, since the beginning, the CGTP has adopted an attitude of some prudence concerning the EWCs, admitting that they would hardly avoid arbitrariness in company restructuring processes (CGTP 1995: 2). Moreover, for many of its leaders, the EWCs were not the greatest of achievements of the European trade union movement. In its 9th Congress (December 1999), without minimizing the importance of the EWCs, the CGTP stated that they are 'one of the possible forms of adapting social structures of worker representation to the changes undergone by the economic rules and structures themselves' (CGTP 1999b: 131). The high degree of attention given to the EWCs by the UGT has largely to do with a stronger tradition of inclusion in transnational trade union spaces and organizations, as is proved by its affiliation with the International Confederation of Free Trade Unions (ICFTU), in 1979 and with the ETUC in 1983. This explains the fact that, unlike the CGTP leaders, UGT leaders consider themselves to be much closer to the ETUC's guidelines.

Although the third factor – which points to the duality between national representativeness (at company level) and transnational affiliation – does, to some extent, emerge as a consequence of the second, it is the one which has, in recent years, most markedly influenced Portuguese trade union participation in the establishment of EWCs in companies or groups of companies whose central management is not located in Portugal.

In the face of Directive 94/45/EC, the CGTP certainly gives more importance to its penetration and representativeness within companies, whereas the UGT tends rather to emphasize 'historical achievements', that is, the above-mentioned transnational affiliations.

From a confederationist point of view, it could be said that transnational affiliation is guaranteed for the reason that the UGT and the CGTP are full members of the ETUC, although the process of affiliation of the CGTP was fraught with contradictions (Costa 2000). However, the sectoral level must not be forgotten, and neither must the role performed by the EIFs, which are also member organizations of the ETUC. In my view, the transnational trade union membership provided by the EIFs constitutes a very important condition for access to information and consultation on the part of the workers in Community-scale companies or groups of companies, and it also reinforces the importance of the Directive's transnational clauses. It so happens that the UGT has always congratulated itself on the fact that most of its structures are affiliated to the EIFs: 'With the creation of the EWCs, it becomes increasingly important for trade unions to participate in European Federations. UGT trade unions should therefore promote their affiliation to their respective Industry Federations, with the UGT coordinating and dynamizing the intervention of its trade unions in those structures' (UGT 1996: 47). The CGTP, in its turn, soon regretted the fact that the absence of affiliation to the EIFs of a great number of its sectoral organizations made it impossible for the Portuguese confederation to have a more dynamic position within the EWCs. However, European sectoral affiliation processes on the part of CGTP organizations have been intensifying, one of the most recent examples being the affiliation of the *Federação Intersindical da Metalúrgia, Metalomecânica, Minas, Química, Farmacêutica, Petróleo e Gás* (FEQUIMETAL) with the European Metalworkers' Federation (EMF), one of the most dynamic EIFs in terms of EWC activation.

Notwithstanding the fact that, in the last few years, transnational affiliation has been considered as more important than national representativeness (it should be remembered that the process of concluding an agreement for the setting up of an EWC is as a rule conducted by an EIF), the CGTP has always sought to maximize its position as the most representative confederation of Portuguese workers, as was the case in its 9th Congress. In an interview I made in 1996 with a member of the technical staff of the CGTP from its department for Community affairs, I was told that one of the main assets of the EWCs rested upon the fact that they permitted 'contacts between trade union representatives at a level which is closer to the grassroots, that is, contacts which are not limited to or monopolized by international departments'. This discourse, which clearly reveals the existence of the confederation's 'grassroots vocation', is still very much alive today: 'at the national level, the process of institutionalization of the EWCs, or of information and consultation mechanisms, should be based upon cooperation between the trade union organizations of the sector – representative federations and trade unions – and the existing workers commissions' (CGTP 1999b: 131–2).

This quotation shows how the CGTP is concerned about the role of the main workers' representation structures in Portuguese companies, that is, shop steward committees (which represent the trade unions present in the company) and the workers commissions (CTs, which represent the entire company workforce). Although not as important as they have been in the past,[15] it should be remembered that, as far as information and consultation of workers is concerned, Law 46/79, of 12 September (which creates and regulates the activities of the CTs), stipulates the 'content of the right to information', in Article 23, and, in Article 24, establishes the 'compulsory character of a prior opinion' issued in writing by the workers' commission, concerning a set of acts on the company's situation and activities. This choice of 'preserving' CTs on the part of the CGTP is justified not only by the fact that the trade union confederation claims to be heavily represented within those commissions, but also because it believes that their working logic is important to the establishment of EWCs.

On the contrary, the UGT believes that the future of CTs ought to be re-thought, so that trade unions can become the only representative organizations in companies. This issue was debated during the 8th UGT Congress (May 2000), with UGT positing as its main goal 'to unify UGT trade union structures in companies', since the objective set in the previous Congress (in 1996), that of establishing pro-UGT commissions in the companies, had not been achieved, 'due both to their own inability and resistance on the part of trade unions' (UGT 2000: 111).

It would certainly be an exaggeration to consider that the positions of the two confederations regarding EWCs are diametrically opposed. What we have here is two different conceptions of trade unionism, or different ways of promoting trade union intervention, depending on whether one is dealing with local/national spaces or with transnational spaces. I would say that both confederations are favourable to the existence of EWCs, if only for the reason that they both believe that these institutions may well signify the possibility of gaining a higher degree of bargaining rights within companies. However, the UGT believes trade unions to be the only levers that can give the EWCs a strong transnational dynamics, whereas the CGTP does not see them as an opportunity for maximizing an exclusively trade union logic.

Seeking Emancipation: Obstacles as Generators of Opportunities

After having identified several of the difficulties facing the EWCs, I would now like to turn to those that stand out more visibly in the Portuguese context. I shall be using examples from the metalworking, textile, footwear and clothing sectors[16] to try and describe the signs of resistance from Portuguese trade unionism. Each of the obstacles identified (and presented as a topic) includes germs of resistance that can help overcome those very obstacles.

The choice of representatives for the EWC: This has been one of the topics which Portuguese trade union leaders have denounced more often and vigorously, and it has to do both with the election of representatives for the EWC and with their participation in the preparatory stage (setting up the SNB). To be rigorous, EWCs should be composed exclusively of employee representatives, although their forms of organization within the company may vary from country to country.[17] What is denounced in concrete terms is some situations where 'the company's personnel management have organized the appointment of some employees who have been accepted as members of the EWC, thereby preventing the participation of the true representatives' (Silva 1998: 5). A situation like this, which involved Portuguese subsidiaries of companies whose central management is situated outside Portugal, did occur in the Ecco Let multinational (footwear) in the preparatory phase of negotiations for the establishment of an EWC in that sector. In 1996, the trade union structures of Ecco Portuguesa began to take the first steps towards the selection of their two workers' representatives, a number calculated on the basis of the total workforce of the multinational. However, the Portuguese Federation of Textiles, Wool, Clothing, Footwear, and Leather Workers Trade Unions (FESETE), which coordinates the trade union activity in the sector, was, after a previous consultation, informed by the European Federation of the Sector, the European Trade Union Federation: Textiles, Clothing, and Leather (ETUF-TCL), of the existence of possible irregularities. The 'alert' was given by the secretary of ETUF-TCL himself in the following terms:

Brussels, October 22, 1996,

Dear Colleagues, we have contacted, as requested, our Danish colleagues concerning the above-mentioned multinational.

> We have just received a short laconic text from the Danish which points out that an agreement was concluded on September 21, 1996, between A/S Ecco Let Sko/Denmark and Ecco Let/Portugal, aiming at informing the workers, and creating a common view regarding decisions with an impact on the different EU countries. The text states that 'the agreement aims to inform and create a common view among all workers in the individual companies of the group so that the entire workforce is given the same information and can benefit from the same opportunities to make themselves heard regarding decisions taken by either the Group or by the individual company'.
>
> Unfortunately, we haven't been able to get the text of the agreement, and we wonder whether there is something else beyond that paragraph.
>
> The paragraph is signed (on behalf of Portugal) by Carolina Santos (Staff representative), Jan W. Hoeg (Staff representative of the Supervisory Board in A/S Eccolet Sko), Michael Vestergaard (Staff representative of the Supervisory Board in A/S Eccolet Sko), and Anne Mette Cristensen (Staff representative of the Supervisory Board in A/S Eccolet Sko).
>
> Can you tell us who the signatories are? Are they workers, shop stewards, employers?
>
> We thank you in advance for your reply. With brotherly greetings,
>
> Patrick Itschert

The content of this letter shows how concerned ETUF-TCL was in finding out the truth about the election of the workers' representatives on the Portuguese side. This trade union solidarity action towards the workers of the company's subsidiary in Portugal was promoted by the Danish trade union of the sector in the parent company (the trade union that called the attention of ETUF-TCL to the existing irregularity), while it also exerted a strong pressure upon the central management (interview, Footwear Trade Union/CGTP leader, 15 February 2000, p.8). The exchange between the Danish and the Portuguese leather/footwear trade unions was intensified with a view to definitively solving the manipulation of identities carried out by the Portuguese management of Ecco Let.

Bredebro, June 9, 1997

Dear Friends!

First of all, we will thank you for our little trip around Portugal to look at Ecco Portugal .... We hope that it was just the beginning of a long and good talk between our two Unions and the two Ecco factories in Portugal and Denmark.

I have talked with the people at Ecco Denmark, and they are also very happy that it now seems to be succeeding, that our two factories are going to talk together, and learn about each other.

We have been talking a lot about what we heard and saw at Ecco Portugal. And we are sure that it is very good and necessary that we are going to start the project about EWCs. Carolina Santos is the person who has signed the EWC contract on the part of the workers. Who is she?

The Union here in Denmark will now make a contact with Patrick in Brussels, so that he can try to get the money for starting the project ...

Good Luck!

Med Venlig Hilsen

Finn P. Hansen

This letter was, if we can put it that way, the culminating point of an impasse that lasted more than a year. The company workers were thus able to get the annulment of the 'agreement' that had been signed by illegitimate workers' representatives, and a democratic election was consequently held. 'After all the pressure and after the agreement was denounced, the company finally caved in. The old agreement was torn up and a new one was signed in December 1998' (interview, Footwear Trade Union/CGTP leader, 30 March 2000, p.6). This example shows how transnational trade union solidarity actions were able to transform an obstacle into an emancipatory opportunity. However, one should not forget that the question was not only one of choosing someone whom the workers could identify with, but also the transparency of the entire process. In fact, even when an EWC is located in another Member State, the Portuguese Ministry of Labour and Solidarity should be informed of the identity of the Portuguese members, as well as of the countries of origin, as is established in no. 2 of Article 14 of the Portuguese law (Law 40/99).

A competitive logic in trade union action: As mentioned at the start of this part of the essay, this topic has marked the system of labour relations for the last 25 years (Ferreira and Costa 1998/99: 146). Although the above-mentioned case of the selection of a workers' representative for the EWC in the footwear sector did not particularly evince competitiveness between the UGT and the CGTP trade unions, a tense relationship between them is not infrequent, especially in cases where both are represented in the same multinational and there is an odd number of eligible Portuguese representatives. However, and although it may seem paradoxical, it is perhaps an exaggeration to speak of insurmountable obstacles, especially because trade union pluralism has become a structural feature with which Portuguese trade unionists have learned to live. In this sense, it might be better to speak of tolerable difficulties instead. In truth, the above-mentioned duality between national representativeness and transnational affiliation can simultaneously constitute both an obstacle and an opportunity, depending on trade union perspectives, the protagonists involved or even the timing of trade union actions.

In a long interview I conducted with a former Portuguese representative elected to the FAG Kugelfisher Group EWC[18] (a multinational company of the metalworking sector with its head office in Germany), I could verify, for example, that she had been elected as a member of the UGT trade union of the Portuguese subsidiary of the company ROL, Rolamentos Portugueses SA. Although it represented only a small share of all trade union members in the company (about 20 per cent), that trade union was affiliated to the EIF of the sector, the EMF (the organization that had started the process of establishing the FAG EWC). However, practically all of the workers recognized her legitimacy as their representative, both for her personal skills (namely in interpersonal relations) and for her abilities (she was fluent in both spoken and written German): 'even those who were members of the other trade union voted for me as the company's representative' (interview, p.8). In a communiqué addressed to the workers and issued shortly before the agreement concerning the establishment of the FAG Group EWC was signed, she said:

> Following the work begun in Brussels regarding the establishment of the FAG Group EWC, for which the creation of an SNB was proposed, this is to inform you that my appointment as representative of the ROL, Rolamentos Portugueses workers was

accepted, after the presentation of results from the referendum held on March 8, 1995.

To continue the process, a meeting will be held in Schweinfurt on April 5 and 6, 1995 with some colleagues (German, Austrian, Italian and Portuguese), as well as a meeting with the FAG Central Management. One of the aims of this meeting is to obtain better cooperation, and the exercise of the right to information and consultation on the part of the FAG Group workers, looking forward to a climate of social conciliation where everyone can enjoy a feeling of fulfilment both in professional and in human terms.

I would like to take this opportunity to thank all of you for your trust, hoping to be able to count also on your active and constructive collaboration with all suggestions you may find relevant. I shall be at your disposal for that.

Your colleague

M. Fátima Gomes

Caldas da Rainha, March 31, 1995

This example shows how, even in a context (which still persists) of competitiveness between trade unions in the same company, it was possible to overcome this difficulty by enabling the election of a representative who was a member of a trade union which represented only a minority of the workers.[19] It is clear enough that this topic is closely related to the first (the choice of representatives for the EWC), although there is one difference: whereas, in the previous case, the choice of the representative was the result of employer manipulation, here it was the object of trade union manipulation which, although it did not obstruct the election, certainly influenced it.

Another important challenge that stems from competitiveness among trade unions is the overcoming of the distance between union leaders and the rank and file, which can be present even in the EWCs modus operandi. And, curiously enough, distrust regarding trade union leaders can exist not only towards the representatives elected by the rival trade union, which would be 'natural' (although it did not happen, as we saw, in the example above), but also towards those elected by the same union.

> People ask, 'What's the aim of that individual there, what does he want?' And even when he belongs to the same union, they still want to know, 'what's his intention?' Some days ago, I happened to hear a comment regarding labour problems and these representatives: 'nowadays, the Portuguese are not involved, or they don't want to be involved, in the problems that exist in their work field'. They go to work in the company, the factory, the shop, the office, they work their hours and don't want to meddle with other problems. However, if someone comes up with different ideas, wishing to solve concrete problems in a different way, and even to gain some benefits, people become suspicious; they are not interested, and they just don't adhere.[20]

This suspiciousness – which also extends in some measure to the role and functions of the trade union – is sometimes accompanied by a lack of interest in labour participation at company level. I will now examine this other obstacle to the operation of the EWCs.

A weak culture of participation at company level: As is generally recognized by trade union organizations, workers' participation is lower at company level, a situation which is even more apparent when compared with the European reality (UGT 2000: 87; Cristovam and Casinhas 1988: 4; Pedersini 1998: 16). The low level of labour participation sometimes goes hand in hand with a culture of subjection that is certainly a remnant of the dictatorship under which Portugal lived during almost half of the twentieth century, and that trade union law (DL 251-B/75), passed soon after democracy was restored in 1974, has not yet been able to really erase it (Estanque 2000; 2004).

In an attempt to overcome this obstacle – a mixture of weak participation and strong subjection – the ROL Portuguesa workers decided to take advantage of the process of establishing an EWC to create a similar structure in the Portuguese subsidiary company, also because there were no CTs in the company:

> Comuniqué. Subject: setting up the 'ROL Works Council'
>
> With the aim of creating the conditions for the establishment of a dialogue between the parties, employers and employees, it becomes necessary to set up an interlocutory body. This need is emphasized in the EWC agreement. The existence of dialogue between the parties, employer/employee, is a recognized basic condition for the resolution of employee problems as well as some management problems on the part of the employers.

> The legal interlocutory organ representing employers is their internal organization in the company, which we would like to call '*Conselho de Empresa ROL*' (CER da ROL – ROL Works Council), similar to the one which is being set up at the level of FAG in Europe. For the establishment of the ROL Works Council, we are counting on the invaluable collaboration of our colleagues in the FAG collaborators council, of the EMF, and of the *Sindicato dos Metalúrgicos e Afins* (Metalwork and Similar Activities Trade Union). We do hope we can also count on the collaboration of the Sindicato dos Metalúrgicos and its members, ROL workers. ...
>
> The Signatories, M. Fátima Gomes and Luís Ferreira.
>
> Caldas da Rainha, May 15, 1995

However, since the ROL Works Council was established (May 1995), their relationship with the local management of the company has not been easy, as I could gather from some statements and documents I collected. In this sense, the importance of the FAG Group EWC and of the meetings between the Portuguese representatives and those of other countries (namely the German ones) had to do with the fact that they would open up the way to an externally more active attitude of participation, as a way of compensating for internal limitations[21] which the ROL Works Council could not solve. In a congress held in December 1996 between the EWC representatives and the representatives of the different works councils of all factories with main offices in Germany, it was possible to see that there was a will to participate, a refusal to be left out, as the following communiqué to the ROL workers clearly demonstrates:

> Communiqué. Dear Colleagues.
>
> As announced, the annual meeting of the EWC took place in Bad Kissigen, Germany, on December 11 and 12, 1996, and, for the first time, there was a meeting with the other European representatives .... In the Congress between EWC/Europe and the representatives of the Councils of the different companies headquartered in Germany there was a discussion and a general presentation of ideas and problems affecting the community in general and in this case the European workers' community in its different fields.
>
> In this Congress, participants were generally interested in learning how labour relations in the different countries worked, and

obviously also in Portugal and in ROL. After having briefly described the position of ROL-Portugal at the level of the FAG Group, I explained how we wish to be recognized as valid human beings, capable of an ever growing commitment, thus contributing to the prosperous continuation of the Consortium, in the hope of having our efforts rewarded both in terms of material and social conditions, so as to be able to build a society without frontiers ....

The ROL-Portugal representative. M. Fátima Gomes.

Caldas da Rainha, December 15, 1996

The passage quoted shows how EWCs can promote a wider and more shared reflection on the tensions between capital and labour, as they offer a higher degree of freedom of expression and, therefore, the opportunity to denounce and discuss problems. Consequently, this became clear in the expression of some of the claims presented to the EWC: 'if a social Europe is what is wanted, why don't you start sharing some of the benefits you have here in Germany with countries like Portugal, Hungary, or Korea? We Portuguese wish that the Portuguese company was not treated as if it were a stepchild, but rather like another daughter of FAG's, because we have belonged to FAG for 30 years now!' It was also clear in the procurement of benefits, for the external influence of the 'German model' – consisting of 'people with a high level of education, knowledge and experience, with the proper qualifications to belong to a body like this and the ability to negotiate' – led to a 'change regarding the way people are treated' internally (that is, in the Portuguese company).[22]

The utilitarian significance given to the EWCs: This obstacle is not really a question of how the EWCs work, for these institutions are not in fact guided by objectives related to salary increases. However, the inequality in wage rates of Portuguese workers, when compared with the EU average (Hoffmann and Mermet 2000: 92), made them start to regard the EWCs as a mechanism for obtaining better wages. In reality, 'people wanted to improve their economic situation, that is, to earn as much as their colleagues in Germany, because we also produce with quality'. Therefore, 'the lack of solidarity or the tendency towards some form of self-centredness are also a consequence of people's feelings of insecurity regarding their jobs, their low income levels, their poor education, their lack of knowledge, their many handicaps. People say, "the Germans earn much more than we do, and so they can afford a reduction of their salaries because they will live all the same, and live comfortably, won't they, but not us!"²³

The Portuguese trade union answer for this 'non-obstacle' has taken the form of a progressive commitment to the reinforcement of trade union training policies. Being an educational tool, training is also a form of being better informed about different subjects and of being able to discuss them in a deeper and more diversified manner, thus reinforcing the workers' critical awareness: 'nowadays, training calls things into question, nowadays, training asks questions, it debates ideas that may all be called into question' (interview, CGTP official, 23 May 2000, p.7). In other words, in spite of how fair the claim for better wages may be considered, 'in trade union training, workers and trade union staff are encouraged to doubt, to analyze, to express their disagreement and to protest, and to know why they are doing it ... thus improving their resistance against the status quo'. Furthermore, 'trade union action increasingly takes the form of reasoning and proposal presentation; intelligence is more necessary than muscle if you are to win' (Garrido 1999: 63; 64). This investment in trade union training constitutes a challenge to trade unionism in general, regardless of the type of action being considered. In the case of the EWCs, training constitutes the necessary substratum for the development of 'an internationalist awareness and perspective. Trade union training that is capable of incorporating international relations into daily practice is an indispensable condition for the development of trade union action grounded in solidarity among workers worldwide' (Barbosa 2000: 8).

Delay in the transposition of the Directive into national law: From the trade union point of view, and following the spirit of the Directive, this was an important point, since an EWC could only be established in a company with central management located in Portugal after the promulgation of appropriate national legislation. The way Portuguese trade union organizations tried to overcome this obstacle was by participating in the discussions held in the *Conselho Económico e Social* (CES-P – Economic and Social Council – a body which includes the government, entrepreneurs, trade unions, and other organization (social solidarity institutions, universities, associations for environmental preservation and so on), as well as by internally analyzing and discussing the content of the proposed legislation. While the UGT proposed that the issue be included in the Short Term Agreement on Social Concertation, celebrated in 1996, the CGTP, which did not subscribe to the agreement, believed that the legislative draft on that matter should be discussed in a wider forum, the *Assembleia da República* (the Portuguese Parliament)

(Cristovam and Casinhas 1998: 1; interview, CGTP leader, 23 May 2000, p.2). Although 'the lack of large scale companies[24] and the lack of practice in participating at the company level' (Cristovam and Casinhas 1998: 4) could partly explain the delay in the transposition of the Directive, this process is no longer an obstacle, because a law is already in force.

For Cristovam (1999b: 3), the transposition of the Directive into the Portuguese law was an important moment for the country's system of industrial relations, because it was 'a first step toward regulating the information and consultation process in Portugal'. In the near future, the fight of Portuguese trade unionism will therefore be directed toward the concrete enforcement of the law and toward the election of workers' representatives in the few Portuguese parent companies (seven according to Table 1) which comply with the Directive's requirements.

The variety of the examples selected[25] clearly illustrates how Portuguese trade unionists do not posit one single obstacle as their point of reference. In truth, the figure of the oppressor may coincide with that of the traditional employer, but it can also be the Portuguese state or state institutions (with historically adverse traditions of industrial relations), or even trade unionism itself. But as I have tried to demonstrate, it has been possible in most cases to react or to create the conditions for reacting against adversity. When that does happen, there are more chances to obtain a reward. From among the main achievements made possible for the Portuguese workers by the EWCs, I would emphasize the following: to be able to share problems of a national scope at a transnational level (in a wider forum) so as to try and seek joint solutions for them; to have a more concrete understanding of the type of involvement manifested by the workers of the same multinational, albeit of different countries, regarding the EWCs; to know the labour realities of other countries better, ensuring better communication and more visibility among all the workers of the same multinational; to learn about the trade union action strategies of the country of the parent company regarding the trade unions of the countries of the subsidiaries, thereby testing the transnational effectiveness of trade union solidarity; to allow access to initiatives or to information which are not limited to a pure model of company management, and so on.

CONCLUSION

The current process of revision of Directive 94/45/EC presents a good opportunity to improve the efficacy of the 'ambassadors of a Social Europe' (Platzer, Rüb and Weiner 2001: 92). Despite the opposition of the European employers (UNICE), 'the review of the Directive has become a prerequisite for positive and successful work by the EWCs still to be created' (Bushack 2000: 165). It is therefore worthwhile to continue believing that EWCs constitute a central element in the building of a 'European-level industrial relations system' and of a social policy in general (Pedersini 1998: 18; Hoffmann 2000: 652; Kowalsky 2000: 43–4; Hyman 2001: 175; Rehfeldt 2001: 346), and an open way for the development of common understandings and for the construction of a common strategic agenda (Hyman 2000: 3). According to the ETUC, the EWCs 'are not only an important instrument for information and consultation with the management of multinational firms', but they are also 'in a position to develop effective cross-border solidarity actions thanks to which unilateral corporate decisions have been successfully challenged and compelled to incorporate interests of the workforce' (ETUC 2003: 31).

Because of its importance, the European EWC experience has in fact served as a reference for the MERCOSUR (Barbosa 2000: 8) through the first MERCOSUR Collective Contract (mentioned earlier), which in one of its items contemplates the exchange of information between capital and labour in that company. Furthermore, the progressive establishment of World Works Councils (WWCs), already in existence in companies like Danone, VW, SKF, among others, is the corollary of EWC experiences (Steiert 2001: 122–6; Kerckhofs and Cox 2002: 161–3). Meanwhile, other legislative initiatives concerning workers' consultation and information have taken place. These initiatives can be seen not only as the corollary of the experiences led by the EWCs, but also as a way of reinforcing their operations, perhaps even more ambitiously. I am referring to both Directive 2002/14/EC of 11 March, which establishes a general framework for information and consultation of workers within the EU, and Directive 2001/86/EC of 8 October, which defines rules concerning the involvement of workers in the activities of European Companies.

In the case of Portugal, where EWCs are still taking their first steps, there is a need for trade unions to recognize their value, especially because Portuguese collective bargaining is known to be not very 'Europeanized' (Naumann 2000: 381). In this sense, there is still much to be done in order to strengthen the literature on globalization (understood here in its social and emancipatory dimensions) with the contributions provided by the Portuguese context. The examples I gathered from the textile, clothing, footwear and metalworking sectors show that it is easier to increase the literature that relates to the negative impact of globalization on labour activity than to contribute, on the basis of concrete experiences, to the strengthening of the literature that has an emancipatory character. In any case, even though no EWCs were established in Portugal from companies with central management in the country, the willingness shown by

Portuguese trade union organizations to participate in EWCs provides an opportunity to illustrate this emancipatory literature.

In fact, the EWC representatives of Portuguese workers as well as their respective trade union organizations have been giving clear signs of a strong trade union predisposition to identify obstacles and expose infringements. It is to a large extent due to the hindrances which still limit the exercise of trade union activity within companies that the Portuguese labour voice preferably makes itself heard through discourses of resistance – or, it might be said, through a sort of discursive cosmopolitanism. After all, as Munck (2000: 391) would put it, all social struggles are also struggles of interpretation at a discursive level. This means that, even when the goals of the struggles of Portuguese workers and trade unions are not achieved, they are nonetheless 'life experiences, and their effects, in impinging upon the reflective reconfiguration of individual or collective identifications, also affect the conditions of future action. Lived experience contains within itself elements of reflectivity that make up the cognitive involvement of the actors in emancipatory struggles' (Estanque 2004: 6, *mimeo*).

The implementation of EWCs in companies whose central management is located in Portugal is a great objective for the future. This would include, for instance, a closer physical proximity to the decision-making centre; a higher level of participation in meetings in the Portuguese language; a probable increase in the number of meetings between entrepreneurs and employees; an increase in the exchange of information amongst Portuguese employees in the company; the possibility of following the EWC operating procedures more closely, starting with the procedure for the election of the workers' representatives; a reinforcement of trade union bargaining capacity, considering that, as was mentioned above, both the level of institutionalization of labour relations and union membership are higher in larger companies; the creation of favourable conditions for influencing company managerial decisions even before they are made, and so on. It is therefore the duty of Portuguese trade unionism to respond to these challenges so as to convert them into real opportunities for social emancipation.

NOTES

1. On the antecedents of Directive 94/45/EC, see, among others, Danis and Hoffman (1995: 183–7); Leite *et al.*(1996: 18–22), Danis (1996: 79–82), Gaspar and Fiolhais (1996: 57–8), Simões (1996: 10–12), Costa (1996: 13–16) and Lecher (1999: 297).
2. For a complete analysis of the general meaning of the Directive, see, for instance, Vol.1, No.2 of *Transfer* (1995), a periodical published by the European Trade Union Institute

(ETUI), or the practical guide edited by Leite et al.(1996). For an analysis of the content and an interpretation of the agreements that have been implemented, see, for example, Krieger and Bonneton (1995), Bonneton et al. (1996), Marginson et al. (1998), some articles in *Transfer*, Vol.5, No.3 (1999), Fondation Européenne pour l'amelioration des conditions de vie et de travail (2000), Carley (2001) and Platzer, Rüb and Weiner (2001).

3. While collecting empirical experiences and examples during my fieldwork, I have focused on the textile, clothes and footwear sectors, as well as on the metalwork industry, for these are the sectors in Portugal with the most significant number of subsidiaries of foreign multinationals in compliance with the EWCs Directive. In those sectors, I interviewed trade union leaders connected with 'EWCs files', international relations and trade union training departments and also local trade unions, as well as Portuguese workers' representatives who had some experience of participation in already established EWCs.

4. (Leisink 1999: 3; Lambert 1999: 213; Moody 2000: 5; Le Roux, Fouquet and Rehfeldt 2000: 213–14; Lambert and Webster 2004: 38–9, *mimeo*).

5. (Munck and Waterman,eds. 1999; Waddington ed. 1999; Leisink ed., 1999; Fouquet, Rehfeldt and Le Roux, eds. 2000; Gills, ed. 2000; Munck, ed. 2004; or Santos, ed. 2004).

6. It should be noted that the EWC Directive does not apply only to trade unions, but also to employees of multinational companies, whatever their form of representation. On European models of workers' representation, see Pichot (1996), Costa (1996: 88–9), Psimmenos (1997), Slomp (1998: 79–90) or Blanke (1999a: 44–5).

7. This is explained, according to Santos (2001: 75), by the different conceptions of emancipatory resistance seen in cosmopolitan initiatives in different regions of the world system, as well as by the permanent demand for self-reflectivity of those who participate in them, since a counterhegemonic action can acquire predominantly hegemonic features.

8. '"Community-scale undertaking" means any undertaking with at least 1,000 employees within the Member States and at least 150 employees in each of at least two Member States' (Article 2. 1. a.). And '"Community-scale group of undertakings" means a group of undertakings with the following characteristics: at least 1,000 employees within the Member States; at least two group undertakings in different Member States; and at least one group undertaking with at least 150 employees in one Member State and at least 150 employees in another Member State' (Article 2. 1. c.).

9. It should also be mentioned that in a first phase there was no legal obligation for the United Kingdom to establish an EWC for the reason that it obtained an 'opt-out'. This situation was changed on 15 December 1997 with the extension of the Directive to the United Kingdom (through Directive 97/74/EC). That is, EU states and EEA states are now covered (Iceland, Norway, and Liechtenstein).

10. Krieger and Bonneton use, in this case, the curious label of 'forced voluntarism' (an expression that tries to combine different industrial relations traditions in Europe and, to a certain extent, to harmonize the interests of social partners). In practical terms, the following advantages would derive from this: a better adaptation of the agreement to the existing structures of the company, to its internal system of labour relations, or to the company's culture; an articulation of the industrial relations of those countries where transnational companies operate; and the building of 'common property' to both sides through the negotiation of an agreement (Krieger and Bonneton 1995: 190).

11. The number of agreements signed according to Article 13 of the Directive (that is, before 22 Sept., 1996) reached 450 (Carley 2001: 1).

12. EWCs are an established phenomenon (Carley 2001: 1; 2002: 652), with an average growth of about 60 per year (Kerckhofs 2001: 137–43; 2002: 46). Although 639 companies have set up EWCs (Table 2), there are 739 EWCs located in those companies. This difference between the number of EWCs and the number of multinational companies at which an EWC has been established 'results from some companies

establishing EWCs at division or some other sub-unit level': 608 multinational companies have one EWC; 36 have established two EWCs; 17 have established three EWCs; and two have established four EWCs (Kerckhofs 2002: 47; Waddington and Kerckhofs, 2003: 325).

13. Personal interview with a CGTP trade union leader who is responsible for the EWCs (23 May 2000, pp.2; 11).
14. (Lecher 1999: 298–301; Miller 1999: 359–62; Blanke 1999a: 49; 54–6; 1999b: 380–82; Bushack 1999a: 386–92; 1999b: 60–65; 2000: 161–72; Kerckhofs 2000: 145–50; Carley 2001: 2; Waddington 2002: 183–6; Hall 2003; Waddington and Kerckhofs 2003: 335–8; ETUC 1999; 2001; 2003: 29).
15. More than 900 were created between 1974 and 1980, with a total of 470 existing at present (Babo 2000: 103). According to Dornelas (1999: 48), in 1998, 16.4 per cent of the workers commissions were operating in companies with 100 or more workers; to this reduced influence was added the asymmetrical geographical distribution of the CTs.
16. Of the 386 EWCs already established on a voluntary basis, 137, that is, 35 per cent (the highest percentage) can be found in the metalwork industry, whereas textiles, footwear, clothing and manufactured products all together accounted for 15 per cent of the agreements (Marginson 1999: 261–2). These values are basically identical to those presented by the agreements signed under Article 6 of the Directive (*Fondation Européenne pour l'amelioration des conditions de vie et de travail*, 2000: 7–8). See also Steiert (2001: 114).
17. In the Portuguese case, the tendency is for 'most of those appointed or elected to be trade union representatives' (CGTP leader responsible for EWCs, personal interview, 23 May 2000, p.8). A similar opinion was expressed by a Footwear Trade Union/CGTP leader in an interview made on 15 Feb. 2000 (p.3).
18. She filled the position for a period of four years, from the establishment of the EWC on 6 May 1995 (according to Article 13 of the Directive).
19. Curiously enough, towards the end of her participation period in the EWC, she withdrew her membership from the UGT trade union and became a member of the CGTP trade union, although she had decided not to run for re-election. At present, and as a consequence of the competitiveness among trade unions, she is not a member of any trade union (personal interview, 9 May 2001).
20. Former representative of the Portuguese workers in the FAG Group EWC (personal interview, 9 May 2001, pp.18–19).
21. In this respect, an example should be mentioned which occurred in the Common Market of South America (MERCOSUR) – the Agreement celebrated on 29 March 1999 at Volkswagen, known as the MERCOSUR Collective Agreement – and which was the result of 'international pressure aiming at the constitution of workers representative bodies worldwide, as well as the celebration of agreements with their respective companies, especially in the automobile industry sector' (Véras 2004: 35, *mimeo*). One of its potentialities resides precisely in the fact that Volkswagen recognizes the workers' right to organize and set up Factory Commissions (Item 6 of the Volkswagen/MERCOSUR Collective Agreement, 1999: 3). That is, it was a transnational initiative which led to a more efficient conflict management within each company as well as an articulation with other struggles at national level (such as, for example, the struggle for a national collective agreement in the metalworking sector). On this, see Oliveira (2004: 26–30, *mimeo*) and Véras (2004). On the possibilities of trade union cooperation at a MERCOSUR scale and articulations between spaces of regional and national bargaining, see Silva (2004) and Costa (2005).
22. Former representative of the Portuguese workers in the FAG Group EWC (personal interview, 9 May 2001, pp.14–15).
23. Former representative of the Portuguese workers in the FAG Group EWC (personal interview, 15 March 2000, pp.24; 33). As Cristovam (1999a: 6) also argues, when referring to the position of the FEQUIMETAL/CGTP, 'the aims of these councils are

very restrictive, providing only for information and consultation, never a discussion of salaries'.
24. According to Barreto and Naumann (1998: 416), there is in Portugal 'a dual system of industrial relations: on the one hand a smallish group of large and some medium-sized companies which practice institutionalized industrial relations; on the other hand a huge mass of small and medium-sized companies where labour relations are regulated by informal methods and where institutionalized systems are largely irrelevant'. See also Stoleroff (1995).
25. In addition to the obstacles I have mentioned, others have been identified by Portuguese trade unionists, also conducive to actions of labour resistance: the absence of databases on the EWCs (which strangely extends to both the Portuguese Ministry of Labour and Solidarity and to the National Institute for Statistics [Ferreira, 2001]); the lack of fluency in foreign languages or the difficulty in providing translation systems; how to gain access to information withheld by the company management or considered as classified information, and so on.

REFERENCES

Babo, M.J. (2000): 'Assim se vê a força das CTs', *Focus*, pp.102–7.
Barbosa, M.S. (2000): 'Sindicalismo no Mercosul: com os pés na estrada', International Seminar *CUT: discutindo novos caminhos*. São Paulo: Sindicato dos Químicos e Plásticos, 14.06.2000 (mimeo): 1–8.
Barreto, J. and R. Naumann (1998): 'Portugal: Industrial Relations under Democracy', in J. Ferner and R. Hyman (eds.), *Changing Industrial Relations in Europe*, Oxford: Blackwell, pp.395–425.
Bonneton, P., et al. (1996): *Review of Current Agreements on Information and Consultation in European Multinationals*, Luxembourg: Office for Official Publications of the European Communities.
Blanke, T. (1999a): 'European Works Councils as an Institution of European Employee Information and Consultation: Overview of Typical Features of National Transposition Provisions, Outstanding Legal Questions and Demands for Amendments to EWC Directive 94/45/EC', European Trade Union Institute, *A Legal Framework for European Industrial Relations* (Report 60), Brussels: ETUI, pp.39–56.
Blanke, T. (1999b): 'European Works Councils as an Institution of European Employee Information and Consultation: Overview of Typical Features of National Transposition Provisions, Outstanding Legal Questions and Demands for Amendments to EWC Directive 94/45/EC', *Transfer – European Review of Labour and Research* 5/3, pp.366–83.
Buschak, W. (1995): 'European Works Councils Open New Horizons', *Transfer – European Review of Labour and Research* 1/1, pp.133–5.
Bushack, W. (1996): *Les Comités d'Enterprises Européens. La Directive européenne: analyse et commentaires de la CES* (mimeo), pp.1–47.
Bushack, W. (1999a): 'Five Years After: a Look Forward to the Revision of the EWC Directive', *Transfer – European Review of Labour and Research* 5/3, pp.384–92.
Bushack, W. (1999b): 'Workers' Involvement in the European Union or What Happened to the Nautilus and Captain Nemo?', in E. Gabaglio and R. Hoffmann (eds.), *European Trade Union Yearbook, 1998*, Brussels: European Trade Union Institute, pp.49–65.
Bushack, W. (2000): 'Review of the EWC Directive', in E. Gabaglio and R. Hoffmann (eds.), *European Trade Union Yearbook, 1999*, Brussels: European Trade Union Institute, pp.161–72.
Carley, M. (2001): *Bargaining at European Level? Joint Texts Negotiated by European Works Councils*, Dublin: European Foundation for the Improvement of Living and Working Conditions.

Carley, M. (2002): 'European-level Bargaining in Action? Joint Texts Negotiated by European Works Councils', *Transfer – European Review of Labour and Research* 8/4, pp.646–53.
CES (1999): *Résolutions. IXème Congrès*, CES: Brussels.
CGTP (1995): *Manual: Comités de Empresa Europeus*, Lisbon: CGTP (mimeo).
CGTP (1999a): *Empresas ou Grupos Multinacionais com Estabelecimentos ou Sede em Portugal*, Lisbon: CGTP (mimeo).
CGTP (1999b): *Programa de Acção e Resoluções do IX Congresso*, Lisbon: CGTP.
Contrato Colectivo da Volkswagen (MERCOSUL) (1999). São Bernardo do Campo. 29.03.1999 (mimeo).
Costa, H.A. (1996): *Os Conselhos de Empresa Europeus: na rota da fábrica global?*, Lisbon: Friedrich Ébert Foundation.
Costa, H.A. (1999): 'Time Regulation, Training and Collective Action: Topics for a Contemporary Trade Union Debate', *Oficina do CES* 142, pp.1–17.
Costa, H.A. (2000): 'Portuguese Trade Union Participation in Europe: The CGTP affiliation with ETUC', *Oficina do CES* 149, pp.1–37.
Costa, H.A. (2005): 'O sindicalismo na UE e MERCOSUL: etapas e caminhos em aberto', in E. Estanque, L.M. Silva, R. Véras, A.C. Ferreira and H.A. Costa (eds.), *Relações laborais e sindicalismo em mudança: Portugal, Brasil e o contexto transnacional*, São Paulo: Contez (forthcoming).
Cristovam, M.L. and A.C. Casinhas (1998): 'Comparative Supplement – European Works Councils. Portugal', Eironline. European Foundation for the Improvement of Living and Working Conditions (http://www.eiro.eurofound.ie/1998/07/study/TN9807201S. html), 23 March 2000.
Cristovam, M.L. (1999a): 'Europeanization of Collective Bargaining: Comparative Study. Portugal', Eironline. European Foundation for the Improvement of Living and Working Conditions (http://www.eiro.eurofound.ie/1998/07/study/TN9807201S.html), on 23 March 2000.
Cristovam, M.L. (1999b): 'European Works Councils and Industrial Relations in Portugal. Eironline', European Foundation for the Improvement of Living and Working Conditions (http://www.eiro.eurofound./1999/12/features/PT9912176F.html), 27 Oct. 2000.
Cruz, G. (1999): 'Igualdade de oportunidade e conselhos de empresa europeus', *Intervenções do Conselho Nacional. IX Congresso da CGTP*, Lisbon: CGTP, pp.37–9.
Danis, J-J. and R. Hoffmann (1995): 'From the Vredeling Directive to the European Works Council Directive', *Transfer – European Review of Labour and Research* 1/2, pp.180–7.
Danis, J.J. (1996): 'European Works Councils', in E. Gabaglio and Hoffmann (eds.), *European Trade Union Yearbook, 1995*, Brussels: European Trade Union Institute, pp.77–94.
DeMartino, G. (1999): 'The Future of the US Labour Movement in an Era of Global Economic Integration', in R. Munck and P. Waterman (eds.), *Labour Worldwide in the Era of Globalization: Alternative Union Models in the New World Order*, London: MacMillan Press, pp.83–96.
Diário da República – I Série A (1999): *Lei 40/99*. Diário da República n° 133 (9.06.1999).
Dornelas, A. (1999): 'As relações industriais em Portugal. É possível mudar? É possível não mudar?', *Sociedade e Trabalho* 7, pp.45–55.
Edwards, T. (1999): 'Cross-border Mergers and Acquisitions: the Implications for Labour', *Transfer – European Review of Labour and Research* 5/3, pp.320–43.
Estanque, E. (2000): *Entre a Fábrica e a Comunidade: subjectividades e práticas de classe no operariado do calçado*, Porto: Afrontamento.
Estanque, E. (2004): 'A reinvenção do sindicalismo e os novos desafios emancipatórios: do despotismo local à mobilização global', in B.S. Santos (ed.), *Trabalhar o mundo: os caminhos do novo internacionalismo operário*, Rio de Janeiro: Civilização Brasileira (forthcoming).

ETUC (1999): 'Review of the Directive on European Works Councils. Resolution adopted by the Executive Committee on 2–3 Dec. 1999' (http://www.etuc.org/Exec/Resolutions/English/120299_ewc.cfm), 3 Nov. 2000.
ETUC (2001): 'The EWC-Directive needs urgently to be revised: Amendments of the ETUC to the Directive' (http://www.etuc.org/EN/Dossiers/EWC/com9445.cfm), 5 Feb. 2002.
ETUC (2003): 'Making Europe work for the people' (http://www.etuc.org/EN/xcongress/fr/docs), 30 May 2003.
ETUI (2001): 'Companies Having Installed European Works Councils', (http://www.etuc.ed.etui/databases/default.cfm), 20 March 2001.
ETUI (2003): *ETUIinfo* (January), 1–6.
Ewing, K.D. (2000): 'Modernizing International Labour Standards: Globalization, Multinational Corporations, and International Trade Union Rights', ICTUR, *Trade union rights for the next millennium (draft discussion paper)*, London: ICTUR, pp.19–56.
Ferreira, A.C. (2001): 'Para uma concepção decente e democrática do trabalho e dos seus direitos: (Re)pensar o direito das relações laborais', in B. de S. Santos (ed.), *Globalização: Fatalidade ou utopia?*, Porto: Afrontamento, pp.255–93.
Ferreira, A.C. and H.A. Costa (1998/99): 'Para uma sociologia das relações laborais em Portugal', *Revista Crítica de Ciênciais Sociais* 52/53, pp.141–71.
Fondation Européenne pour l'amelioration des conditions de vie et de travail (2000): *Comités d'entreprise européens: une étude comparative entre les acords visés à l'article 6 et à l'article 13*, Luxembourg: Office des publications officielles des Commnuautés européennes.
Fouquet, A., U. Rehfeldt and S. Le Roux (eds.) (2000): *Le Syndicalisme dans la Mondialisation*, Paris: Éditions de l'Atelier.
Garrido, U. (1999): 'Formação e comunicação sindical', *Intervenções do Conselho Nacional* (IX Congresso da CGTP), Lisbon: CGTP, pp.63–7.
Gaspar, L. and R. Fiolhais (1996): *Europa Social (1957–1992): Evolução e Perspectivas na Área das Relações e Condições de Trabalho*, Lisbon: Ministério para a Qualificação e o Emprego.
Gills, B.K. (ed.) (2000): *Globalization and the Politics of Resistance*, London: MacMillan Press.
Hall, M. (2003): 'Unions Seek More Influence for EWCs', *International Union Rights* 10/1, pp.6–7.
Hoffmann, R. (2000): 'European Trade Union Structures and Prospects for Labour Relation in Europe', in J. Waddington and R. Hoffmann (eds.), *Trade Unions in Europe: Facing Challenges and Searching for Solutions*, Brussels: European Trade Union Institute.
Hoffmann, R. and E. Mermet (2000): 'Wage coordination in the European Union – Challenges for the Coordination of Collective Bargaining', in E. Gabaglio and R. Hoffmann (eds.), *European Trade Union Yearbook, 1999*, Brussels: European Trade Union Institute, pp.87–111.
Hyman, R. (2000): 'The Research Agenda: The Impact of European Integration', *Labour Movements*, Research Committee (RC) 44 (December) of the International Sociological Association. Madrid: Universidad Complutense, 3.
Hyman, R. (2001): 'European Integration and Industrial Relations: A Case of Variable Geometry?', in P. Waterman and J. Wills (eds.), *Place, Space and the New Labour Internationalisms*, Oxford: Blackwell, pp.164–79.
Jornal Oficial das Comunidades Europeias (1994): *Directiva 94/45/CE do Conselho de 22.09.1994*. JOC n° L 254/64 de 30.09.1994.
Kerckhofs, P. (1999): 'Social Partners' Conference on European Works Councils, Brussels, 28–30 April 1999' (Report), *Transfer – European Review of Labour and Research* 5/3, pp.441–4.
Kerckhofs, P. (2000): 'European Works Councils Developments in 1999', in E. Gabaglio and R. Hoffmann (eds.), *European Trade Union Yearbook, 1999*, Brussels: European Trade Union Institute, pp.133–60.

Kerckhofs, P. (2001): 'European Works Councils Developments in 2000', in E. Gabaglio and R. Hoffmann (eds.), *European Trade Union Yearbook, 2000*, Brussels: European Trade Union Institute, pp.135–64.
Kerckhofs, P. (2002): *European Works Councils: Facts and Figures*, Brussels: ETUI.
Kerckhofs, P. and S. Cox (2002): 'European Works Councils: Developments in 2001', in E. Gabaglio and R. Hoffmann (eds.), *European Trade Union Yearbook, 2001*, Brussels: European Trade Union Institute, pp.153–72.
Kowalsky, W. (2000): *Focus on European Social Policy: Countering Europessimism*, Brussels: European Trade Union Institute.
Krieger, H. and P. Bonneton (1995): 'Analysis of Existing Voluntary Agreements on Information and Consultation in European Multinationals', *Transfer – European Review of Labour and Research* 1/2, pp.188–206.
Laclau, E. (1996): *Emancipation(s)*, London and New York: Verso.
Lambert, R. and A. Chan (1999): 'Global Dance: Factory Regimes, Asian Labour Standards and Corporate Restructuring', in J. Waddington (ed.), *Globalization and the Politics of Resistance*, London: Mansell, pp.72–104.
Lambert, R. and E. Webster (2004): 'Emancipação social e novo internacionalismo operário', in B. de S. Santos (ed.), *Trabalhar o Mundo: Os Caminhos do Novo Internacionalismo Operário*, Rio de Janeiro: Civilização Brasileira (forthcoming).
Le Roux, S., A. Fouquet and U. Rehfeldt (2000): 'Conclusion', in A. Fouquet, U. Rehfeldt and S. Le Roux (eds.), *Le syndicalisme dans la modialisation*, Paris: Éditions de l'Atelier, pp.213–18.
Lecher, W. (1999): 'Resources of the European Works Council – Empirical Knowledge and Prospects', *Transfer – European Review of Labour and Research* 5/3, pp.278–301.
Leisink, P. (1999): 'Introduction', in P. Leisink (ed.), *Globalization and Labour Relations* Cheltenham: Edward Elgar, pp.1–35.
Leisink, P. (ed.) (1999): *Globalization and Labour Relations*, Cheltenham: Edward Elgar.
Leite, J. (1996): *Conselhos de Empresa Europeus: comentários à Directiva 94/45/CE*, Lisbon: Cosmos.
Marginson, P. (1999): 'CEE Agreements Under Review: Arrangements in Companies Based in Four Countries Compared', *Transfer – European Review of Labour and Research* 5/3, pp.256–77.
Marginson, P., M. Gilman, O. Jacobi and H. Krieger (1998): *Negotiating European Works Councils: an Analysis of Agreements Under Article 13*, Luxembourg: Office for Official Publications of the European Communities.
Mazur, J. (2000): 'Labour's New Internationalism', *Foreign Affairs* 79/1, pp.79–93.
Miller, D. and J. Stirling (1998): 'European Works Council Training: An Opportunity Missed?', *European Journal of Industrial Relations* 4/1, pp.35–56.
Miller, D. (1999): 'Towards a "European" Works Council', *Transfer – European Review of Labour and Research* 5/3, pp.344–65.
Moody, K. (2000): 'Global Capital and Economic Nationalism. Protectionism or Solidarity?', Global Solidarity Dialogue (http://www.igc.org/solidarity/atc/87Moody.html), 19 Jan. 2001.
Munck, R. (1999): 'Labour Dilemmas and Labour Futures', in R. Munck and P. Waterman (eds.), *Labour Worldwide in the Era of Globalization: Alternative Union Models in the New World Order*, London: MacMillan Press, pp.3–23.
Munck, R. (2000): 'Labour and Globalization: Results and Prospects', *Work, Employment and Society* 14/2, pp.385–93.
Munck, R. (ed.) (2004): *Labour and Globalization: Results and Prospects*, Liverpool: Liverpool University Press.
Munck, R. and P. Waterman (eds.) (1999): *Labour Worldwide in the Era of Globalization: Alternative Union Models in the New World Order*, London: MacMillan Press LTD.
Naumann, R. (2000): "Portugal", in G. Fajertag (ed.), *Collective Bargaining in Western Europe 1998–1999*, Brussels: European Trade Union Institute, pp.369–84.

Oliveira, F. (2004): 'Quem canta de novo *L'Internationale?*', in B. de S. Santos (ed.), *Trabalhar o Mundo: Os Caminhos do Novo Internacionalismo Operário*, Rio de Janeiro: Civilização Brasileira (forthcoming).
Pedersini, R. (1998): 'The Impact of European Works Councils', Eiro-online. European Foundation for the Improvement of Living and Working Conditions (http://www.eiro.eurofound.ie/1998/07/study/TN9807201S.html), 3 March 2000.
Pasture, P. (1996): 'Conclusion: Reflections on the Fate of Ideologies and Trade Unions', in P. Pasture, J. Verberckmoes and H. De Witte (eds.), *The Lost Perspective?*, Aldershot: Avebury, pp.377–403.
Pichot, E. (1996): *L'Europe des representants du personnel et de leurs attributions economiques*, Report for the European Commission, Luxembourg: Office for Official Publications of the European Communities.
Platzer, H.F., S.Rüb and K.P. Weiner (2001): 'European Works Councils – Article 6 Agreements Quantitative and Qualitative Developments', *Transfer – European Review of Labour and Research* 7/1, pp.90–113.
Psimmenos, I. (1997): *Globalization and Employee Participation*, Aldershot: Ashgate.
Ramsay, H. (1997): 'Solidarity at Last? International Trade Unionism Approching the Millennium', *Economic and Industrial Democracy* 18/4, pp.503–17.
Ramsay, H. (1999): 'In Search of International Union Theory', in J. Waddington (ed.), *Globalization Patterns of Labour Resistance*, London: Mansell, pp.192–219.
Rehfeldt, U. (2001): 'European Works Councils and Union Bargaining Strategies', in D. Foden, J. Hoffmann and R. Scott (eds.), *Globalization and the Social Contract*, Brussels: European Trade Union Institute, pp.343–53.
Santos, B.S. (1995): *Toward a New Common Sense: Law, Science and Politics in the Paradigmatic Transition*, London: Routledge.
Santos, B.S. (1997): 'Por uma concepção multicultural dos direitos humanos', *Revista Crítica de Ciências Sociais* 48, pp.11–32.
Santos, B.S. (2001): 'Os Processos da globalização', in B.S. Santos (ed.), *Globalização: Fatalidade ou Utopia?*, 31, Porto: Afrontamento, pp.31–106.
Santos, B.S. (ed.) (2004): *Trabalhar o mundo: os caminhos do novo internacionalismo operário*, Rio de Janeiro: Civilização Brasileira (forthcoming).
Savoini, C. (1995): 'The Prospects of the Enactment of Directive 94/45/EC in the Member States of the European Union', *Transfer – European Review of Labour and Research* 1/2, pp.245–51.
Silva, L.M. (2004): 'Trabalhadores do Mercosul, uni-vos! A construção de uma voz colectiva contra-hegemónica: quando o dissenso é "pôr-se de acordo com, a propósito de"', *Trabalhar o Mundo: Os Caminhos do Novo Internacionalismo Operário*, Rio de Janeiro: Civilização Brasileira (forthcoming).
Silva, M.C. (1998): 'Syndicalisme Europeen et International au XXI Siècle' (http://www.cgtp.pt/temas/sindical/sindical.html), 29.01.2000.
Simões, N. (1996): *Informação e Consulta dos Trabalhadores nas Empresas ou Grupos de Empresas de Dimensão Comunitária: um Modelo Negocial*, Lisbon: Conselho Económico e Social, pp.7–55.
Slomp, H. (1998): *Between Bargaining and Politics: An Introduction to European Labour Relations*, London: Praeger.
Steiert, R. (2001): 'European Works Councils, World Works Councils and the Liaison Role of the Trade Unions: a Test of International Union Policy', *Transfer – European Review of Labour and Research* 7/1, pp.114–31.
Stoleroff, A. (1995): 'Elementos do padrão emergente das relações industriais em Portugal', *Organizações e Trabalho* 13, pp.11–41.
Streeck, Wolfgang (1998): 'The Internationalization of Industrial Relations in Europe: Prospects and Problems', *Politics and Society* 26/4, pp.429–59.
UGT (1996): *Resolução Programática do VII Congresso*, Lisbon: UGT.
UGT (2000): *Resolução Programática do VIII Congresso*, Lisbon: UGT.

Véras, R. (2004): 'O Sindicalimo metalúrgico, o "festival de greves" e as possibilidades do contrato coletivo nacional', in B.S. Santos (ed.), *Trabalhar o Mundo: Os Caminhos do Novo Internacionalismo Operário*, Rio de Janeiro: Civilização Brasileira (forthcoming).

VW Brasil Ltda.; VW Argentina SA; CNM-CUT; SMABC; STIMSATT; SMATA; Comissões de Fábrica da VW brasileira e argentina (1999): *Contrato Coletivo*. Buenos Aires. 29.03.1999 (mimeo), pp. 1–5

Waddington, J. (ed.) (1999): *Globalization and Patterns of Labour Resistance*, London: Mansell.

Waddington, J. (2002): 'Views on the Agenda of European Works Councils and on the Revision of the Directive: a Perspective from Five Countries', in E. Gabaglio and R. Hoffmann, (orgs.), *European Trade Union Yearbook, 2001*, Brussels: European Trade Union Institute, pp.173–88.

Waddington, J. and P. Kerckhofs (2003): 'European Works Councils: What is the Current State of Play?', *Transfer – European Review of Labour and Research* 9/2, pp.322–39.

Waterman, P. (1998): *Globalization, Social Movements and the New Internationalisms*, London: Mansell.

Waterman, P. (2000a): 'Social Movements, Local Places and Globalized Spaces: Implications for Globalization from Below', in B. Gills (ed.), *Globalization and the Politics of Resistance*, London: MacMillan Press, pp.135–49.

Waterman, P. (2000b): 'Trade Union Internationalism in the Age of Seattle', Global Solidarity Dialogue (http://www.antenna.nl/ ~ waterman/ageseattle.html#top), 17 Jan. 2001.

Waterman, P. (2002): 'Internacionalismo Sindical na Era de Seattle', *Revista Crítica de Ciências Sociais* 62, pp.33–68.

Wills, J. (2001): 'Uneven Geographies of Capital and Labour: the Lessons of European Works Councils', in P. Waterman and J. Wills (eds.), *Place, Space and the New Labour Internationalisms*, Oxford: Blackwell, pp.180–205.

The Reinvention of Trade Unionism and the New Challenges of Emancipation

ELÍSIO ESTANQUE

This essay analyzes a case study which needs to be presented in context. The impacts of the neoliberal trends of the world economy are polymorphic – multiple and changing in different regional, spatial and social contexts. Globalization itself is paradoxical, causing new forms of localization, in which new opportunities for social inclusion combine with new forms of oppression and exclusion (Boyer and Hollingsworth 1997; Santos 1995 and 2000). There is an evident contrast between the apparent scope and strength of international capital, on the one hand, and the apparent limits and fragility of the trade union movement, on the other. Of course, the strength of the former tends to debilitate the latter. But the local effects are not uniform: they depend on a complex set of interactions within both the workplace and local civil society, thus providing international trade union movements with different possibilities of response.

The approach taken in this essay closely follows the proposals of Boaventura Sousa Santos in trying to go beyond *sub-paradigmatic* interpretations towards a *paradigmatic* stance capable of challenging hegemonic globalization by making counterhegemonic tendencies and movements visible (Santos 1995b: 258 ff.; 2000: 70–110). This framework suggests that globalization creates varied contrasts and connections within society, in its geographic, political, economic and cultural dimensions. In this process of reciprocal interaction, 'globalization' is the counterpart of 'localization', in which 'local sub-classes' are the counterpart of 'global over-classes' (Lash 1999). The analytic challenge for social science and critical theory is to illuminate such reciprocal interactions and local alternatives which, in a fragmentary fashion, have begun to emerge in the present global context. This implies listening to the voices of the margin, shedding light on the micro-examples that emphasize differences, thus contributing to their visibility as 'models of utopian realism' (Giddens 1990).

The case study analyzed in this essay – the trade union of the footwear industry in the industrial district of São João da Madeira (SJM) in Portugal – offers an example of resistance, in which different forms of local connections between industry and community, between work and cultural activism, constitute the basis for a form of social struggle which can inform and amplify networks of solidarity from the local to the international level. It is an example of how countering the liberal utopia with a heterotopia of resistance can contain an emancipatory potential. In spite of all the disciplinary mechanisms and strong ideological constraints with which workers have to cope, the strategy followed by the trade union leadership shows how such experience on the margins of the system can lead to new connections between trade unions, social movements, local associations, and so on, and at the same time provide new forms of articulation between roots and options (Santos 2000: 307).

Closely related to the neoliberal trends of the global economy and also as a result of the collapse of Communist mythology, 'class unionism' is fragile and currently riven by countless problems. Not only have the working-class struggles been 'cannibalized' by capitalism, the administrative structures of the main trade unions have also largely become instruments of state regulatory action. The trade unions themselves have also contributed to this process, by 'cannibalizing' the old proposals of revolutionary action. In the midst of all this, the conquests made by workers and by the traditional trade union movement have largely given way before the pressures of co-option, and have imperceptibly entered the dynamics of the system, becoming absorbed by the logic of regulation (Santos 2000: 335). However, side by side with the discrediting of the 'old' worker- and nation-based trade unionism, there have appeared signs of renewal, especially at the level of ideas and political debate, both in the academic sphere and in the trade union field, which point towards the emergence of a 'new' social trade union movement of global or international scope (Ashwin 2000; Bezuidenhout 1999; Moody 1997).

Recent approaches by Peter Waterman are precisely in this direction. In order to reconceptualize the old trade union internationalism with a national/industrial/colonial basis so as to adapt it to the present capitalist era of globalized information networks, a new social trade unionism is necessary, founded upon a new labour internationalism. Its main features will have to involve democratic and pluralist strategies and struggles capable of linking the workers' problems to those of other social segments, movements and communities,[1] within the framework of the construction of an ethics of international solidarity that 'surpass[es] an 'export solidarity' model by practising 'international solidarity at home', combating the local causes/effects of international exploitation and repression' (Waterman 2000). As we can see, these proposals are part of the theses about Portuguese trade unionism presented by Santos in 1995. He emphasizes the principle of solidarity as a necessary response to the growing reinforcement of local and transnational regulations, at the expense of national regulatory mechanisms. The construction of an active citizenship would imply the combination of a greater direct involvement of trade unionism in the space of production, namely through the reinforcement of the role of workers' committees, with a greater intervention outside the space of production by establishing connections with 'other progressive social movements, consumer movements, feminist movements, and so on... the trade union movement's energies for protest should shift towards the articulation with these other movements' (Santos 1995a: 135). This means that trade unionism, if it is to be reinvented, will have to open up to fields outside production and free itself from the national and sectorial format in which it is imprisoned. As José Manuel Pureza suggests, there are now two alternatives for the transforming and emancipatory intervention of trade unionism: either it remains enmeshed in national social pacts, or it rebuilds itself as a social movement dedicated to combating the logic of the internationalization of capital (Pureza 2001).

While emancipation has been a somewhat paradoxical notion, the experiences of the life world, whether framed by the spheres of the community, production or household, may present themselves as fields of struggle between the contamination of the system and the contamination of emancipatory action. Experiences of struggle are always important life experiences, even when their material aims are not achieved, and their effects, particularly upon the reflective reconfiguration of individual or collective identifications, also affect the conditions of future action. Lived experience contains within itself elements of reflexivity that make up the cognitive involvement of the actors in emancipatory struggles. That is why leaders repeatedly exalt past struggles. Building a patrimony of identity out of the memory of historical experience is a way of restoring collective dignity and opening up paths to the future. Even when the past was not satisfying, it is always preferable to reflect upon it and try to understand it than to allow it to sink into oblivion.

FROM REGULATION TO EMANCIPATION: BETWEEN INDUSTRY AND COMMUNITY, BETWEEN THE LOCAL AND THE GLOBAL

In the light of these concerns, I will seek to analyze the main processes and mechanisms of social regulation, as well as forms of resistance and moments of struggle and emancipatory rebellion, which, with all their contradictions and ambiguities, led to the shaping of the working class of the region of São João da Madeira (henceforth, SJM). The interpretation of these processes is based upon a double articulation: the connection between industry and community, and between the local and the global. These two dynamics obviously do not constitute separate realities, given that industry has asserted itself as the principal mediator between the local and the global, facilitating the penetration of local communities by external factors – namely the market at national and international levels. However, I take them as analytically distinct dimensions, as they operate on different scales and allow us to visualize the way this double logic has acted upon the socio-cultural complexity of the region. To a large extent, the processes of structuring of community identities and collective subjectivities of local actors take place within these two dimensions. As I will show, this explains the selection of the footwear workers' union (the most representative industrial sector of the region) as a privileged collective actor, since it has, at different times, been the main stimulus of resistance vis-à-vis the hegemonic logic exerted through those two articulations. Either of them, therefore, may constitute a model of regulation within the current dominant paradigm, while, at the same time, being susceptible to producing orientations and subjectivities of an emancipatory nature. This also justifies the importance given to the reconstruction of historical experience, which means attempting to carry out an operation 'of archaeological excavation in the regulatory magma in order to recover the emancipatory flame, no matter how weak it might be' (Santos 2000: 335). It is based on the analysis of this double articulation that I will, first, describe the way in which the main social mechanisms were produced for the framing and domination of the workers in the region, and secondly, outline the present challenges, which continue to reveal the dialectical conjugation of the new tendencies of hegemonic globalization and the new networks of emancipatory solidarity.

In the first articulation, industry worked as a determining factor in the reshaping of the territorialized community, restructuring it and adapting it to the logic of production and of the market, and managing it in such a way as to neutralize the formation of strong communities of resistance. This means that the economicist and individualistic perspective that supports capitalism was able to penetrate into worker collectivities more profoundly and efficiently than was the collectivist socio-political perspective underlying trade union struggle. This is to say that it was mostly under the pressure of capital and not of labour (or class) that rural communities approached industry. However, this articulation was never static, but rather marked by multiple dynamics and forms of resistance, latent or explicit.

As has already been made clear, the perspective adopted here concerning the concept of community, namely when discussing its relation with industry, is to view it as a set of discursive constructions, often conflictual, which support the structuring of its identity. One must, then, avoid conceiving community in a merely territorial, substantive or static sense. Community is a dynamic socio-cultural process involving multiple struggles, discourses and identification dynamics, which oscillate between localized subordination, dependent on the demands of production, and *the community in movement*, which asserts its originality and demands recognition, dignity and expansion opportunities vis-à-vis the dominant powers. It is in this sense that we may be able to anticipate a new turn in the articulation between industry and community, which will allow the latter to impose forms of 'cosmopolitan' pressure on the former to prevent the violation of rights and achieve new rights for workers and collectivities.

Of course this can only occur if future social conditions in the labour market, as well as in the leadership structures of the trade union, favour the renewal of its collective action. For that, activist initiatives will have to combine workers' resistance from within companies with other forms of grassroots and local associations outside the sphere of industrial relations, in order to reinforce its capacity to intervene. Only by restructuring the role of the community will labour collectivities be able to restructure their leading role within enterprises. This means that the future of trade union action will cease to be supported primarily by 'class' action, becoming an aggregation of local movements, whose struggles will be aimed not only at (and within) the company, but also, simultaneously, towards other social movements and state institutions, from the local to the transnational level (as I seek to show in the next section).

As regards the articulation between the global and the local, the impact of industrialization and market dynamics established in the region over the years has resulted in the growing hegemony of a global logic over the local. It must be added, first, that such logic was, and still is, strongly mediated by the national; and, secondly, that such overdetermination of the global was only effective to the extent that it was able to incorporate and co-opt significant elements of the local dynamic, harnessing them to the needs of industry (as I mentioned above) and thus maximizing their modelling effects. These can be seen as forms of localized globalism (Santos 1995b: 263) which, through diverse agents and frameworks, have prevented local cultures and worker collectivities from asserting themselves and extending their rights into wider spheres, moving from the local to the global by way of the national. At different times, it was the general interests of the economy, of state institutions and of global markets which most marked local identities and subjectivities, circumscribing them to the region or to fortress communities (Santos 2000: 314). Although this articulation still involves the hegemony of the global over the local, it might also be inverted in the medium term. If this happens, it will entail the reinvention of trade unionism in the sector and the latter's capacity to introduce local elements, with their sociocultural specificities and dynamics, into its programmes of global struggle. If the footwear workers' union is able put into practice new forms of transnationalization and enlarging solidarity networks in which it participates, it may become the main mediator between the local and the global, in a counterhegemonic sense. In this way, trade union action and the local movements with which it seeks to ally itself would effectively function as brakes to the present logic of hegemonic globalization, counteracting it with a new logic of global solidarity promoted through new emancipatory dynamics and new coalitions and alliances, oriented towards the defence of the dignity of work and the recognition of the community.

THE CONNECTION BETWEEN INDUSTRY AND COMMUNITY: BUILDING AUTHORITARIAN PATERNALISM

Despite the social and political importance of early working class movements in Portugal, their rather dispersed and fragile character in organizational terms is well known (Cabral 1979; Tengarrinha 1981). Beyond their dramatized discourse and even the emancipatory possibilities that they opened up for the Portuguese working class, these experiences introduced a working class language in Portugal. However, as happened in England in the first half of the nineteenth century, these movements were clearly marked by the logic of local communities, by a defensive and even conservative stance towards the threat of modern machinery and industry (Thompson 1963; Hobsbawm 1984; Jones 1989).

It was by means of a similar process that, in this region, diverse sociocultural elements were transferred from the sphere of the household and domestic crafts to industry, particularly during the first stage of industrial and commercial growth in the final years of the nineteenth century. In the first phase, units of production multiplied, based on the same family matrix in which the traditional craft of shoemaking operated. Located in the household, and resorting to the help of their children and of apprentices hired through neighbourhood networks, masters only needed to create the conditions to respond to a growing number of orders.

Even after the first manufacturing units were set up, most workers continued to produce from their homes, and, when they did eventually start to work in larger units, some of the tools belonged to the workers themselves, which clearly illustrates the persistence of the craftsman logic. Moreover, the implantation of companies already supplied with mechanized equipment did not immediately prevent production from continuing to depend largely on isolated producers, who resisted having to travel every day to the factory. Pressure for a greater concentration of the work force only came later, both from entrepreneurs, who were investing in mechanization, and from trade union activists, who saw that this provided better conditions for union action.

It might be said, therefore, that the first phase of expansion of the footwear industry essentially obeyed a patriarchal logic, which continued to shape the production demands and structuring processes of industrial relations, remaining under the strong influence of family ties. However, if the family was the first structural mediator between the community and production, the strongest pole of structural power was gradually displaced as industry grew and market demands increased. It is known that the dynamics of family-rooted affinities and loyalties are still present in enterprises, but there has been a slow but persistent movement away from family rule to rule through the family. With the gradual loss of family autonomy, the community also turned from being a bastion of resistance to a vehicle of domination (Burawoy 1985).

As workshop production gradually lost its initial hegemony, the family logic and communities themselves gradually gave way to a new type of paternalism, of a neofeudal nature, by means of which entrepreneurial despotism extended its control mechanisms over the working class, through the family and the community. Such despotism conveyed a mercantilist logic, whilst retaining its paternalistic dimension. Indeed, it could be said that this double logic, precisely because it was ambiguous, was able to impose framing mechanisms upon the community through the paternalistic dimension, in order to simultaneously exercise despotic power over the workers on the shop floor. Far from being linear, this process took on interesting contours, which demonstrate not only the reasons for its strength and efficacy, but also the way in which, to be effective according to the logic of regulatory modeling, it had to produce and assimilate emancipatory experiences.

It is important to point out that most of the entrepreneurs of SJM (even the wealthiest) had their social roots in the working class. Some had begun their activities with small units of production in the region, but those who contributed most at that time to the acceleration of the process of industrial modernization had accumulated most of their wealth through business in Brazil, which had been the main destination for migrants since the nineteenth century. Many employees saw in the entrepreneurs, from the smallest to the largest, successful examples of what could be achieved, in terms of upward social mobility, through dedication to hard work and productive discipline. A central nucleus of that recomposition was based on the defence of the productivist idea, which led to the development of SJM as 'the Land of Labour', a formula still displayed on the local flag. The adaptation of the old community to the new mechanisms of regulation thus entailed the conversion of the traditional paternalism, which characterized the relationship between the local elites and the people, into a form of neopaternalism between employers and employees. As the demands of the market and productivity grew stronger, paternalism gradually gave way to company despotism.

In this respect, it is also convenient to mention the repressive role of the Salazar regime, with its project of corporatism, which, from 1933, outlawed the old class-based unions and imposed corporatist trade unions, which brought together workers and employers in the same organization (including mandatory affiliation for all the workers). All of this took place within a framework of strict authoritarian and ideological control, of conservative, rural and Catholic inspiration, which, until 1974, kept the country in a position of great socio-economic backwardness, with no political freedoms.

However, that process was always accompanied by a dialectic of conflict. Just as regulatory formulas sometimes took on the contours of emancipation, so emancipatory dynamics sometimes rose out of the official institutional framework. This happened, for instance, with the corporatist trade union created in 1933, which involved the co-optation of a new leader who was a sympathizer with communist ideals.[2] The handcraft origins of shoemaking, and the proximity between workers and small employers within the same communitarian matrix also contributed to the creation of unusual alliances. The community's subjection to the hegemonic powers was achieved by means of a double control: repressive, disciplinary action, exercized mainly through the suppression of autonomous trade unionism and the disciplinary framing of workers within companies; and doctrinal and ideological action exercized by state and church institutions over worker and community associations (organized as free time organizations for workers).

Over the last four decades (mainly since the 1960s), there has been a diffuse growth of the industry from the town to the outskirts, and from there to the most rural collectivities. This has permitted semi-wage workers to keep their connections with agriculture and with an innocuous religious and recreational activities. At the same time, the force of the market has become more overwhelming, injecting into the community a whole set of consumer references and codes that promote individualistic alienation and inhibit collective participation. Nevertheless, despite the neutralization or co-option of some of the struggles and acts of resistance of the past by regulatory mechanisms, it should not be concluded that the community has lost all of its emancipatory potentialities. It is in this context that trade union action has played an essential role in recent decades.

THE POTENTIALITIES OF COMMUNITY-ORIENTED TRADE UNIONISM

One of the main virtues of this union structure – the *Trade Union of Workers in Footwear, Bags and Related Articles of the Districts of Aveiro and Coimbra* – lies in the attention that it has given to grassroots work and to the proximity with the workers' collectivities, not only within companies, but also as regards the articulation with other associational and cultural activities. The very fact that the main leader of this trade union (M. Graça) since the late 1970s initiated his associational activity in the sphere of community-based cultural associationalism shows us that we have here a concept of trade unionism that is, in many ways, different from the traditional model in Portugal.

Workers' struggles in this region before 25 April 1974 only occasionally went as far as open contestation, as in the case of the 1943 strike, or the strike movements at the end of the 1960s in the metalworking sector (in the Oliva sewing-machine company). In the so-called 'hot summer' of 1975, when diverse anti-communist protests appeared throughout the country, SJM was one of the first places where the headquarters of left-wing parties were attacked and vandalized. These protests were associated with the conservative right. These sectors of the local workforce were undoubtedly dominated by the interests of employers.[3] In a scenario characterized by profound political and ideological divisions, it is not surprising that, alongside those events there were also various workers' protests, factory occupations, and a massive affiliation to trade unions in this region,[4] as happened all over the country in the agitated years of 1974–75. However, following the political about-turn which occurred in the country at the end of 1975, there was a period of reflux in popular and trade union mobilization (as mentioned before, never very strong in this region), which was favourable to the climate of persecution of activists within companies, or, in some cases, their co-optation into better-paying positions in exchange for the abandonment of trade union activity.

It was in this scenario that the new directorate of the footwear workers' union outlined a plan of action that was more suitable for the reality of this sector, under the influence of M. Graça. His trajectory deserves to be mentioned in a brief note. Although he was a working-class leader, Graça had become involved in associational activism and political intervention very early in his life, which explains the attention that the trade union has lately given to cultural intervention and to the establishment of alliances between the union and other associations and NGOs in different fields. It is precisely this effort to combine initiatives geared towards other community spheres, which, when closely articulated with intervention in companies, could become the main capacitating factor of emancipatory energies, enabling the union to oppose the regulatory logic to which the community has been subjected.

Various initiatives of this kind have been promoted, many of which reveal the same contradictory features that have marked the articulation between 'new' and 'old' social movements in Portugal (Santos 1994). In this trade union, whose main leader, of working class background, demonstrated early on a particular interest in the cultural dimension,[5] the ideological values of the radical left are combined with a refined pragmatic sense; its orientation appeals to popular participation, assuming the importance of dialogue and negotiation; and advocating a combination of participatory and representative democracy. This is largely the result of the present leader's experiences in the revolutionary period following 25 April 1974.[6]

> I used to believe in immediate struggles, but I also defended – against many, who did not believe in them – legislative elections and representative democracy, because I thought (as I still do) that these things are not incompatible. It is possible to combine this with participatory democracy, with the intervention of the masses, of grassroots popular organizations. They are not at all incompatible. I believe that the people have the right to organize themselves into political parties and organizations. It is, in my opinion, a ... sacred right! I am not a Catholic, but it is ... sacred. Now, in specific cases, it is clear that I was always on the side of those who argued for popular participation, there's no doubt about that. (Trade union leader, SJM, July 2000)

These characteristics have clearly had a strong influence on the functioning of the trade union structure since the beginning of the 1980s, and this is undoubtedly related to the growing levels of sympathy and support that it has achieved amongst workers of the sector.

It was this concept of militancy that allowed the union to withstand a particularly difficult climate for the industry two decades ago:

> There was great repression in companies and the trade union movement generally began to go into decline, didn't it? ... So, many activists were fired ... although the strike had a huge number of participants and lasted two weeks. That's why there was a cycle of dismissals afterwards. It was the period of greatest repression and lots of people got laid off, mostly activists, those that manned the pickets. At that time, there was a very brutal direct repression in the companies. Now it's subtler, isn't it? It was a 'cleaning job', which lasted about four years, so a period of great backsliding. (Trade union leader, SJM, July 2000)

Given the difficulty of creating strong, organized and cohesive structures inside the companies, particularly in the small and medium-sized businesses that are predominant in the sector, trade union leaders travel daily to the gates of factories to hear what workers have to say and inform them of their rights. Faced with illegalities and the suppression of rights, the union responds by combining the discourse of indignation with legal action, with largely positive results for the workers. It exposes and protests against despotic attitudes or even acts of violence exercized by many proprietors over the workers, whilst trying to keep open channels for dialogue; it defends women's rights by denouncing discriminatory practices and making use of the legal channel; and in cases of child labour, it seeks to pressure the *Inspecção Geral do Trabalho* (General Inspection of Work) and launches media campaigns, which, since the mid-1990s have had remarkable success. Given the production logic based upon intensive labour and a cheap work force which prevails in the sector, the union seeks to ensure that workers' interests are protected, while at the same time participating in negotiations concerning reorganisation programmes in larger companies.

Many repressive practices continue to prevail in the enterprises of the sector,[7] but legal action (with many cases resolved in favour of the workers) seems to be having a dissuasive effect upon employers. This clearly shows why this trade union can be taken as an exemplary case as regards the way in which it has managed to coherently combine the different components of its activity. In addition to its ability to carry out the traditional functions of trade unions – defending members, establishing a dialogue with social partners, and political activation (Rosanvallon 1988) – this trade union has provided consistent proof of its efforts to ally the firm defence of emancipatory principles with a realistic sense of action, thus allowing it to achieve a fair balance between protest and negotiation.

For instance, despite the disciplinary power and despotic authoritarianism of the factory, workers have often succeeded in eluding this through multiple tactics of a subversive game (Estanque 2000: 270 ff.). During the three months in which I worked and lived with the workers of one footwear factory, I witnessed many signs of how 'consent' is accompanied by forms of 'tacit resistance' that sought to undermine despotism and subvert structures of power. While recognizing the fragility of the class-consciousness of these workers, the restructuring of their collective identity in the factory has produced many forms of *escapism* and games that subvert disciplinary power through collective daily practices (Linstead 1985). The assembly line supervisor complained that the workers always tried to do things their own way and said that some of them were trying to 'make my life a misery ... and test me to see how soft I was. And the more they felt I was soft, the more they took advantage... sometimes I pretended not to notice but I understood what was going on all right!' When I asked him why he shouted at the workers from a distance when they were, as he put it, 'filing their nails' (meaning that they were chatting or slacking), he gave me the following explanation: 'before, I used to go up to them and point out what they were doing and control things. But I began to realise that they just wanted to give me the runaround. When I went up to someone who was talking or fooling around, they understood and so the others behind me would call me over to sort something out as well...'

Still, some arrogant shouts over the workers (which I witnessed) were much more in evidence when the boss was around and were usually directed at the youngest and least qualified workers, especially the young women. Resistance varied according to individual cases and could involve more dramatic reactions or more subtle kinds of games. *Uncle* António (a 60-year old who worked next to me) would sometimes yell in desperation to the supervisor when the belt was running too fast, but never straight to his face and not when he was nearby: 'can't he see he can't do this? Any minute now, I'm going to walk out of here!!'

Such practices clearly reveal that this is not a working class that accepts exploitation passively, but rather, one that resists it in a subtle manner, trying to preserve and recreate zones of freedom in order to protect their collective dignity, which is constantly being offended on the shop floor. Although open and organized forms of collective action are few and far between, these guerilla micro-tactics (De Certeau 1984) illustrate that emancipatory potentialities are not dead.

Certainly, the difficulties of organization and struggle currently faced by the trade union movement in general are also present in this region. But the specifics of this case set it apart from other industrial contexts where political conditions were particularly favourable to radical struggles in the 1970s (as, for instance, in the industrial belts of Lisbon and Setúbal). However, exactly because in this region workers were never familiarized with those experiences, that is to say, exactly because in this case the trade union had to deal with structurally adverse conditions in the past, it had an opportunity to accumulate considerable organizational experience in re-inventing its forms of intervention and this can be considered an advantage. Portuguese trade unionism as a whole benefited from the revolutionary climate and class language that became widespread in Portuguese society after 25 April (Estanque 1999), but now most of the union structures are still tied to a traditional model of action and that is why they have greater difficulties in dealing with the current crisis. In the case of the footwear sector, and particularly in SJM and in other regions of diffuse industrialization, the atmosphere of claims-making had little penetration. The instability, mobility and dispersion of the productive process, and the reserve and distrust of a semi-rural workforce have meant that trade unions have always had to resort to different strategies.[8] The fact of the matter is that many of the problems that have always existed in the region prevail, at present, in traditional industrial environments, where, in recent decades, multiple processes of industrial privatization and industrial reconversion have occurred (Lima *et al.*, 1992; Rosa 1998).

This explains the leader's fine sensitivity regarding the new challenges of trade union action in a context like this. It also explains the refusal to resort to long 'demagogic' speeches in a sector characterized by a low-skilled and poorly educated work force.

> The problem is this: if you begin to speak about things too much, you end up alienating people. If you are too demagogic about it, it doesn't work. So, people, the leaders, have to see the level of the workers. They have to see that the workers of a footwear factory are not on the same level as an activist or trade union leader. They have very little education and I understand this. It is often difficult for me to make that kind of speech. I prefer more concrete discussions. I've always had this principle, of trying to create a more just society, but speaking about that systematically, and more deeply, is another matter, because I think that this becomes demagogic. (Trade union leader, SJM, July 2000)

These are the problems that oblige trade union leaders to look for new ways of consolidating the levels of implantation already achieved, by developing a critical sense and exposing cases of employer abuse, without sacrificing the pragmatism required by socio-economic conditions.

While mobilizing workers and contesting undesirable situations, the trade union also supports and participates, for example, in programmes of technological modernization and professional training, developed through company agreements (particularly in the case of large companies) or through the Technological Footwear Centre (whose board of directors includes trade union representatives) in partnership with the entrepreneurial association of the sector (APICCAPS). While promoting assemblies and struggles in many companies, it does not neglect cultural activities and relationships with other associations in the community.

This strategy of developing different forms and spheres of intervention has arisen from the need to encourage collective participation in spaces where apathy has prevailed. Intervention in this field may produce a new synthesis based on the split between an industrial activity subjected to rapid and abrupt change, and a community activity which is still sheltered in the profound stagnation of its rural roots.

Many public events throughout the region involving local or national associations can be mentioned to illustrate the dynamics of this trade union.[9] Other initiatives, especially in the field of cultural intervention, have been organized at the headquarters of the footwear workers' union in SJM, most of them taking place in its new auditorium called José Afonso (a well-known left-wing singer of popular ballads), which was inaugurated in 1999. These included recitals, concerts, exhibitions, debates, theatrical performances and book fairs.

This variety of networks and activities clearly shows the importance given to cultural activities, as a fundamental backdrop to trade union strategy. There is an obvious openness to plural languages and forms of intervention and denunciation, which, while preserving a profound belief in the anti-capitalist struggle, also appeals to the need for political alliances outside the trade union field: 'at the political level [it is necessary to recover the role of] NGOs, of organizations related to ecology, to the rights of women, minorities, the protection of the poor and homeless ... There has to be some connection between these movements, which at present does not exist; they are all dispersed and unconnected ...' (Trade Union Leader, 12 June 2000). This orientation, which is far removed from the orthodoxy and dogmatism which undermined the Portuguese trade union movement, points precisely towards a quest for 'heterotopias of resistance', in the sense proposed by Santos (2000: 311). It can be seen as an example of an alternative experience that stimulates new coalitions with different actors and movements, overcoming resentment by means of a creative imagination and reinventing new paths for trade unionism towards emancipation. Only under these conditions is it possible to identify social arenas where actors are not limited to accepting submission and exploitation, but where they may tackle the system through innovative forms of resistance.

Undoubtedly there are many obstacles confronting the trade union in this kind of grassroots work, and it is difficult to predict a scenario of generalized emancipatory struggles. But, as we know, the new movements, which are today perhaps more active and efficient in the promotion of collective emancipatory action, operate by opposing the connections of hegemonic domination with new antihegemonic connections of resistance – between exploitation and exclusion, the economy and culture, the factory and the community, the local and the global.

BETWEEN THE LOCAL AND THE GLOBAL

The footwear sector has become one of the most dynamic within Portuguese industry in recent decades and this dynamism is largely due to its vocation for exports.[10] However, we should begin by pointing out that this orientation towards international markets is far from being a recent trend; on the contrary, it has been present throughout the development of the sector since its first steps towards mechanization and modernization in the early decades of the twentieth century. Besides, it is this traditional connection to international economic transactions that justifies this line of analysis. The aim is, on the one hand, to understand the way in which local and global dynamics have interacted in the production of adaptive regulatory mechanisms (of the global upon the local), and, on the other hand, to identify and analyze the most recent experiments originating in the community, particularly those which have been activated by means of trade union action, in order to bring together local resistance and global action and direct them towards an antihegemonic and cosmopolitan perspective.

As mentioned above, modern industry in this region, and the footwear industry in particular, was initially launched with the support of capital accumulated by the generation of local emigrants who had made their fortune in Brazil.[11] Many of these figures today are commemorated in the street names of the city of SJM, in recognition of their important role in promoting local development since the first decades of the twentieth century.

Their considerable investments in industrial development and their contributions to the creation of different infrastructures followed a strategy that fed a philanthropic discourse and helped to legitimize the leading role that some of these personalities were to assume in local politics. If it is true that their apparent voluntarism would probably not have been successful if market dynamics had not already begun to make their mark upon the economic activity in the region, it can also be argued that these early industrialists made an important contribution to the transformation of traditional rural communities by bringing them closer to industry. In addition, the fact that the intensification of national and regional commercial relations was a decisive factor for industrial development was also strongly mediated by the transnational circulation of capitals, which means that, in that period, global economic transactions profoundly marked local processes. It may also be added that the very process of mobility (the departure and return of emigrants) which made this social sector a pivot of modernization, contains a contradictory logic of de-territorialization/re-territorialization, which is inscribed in the identities of the communities and in their adaptation to a regulation subordinated to the demands of capitalist accumulation.

Another dimension that testifies to the way in which the local impact of industrial expansion has always been combined with global factors can be found in the export of footwear. The first industrialists of the sector, many of whom had developed businesses in Brazil, as we have seen, sought to consolidate that market as a privileged destination for their products. But most of the Portuguese footwear manufactured in this region was destined for the Portuguese army, for use by troops taking part in World War I. Although this was not exactly export, it obviously responded to demands of a global nature that concerned a geopolitical context which, beyond its dramatic consequences, had widespread local repercussions. This was not only because it promoted the first mechanical units of the sector, but also because it indirectly led to the development of several small businesses that began their operations as subcontractors.

This situation, although arising from a particular context, structured local industrial activity and its impact upon the communities. While enabling the sector to gradually orient itself towards export, it also laid the foundations for the increasing vulnerability of the working class and the industry in general to international oscillations in the political and economic sphere. More and more sectors of the traditional agricultural workforce were gradually absorbed industry, which led to the emergence of a highly exploited semi-proletariat, which was docile and dependent, and which saw the factory as an attractive alternative or complement to their traditional means of subsistence. Precisely because the exports of Portuguese footwear to other European countries increased significantly throughout the 1930s and 1940s, the economic recession and market contraction brought about by war and social and political upheaval had repercussions on the local level, in the form of the closure of many companies and waves of hunger, disease and misery for the working class of the region (as happened during the Spanish Civil War and particularly during World War II).

The devastating consequences of international crisis in this region clearly illustrate the interdependence that had gradually been established between the global markets and the wage relation in the sector. Despite the restrictive, repressive and nationalist policies of the Salazar regime, the footwear industry managed to keep a window of internationalization open.[12] The segments of the world market that had been conquered by the sector were naturally continued in the post-war period of international growth and stability.

After the 1950s, and particularly throughout the 1960s, footwear exports expanded substantially, managing to penetrate the American market and countries of the Soviet bloc, while still keeping commercial links with western Europe, the African colonies and Brazil. However, the international division of labour, despite these ties of interdependence, gradually gave rise to systems of production and experiments in trade union action that were widely divergent. And these past experiences have repercussions in the present. Whereas, in the countries and regions in which the labour movement and industrial systems experienced 'fordism', the old model of trade unionism is now desperate to develop strategies adequate to deal with the current global trends of labour fragmentation and crisis in union mobilization, one can say that, in this region, from the 1960s, despite the policies of the Salazar regime, there was a direct entrance into a 'post-fordist' phase without having ever passed through 'fordism'. However, the profound imbalances, socio-cultural divisions and identity recompositions that these changes brought about, can become a potential advantage to the renovation of trade unionism, and through it, for the revival of the principle of community.[13]

Although the discourse that produced the 'adapted community' of SJM in the first decades of the twentieth century was centred on the articulations between the local and the national, it also brought representations concerning a subjective sense of universalization into which the local/global binomial was inscribed. The first local movements, set in motion by the important personalities and 'nouveaux riches' of the region in an attempt to achieve the classification of town and municipality for SJM,[14] were accompanied by a discourse that glorified the 'spirit of sacrifice' and dedication to work carried out in the name of 'progress' and industrial modernization. The new status of the town that was now displayed upon the map of Portugal no doubt resulted from deliberate attempts to give it greater visibility. But, as we know, the important role played by the dominant classes should not be confused with the emancipation of the people. It may have been an important achievement for the local elite, but perhaps its greatest significance lay in the way it reinforced top-down regulatory mechanisms vis-à-vis the working classes, rather than in the assertion of a type of 'bottom-up' power in their relations with the official power structure. A reflection of this is the fact that this kind of discourse, which was essentially parochial, soon started to become confused with the nationalist doctrine that was then emerging; both had paternalistic contours, and functioned as an ideological support to the Salazar regime and as a fundamental link between disciplinary policies and local powers. It had a considerable impact on the framing of communities, in the spheres of both labour and recreation, namely through the local application of the famous Fascist formula, cynically called 'Joy at Work'.[15]

From the viewpoint of state action, this was a doctrinal and repressive measure, which sought, like the Nazi experiment, to convert the myth of the old medieval-type community into a new 'aestheticized' 'folk' community at the service of the Salazar regime. But from the perspective of local dynamics already in operation, it is important to note that this kind of 'reactionary modernism' creates a fictitious community, adapted and regulated from within. That is to say, it emanates from the 'hard core' of established local power, and responds in large measure to the expansion needs of local industry based upon the fabrication of a new disciplinary logic, of mechanisms of consent, which resulted in the subjugation of the working class and in the 'localization' or 'colonization' of the community, not only by the national state, but also in response to wider economic connections subjected to the principle of the market and to the export strategy of the local footwear industry.

Although, as I have pointed out, the local impacts of globalization have been felt for some time, the new global liberalism of recent decades has also had visible consequences in this region. These are part of the general logic of exponential growth of central economies, and naturally result in the domination of more fragile economies, namely those situated on the periphery of the world system. If Portugal reflects the contradictions inherent in a semiperipheral society integrated within a central bloc (the European Union), some productive sectors within it (such as this example of the footwear industry) show those contradictions particularly sharply. While exports in the sector continue to account for more than 80 per cent of production, external investment, which, especially since the 1960s, has been benefiting from the low cost of labour, has in the last decade shifted to the countries of the South, particularly to Asia, for exactly the same reasons. Competition from those countries has had repercussions in Portugal, resulting in many cases of company relocation, abrupt closure and fraudulent bankruptcies.

Although the footwear sector as a whole has continued to resist the new conditions of global competition, salaries account for only 17 per cent of production costs, which reflects the fact that it continues to be largely labour intensive, with the average salary of the sector around €375 per month. The heterogeneous nature of the entrepreneurial fabric continues to nourish deep divisions and interdependencies between the large companies and the vast majority of small units whose subsistence depends on the larger ones, operating according to a system of subcontracting, which encourages home-based labour and illegal production (even including child labour). While there are signs that some producers are beginning to invest in technological reconversion, design and differentiated competitiveness based on quality, many companies, including the most modern, produce mostly for international, European and American brands, which distribute Portuguese products worldwide through large commercial chains and distribution depots, where the label 'made in' disappears. The owners of the major brands, namely English and Scandinavian, have developed franchising contracts with extraordinary marketing gains, selling products that have been manufactured wherever it is most convenient (INOFOR 2001) and conquering vast segments of the global markets through their logos and images, without the place of origin or manufacturers' names ever being revealed. We are thus confronted with a strategy of global marketing which is inserted into the primacy of cyberspace over geography, the primacy of global networks over the classical concepts of exchange and market. This is a similar strategy to that of the prestigious brand Nike, which, as Jeremy Rifkin says, 'has no productive capital: its shoes are made through anonymous contractors in Southeast Asia – it is an operational cost. The brand's customers pay the price of entering into its legend' (Rifkin 2001: 18).

It could be argued that, in this case, the 'globalized localisms' are not exactly 'localisms' but rather diffuse and complex processes that enable transnational capital to perfect mechanisms for the 'draining' of resources, thus exponentially increasing their domination and accumulation of wealth. As a result of this, the country or place of production is completely erased, and millions of workers are silently excluded, in a process in which 'living work' disappears and what remains is the aesthetic hyper-realism of a product adorned with the colours of the 'global' middle class. It could be said that 'localized globalisms' correspond in this case to the local impact of economic power on these workers and their communities, some of whom are cumulatively exploited in their work, others silenced and relegated to the margins of society and of the system. The hegemonic globalization of the last decade has merely accentuated and rendered more complex the whole web of interdependencies; the intensity of exploitation is now protected by subtler forms of power, better hidden forms of oppression and more sophisticated forms of domination, which are reproduced in a chain from the international centres of economic power to the domestic sphere of the poorest worker. It is in this sense that the subordination of communities to industry follows the same logic of the 'colonization' of the local by the global, that is, the domination of workers' collectivities and their community and family ways of life by the power of global capital. For this reason, it makes sense, in my opinion, to interpret the problems and potentialities of the trade union's new strategies of internationalization through solidarity as a counterpart to the powerful impact of the global markets upon the region and the working classes, as we have seen.

TOWARDS A NEW GLOBAL AND ANTIHEGEMONIC LABOUR INTERNATIONALISM

As we know, the crisis in the trade union movement has become more accentuated over the last two decades (Hyman 1994). After a phase of relative euphoria during the 1960s and 1970s, statistics show an ebb between 1980 and 1990. According to OECD data, there was a drop during this period in all member countries of approximately 7 per cent of wage workers (OECD 1991). From 1974 to 1995, membership rates in Portugal decreased from 52 per cent to 30 per cent (Cerdeira 1997: 51). The reduction in union membership is combined with models of competitive union pluralism, which contributes to weakening the unions' negotiating power (Ferreira 2001: 270–77). In the footwear union, this trend towards increased disaffiliation can also be seen. While at the beginning of the 1990s the membership rate was close to 55 per cent (a figure much above the national average at that time), the percentage of members is today nearer 35 per cent, according to the most recent information from the union.

Nevertheless, while it is clearly true that labour is today more divided and precarious, and capital more united and coordinated on the global level, it does not necessarily follow that, as Castells argues (1996: 360), the 'workers' movement was historically suppressed', or that it has even lost its capacity to transform and emancipate (Waterman 1999). It is true that traditional trade unionism seems to be collapsing, but there is also evidence that it may be possible to revive it, although under new bases of intervention.

For example, the European experiment of implementation of European Works Councils (EWCs), although limited to large companies and subject to many difficulties, demonstrates a potential that constitutes a challenge for Portuguese workers and Portuguese trade unionism, with possible emancipatory consequences (Costa 2000); and the trade union network SIGTUR (Southern Initiative on Globalization and Trade Union Rights), studied by Lambert and Webster (2000), clearly illustrates the virtues of an antihegemonic global social movement, based on a new labour internationalism which tries to combine traditional trade union organization with modern information networks.

Similarly, the case analyzed here also shows innovative potential in this area. I have already shown how the footwear workers' union has made a mark on the region, not only through its exposure of abused rights and the unbridled exploitation of workers, but also as a decisive pivot of solidarity and as a catalyst for numerous community initiatives. Following the line of analysis I have been developing, it is important to stress the efforts that the footwear workers' union has been making to counteract the destructive effects of neoliberal globalization through innovative forms of counterhegemonic globalization, which seek to converge with new global movements of resistance through participation in international networks of collective mobilization.

Throughout the 1990s, the trade union began to extend its local coalitions on a global scale, involving the participation of different actors and plural forms of intervention. This was what happened when, in 1997, the trade union leadership joined the project of the European Marches against Unemployment and Precariousness,[16] well before the main confederation CGTP-IN[17] joined the movement. This intervention in international networks (mainly in Europe but also extending to Brazil) clearly illustrates the importance attributed both to the institutional framework of labour policies within the European Union, and to initiatives promoted by trade union organizations on the transnational level. Such an intervention is thus reflected at the level of dialogue and negotiation mechanisms, as well as in protest demonstrations. For example, as regards the EU Directive on the European Works Councils (EWCs), the trade union was represented in different meetings dealing with the application of the directive in multinational companies of the sector established in the region (such as the firms Ecco Let, C. & J. Clark, and Rhode), and followed these proceedings closely. In particular, it exposed attempts to manipulate the respective electoral acts designed to elect workers' representatives in the EWCs,[18] and, as a result, those illegal acts were annulled. It is this type of intervention that reinforces the mediating role of the trade union in negotiating processes, and strengthens its international position among similar unions in Europe.

In addition, it has forged closer connections with the Brazilian trade union movement, maintaining contacts with the federation CUT and with the Shoemakers' Union of Nova Amburgo, and participating in December 1999 in various trade union meetings in Rio Grande do Sul.

Following a similar course of action to the current global social movements, the leaders of the SJM footwear workers' union are making increasing use of cyber networks on the worldwide web for access to up-to-date information, which they then divulge to their members and to the local population. Thus, they seek to show how local problems frequently originate in global factors, thereby stimulating sentiments of solidarity with the victims of hegemonic globalization worldwide. Various international associations and movements are on the list of partners and agreements that have been made in recent years.

- MST – *Movimento dos Sem Terra* (Landless Workers Movement) Brazil;
- CUT – *Central Única dos Trabalhadores* (Unified Workers Confederation) Brazil;
- *Viento Sur* – Journal of Economic and Social Affairs, Brazil;
- *Mouvement des 'sans papiers'* (Movement of illegal immigrants), France;
- *Agir Contre le Chômage* (Movement against unemployment), France;
- *Plataforma 0,7* – Madrid;
- CGT – *Confederatión General de Trabajo* (General Confederation of Labour) Madrid;
- *Derechos para tod@s*, (Rights for All), Madrid;
- *Paz Ahora* (Peace Now), Madrid;
- European Homeworking Group, Leeds, England;
- *Comissión Obrera Nacional de Catalunha*, (National Committee of Workers of Catalonia), Barcelona;
- *Oibrí Baile* (Group for home-based labour), Ireland;
- Maquila Solidarity Network (Group for home-based labour), Toronto;
- Homenet (Groups for home-based labour), India, Thailand, Santiago do Chile;
- Outwork TCFUA (Group for home-based labour), Carlon, Australia;
(SOURCE: Trade Union of Workers in Footwear, Bags and Related Articles of the Districts of Aveiro and Coimbra)

Many of these organizations have joined in different demonstrations and collective protests (such as the previously mentioned European Marches), and, like the trade union analyzed here, have a place within the broader movement of peaceful protest against hegemonic globalization. This intervention effort, which oscillates between the local and the global and which seeks to connect both types of logic within the same process, may be read not only according to the old ecological motto 'think globally, act locally', but also as an attempt to reinterpret the notion in a way which is perhaps more suitable to the current context – 'think locally, act globally'. This perspective rests, then, on the idea that today, thought and action can, more than ever, cross borders and dialectically produce solutions for current problems, either by discovering alternatives for local questions on the basis of global action, or by contributing to a new universal humanism of solidarity based on local action. One might say that, when the reality of SJM footwear workers is exposed in international forums, it is not only the world of industrial production that is put into question, but the whole local context surrounding this reality.

The emancipatory orientation that has been followed is based, therefore, not only upon the construction of platforms and local alliances, but also upon expansion to the global level of intervention; and this has been the strategy underlying the actions of this union and its leadership over the last decade. In other words, it is a strategy that brings together the concerns of both the 'old' and new types of internationalism, conveying a labour solidarity of the 'revolutionary' type and also a sentiment drawn from experiences that are not restricted to union militancy. It is useful to bear in mind here that the principal leader of the union was in the past very active in party politics and associations, combining cultural intervention (mentioned in the previous section) and membership of parties of the extreme left (of Trotskyist inspiration, such as the LCI and PSR), not to mention an identification with grassroots union currents (such as BASE-FUT). It is not surprising, therefore, that his stance combines a 'culturalist' and 'grass roots' vocation with a great openness vis-à-vis current movements of global solidarity. This is evident in his discourse, which contains both a radical critique of capitalist globalization and the profound conviction that nothing is achieved without the hard work of organization and mobilization. It is thus a discourse that basically links an updated and open form of ideological radicalism with a pragmatic sense of immediate action.

> There is a need to create alternatives to this system. If we take ecologist measures to their extreme, it is clear that the movement has to be anti-capitalist, in the strict sense of capitalism, as a system existing only for accumulation and not serving human beings. Because today, with the present state of knowledge and technology, human beings are on a level where there is no need for so much poverty ... But the system is made to create this poverty and this wealth...

> Nothing can be done without the work of organization... So, there has to be an articulation between these movements, both in Portugal and internationally. That is to say, nothing will happen if great efforts are not made to mobilize, organize, reflect, so that everyone together manages to put a spoke in the works, try to create stronger and more powerful movements in Portugal and in Europe and worldwide. There are millions of people in the world who are acting now! They are acting, like that peasant leader in France who recently invaded McDonald's. That was not banditry, it was an act against this system of normalization and globalization, which bars everyone, fires everyone, makes everyone unemployed, and is in favour of large economic groups and the brutal accumulation of great fortunes, isn't it? That action provoked sympathy in millions of people, and now what is necessary is to articulate those forces in all areas. (Trade union leader, SJM, July 2000)

In this vision, what stands out is clearly the importance given to the counterhegemonic movements appearing in the world today, together with the need to articulate the trade union movement with other movements, local and national problems with the global logic. In addition, we also get a clear idea that current social and cultural movements are scattered, and that a great effort will be needed to articulate the different fields of collective action, otherwise trade unions will have difficulty in finding alternative routes to social justice and solidarity.

As this conception is, in the end, the product of the cultural and socioeconomic reality of the region, it cannot but be taken as an example that provides empirical proof of the arguments developed throughout this essay. The local framework that, over the years, was an important mainstay of regulatory normalization, also produced underground sites of contestation and dissident voices. Although these may be no more than the expression of an emancipation that has been subjugated and absorbed by regulation (Santos 2000: 335), they have a tendency to persist as silent germs of latent resistance. Born in the silence of the margins, the voice of the trade union finds an echo in the hidden vibrations of the 'localized' community in order to become a great resonating sound in the centres of 'cosmopolitan' contestation. In this sense, cosmopolitanism is no more than another name for universalized localism.

CONCLUSION

The growing fragmentation and weakening of labour and of the traditional union movement is bringing to the fore the need to study the new challenges that this field has been facing, as well as the urgent need to find alternative ways to revitalize and reinvent it. A critical analysis that is also politically committed cannot limit itself to the underlining of difficulties and the dramatization of situations that are already dramatic. It also cannot override reality and invent something that does not exist. But it can, and to my mind should, if it wishes to remain faithful to the critical theory that provided the main analytical support to this collective project, reveal the other side of what exists but does not let itself be seen, making visible both the human dramas hidden under the mantle of multiple oppressions and the experiences, struggles and initiatives which, by their exemplary nature, can open up new paths to emancipation and solidaristic new humanist forms of internationalism.

In this essay, I have analyzed a case in which old and new forms of oppression, exploitation and exclusion are clearly inscribed within the logic of global economic domination. I have sought to understand them on the basis of the historical and socio-cultural factors that accompanied the industrial development of the region from the beginning of the twentieth century, showing their power and ability to frame industrial production in local communities, and also the way in which this framework obeyed the economicist dictates of the markets and was influenced by international political conjunctures. Despite the efficacy with which these factors managed to connect transnational structures of economic power to mechanisms of local control, and notwithstanding the regulatory force of the local capitalist elite and its triumph over class-based practices and struggles and community rebellion, the exercise of this economic, social and symbolic power has always been opposed by forces of rebellion and resistance arising from the grassroots.

The way in which the principle of the market has imposed itself upon the principle of community has exposed the contradictions of the former and the creativity of the latter. While the adaptation of the community had to be accompanied by solidarity initiatives controlled by industrialists, the hegemony of the market had to be supported by state action (notably the repressive authoritarianism used by the Salazar regime) in order to manufacture the sort of consent that suited its designs. At the same time, the local impacts of different global mechanisms translated themselves into factors of oppressive regulatory pressure, which, from the 1980s, were greatly reinforced. This is an alarming trend, which has given rise to new union policies as regards alliances, and a reorientation of union intervention towards the transnational level in an attempt to oppose the localism of exclusion with a globalist, inclusive and cosmopolitan approach, which tries to overcome local oppression through global solidarity.

Community recomposition has also been affected by contradictory influences over the years, which have sometimes opened up the way for initiatives of resistance and acts of rebellion. It was indeed in the gaps between these contradictions that union action has intruded in order to promote labour struggles. However, confronted with forms of regulation that evolved from old patriarchal allegiances into modern employer despotism, workers rarely supported union initiatives that were limited to the world of production. This is why the union (despite its important victories during the 1980s in struggles against arbitrary violence from entrepreneurs, discrimination against women and child labour) began to move increasingly in the sphere of associationalism and cultural work in the community as a way of reinforcing its capacity to intervene on behalf of workers. Although this opening-up of horizons has not yet yielded great results in mobilization, it clearly illustrates the imaginative potential and heterodox creativity of a leadership able to ally the everyday issues of labour and proximity with workers both inside and outside the companies with a great sensitivity towards cultural intervention in collectivities and associations in the region. It is a strategy which not only offers resistance to unsociable and individualist indifference but also promotes emancipation in the community by building new alliances and bringing together the most precarious and vulnerable segments of the workforce (such as the unemployed, the aged, young people and women working at home, and so on).

This strategy of multiple intervention contributes to the strengthening of conditions and programmes of negotiation which the union pursues in other ways (through dialogue with employers, the state and other social partners), revealing how the paradigmatic struggle operates both from within and without, gathering strength on the margins in order to undermine the centres of power within the mechanisms of regulation themselves. This orientation also promotes the articulation between labour action and different social and cultural movements. Indeed, this is one of the paths generally indicated for the revitalization of unionism. However, if this type of response reveals creative potential for the reinvention of union action, it can still be complemented by other forms of participation, namely at the transnational and global level.

Therefore, the internationalist praxis of this union, in assuming a greater role in struggles against neoliberal hegemonic globalization alongside other types of activism and other social movements, is guided by a course of action aimed at counteracting and resisting the destructive effects of the multinational companies in the sector, while seeking to invert the process of 'oppressive localization' which has maintained labour collectivities and their communities subjected to 'conformist sociabilities'; it seeks to orient its action in an antihegemonic direction, thus contributing to a new visibility of workers' problems and a reinforcing the new dimensions and networks of international solidarity. Well ahead of most Portuguese unions, the SJM footwear workers' union and its leadership have revealed an imaginativeness and a potential that justify its placement on the front line of present-day internationalist emancipatory movements.

We may conclude by saying that this union's struggle for emancipation clearly illustrates the potential hidden behind the logic of regulation which developed over the years out of the hegemonic forces that subjected the community to industry, and the local to the global. By seeking to rejoin what has been separated, it hopes to restore the dignity of labour through community intervention, and to promote the emancipation of the local by intervening in the global counterhegemonic networks, struggles and social movements.

NOTES

1. Among other things, the new trade unionism proposed here requires that the struggle within the work force be linked to actions concerning the issue of wage labour; that demands for better wages and better working conditions be accompanied by more control over the production process, investments, new technologies, relocation, subcontracting, and education and training policies; that the struggle against authoritarian and technocratic methods of control be based on alliances with other non-union sectors, movements and communities; and that there be dialogue and cooperation with other forces and democratic non-class-based or multi-class movements, while refusing to be – or to be subordinated to – some vanguard or 'sovereign' power (Waterman 2000).
2. Although he was officially subordinated to the structures of the Salazar regime, the National Trade Union of Footwear Workers of the District of Aveiro, this leader (António Carreirinha) used his position for approximately ten years as a legal cover for a whole clandestine activity, organizing and mobilizing footwear workers (which culminated in the August 1943 strike), a process set in motion by the local branch of the Portuguese Communist Party (PCP) to which he belonged.
3. Not only the employers but also significant segments of the local population were at that time particularly alarmed at the power that the revolutionary discourse and the role of the PCP were achieving in Portuguese society.
4. It should be noted that at the beginning of the 1980s trade union membership was at about 60 per cent.
5. He began his activity in the cultural association ARCA – Cultural and Recreational Association of Oliveira de Azeméis, a few years after starting work in the sector, in the second half of the 1960s.
6. It should be pointed out that this trade union leader was doing his military service at that time and therefore represented the MFA in the resolution of various labour conflicts in the greater Lisbon area. This context, which was marked by 'revolutionary' discourse and by the presence of strong but contradictory popular movements, was undoubtedly an important moment in the political education of this leader. Despite the experience he had already accumulated, his arguments for the articulation between the trade union movement and the new social movements, as well as between local and global

dimensions, have been fundamentally influenced by that period and that intense experience.
7. A glance at the newspaper headlines reveals the repressive conditions in companies and some of the struggles that the union has faced: 'Trade unionist stabbed by footwear entrepreneur' (*Jornal de Notícias*, 15 March 1988); '"Security guards" attack trade unionists in a factory in S. João da Madeira' (*Jornal de Notícias*, 20 July 1990); 'S. João da Madeira – Violence in the footwear strike' (*Público*, 1 Sept. 1993); 'Workers prevent machines leaving factory in Arouca – Vigilance in the footwear industry' (*Público*, 28 Oct. 95); 'Workers from company in Arouca without wages – Factory closure leads to demonstration' (*Jornal de Notícias*, 27 Sept. 1995); 'Worker suspended from footwear factory – Supreme Court overturns sanctions on union representative' (*Público*, 19 Nov. 1996); 'Trial of alleged unionist attackers – to be or not to be the moral author, that is the question' (*Público*, 5 Nov. 1996); 'Employer and "security guards" condemned for aggression against trade unionists' (*Jornal de Notícias*, 15 Nov. 1996); 'GNR [Republican National Guard] says it saw nothing – unionists "sequestrated" by employer' (*Jornal da Feira*, 8 May 1998); "Basilius" Company in the defendant's chair – "Let justice be done", says the union' (*O Regional*, 22 Jan. 2000); 'Footwear employer condemned for sequestering trade unionists' (*Jornal de Notícias*, 25 March 2000); 'Demonstration of Clark's workers attracts far less support than in Arouca – To say that there is no work is a bluff' (*Comércio do Porto*, 4 March, 2001).
8. One can say that, contrary to former hopes that the gradual development of 'consciousness' would result in radical social emancipation, the present scenario reveals that those who were supposed to have achieved such a 'consciousness' have been gradually losing it, while those who had never had it, might now promote their own struggle for dignity without paying the cost of disillusionment suffered by those who had assimilated such a utopia.
9. Associations with which the trade union maintains a regular collaboration, or with which it has established agreements, include: Associação Abril em Maio (a Lisbon cultural association); Associação Recreativa e Cultural de Arouca (a recreational and cultural association); O Sítio – Associação de Jovens 'Ecos Urbanos', of S. João da Madeira (a youth association); the Academy of Music of São João da Madeira; SOS-Racismo and Olho Vivo – Associação Anti-Racismo (anti-racist associations); APCC – Associação de Apoio às Crianças Carenciadas (an association for the support of children in need); Escola de Bailado e Artes Cénicas, Vila da Feira (a ballet and theatre school); IGRECA – Grupo de Estudo do Trabalho ao Domicílio (a study group for home-based work); Centro de Documentação 25 de Abril (a documentation centre); and Mutualidades – Associação Cultural, Esmoriz/Ovar (a cultural association).
10. See *A Indústria Portuguesa de Calçado*. Edition APICCAPS, Oporto, 1997; INOFOR – *Evolução das Qualificações e Diagnóstico das Necessidades de Formação*, Sector Report on Tanning, Footwear and Other Leather Products, 2001; APICCAPS, *Plano Estratégico para os Próximos cinco Anos*, in *Expresso*, 16 June 2001.
11. As some studies have noted, the experience of migration tends to result in a 'border discourse' which shapes the emigrant's 'multiplicity of identity' (Capinha 1997). In this case, it could be said that this multiplicity resulted in a reinforcement of the identification with the community of origin; that is to say, the transnational experience found in mobility a factor for the consolidation of local identity (the strength of roots), demonstrating how connections between the global and the local may relegate the national to second rank (Feldman-Bianco 1993).
12. I will refer below to some of the local effects of the policies of the so-called *Estado Novo*, and the way in which, by means of a narrow discourse of local interests and 'reactionary progressivism', the local subjectivities evolved towards a community subjected to official ideology, which mediated between the local and the global.
13. It is appropriate to recall my initial statements about the 'community', which is not taken here as something substantive; rather, the 'realization of community means, in this sense, the presence of discursive formulas or processes under construction which aspire

to achieve a new collective identity' (Estanque 2000: 56). If traditional small-town 'fortress communities' have been destroyed and if the de-territorialization of the community has produced more 'amoeba communities', then these may develop either according to a logic of adaptation, bound by roots, 'localized' and of 'descent', or according to a logic of emancipation, oriented by a sense of mission, of 'ascent' and in search of 'cosmopolitanism' (Santos 1995b; Morris 1996; Bellah 1997). In a certain way, the construction of the local community faced this type of contradictory tendencies.

14. SJM became a town in 1924 and a municipality (*concelho*) two years later (see Estanque 2000: 147).
15. I am referring here to the main organization for the workers' leisure time, established by the Salazar State in 1935 and inspired by similar experiments by Hitler's and Mussolini's regimes, the so-called National Foundation for Joy at Work (FNAT) (see Rosas 1992).
16. Participating in demonstrations such as Brussels, April 1997; the Zurich–Marseilles march, May 1997; Oporto, January 2000; and in Nice, December 2000.
17. The footwear trade union of S. João da Madeira is affiliated to the General Confederation of Portuguese Workers [CGTP-IN], but it has maintained an independent position in relation to the hegemonic current of its directorate, politically closer to the PCP. The other large federation rivaling this one (the General Union of Workers/UGT) takes a more reformist and moderate stance, and supports negotiation and social 'concertation' rather than mass mobilization; it is politically aligned with the Socialist Party.
18. See the case of the annulment of an agreement with the headquarters of Ecco Let in Denmark, which had been signed by delegates 'nominated' by the management instead of democratically elected by their peers, as mentioned by Hermes Costa (2000).

REFERENCES

Ashwin, S. (2000): 'International Labour Solidarity After the Cold War', in R. Cohen and S. Rai (eds.), *Global Social Movements*, London: Athlone, pp.101–16.
Bellah, R. (1997): 'The Necessity of Opportunity and Community in a Good Society', *International Sociology* 12/4, pp.387–93.
Bezuidenhout, A. (1999): 'Towards Global Social Movement Unionism? Trade Union Responses to Globalization in South Africa', Geneva: International Labour Organization (www.ilo.org/public/english/bureauc/inst/papers/2000/dp115/), 11 July 2001.
Burawoy, M. (1985): *The Politics of Production*, London: Verso.
Cabral, M.V. (1979): *Portugal na Alvorada do Século XX*, Lisbon: A Regra do Jogo.
Capinha, G. (1997): 'Ficções credíveis no campo da(s) identidade(s): a poesia dos emigrantes portugueses no Brasil', *Revista Crítica de Ciências Sociais* 48, pp.103–46.
Castells, M. (1998): *End of Millenium. The Information Age: Economy, Society and Culture* (Vol. III), Oxford: Blackwell.
Cerdeira, M. da C. (1997): 'A sindicalização portuguesa de 1974 a 1995', *Sociedade e Trabalho* Ministério para a Qualificação e o Emprego, 1, pp.46–53.
Costa, H.A. (2000): 'O Sindicalismo Português face aos Conselhos de Empresa Europeus', International Symposium *Reinventing Social Emancipation*. University of Coimbra, November 2000.
De Certeau, M. (1984): *The Practice of Everyday Life*, Berkeley: University of California Press.
Estanque, E. (1999): 'Acção colectiva, comunidade e movimentos sociais: para um estudo dos movimentos de protesto público', *Revista Crítica de Ciências Sociais* 55, pp.85–111.
Estanque, E. (2000): *Entre a Fábrica e a Comunidade: subjectividades e práticas de classe no operariado do calçado*, Oporto: Afrontamento.
Featherstone, M., S. Lash and R. Robertson (eds.) (1995): *Global Modernities*, London: Sage.

Feldman-Bianco, B. (1993): 'Múltiplas camadas de tempo e espaço: (re)construções da classe, da etnicidade e do nacionalismo entre imigrantes portugueses', *Revista Crítica de Ciências Sociais* 38, pp.193-223.
Ferreira, A.C. (2001): 'Para uma concepção decente e democrática do trabalho e dos seus direitos: (re)pensar o direito das relações laborais', in B. de S. Santos (ed.), *Globalização: Fatalidade ou Utopia?*, Oporto: Afrontamento, pp.259-96.
Gentili, P. (org.) (1999): *Globalização Excludente: Desigualdade, Exclusão e Democracia na Nova Ordem Mundial*, Petrópolis: Editora Vozes.
Giddens, A. (1990): *The Consequences of Modernity*, Stanford: Stanford University Press.
Habermas, J. (1989): *The Theory of Communicative Action: Lifeworld and System. A Critique of Funcionalist Reason*, Cambridge: Polity Press.
Habermas, J. (1998): *O Discurso Filosófico da Modernidade*, Lisbon: Publicações Dom Quixote.
Held, D. and A. McGrew (2001): *Prós e Contras da Globalização*, Rio de Janeiro: Zahar.
Hirst, P. and G. Thompson (1996): *Globalization in Question*, Cambridge: Polity Press.
Hobsbawm, E.J. (1984): *Worlds of Labour: Further Studies in the History of Labour*, London: Weidenfeld.
Hyman, R. (1994): 'Trade Unions and the Disaggregation of the Working Class', in Marino Regini (ed.), *The Labour Movements*, London: Sage, pp.150-68.
INOFOR (2001): *Evolução das Qualificações e Diagnóstico das Necessidades de Formação*, Sectoral report on tanning, footwear, and other leather products, Lisbon: Ministério do Trabalho e da Solidariedade.
Jones, G.S. (1989): *Languages of Class – Studies in English Working Class History 1832-1982*, Cambridge: Cambridge University Press.
Laclau, E. (1996): *Emancipation(s)*, London: Verso.
Lash, S. (1999): 'Crítica da informação', *Revista Crítica de Ciências Sociais* 54, pp.13-30.
Lambert, R. and E. Webster (2000): 'Social Emancipation and the New Labor Internationalism: a Southern Perspective' International Symposium *Reinventing Social Emancipation*. University of Coimbra, November 2000.
Lima, M.P. de, José G. Oliveira, L. Oliveira, M. da C. Cerdeira and M.T.S. Rosa (1992): *A Acção Sindical e o Desenvolvimento*, Lisbon: Edições Salamandra.
Linstead, S. (1985): 'Jokers wild: the importance of humor in the maintenance of organizational culture', *The Sociological Review* 33/4, pp.741-67.
Moody, K. (1997): *Workers in a Lean World: Unions in the International Economy*, London: Verso.
Morris, P. (1996): 'Community Beyond Tradition', in Paul Heelas (ed.), *Detraditionalization*, Oxford: Blackwell Publishers, pp.223-49.
O'Hearn, D. (2000): 'Globalization, the 'New Tigers' and the End of the Developmental State? The Case of the Celtic Tiger', *Politics and Society* 28/1, pp.67-92.
OECD (1991): *Perspectives de L'Emploi*, Geneva: OECD.
Pureza, J.M. (2001): 'Para um internacionalismo pós-vestfaliano', in Santos, Boaventura de Sousa (ed.), *Globalização: Fatalidade ou Utopia?*, Oporto: Afrontamento, pp. 238-58.
Ray, L.J. (1993): *Rethinking Critical Theory: Emancipation in the Age of Global Social Movements*, London: Sage.
Rifkin, J. (2001): 'Quando os Mercados se Apagam ante as Redes: uma transformação radical do capitalismo', *Le Monde Diplomatique* – Portuguese edition, Year 3, No. 28 July, pp.18-19.
Rosanvallon, P. (1988): *La Question Syndicale*, Paris: Calmann-Lévy.
Rosa, M.T.S. (1998): *Relações de Trabalho e Sindicalismo Operário em Setúbal*, Oporto: Afrontamento.
Rosas, F. (ed.) (1992): *Portugal e o Estado Novo (1930-1960)*, Lisbon: Editorial Presença.
Santos, B. de S. (1994): *Pela Mão de Alice – O social e o político na pós-modernidade*, Oporto: Afrontamento.
Santos, B. de S. (1995a): 'Teses para a Reinvenção do Sindicalismo em Portugal, seguidas de um apelo', *Vértice* 68, pp.132-9.

Santos, B. de S. (1995b): *Toward a New Common Sense: Law, Science and Politics in the Paradgmatic Transition*, London/New York: Routledge.

Santos, B. de S. (2000): *A Crítica da Razão Indolente: contra o desperdício da experiência*, Oporto: Afrontamento.

Tengarrinha, J. (1981): 'As greves em Portugal: uma perspectiva histórica do século XVIII a 1920', *Análise Social* 67/68/69, pp.573–601.

Thompson, E.P. (1987) [1963]: *A Formação da Classe Operária Inglesa*, Rio de Janeiro: Paz e Terra (vols. I, II e III). English edition: *The Making of the English Working Class*, London: Harmondsworth/Penguin.

Waterman, P. (2000): 'Trade Union Internationalism in the Age of Seattle' (http://www.antenna.nl/~ waterman/), 11 July 2001.

INDEX

Note: Page numbers in bold type refer to figures

abortion: decriminalization 168–9
Abraço 175–6
accountability: limited 9
active citizenship 6–9; decline and revitalization 11; lessons from Spinoza 39–40; state co-operation 59; and trade unionism 255; worldwide movement 40, *see also* collective action; neighbourhood movements; social movements; trade unions
administration agencies: counterhegemonic strategies 58–9
African colonies: independence 51; liberation movements 50
Agenda for Peace (UN) 200
aggregative democracy 5
agonistic pluralism 7
Algarve: contrasts 18; *Feiras da Serra* 26, 33; public services 22
Amnesty International 183
Anderson, Benedict 197
Angola: liberation movement 10, 50
ANIMAR (Portuguese Association for Local Development) 32, 38
Annan, Kofi 211
anti-hegemony *see* counterhegemonic strategies
anti-war demonstrations (2003) 8
architecture: community role 56
armed forces *see* MFA
associations: ecological 88; entrepreneurial 88–9; local 86–7; local development 37, 89; strength/mobilization 90
associative participation 79–81
asymmetric developmental framework 43

Balo, Bishop Carlos 199
Barry, Andrew 8
Beck, Ulrich 46
Beira: female activism 116, *see also* Canas de Senhorim
Bernard van Leer Foundation 21
black movement: and LGBT movement 180
Braudel, Fernand 41
Brazil: LGBT movement support 165

Caetano, Marcello 10
Canas de Senhorim: committee demands 102; municipality status 99–100; Parliamentary bill 102–4, *see also* MRCSS
capitalist system: facilitation of new family models 162–3; and gay identity 162–6; and information exchange 163; and sexual oppression 164
Carnations Revolution (1974) *see* revolution
Carvalho, Otelo Saraiva de 52
Castells, Manuel 49
Catholic Church: social mobilization 168–9; Timorese support 204–5

285

Catholicism: and sexuality 168–71
CCI (Independent Scientific Commission): error 146; legal framework 142; report criticism 143–5
CCRLVT (Coordinating Committee of Region of Lisbon and Tagus Valley) 82–3, 86
CDPM (Maubere People's Rights Commission) 204
CDS (Social Democratic Centre) 102
CEP (Portuguese Episcopal Council) 168, 170
CET (Centre for Territorial Studies) 82
CGTP (General Confederation of Portuguese Workers): EWCs position 230–3
chains of transmission 60
Chomsky, Noam 191
Chueca (Madrid): gay consumerism 165–6
Cimpor 139, 145
citizen action: necessity 27
citizen movements: emergence 12
claiming action 86–7
claims movements: motivation 64
CLCC (Committee for the Fight against Co-incineration) 133, 140–1
co-incineration: CCI study 143–6; *Diário de Coimbra* petition 141; government strategy 139–40; international forum 143; legislation 142; media attitudes 143; ministerial statement 143; POP production 147; risk assessment 146, *see also* CLCC; Coimbra; Souselas; Souselas protest movement
cognitive justice: indispensability 3
Coimbra: co-incineration petition 141; discrimination 141
Coimbra Civic Association Pro Urbe: parliamentary negotiations 141–2; presidential statement 145
Coimbra Federation of Trade Unions: cement plant mediation 141
collective action: subversive games 264; typology 85–91
Common Agricultural Policy (EU) 33

Communist Party 59
community: industry impact 258–61
concerted negotiation action 88–9
consensus: culture 94; supreme value of democracy 68; through deliberation 6
Constitution: drafting 10, 11; explicit aims 71; housing rights 59; and participatory democracy 51–2; sexual orientation legislation 172; successive revisions 69, 71
contentions politics: study territory 8
Coordinating Committee of Region of Lisbon and Tagus Valley (CCRLVT) 82–3, 86
corporate interests: reinforcement 80
Correia, José Lopes 102, 105
cosmopolitanism 221
Council Directive 94/45/EC: cross-border influence 227; emancipatory potential 225; information rights 222–4; main objective 222; Portuguese compliance 229; revision process 242–3; and voluntary agreements 225–6, 228, *see also* EWCs
counterhegemonic strategies 8, 159, 191, 193, 253; administration agencies 58–9; trade unions 258, 267, 273
critical action 87–8
critical education 17–18
CSOs (civic and solidarity organizations): outlook 37–8; relationships with formal powers 37

decentralization 61–2; process 99
decision making: urban planning 82
deliberative processes 5–6
D'Emilio, John 162, 182
democracy: aggregative 5; epistemic 3; forms 7; managerial 93; neoliberal challenges 4–6; normalizing chronology 70; pathologies 6; thin 4, *see also* participatory democracy
democratic order: affecting pathologies 4
Democratic Republic of East Timor (RDTL) 204
democratization: path diversity 1

INDEX

demonstrations 273; anti-war (2003) 8; LGBT movement 161, 177; MRCSS 102–4, 112–15, 119–20; Souselas 141–2
Diário de Coimbra 141
duality of impotences 51, 57, 59

East Timor: 1999 massacres 212; campaigning groups 204, 205–6; colonial rule 195; cultural specificity 204; demonstrations 212; EU position 209–10; *fait accompli* 196–7; founding principles of resistance 197; genocide 196, 200, 201; geopolitical factors 198–200; INTERFET 201, 202; international law 199; international support 205; New York Agreements 211; political shift in resistance movement 2–6; Portuguese role 195–6, 206–12; Santa Cruz massacre 199, 205, 210; solidarity movements 203–6; strategic relevance 210–11; TAPOL 205; UN legislation 195, 207–8; UN referendum (1999) 191; UNTAET 212–13
Ecco Let: EWC experience 233–6
ecological associations: critical action 88
economic recession: repercussions 268–9
education: social movements' role 17–18
election boycott: MRCSS 113, 126
electoral participation: levels 79–80
emancipation: multiple option view 220–1
emancipatory struggle: transformations associated with 136
employees: information/consultation mechanisms 218
entrepreneurial associations: advantages 88–9
entrepreneurial despotism 259
environmental issues: risk perception 134
episodic framing 114
epistemic democracy: indispensability 3
Escarameia, Paula 195, 199

Estado Novo 10; housing policies 53–4; opposition forms 50, *see also* Salazar regime
ETUC (European Trade Union Confederation) 220
Euroletter 184
European Marches against Unemployment and Precariousness 273
European Union (EU): East Timor position 209–10; education funding 24; legal frameworks 135; and legislation 135, 166–7; Portugal's entry 10–11; protest within 8; as social movement resource 135–6; waste management directives 147–8
EWCs (European Works Councils): anticipation strategies 222; and consultation 228; Ecco Let experience 233–6; emancipatory aspect 221–2, 272–3; establishment 229–42; FAG Group experience 236–40; limitations 227–9; national legislation 241–2; organisatory potential 226; overview 224–9; perception 240–1; personal observations 238; regulatory aspect 221; summarizing 242–4; trade union responses 219–20, 230–3, *see also* Council Directive 94/45/EC
exclusion 46
expert/lay alliances 47–8, 57, 72–3, 133, 148–9
expression: modes 6
Eymard-Duvernay, François 78

FAG Group: EWC experience 236–40
Falk, Richard 192, 199
Faro Polytechnic Institute 20, 27
Feiras da Serra 33
feminist movement: and LGBT movement 175, 180
Ferreira, Vitor Matias 64
FHH (Fund for Promotion of Housing) 62
footwear industry: development 258–61; export strategy 267, 268–9; global marketing system 271; repressive practices 263;

salaries 270–1; subcontracting system 271
footwear workers' union: community oriented potentialities 261–7; counterhegemonic strategies 258, 273; cultural intervention 266; international partners 274–5; legal action 263; personal observations 262, 263, 264, 265, 266, 275–6; summarizing 276–9; training policies 266, *see also* São Joã da Madeira
force: discretionary use 201
forcible relocation: struggle against 72
Fordism 269
forms of democracy 7
Foucault, M.: influence 6; specific intellectual 48
free elections 10, 51, 102
Freire, Paulo 40
Fund for the Promotion of Housing (FHH) 62

gay consumerism: and emancipation 165–6; and globalization 159–60, 177; Portuguese market 163
General Confederation of Portuguese Workers (CGTP): EWCs position 230–3
General Workers' Union (GWU): EWCs position 230–3
geopolitics 198–200
Giddens, Anthony 46
globalization: emancipatory advantages 219; labour impacts 219; paradoxical nature 253
globalized localism 221
GNR (Republican National Guard): Canas de Senhorim 103, 119, 120
Godet, Michel 82; actors' strategy 82–3, 85, 86
grassroots organizations: action typology 85–91
Green Party 145
Green-Blue Project 19–20
Greenpeace 147
group restructuring 92
GTM (Medical Working Group): formation 146
Guerra, Isabel 35

Guinea-Bissau: liberation movement 10, 50
Gusmão, Xanana 206, 210, 213
Guterres, António 120
Guterres, Eurico 202

Habibie, President B.J. 211
hegemonic globalization: exploitation 271–2; minority counterhegemony 159; resistance 8
heterosexual hegemony 165
homophobia 164
homosexuality: Catholic position 169–71; economic status 163, 165, 166; legislation 161; positive discrimination 161; and poverty 162, *see also* LGBT movement
housing: struggle for 49–50, 52, 55
housing policies: counteracting urban impacts 62; forcible relocation 7; public intervention model 53–4; as social control tool 54
housing problems: popular cooperation 59
humanitarian intervention 200–1
hunger strike: MRCSS 112, 113

ILGA-Portugal (International Lesbian and Gay Association): official recognition 172
ilhas 55
In Loco Association: beginnings 19–28; bureaucracy 31–2, 36; catchment area 28; central mission 27; coherent strategy 30–1; external impact 32–3; external support 36–7; formal creation 26–7; independent nature 27; integrated strategy 26; internal democracy 32; lobbying initiative 33–4; networking 38; official recognition 28; outlook 45; partnerships 34; sustainable development promotion 27–8; towards local democracy 34–6; trainee grants 25; two-tier methodology 29
inclusive society: route to 161
Independent Scientific Commission (CCI) *see* CCI

INDEX

Indonesia: financial crisis 210; militia groups 202; UN support 196–7, 201–2; use of *fait accompli* 197–8
industrial growth: nineteenth century 258–9
industrial waste treatment 135
industrial working class: urban increase 10
information: local empowerment 144–5, 149
innovative action 89–91
integrated local development: strategy development 30–1
Integrated System for Management of Industrial Waste (SIGRI) 135
intellectuals: specific *see* specific intellectuals
interactionist sociology: objective 78
International Forum on Co-Incineration 143
international law: emancipatory role 199; post-Westphalian transition 194–5
International Monetary Fund (IMF) 200
Iyengar, Shanto 114

Jobert, Bruno 92
Joy at Work 270

Kerckhofs, Peter 229
knowledge: local empowerment 144–5, 149
Koskenniemi, Martin 194
Krickler, K. 183–4

law: application consistency 167
lay/expert alliances 47–8, 57, 72–3, 133, 148–9
LEADER Programme (EU): funding 29, 30–1; preparatory stage 28–9; public policy impact 32–3
Lecher, Wolfgang 223–4
Lefèbvre, Henri 49
Lefèvre, Christian 95
left-wing organizations 59; and popular initiatives 59–60
LGBT movement (lesbian/gay/bisexual/transgender): agenda 174–5, 184–5; demonstrations 161, 177; discrimination 164–5; emancipatory potential 178–84; emergence 171–7; equality discourse criticism 161; globalization context 159; parliamentary legislation 179; personal observations 176, 180, 181, 182; political allies 176–7; summarizing 184–6; support network 174–7, 178–80, 182–4
liberticide measures 4–5
Lilás 172
Lisbon: research study 82–3
Lisbon/Tagus Valley: coordinating committee 82–3, 86; MACTOR software 82–3, 84; planning process 83–6; structure 84
local associations: claiming action 86–7
local authorities: legitimate representation 99
local committees 79–80
local consensus: role in territorial fieldwork 23
local development 18–19
local development associations: grant entitlement 37; innovative action 89
local development plans: importance 34
local economies: protection 43–4
local entrepreneurship: sustainable development 27
local health care provision 28
local knowledge: legitimacy 137
local money 43–4
local populations: access to information 144–5, 149; anomie 79
local production: development initiatives 26; problems of scale 25–6; regulatory conditions 33
localized globalism 257, 271

Maastricht 218
MACTOR software 82–3, 84
managerial democracy: opposition 93
Manifesta 32

manufactured risks 46–7
Maubere People's Rights Commission (CDPM) 204
media: East Timor 198
Medical Working Group (GTM): formation 146
Melo, Alberto: critical education 17–18; political development 16–19
MERCOSUR 243
Mexico: Catholic Church 169
MFA (Movement of Armed Forces) 10; Division for Civil Affairs 60; internal tensions 50; MRCSS role 101; SAAL role 55
military coup 10
military coup (1974) 50
minimum wage: income level 24
minorities: resistance potential 159
mobile education 28
Mobile Service for Local Support (SAAL) *see* SAAL
modernity: unfulfilled promises 1
Monteiro, António 202, 208
Monteiro, Cáceres 114
Movement for Restoration of the Municipality of Canas de Senhorim (MRCSS) *see* MRCSS
Mozambique: liberation movement 10, 50
MRCSS (Movement for Restoration of Municipality of Canas de Senhorim): action strategies 111–16; demonstrations 102–4, 112–15, 119–20; election boycott 113, 126; hunger strike 112, 113; identity processes 122–4; main objective 98; media coverage 112–13, 114–16, 120, 121, 122; organization/leadership 105–11, 116, 124–5; personal observations 104, 107, 109–10, 112, 115, 117, 118, 122; violence 118–20; women's participation 116–18, 125
Muller, Pierre 92
multicultural citizenship: overview 2; promoting 7–8
Municipalities, Law on Creation of 101

National Solidarity Movement (PSN): Canas de Senhorim 119
neighbourhood movements: contradictory dynamics 65; female activism 55–6, 72; military's role 60–1; political organizations' role 59–60; professionals' interest 56, 72–3
Nelas: municipality status 99–100
neoliberal globalization 192–3; and *Agenda for Peace* 200
neoliberalism: democracy challenges 4–6
new conquistadors 41
new technology: careful introduction 25; impact 7
NIABY (Not In Anyone's Back Yard) 151
NIMBY (Not In My Back Yard) 138–9, 145, 151
Nogueira, D. Eurico Dias 169–70
normalization period 10–11

Oporto: forcible relocation 72; public/state cooperation 63; resistance history 55, 57; SAAL development 52, 55
Oppenheimer, J. Robert 48
Opus Gay 163, 172–3, 182
Organa 171–2
organized scepticism 152

participation: associative 79–81; electoral 79–80; focus forms 132–3; models 134; political 48–50, 79–81; problems 46–7; reinvention 69; women 55–6, 72, 116–18, 125; workplace 70
participatory democracy 2; and Constitution 51–2; emancipatory potential 136; expanding 81; memory deletion 69–70; overview 9–12; questions 94–5; revolutionary period 47, 52; SAAL 64–6, 73; trade union promotion 262
participatory management action 88–9
Pasture, Patrick 221

INDEX

pathologies of democracy: European context 6
persistent organic pollutants (POP) 147
personal observations: LGBT movement 176, 180, 181, 182; Serro do Caldeirão 30; Souselas 140, 148, 149, 150, 151–2
PESGRI (Strategic Plan for Management of Industrial Waste) 139–40
pilgrim citizenship: East Timor 203–6
Pinheiro, Luís 105, 107, 109–10, 115
pink industry 159–60, 177; Portugal 181
planning methodologies: comparison 86
planning processes: legitimacy 88–9
planning technicians: central questions 78–9
political activism 10
political participation 79–81; intellectuals' role 48–50
political parties: and popular initiatives 59–60
political-administrative system: fragmentation 81
politics: precautionary approach 46–7
POP (persistent organic pollutants) 147
popular epidemiology 145
popular mobilization 12
popular movements: military support 60; state support 59
population: post-war changes 10
Portas, Nuno 59, 61, 67
Porto Alegre 8
Portugal: intermediary role 9; post-war experience 10; semiperipheral condition 47, 133, 135, 166, 270
Portuguese Association for Local Development (ANIMAR) 32, 38
Portuguese Electric Oven Company 101, 104
Portuguese Episcopal Council (CEP) 168, 170
positivism 193–5
post-revolutionary period: infrastructure preoccupation 20; normalization process 61, 68, 70, 102; trade union reflux 261; weaknesses 9
presidential election 52
proscription: of social groups 160
protest movements: effects on Portuguese society 152; local activism 138–9; motivation 64; and science/technology 136–7; successes 141
provisional governments 51
PSD (Social Democratic Party): co-incineration bill 141
PSN (National Solidarity Movement): Canas de Senhorim 119
public action: value system 78
public policies: territorializing 77
Pureza, José Manuel 255

QUEERS (Queers United to Eradicate Economic Rationalism) 165

Rabinow, Paul 48–9
RADIAL Project: action plan 22–3; children activity centres 23–4; creation of In Loco Association 26–7; marketing strategy 25–6; preliminary consultation 21; self-employment training 24; trainee grants 23–4; training methodology 23–4
Ramos Horta, José 199, 207
RDTL (Democratic Republic of East Timor) 204
real estate groups: growing prominence 79
realism 194
realpolitik 198
recession: repercussions 268–9
Reinventing Social Emancipation (research project): critical engagement 3–4; methodology 2; selected countries 2; thematic areas 2–3
relocation: forcible 7, 57, 72
Republican National Guard (GNR): Canas de Senhorim 103, 119, 120
revolution: and colonial policy 196; official narratives 68–74, *see also* post-revolutionary period; revolutionary period

revolutionary legitimacy 61
revolutionary period 10–11;
  homosexual mobilization 171;
  Operation SAAL context 50–3;
  participatory democracy experience 47, 52
right to difference 161
right to place 52; defining 57; SAAL perspective 62
right-wing regimes: policies 16–17
risk management: state experience 136
rogue states 4
Rubin, Jeffrey 106
rural areas: integrated local development 25–6

SAAL (Mobile Service for Local Support): aims/operational logic 61–4; ambiguous dynamic 64–5; demise 66–8; lay/expert participation 57; methodology 62–3, 65–6; objectives 61–2; overview 52; social emancipation/participatory democracy 64–6, *see also* Oporto; SAAL/Norte; specific intellectuals
SAAL/Norte: actors 54–5; development context 53–4; fostering participatory democracy 73; legislative production 63–4; lessons 72; memory invocation 52–3; positive results 63; state relationship 58, 73–4; technical solutions 56
Salazar regime: repressive role 260, *see also* Estado Novo
Santa Cruz massacre 199, 205, 210
Santos, Boaventura de Sousa 57–8, 69, 125, 126, 221, 253
São Joã da Madeira (SJM) 254, 256; Brazilian connection 259–60, 267; entrepreneurs social roots 259–60; local movements 269–70; vandalism 261
science: credibility 133; legitimizing instrument 150; vulnerability to appropriation 137–8
science/technology: decision making mechanisms 134–5; and exclusion 46–7; and protest movements 136–7
Scoreco: formation 139; relationship with population 140
Scott, James 134, 153
Seattle 8
Secil 139, 145
secrecy: in political decisions 46
Security Council: East Timor 196–7, 201–2
self-regulation 194
semiperipheral condition of Portugal 47, 133, 135, 166, 270
September 11 attacks: and citizens' rights 4
Serro do Caldeirão 20; emigration 21; *Feiras da Serra* 33; integrated local development 25–6; population identity 20–1; public consultation 34; training schemes 24
Serzedelo, António 163, 182
sexual acts: decriminalization 166–7
sexual emancipation: and Catholic Church 168–71
sexual orientation: discrimination 164; and economic power 162–6; employment protection 165, 179; and oppression 159, *see also* LGBT movement
shoe industry *see* footwear industry
SIGRI (Integrated System for the Management of Industrial Waste) 135
small-scale tourism: supplementary income 32
social action: overview 18
Social Democratic Centre (CDS) 102
Social Democratic Party (PSD): co-incineration bill 141
social emancipation: SAAL experience 64–6
social groups: proscription 160
social housing: design 73
social intervention 91–5; emancipation/integration paradox 91–3; managerial/project democracy 93–5
social movement: EU as resource 135–6

INDEX

social movements: educational role 17–18; motivation 64; networking 176–7; strength 167, see also neighbourhood movements
social regulation: community/industry articulation 256–7; global/local articulation 257–8
solidaristic globalization 3
solidarity movements: East Timor 203–6
Souselas (Coimbra): Anti-Pollution Commission 140, 149; as co-incineration site 133, 139; environmental impact assessment 139
Souselas protest movement: alliances 138–9; antecedents 139–40; CCI criticisms 143–5; implications from knowledge/power viewpoint 148–52; initiatives 140–2; personal observations 140, 148, 149, 150, 151–2; public health focus 146–8; scientific focus 142–6; state/civic relations 150–1; summarizing 152–4; working hypotheses 137–9
South of the North 47
specific intellectuals: convergence with popular movements 56; perception of SAAL process 66; and popular struggle 49–50; role 48–9; state agencies 57, 59; vision 56–7
Spinoza, Baruch 39–40
state: and heterogeneity 58–60; and social participation 65; transformation 58, 65
state socialism: collapse 5
Stockholm Convention (2001) 147
strategic game of actors 77, 95
Strategic Plan for Management of Industrial Waste (PESGRI) 139–40
struggle: emancipatory potential 124–7
struggle for housing 49–50, 52, 55, see also SAAL; SAAL/Norte
subalugas 55
subversive games 264
suffering: phenomenology 127
Suharto 197
sustainable development: local entrepreneurship 27

Sustainable Local Development: bottom-up approach 41–3; Braudelian structure 40–1; external support requirements 44–5; political context 43–4

tacit resistance 264
Taylor, John 200, 206–7
territorial planning: local strategic game of actors 77–8
territorial policies: crisis 77
thin democracy 4
think locally: act globally 275
Third Community Support Network 83
Third Sector Forum 36
trade unionism: summarizing reinvention 276–9
trade unions: competitiveness 236–8; corporatist imposition 260; counterhegemonic strategies 267; crisis 272; Ecco Let EWC experience 233–6; emancipatory options 220–1; EWC representative selection 233–6; FAG Group EWC experience 236–40; globalization impact 219; involvement with social struggle 141, 165; responses to EWCs 219–20, 230–3; strategy development 265–7; strategy requirements 254–5; training policies 241, 266; transnational affiliation 231–2, see also footwear workers' union
training programmes: European-funded 24
training schemes: Serro do Caldeirão 24
transnational corporations: power 41

UGT (General Workers' Union): EWCs position 230–3
UN (United Nations): legitimizing use of force 201; multilateral interventions 213
United Kingdom (UK): LGBT movement strategy 181
United States of America (USA): LGBT movement strategy 181; Proposition 187 182–3

urban management: growing crisis 79
urban planning: as commodity 78; decision making 82; decision processes 90–1; interlocutor selection 90; participatory 90, 94
urban politics: participation 79–81
urban social movements: categorizing 64
useful universalism 161

violence: MRCSS 118–20
Vitorino, Sérgio 166, 176, 181

Wachter, Serge 78, 93, 94, 97
waste management: legislation 142; national policy 135, *see also* SIGRI
Waterman, Peter 254

welfare state: core countries' experience 5
western-style democracy: low intensity model 46
Westphalia Peace Treaties (1648) 192
Westphalian legacy 192–3
women: active participation 55–6, 72, 116–18, 125; inequality 164
women's rights 173
working class movements: fragility 258, *see also* MRCSS
workplace participation 70
World Bank 1, 200
World Economic Forum 8
world economy 41
World Social Forum 8

young adults: positive influence 29